M000098698

NEW ENGLAND
GARDENER'S HANDBOOK

ALL YOU NEED TO KNOW TO PLAN, PLANT,
& MAINTAIN A NEW ENGLAND GARDEN

Inspiring | Educating | Creating | Entertaining

Brimming with creative inspiration, how-to projects, and useful
information to enrich your everyday life, Quarto Knows is a favorite
destination for those pursuing their interests and passions. Visit our
site and dig deeper with our books into your area of interest:
Quarto Creates, Quarto Cooks, Quarto Homes, Quarto Lives,
Quarto Drives, Quarto Explores, Quarto Gifts, or Quarto Kids.

© 2012 Quarto Publishing Group USA Inc. Text © 2009 Jacqueline Hériteau;
© 2009 Holly Hunter Stonehill; © Liz Ball; © James Fizzell; © 2009 Joe Lamp'l

First published as New England Gardener's Resource, 2009. This edition published in 2012
by Cool Springs Press, an imprint of The Quarto Group, 401 Second Avenue North, Suite
310, Minneapolis, MN 55401 USA. T (612) 344-8100 F (612) 344-8692
www.QuartoKnows.com

All rights reserved. No part of this book may be reproduced in any form without written
permission of the copyright owners. All images in this book have been reproduced with the
knowledge and prior consent of the artists concerned, and no responsibility is accepted by
producer, publisher, or printer for any infringement of copyright or otherwise, arising from
the contents of this publication. Every effort has been made to ensure that credits
accurately comply with information supplied. We apologize for any inaccuracies that may
have occurred and will resolve inaccurate or missing information in a subsequent reprinting
of the book.

Cool Springs Press titles are also available at discount for retail, wholesale, promotional,
and bulk purchase. For details, contact the Special Sales Manager by email at specialsales@
quarto.com or by mail at The Quarto Group, Attn: Special Sales Manager, 401 Second
Avenue North, Suite 310, Minneapolis, MN 55401 USA.

ISBN: 978-1-59186-544-5

Library of Congress Cataloging-in-Publication Data on file

Associate Publisher: Mark Johanson
Design Manager: Brad Springer
Design: S. E. Anderson
Page Layout: Danielle Smith

Cool Springs Press would like to thank the following photography and illustration
contributors to the *New England Gardener's Handbook:*

William Adams
Liz Ball
Ken Cole/Dreamstime.com
Michael Dirr
Steve Dobbs
Thomas Eltzroth
Dan Gill
Lorenzo Gunn
Pamela Harper
Heirloom Roses, Inc.
Steve Holsderfield/Dreamstime.com
iStockphoto and its artists
Jackson & Perkins
Dency Kane
Bill Kersey Graphics

Todd Koske
Charles Mann
Kevin Mathias
Judy Mielke
Scott Millard
iStockphoto.com/Stephen Muskie
Jerry Pavia
Rick Ray
Felder Rushing
Guy J. Sagi/Shutterstock.com
Ralph Snodsmith
Neil Soderstrom
Michael Turner
André Viette

NEW ENGLAND
GARDENER'S HANDBOOK

ALL YOU NEED TO KNOW TO PLAN, PLANT, & MAINTAIN A NEW ENGLAND GARDEN

JACQUELINE HÉRITEAU AND HOLLY HUNTER STONEHILL

WITH LIZ BALL, JAMES FIZZELL AND JOE LAMP'L

COOL
SPRINGS
PRESS

CONTENTS

WELCOME TO GARDENING
in New England

Our very first real garden was in Vermont, close to Montpelier. That's not far from the Canadian border, Zone 3. In winter the fields were knee-deep in snow and temperatures now and then went to thirty below zero. As far as knowing anything about gardens or plants, we were "buck naked" at the time. So when the bulblike things we had transplanted from the previous owner's garden sent up single stems topped with clusters of small dainty white flowers with an unforgettable perfume, we decided they were tuberoses—they were the only heavily perfumed bulb flowers we knew by name. Our gardening friends laughed, of course. They knew what we didn't—that tuberoses, *Polianthes tuberosa,* came originally from Mexico, and no way could they winter in the ground north of Zone 8 or 9. Someone suggested our perfumed posies must be narcissus, the very perfumed Poetaz or Polyanthus types. A fine suggestion—except those can't survive Zone 3 winters either, nothing north of Zone 5.

Yes, well, whether or not these plants could, one or the other did make it in our garden in hilly northern Vermont. The moral of this story is, the weather that governs our gardens, is, like much else in New England, idiosyncratic. Its outrageous eccentricities are our favorite small talk. So seize the moment. Take a chance. If the butterfly bush you must have dies over the winter in your garden, grow it as an annual, like a geranium. If it survives, cheer. If not, replant next year.

To help gardeners choose plants that will survive winters in their gardens, the USDA has created a climate zone map that identifies regions according to their average lowest winter temperature. Zone 1 has the coldest climate, Zone 11 the warmest. But New England topography requires that you use your noggin. The plains and the coasts are one or two zones warmer than the hills—and we have lots of hills. Can you count on lots of snow? Under a protective blanket of snow, plants can survive more cold than where the earth is bare and frigid. High hills are colder than their respective zones. For every additional 1,000 feet of elevation, you are one zone colder. The authors'

gardens are about ten minutes apart as the crow flies, but Jacqui lives in a narrow valley that follows the Housatonic River, while Holly lives on the tip-top of a hill at least 1,000 feet higher up: Jacqui's in Zone 5, Holly's in Zone 4.

The dynamic of mountainous areas versus valley areas can be baffling: mountaintops hold the extremes of temperatures while valleys hold the best of circumstances. When the weather is hot, the mountaintops are hotter than the valleys because the valleys hold the cool evening air longer. Conversely, when the weather is cold, the mountains are colder than the valleys because the valleys hold the heat from the previous day's sun. Mountaintops = extremes: valleys = insulated havens. The north side of a hill is subject to more cold than the south-facing slope below the crest. Cities are five to ten degrees warmer than the suburbs and the countryside. Large bodies of water also modify temperatures. In winter the coast and ten to twenty miles inland is warmer than the landmass behind. But as spring warms the air, the shore and ten to twenty miles inland is colder by ten degrees or more than farther inland because the ocean holds winter's cold. In summer the shore is cooler because the ocean is cooler than the air.

That said, it's our experience that putting the right plant in the right place is the key to having a garden that will give you joy for years. Knowing your own backyard and its potentially unconventional reaction to the weather has to dictate most of your plant choices, especially long-lived trees and shrubs. This is why New England gardeners have so much fun! There is ALWAYS room for experimental zone choices. No one ever has the "final word" on what will grow.

OUTWITTING YOUR CLIMATE

Since the zone the USDA map assigns to you isn't the last word on plant survival, if a plant you really want seems successful just outside your climate zone, give it a try. Large trees need open space all around, so they are vulnerable to whatever the zone tag on the plant and the USDA map says about your area. But plants that can be protected, or are small enough to inhabit a microclimate—small flowering trees, shrubs, perennials—often will make it. Within every garden there are microclimates hospitable to plants normally a bit outside your zone. For example, a south-facing wall can warm a corner, and shade can cool it. You can even create microclimates: a wall painted white, a reflective surface, increases light and heat. A vine-covered pergola, a trellis, a tree, or a high hedge can provide protection from early and late frost. Walls and windbreaks—and a position below the crest of a south-facing slope—protect plants from sweeping winds that intensify cold. A burlap wrap and an anti-dessicant spray can save evergreens from the wind, and also from deer. Mulch protects roots from extremes of cold and from heat as well.

If you live in a borderline area—almost in cooler Zone 4, but not quite, for example—the safest choices are species that are well within their cold hardiness range in your garden. Borderline plants may live but not always bloom in a satisfying way. Forsythia, for instance, will leaf out in northern Vermont, but will generally bloom only on the portion of the plant below the snow line. Late frosts can devastate the flower buds on a hardy magnolia though the plant itself may do well year after year. Many plants are offered in varieties described as blooming early, midseason, or late. Where the growing season is short, choose varieties that will bloom early. If you wish to enjoy a very long season of bloom of any particular plant, plant varieties of all three types: early, midseason, and late.

You can also outwit the climate by covering plants to protect them from late spring and early fall frosts, and by starting seeds indoors weeks before they can be sown in the open garden. (Seed starting is detailed in the Appendix.) Garden centers and catalogs offer seed starting equipment, as well as protective covers of all sorts. To protect individual plants, we use plastic cones called "hot caps;" and we add, for elegance, a Victorian glass cloche or two. To protect whole rows of seedlings, we use filmy tenting, the Reemay® type. Hot beds and cold frames, though simple enough to make, are projects beyond the scope of this book.

PLANTS THAT SUCCEED

The plants we recommend are the best of the best for New England. There are 180 featured plants, and information on another 500 species and cultivars we recommend. We chose them for their lasting beauty, ease of maintenance, and immunity or strong resistance to pests and diseases. We're not recommending pesticides and other deterrents—they come and go too frequently. But more important to us is that we have learned from decades of experience that the best protection you can give your garden is 1) to choose pest- and disease-resistant plants that thrive in New England, and 2) to give them the light, nutrients, and moisture they need. We do everything possible at the start to provide the right growing environment: after that, either it grows, or it's gotta go!

LIGHT

After climate, the next most important element for success in a garden is the light. On each plant page we tell you the light in which that plant thrives. When a flowering species fails to flower, check the hours of direct sun it receives: unless we say a plant flowers in part or full shade, it requires at least six hours of direct sun to bloom well. Full sun occurs between 10 a.m. and 6 p.m. through mid-August. Plants receiving full sunlight are often the most cold hardy. Plants that flop forward are telling you they need more light. You can increase the amount of light the plants receive by planting them near a wall painted white or a reflective surface. Plants that do best in partial sun or shade (New Guinea impatiens, hostas, and daphnes, for example) can be grown in full sun, if you provide an overhead trellis, a pergola, or something to shade them from the hottest sun of the day—noonday and late afternoon sun.

SOIL PREPARATION AND IMPROVEMENT

Soil is your plant's support system, its drinking fountain, and its larder. In New England acid soils prevail, becoming sandy as you approach the coast. And there's often a layer of hardpan under thin topsoil in new housing developments. Sandy soils are easy to dig and drain well, which is essential for a great many plants. On the other hand, they don't retain water or the nutrients dissolved in it. Whichever your soil type, the way to make it right is to mix it with humusy organic materials—such as compost, leaf mold (rotted leaves), or peat— and slow-release fertilizers.

The ideal garden soil has good drainage, lots of water-holding humus, and is loose enough so you can dig in it with your fingers. We evaluate garden soil in terms of its structure or composition, its pH, and its fertility. Structure governs the soil's ability to absorb and maintain moisture. Gritty particles create air spaces, allowing tender rootlets to seek oxygen, moisture, and the nutrients dissolved in it. They also allow water to drain. Soil containing humus retains enough moisture to keep the rootlets from drying out and starving: roots "drink" nutrients dissolved in water. We add lots of humusy organic amendments to new planting beds to improve the soil's structure.

A plant's access to nutrients also depends on the soil's pH (potential of hydrogen), its relative acidity or alkalinity. A pH of 7.0 is neutral; a pH of 4.0 is very, very acid; a pH of 8.0 is very alkaline. Most garden ornamentals do best in soil whose pH is between 5.5 and 6.5. Trees and shrubs are apt to be more finicky about pH than herbaceous plants. You can use relatively inexpensive testing kits to determine the pH of your soil. If it's above pH 6.5, and you are preparing a bed for plants that do not do well in alkaline ("sweet") soil, apply water soluble sulfur or iron sulfate. If the soil is below pH 5.5, and the plants need "sweeter" soil, spread finely ground limestone or hydrated lime. Ask your garden center or nursery for recommendations.

Plants empty their larder of nutrients every season. If you want plants to be all they can be, you must fertilize a new bed before planting, and all beds every year. The fertilizers we use are organic and release their nutrients slowly during the season, so we get solid stocky plants with loads of gorgeous foliage and flowers.

We mostly plant in raised beds of improved soil. When we're digging a planting hole, we add the same soil amendments and fertilizers in the same proportions. The best times to prepare a new bed are fall, and also spring as soon as cold and moisture are out of the ground. Here's how:

1. Use a garden hose to outline the bed. A bed beside a fence, a wall, or a path can be formal or informal. For an informal look, lay out long, slow, gentle curves rather than scallops or straight lines. For a formal look, make the bed symmetrical—a half circle, oval, square, or rectangle. An island bed can be a large oval, an elongated S, or kidney- shaped. Island beds are the easiest to work since you can get at the middle from either side.
2. Thoroughly water the turf covering the area to get the grass roots activated.

3. Spray the entire area with a weed killer, following the instructions on the label. It takes about two weeks for the weeds to die completely. Alternately, you can remove the turf—the top layer of growth and its roots—but that's pretty hard work.

4. Cover the area with enough of the most weed-free garden soil you can find to raise the soil level about 12 to 16 inches above ground.

5. Cover the bed with 3 to 4 inches of humus, enough so that one quarter of the content of the soil is organic matter. The humus can be decomposed bark, compost, partially decomposed leaves or seaweed, sphagnum peat moss, black peat humus, decomposed animal manures, or other decomposed organic material.

6. Next, with a rear-tine rototiller, which you can rent from a garden center, mix all this deeply and thoroughly. The bed should now be so soft you can dig in it with your bare hands.

7. The next step is to determine the pH reaction of the soil and amend it as needed to reach a pH between 5.5 and 6.5 by following the steps described under Soil Preparation and Improvement.

8. Next, for each 10 by 10 foot area (100 square feet), mix in your amendments and rototill or fork into the improved soil.

9. When you are ready to plant, rake the bed smooth and discard rocks, lumps, and bumps.

10. Finally, tamp the edge of the bed into a long, gradual slope and cover it with mulch to keep the soil from eroding. Or frame the bed with low retaining walls of stone or painted cement blocks, 2 × 2 red cedar or pressure-treated wood, or railroad ties.

PLANTING

When you are planting in a new raised bed with improved, fluffed-up soil, digging a generous planting hole is easy. Digging a big hole in an unimproved spot, even in an old established garden, is tough. But the plant still needs a big planting hole, and soil mixed with 3 to 4 inches of

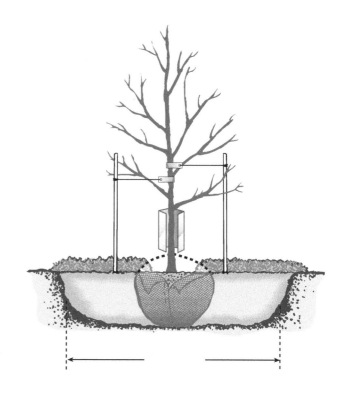

humus (previous Step 5), enough so that one quarter of the content of the soil is organic matter mixed with slow-release organic fertilizers. Each chapter introduction has directions for planting the type of plants in that chapter. Whether the plants are large or small our basic approach is this:

1. Make the planting hole BIG. For trees and shrubs, make it three times as wide and two times as deep as the rootball. For perennials and annuals, dig a hole two times as wide and two times as deep as the rootball.

2. For perennials, annuals, and bulbs provide a base of improved soil for the rootball to rest on by half-filling the planting hole with improved soil before setting the plant in it. For shrubs and trees, half-fill the hole with improved soil, and tamp it down very firmly before setting the plant into the hole.

3. Free the plant from matted roots. When it's possible, unwind roots that may be circling the rootball. If you can't untangle them, make four shallow vertical slashes in the mass. Cut off about a half inch of the matted roots on the bottom. Soak the rootball in a bucket containing starter solution.

4. Set the plant in the hole. Half-fill the hole with soil, tamp it down firmly; fill the hole all the way to the top with soil, and tamp it firmly again. Shape the soil around the stem or the crown into a wide saucer. The saucer is really important for shrubs and trees, less so for perennials and annuals.

WATERING

Deep, slow, gentle watering is what keeps plants growing well. After planting, water the bed deeply, gently, and slowly. Ideal for a new bed is to put down 1½ inches of water after planting. Set an empty coffee tin, regular size, to catch the water and record how long it takes your sprinkler to deliver 1½ inches. Water a newly planted shrub or tree by slowly pouring 10 to 15 gallons of water into the saucer around the plant. For a tree or a shrub's first season, unless there's a soaking rain, in spring and fall slowly and gently pour two to three bucketsful of water around the roots every two weeks; in summer, every week or ten days. Flower beds thrive with two to three hours of gentle rain every ten days to two weeks. If the sky fails you, water long enough to lay down 1½ inches of water gently over a long period of time, at least six to eight hours, every ten days to two weeks. And, of course, water any time the plants show signs of wilting.

Overhead watering is fine as long as you water deeply. There's less waste if you water before the sun reaches the garden in the early morning, or in the late afternoon or evening. In hot dry periods, however, you need to water during the day. Daytime watering lowers leaf temperatures and reduces stress in extreme heat. Evening watering is fine—dew does it and plants like it. We do not recommend electrically timed mechanical watering systems that ignore the weather and water too often and shallowly. However, they can do a good job if they are set up with the correct nozzles, and timed to run long enough to water deeply every week or ten days. Windy, hot times, such as occur in summer, require more water, and the cool spring and fall days less.

STAKING AND STEM PROTECTION

Growing in improved soil and fertilized with slow-release organic fertilizers, only a few of the tallest flowers should need staking. Tall, weak growth is often caused by force-feeding with non-organic fertilizers. Wide spacing improves air circulation, and reduces the risk of disease and mildew. Staking is easy: set a wood, bamboo, or metal stake close to the plant stem while it is still young. As it leafs out, it will hide the stake. Use soft green wool, raffia, or cotton string and tie the main stem loosely to the stake. Staking a tree isn't necessary unless the stem or trunk shows a tendency to lean over or to grow at an angle—and it should not need the stake for more than a year. In cold regions a burlap windbreak is helpful to young shrubs and trees for their first winter. You may need to protect a young tree trunk from rubbing or nibbling by deer: you can surround it with stakes wrapped with mesh, or attach a rubber or plastic stem guard. Remove the wrap in spring when growth starts. To protect the tender bark of a young tree from sunscald, paint it with a wash of calcium carbonate.

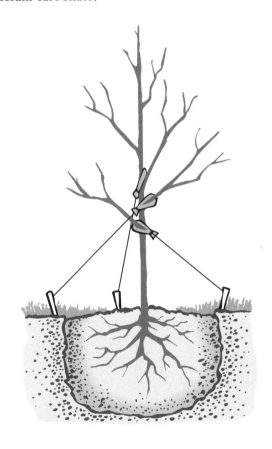

MULCHES

If you love your plants, maintain a 2- to 3-inch layer of organic mulch over the roots from early spring through fall and winter. Start the mulch about 3 inches from the main stem or stems. We mulch in part to buffer soil temperatures and maintain soil moisture, to prevent erosion and control weeds. An organic mulch does more: as it decomposes on the underside it replenishes the soil's supply of humus, which is dissipated during the growing season. The mulches we use suit all plants equally well. Tests have shown that an acid mulch, such as pine needles, has no lasting impact on the pH of the soil beneath.

You can mulch with almost any healthy organic material available—seaweed or chopped leaves for example—as long as it is at least partially decomposed. The commercial mulches we recommend include cypress mulch, pine needles, fir, hardwood, pine bark, and cocoa mulch.

MAINTAINING FERTILITY

We fertilize planting beds, not individual plants. The rule of thumb is to apply a slow- release organic fertilizer to the bed before growth begins in early spring; for some plants you'll see we recommend fertilizing again in the fall. The fertilizer we recommend for general garden use is a complete organic fertilizer, not one for acid-loving plants—that tends to balance out New England's generally acid pH. For plants that do best in quite acid soil, we apply a complete organic fertilizer. For bulbs we use a complete organic fertilizer for bulbs. If plants need a boost in midseason, we apply a water-soluble organic fertilizer such as fish emulsion. In high heat we don't try to force plant growth by feeding, and we avoid pruning at that time, which stimulates growth. The plants will naturally slow their growth in extremes of weather.

GROOMING AND WEEDING

To realize their potential, plants need grooming. In early spring gardens must be cleared of last year's dead foliage. In summer we deadhead and shear spent blooms to encourage flowering this year or next. We prune woody plants to keep them shapely and healthy. We weed, eliminating the competition. Weeds can even be volunteers from last year's cosmos or phlox. They start up in spring and come into their own in midsummer, along with drought and high heat. Although a permanent mulch discourages weeds, you can easily rake up the little green heads if you do it before they're 1 inch high. When they're 8 inches high, you'll need a hoe. After that you'll just be sorry you didn't get to it earlier.

Let weeds flourish in or near a newly established garden and go to seed, and they'll haunt you for years. If some get away from you, don't pull big weeds from bone-dry soil during a drought—they are made difficult to dig out, and the upheaval of soil can cost precious moisture. Water the garden first, then gently free the weeds and their roots.

Looking back on years of gardening, the moments that stand out in memory are those spent grooming the garden. Grooming is a quiet time. Pruning boxwoods in the cool early morning, birds a-twitter, strolling the flower beds at sunset checking for spent blooms that need deadheading, weeding in summer, and raking leaves in autumn. These homely chores lift us out of our everyday lives and into the life of the garden and a potential for beauty that nourishes the soul.

HOW TO USE THE NEW ENGLAND GARDENER'S RESOURCE

Each entry in this guide provides information about a plant's characteristics, habits, and requirements for growth, as well as our personal experience and knowledge of the plant. Use this information to realize each plant's potential. You will find such pertinent information as mature height and spread, bloom period and seasonal colors, sun and soil preferences, water requirements, fertilizing needs, pruning and care tips. and pest information. Each section is clearly marked for reference.

SUN PREFERENCES

Symbols represent the range of sunlight suitable for each plant. The symbol representing "Full Sun" means the plant needs six or more hours of sun daily. A ranking of "Part Sun" means the plant can thrive in four to six hours of sun a day. "Full Shade" means the plant needs protection from direct sunlight. Some plants can be grown successfully in more than one exposure, so you will sometimes see more than one light icon with an entry.

 Full Sun   Part Sun   Full Shade

ADDITIONAL BENEFITS

Many plants offer benefits that further enhance their appeal. These symbols indicate some of these benefits.

 Attracts Butterflies

 Attracts Hummingbirds

 Provides Edible Fruit

 Provides Food for Wildlife

 Has Fragrance

 Suitable for Cut Flowers or Arrangements

 Long Bloom Period

 Native Plant

 Attracts Honeybees

 Provides Shelter for Wildlife

 Good Fall Color

 Waterwise Choice

LANDSCAPING TIPS AND IDEAS

For most of the entries, we provide landscape design ideas as well as suggestions for companion plants and/or recommended varieties, to help you achieve striking and personal results in your New England garden.

USDA COLD HARDINESS ZONES

ZONE	Avg. Annual Minimum Temperature (°F)
3b	-30 to -35
4a	-25 to -30
4b	-20 to -25
5a	-15 to -20
5b	-10 to -15
6a	-5 to -10
6b	0 to -5
7a	5 to 0

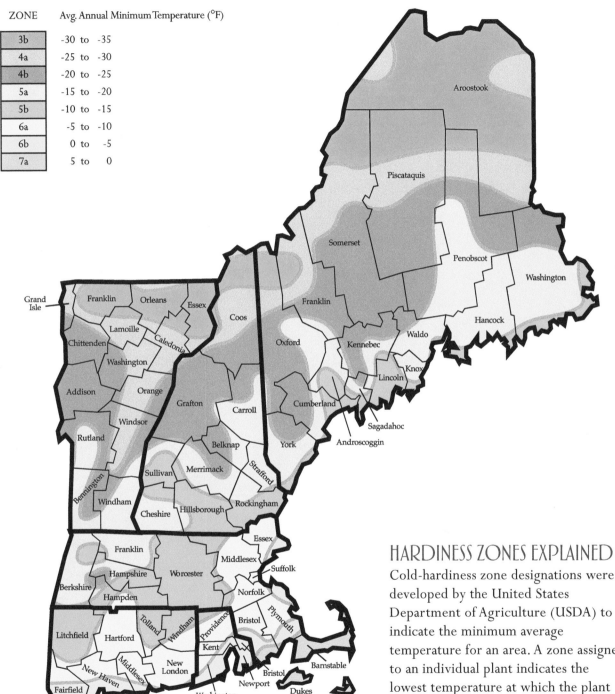

HARDINESS ZONES EXPLAINED

Cold-hardiness zone designations were developed by the United States Department of Agriculture (USDA) to indicate the minimum average temperature for an area. A zone assigned to an individual plant indicates the lowest temperature at which the plant can be expected to survive over the winter. New England has zones ranging from 3b to 7a. Though a plant may grow (and grow well) in zones other than its recommended cold-hardiness zone, zones are a good indication of which plants to consider for your landscape.

TURNING WASTE INTO GARDENING GOLD

At home, my family and I compost or recycle just about everything we can, from inside and outside the house. It's hard to believe just how much waste is generated each day, not only at our house but in homes around the world.

As gardeners, we have such a wonderful opportunity to do something good for ourselves and our gardens, while at the same time doing our part to relieve the pressure of overburdened landfill space and reduce emissions from carbon dioxide and methane gas. So much of what we need and can use ends up as municipal solid waste and discarded junk and is just what we need and can use in our eco-friendly gardens and landscapes.

COMPOST YOUR GARDEN WASTE

For every item that you can throw in the compost pile, that's one less for the landfill.

Fortunately there is measurable progress in reducing the amount of yard waste we are keeping out of our landfills, and there are a number of reasons why. First, many municipalities no longer allow yard debris to be included with other household waste. Instead, trimmings are set aside in biodegradable paper bags and collected separately. They're then taken to a municipal composting site where they are deposited for the slow decomposition process.

Elsewhere, many cities and counties across New England and indeed across the country offer curbside pickup of items too bulky for the paper sacks. Tree limbs, shrubs, and other such items are the usual components of this part of the recycling campaign. Even fall leaves are sucked up and hauled off to a composting facility by some solid waste departments.

For me, surrendering my yard trimmings to a third party is only a measure of last resort. After all, I want as much compostable material as I can get. The thought of handing it over, even the big stuff, seems ludicrous. I admit, it is sometimes tempting to leave cumbersome branches and bags of leaves on the curb rather than haul them to the backyard compost pile, but like most things in life—no pain, no gain.

When you're outside working in the yard. it's always surprising how much yard debris accumulates so quickly. Can it all go into the compost pile? Yes, it probably could, but should it? Well, that's another story.

WHAT GOES IN THE COMPOST PILE, WHAT DOESN'T

Outside, anything that was growing is fair game… almost. A few exceptions are mentioned below. First, however, great additions to a compost pile from outside the house include grass clippings, hay, straw, pine needles, leaves, wood chips, bark, and other yard trimmings.

You may have heard that for compost to break down quickly, there needs to be the right ratio between carbon (the brown stuff) and nitrogen (the green stuff). Although that is true, compost happens in nature with no help from us, although it may take longer.

Rather than get bogged down in trying to provide the perfect ratio, just be sure always to have some of both working all the time. The rate of composting can be accelerated by simply keeping the pile moist (like a damp sponge) and turning it often to provide oxygen to the center of the pile.

Now, the outdoors has a few limitations on what not to put in a compost pile. First, avoid adding weeds that have gone to seed. Weed seeds often survive the decomposition process, only to be spread next season under the cloak of perfect compost.

Diseased plant material also poses risks to your compost. The pathogens may survive the composting process and reinfect other plants as they are distributed about your garden. Play it safe and remove this material from your property completely. Although burning would destroy the pathogens and infected plant material, it's not an option in the eco-friendly garden.

Fireplace ashes present yet another problem. Ashes are highly alkaline. More harm could be done by raising the soil pH of acid-loving plants than the small benefit from potassium inherent with ash. I leave them out of my compost.

Personally, I don't add twigs or branches to my pile that are thicker than a pencil. It's not that they won't become compost; it's that I'm too impatient. Instead, I toss all my thicker branches into a pile of their own. As they slowly break down, the added benefit is that they provide cover and protection for birds and many of the smaller wildlife that live in the area. I also keep thorny branches and twigs such as roses and briars out of my compost. They go into that separate pile and provide additional protection for the smaller animals.

So although there are some don'ts when it comes to what to put into your compost, the exceptions are very few. Just remember that for every item that you can throw in the compost pile, that's one less for the landfill. If that's not motivating enough, know what you are putting in your compost pile will provide the very best soil amendment you can give to your garden, and no store-bought product can match it!

COMPOSTABLE MATERIALS

Rather than being viewed as unnecessary trash, fallen leaves, grass clippings, and other garden trimmings, as well as biodegradable items from inside our kitchens and homes, should be going into our own gardens. There, they can and will enrich the soil while reducing the need for supplemental fertilizers and other harmful chemicals.

GRASS CLIPPINGS

Can you imagine how many bags of grass clippings are collected on any spring or summer day? The EPA tells us yard clippings make up over 20 percent of the entire waste stream entering public landfills. If it were up to me, I'd take them all at my house. Grass clippings are loaded with nitrogen, a key nutrient to lush growth and deep green color. They're also a necessary part of helping other organic material break down quickly.

Nitrogen provides the food source for microorganisms to decompose carbon, that brown waste in our compost such as twigs and leaves. You only need about 20 percent as much nitrogen as carbon, but it is essential that you have both for efficient decomposition. In fact, a compost pile without green waste will seem to just sit there. It will eventually break down, but it takes much longer. Add some grass clippings to the mix and watch the pile start to cook! That heat is from the microbes hard at work again, nourished and fortified from the addition of their essential food source.

Now, even though I've said I'd take all the grass clippings I would get, that's not exactly true. In my eco-friendly garden, I don't want to add clippings that have been doused with herbicides and pesticides. Some of those chemicals don't break down in the heat of composting, and I'm not interested in adding tainted compost to my otherwise chemical-free garden.

The same goes for grass containing a lot of weeds. It's not the weeds I'm worried about as much as the seeds they make. Weed seeds have the ability to survive some pretty harsh conditions, including a hot compost pile. The seeds could remain viable, only to germinate later in other parts of the garden when you apply the finished compost. If I keep my grass cut often enough, though, weeds are rarely a problem since frequent mowing cuts off emerging seedheads.

Finally, too much of a good thing can be, well…too much. If you've ever placed a large amount of grass clippings in a pile, added water, and come back later, you may have noticed a strong and not-so-pleasant aroma much like the smell of ammonia. It's simply a matter of chemistry—too much moisture and not enough oxygen to process the decomposition of the nitrogen-rich grass clippings. But it's an easy fix. Just spread the pile out to allow more oxygen in, add some carbon-based brown ingredients, and then mix it all together. The problem should resolve itself in a day or two.

KITCHEN WASTE, PAPER AND OTHER HOUSEHOLD ITEMS

From inside the house, just about anything that once came from a living source can be composted. From the kitchen, add all fruit and vegetable scraps, coffee grounds and filters, paper towels and the roll, napkins, oatmeal, rice, banana peels, eggshells, and teabags. You'll find more items.

From around the house, add vacuum cleaner bags and contents, dryer lint, cardboard rolls, clean paper (shredded is best), newspaper, cotton and wool rags, hair and fur, and houseplants.

As with everything in life, there are exceptions to the rule, including household compost. First, don't add any meat products, bones, fats, grease, oils (including salad dressing), or dairy products to compost. They create odors that can attract pests such as rodents and flies. And don't compost pet or human wastes. These can contain parasites, bacteria, germs, pathogens, and viruses that are harmful to humans.

LEAVES

As lovely as hardwood trees appear with their leaves in glorious shades of red, yellow, orange, and rust, my favorite part of the autumn season is after they have fallen. The now-brown leaves begin to blanket my lawn and beds, and I know that it is compost time!

No, I haven't lost my mind. I don't relish the work of clearing off those leaves any more than you do. But, I do have a deep appreciation for what they will mean to my garden and landscape in just a few months.

I suppose it goes back to that old saying, "Beauty is in the eye of the beholder." Where most people see leaf debris, along with hours of raking, bagging, and hauling, I see garden beds blanketed in rich organic compost. These leaves contain 50 to 80 percent of the nutrients that their trees extracted from the earth this past season. I will use them to replenish the soil and nourish all that grows within it.

Earthworms will feast on this debris, burrow deeper into the soil, and then deposit the matter as castings, adding even more valuable nutrients, oxygen, and drainage in the process. Beneficial fungi and bacteria will assist in the decomposition process, consuming this raw leaf material and returning it in a nutrient-rich form that can be utilized by plant and tree roots more efficiently and effectively than anything man has ever created.

Mere months after these shredded leaves are applied around my garden, they'll transform into matter that promotes the life of the soil-dwelling organisms, which in turn will fortify my plants and trees to be more pest- and disease-resistant . . . ah, I can see springtime already.

But let me interrupt this vision to ask you a question: Have you ever stopped to consider that no matter what condition the soil is in, leaf compost will help make loose soil retain moisture and compacted soil drain better?

Yes, I'll look forward to gathering up and shredding not only the leaves falling from my trees but from my neighbor's as well. What leaves I don't spread into the beds, I'll store somewhere else in my yard. I'll worry about them later. Shredded autumn leaves are my organic fertilizer, multi-vitamin, and soil conditioner all-in-one, both plentiful and free. It doesn't get any better.

GARDENING TO PROTECT THE ECOSYSTEM

"With a garden, there is hope."
—*Grace Firth*

If we were to step outside our green bubble for a moment and look at the reasons we are facing such an ecological crisis today, we'd realize that biodiversity indeed contributes to so many facets of our human health and the comforts of life. And although many people enjoy and benefit from activities that lead to the loss of biodiversity and cause ecological damage, our actions' true cost to our planet often far exceeds the benefit to us.

At least as gardeners, we can identify some of the most direct benefits to preserving and protecting these relationships. Healthy ecosystems improve the chance for plant and animal populations to recover from the threat of increasingly catastrophic and often unpredictable events such as hurricanes, fires, floods, and other natural and man-induced disasters.

Maintaining natural habitats also provides protection for breeding and migrating populations of birds, as well as offering shelter from predators. Insect pests are kept in check, reducing the need for chemical control measures. The gene pool of plants vital for food and medicine is preserved, while pollinating insects continue to sustain these ecosystems as they work and breed in their diverse habitats.

Today, virtually all of the earth's ecosystems have been altered through human actions, and yet the interruptions seem to continue at a faster rate than ever before. As our interference persists, many plant and animal species have declined in population and scope, and the rate of extinction has increased. Biodiversity loss has occurred more rapidly in the last fifty years than at any other time in history, and these changes are expected to continue at the same pace or even accelerate.

So what can be done? For you and me, the most direct and significant actions must be taken at the local, regional, and national levels while always being mindful that our actions will contribute to the bigger picture. Starting right at home is a simple yet important place to begin. Below are some tangible actions you can take to make a difference.

PROMOTE COMPLEXITY AND AVOID MONOCULTURES

What do the Irish potato famine and the Dust Bowl of the 1930s have in common? You guessed it— they were the result of monocultures.

Our own backyards and neighborhoods can become microcosms of these global events. When we plant too much of a good thing, either too close together or year after year, significant problems may result. We are creating the perfect environment for a population explosion of pests or pathogens by inviting them to latch onto a single host. In monocultures, the relative abundance of a host, combined with the absence of natural predators in sufficient numbers, can have devastating results.

At home, we see dangerous scenarios played out every day, right where we live. Mini-monocultures of turfgrass are a ubiquitous feature in just about every landscape in New England, and indeed throughout the country. Few are the homes that don't have some amount of turf occupying a portion of their landscape. As lovely as a well-manicured lawn can be to look at, it replaces the habitats of native plants and wildlife for birds or beneficial insects.

Another threat to biodiversity in home landscapes is the introduction of exotic and invasive species which out-complete native plants for sunlight, water, and nutrients, destroying entire ecosystems in their wake.

The balance of nature is indeed a concert of all its inhabitants. The natural environment around us is never a monoculture on its own. When we destroy this highly sophisticated yet delicate balance by precluding diversity, ecosystems falter. Yet when biodiversity is protected and promoted in our own yards and neighborhoods, so is the stability of the ecosystems that give us fresh water, clean air, productive soil, and healthy forests.

Action items:
- Limit the size of your lawn.
- Assess the diversity of your flower beds, and make them more diverse if you can.
- Assess the diversity of your kitchen garden, and practice crop rotation.

PROTECT THE GENE POOL

America has been the great melting pot in more ways than one. With each wave of immigrants came a wave of new plants, many in the form of a packet of generations-old seed tucked carefully into a pocket. Each settler planted a favorite tomato, a favorite apple, a particular type of morning glory or an especially striking sunflower, and as a result, they added to the amazing horticultural variety in their new home.

In the middle part of the last century, however, people stopped saving seeds from year to year. With the advent of hybridization, large seed companies began selling seeds that didn't come from seeds saved year after year. Hybrid varieties had many advantages to farmers and home gardeners in terms of consistency, yields, or pest- and disease-resistance, but there was also a disadvantage. They had to be purchased new each year or whenever current supplies were exhausted. This method of seed acquisition replaced much of the traditional swapping and passing on to the next generation of our treasured seeds.

Typically the results from planting a hybridized plant from seed will be iffy. That snapdragon which was such a gorgeous peach-yellow blend this year might reseed next year, but the flower color can be dramatically different. This is not necessarily a bad thing, just something to be aware of. And don't expect that hybrid tomato seed to produce offspring identical to its parent.

Open-pollinated varieties are different. These seeds have not been manipulated by man. Their pollination takes place naturally through insects, birds, wind, and other means. The seeds of open-pollinated plants can produce new generations of the same plant, which is how we can save and plant seeds from one generation to another.

There's another reason for saving seeds that reaches far beyond our flower or vegetable gardens. The entire diversity of plant life on our planet is shrinking rapidly. Climate change is expected to exacerbate the loss of plant diversity and increase the risk of extinction for many more species, especially those already at risk from other threats. Regions of the planet that provide much of the genetic material for our cultivated crop plants are quickly being damaged or destroyed. Many times the effects are irreversible. Unfortunately, pressures on the environment no longer allow plants to remain protected in their natural habitats. Saving seeds is a significant way to preserve these plants from one generation to another.

By saving seeds, we save plants that make up the basis of ecosystems in which all animals, including humans, survive and grow. Since human actions are fundamentally responsible for changing the diversity of life on earth, doing what we can to protect and preserve life only seems right, even the life of a tiny seed. It really is the little things that matter.

Action items:
- Educate yourself—and, eventually, others—about non-hybrid, heirloom, and open-pollinated varieties of plants you like to grow or might like to try. Do Internet research, find seed and nursery sources, ask your friends and neighbors, or ask your favorite farmstand or farmer's market.
- Pick out and grow a few of these. Learn how to save seeds yourself from one year to the next.
- Financially support seed banks, which helps fund their efforts to continue as they collaborate on their worldwide mission to collect and store thousands of species of plants and save them from extinction. Search "seed bank" or "seed preservation" on the Internet.

DISCOURAGE POACHING OF PLANTS FROM THE WILD

How can anyone take a walk in a wooded area and not appreciate the beauty around them? In a healthy, moist, diverse New England hardwood forest, for instance, plant lovers may spot wild lilies, trilliums, bluebells, gingers, bloodroot, hepaticas, calochortus, native irises, and perhaps lady's-slipper orchids.

Sadly there exists and small but disturbing number of nurseries that have decided to capitalize on our appreciation of wild beauties by collecting them in unscrupulous ways. They take advantage of the fact that as we observe these fascinating plants in their native habitat we naturally want to grow them ourselves—we're gardeners, after all! But instead of propagating them from seed, cuttings, or divisions, they dig them up, pot them up, and sell them, usually at an enticing price.

But that price is actually high. The practice of collecting plants in the wild has been compared to that of fishing in the North Atlantic. Perhaps because of its vastness, we've viewed the ocean as a source of infinite resources. The fact is, populations of many species that inhabit it are decreasing at an unsustainable rate, resulting in many now being listed as endangered and threatened with extinction. As is often the case, overexploitation and habitat destruction by humans is to blame.

And so it is with plants. Two of the key reasons cited for the loss of biodiversity and ecosystems around the world are directly related to commercial exploitation and habitat destruction. Too often, when plant explorers, collectors, or other individuals remove plants from their native habitat, they are removing a critical component of the ecosystem and destroying the environment that supports it.

Action items:
- Ask the nurseries where you shop about their source(s) of woodland plants. Be suspicious of very low prices of certain plants, as this could be a sign that they are collecting from the wild. Buy only "nursery-propagated" plants.

- Do not pick or dig up wild plants on your walks or hikes.
- Join or financially support the New England Wild Flower Society in Framingham, Massachusetts. If practical, attend their talks, guided hikes, and special plant sales.

DO YOUR HOMEWORK BEFORE USING TRAPS FOR INSECT PESTS

In an eco-friendly garden, the more chemicals you can keep out of your landscape, the better, even organic and natural ones. So what do you do to control those destructive Japanese beetles, pesky flies, and annoying mosquitoes? Do we trap, zap, or gas these creatures with a botanical-based insecticide? The answers may surprise you.

JAPANESE BEETLE TRAPS

Commercially available, these traps attract the beetles with two types of baits. One mimics the scent of virgin female beetles. Not surprisingly, it's highly effective at attracting males! The other bait is a sweet-smelling, food-type lure that attracts both sexes. This combination of ingredients is such a powerful attractant that traps can draw thousands of beetles in a day.

There is plenty of information available on the effectiveness of these traps. And it's unanimous— they work! In fact, they work too well. Research conducted by universities, laboratories, and even commercial airports has shown that the traps attract many more beetles than are actually caught. Consequently, susceptible plants along the flight path of the beetles and in the vicinity of traps are likely to suffer much more damage than if no traps are used at all.

Action items:
- Don't use Japanese beetle traps at all.
- If you choose to experiment with them, be sure to place them away from the plants you are trying to protect. (Better yet, encourage your neighbors to buy them instead.)
- Watch your susceptible plants. Intervene early in an infestation; handpicking might just work!

- If this pest problem is chronic in your garden, don't grow susceptible plants.

BUG ZAPPERS

If you grew up in my generation, you remember bug zappers as the sweet sound of success on a summer evening. You know the sound, and you loved it. It made for some very entertaining evenings.

But in 1996, some researchers at the University of Delaware collected and identified the kills from six bug zappers at various sites. Of the nearly 14,000 insects that were electrocuted and counted, only 31 were mosquitoes and biting gnats. Most were midges and harmless aquatic insects from nearby bodies of water. Too bad, because those insects are vital to the aquatic food chain. Another important group caught in the traps were predators and parasites. These biological control organisms are the very insects the help keep pest populations down naturally.

In short, and ironically, bug zappers aren't effective on their mosquito targets, and they are bad for the ecosystem. The researchers basically concluded that the number of mosquitoes would still be the same—with or without the zapper.

Action items:
- Don't use bug zappers.
- Pass this information on to your neighbors and friends so they don't use them, either.
- Help reduce the mosquito population in your yard by removing or dumping out all sources of standing water where they breed. In particular, patrol your yard after running the sprinkler or a summer rain shower, and take care of this. You can fill or cover standing puddles.
- Explore alternative traps (be aware that "mosquito misters" that emit organic pyrethrin or permethrin are harmful to beneficial insects, pets, and fish). The newer CO_2 traps can work, depending on placement (upwind of the desired protected are), constant use vs. intermittent use, and even the species of mosquito.

USE ENVIRONMENTALLY RESPONSIBLE WOOD

For many years, redwood has been the most popular building material for decks and other outdoor structures in our home landscapes. In just three generations, its population has been dramatically reduced (by 40 percent). Even as land is often converted to other uses after logging, the early population reductions are in many cases irreversible.

There are also endangered exotic wood species, ones that lure us with irresistible grain patterns and interesting colors. Teak is the best known of these. The American and European appetite for this strong and beautiful wood has nearly eradicated it from its natural range in Southeast Asia and Central America.

Other rainforest woods you may see offered, either in lumber form or already fashioned into patio and garden furniture, include mahogany, nyatoh, balau, jatoba (also called Brazilian cherry), papapera, kempas, iroko, and ipe.

Some of the most beautiful and weather-resistant woods for our landscapes, unfortunately, are also those whose loss can wreak havoc on climate change, biodiversity, and the ecosystems so vital to preserving and protecting our planet. But there are ways to shop for attractive, useful wood with sustainability in mind that will have less impact on the environment.

We gardeners enjoy nice garden furniture, fences, decks, planter boxes, and the like—but it is important that we shop wisely.

Action items:
- Seek out products that are labeled or marketed as certified by the FSC (Forest Stewardship Council); this label certifies that the wood in a product has been sustainably produced.
- Another label to look for is the SFI (Sustainable Forestry Initiative), which was put in place by the timber industry. The Consumer's Union doesn't give it as high marks as the FSC, but it still indicates some progress in protecting forest environments at home and abroad.
- If you buy teak, confirm that it is plantation-grown rather than wild-harvested. Reputable suppliers are eager to point out this benefit, so be suspicious if the information is missing or the dealer is not sure.
- Use recycled wood products from old buildings, fallen or removed trees, or other tree-culling events. A lumberyard should have a "SmartWood Rediscovered" label on wood or finished products.
- Look for environmentally sound wood substitutes. The relatively new so-called synthetic lumber made from recycled wood and plastics (sold by brand names such as Trex® and Timbertec®) is a more forest-friendly alternative.

AVOID INVASIVE, NON-NATIVE PLANTS

Invasive plants are introduced species that can thrive in areas beyond their natural range of dispersal. These plants are characteristically adaptable, aggressive, and have a high capacity to propagate. Because they evolved in completely different habitats elsewhere in the world, these exotics often have few natural enemies and contribute little to the support of native wildlife. Their vigor combined with a lack of natural enemies often leads to outbreaks in populations. Invasive plants can totally overwhelm and devastate established native plants and their habitats by outcompeting them for nutrients, water, and light—and because they offer so little food value to native wildlife, they are destructive to biodiversity on every level.

These can also wreak havoc on our home landscapes, especially if they gain a foothold in our garden beds. Just one gardener planting one invasive plant can have a huge negative effect. Birds can devour hundreds of seeds from this plant and spread them throughout your area as well as up and down their migratory routes.

If you find you need to eradicate an unwanted exotic, you must be careful not to spread the problem further by tossing the uprooted or chopped-up plants into the woods or wetlands in your neighborhood! Herbicides may or may not work, but if used, should be employed with an eye to minimizing any environmental or ecosystem damage.

Kudzu and Japanese honeysuckle are notoriously rampant exotics, but here in New England there are others to look out for. Some of the biggest culprits in this region include: purple loosestrife *(Lythrum salicaria),* Japanese barberry *(Berberis thunbergii),* Oriental bittersweet *(Celastrus orbiculatus),* glossy buckthorn *(Frangula alnus),* common buckthorn *(Rhamnus cathartica),* Japanese knotweed *(Polygonum cuspidatum,* syn. *Fallopia japonica),* and multiflora rose *(Rosa multiflora).*

Action items:
- Learn which plants are invasive in your area.
- Do not buy or grow exotic, invasive plants.
- If you already have an unwanted exotic invasive in your home landscape, get some expert advice on eradication, perhaps from your local Cooperative Extension Service or a conservation organization.
- Ask your local nursery to stop selling these plants. If demand drops or goes away, they will stop carrying them.
- Volunteer to help with local eradication efforts, sometimes run by organizations such as the Audubon Society, with expert supervision.
- Support organizations that promote native plants and habitats, including the New England Wild Flower Society, the Audubon Society, the Nature Conservancy, and local and regional land trusts.

SOME ADDITIONAL THINGS GARDENERS CAN DO

Gardeners may be more attuned to nature than other people, and we certainly should be. Let's make sure our home landscapes are part of the solution, not part of the problem. Here are a few more ideas or "action items" to consider implementing as you work to make your landscape more sustainable, low-impact, and biologically diverse and healthy.

Protect standing dead trees whenever possible. If there is any possibility that people may be in harm's way, especially children who frequent the area, or the tree or its limbs are at risk of falling on a house, driveway, or sidewalk, do remove it. But if it's in the back of your yard or especially, if it's in a wooded spot, leave it alone. Birds, insects, and many other creatures may depend on the tree or call it home. Dying trees and branches are all part of the cycle of a natural woodland habitat. As a gardener, trying to be too clean and tidy, in this case, is working against nature.

Provide a variety of water sources for wildlife. The presence of water can mean the difference between life and death for animals in the wild. Provide a birdbath for birds, or install a small or large water garden that attracts not only birds, but also may attract and provide sanctuary for dragonflies, butterflies, frogs, and even turtles.

Plant to support butterflies. You can help reverse an alarming trend of butterfly endangerment and population decline. Butterflies need nectar throughout their life, and adults feed primarily in sunny areas. Grow beautiful flowers they like, including but not limited to the following: zinnia, verbena, black-eyed Susan, purple coneflower, butterfly bush, beebalm, passion vine, and lantana—all of these are profiled later in this book. Less ornamental but enticing (at the caterpillar and larval stages of the life cycle) plants you can add judiciously to your garden beds include milkweed, parsley, dill, fennel, Queen Anne's lace, and many grasses. The more we can do to attract and keep butterflies in our gardens, the more enjoyment we'll have from these beautiful creatures.

Participate in the National Wildlife Federation's Wildlife Habitat Program. Perhaps you've seen them. Those small but attractive signs near a schoolyard, a backyard, or by the street. The people that display them are proud to show that they are part of this worthy program and have a "Certified Wildlife Habitat." Chances are if you're an environmentally aware gardener, you're already doing many of the things in your landscape that could get it certified, too. Go to their Web site at www.nwl.org or call them at 1-800-822-9919, learn their guidelines, apply, and get your own proud sign!

ANNUALS
for New England

Annuals and tender perennials last just one season but they're a delight to grow and dear to every gardener's heart. Just weeks after planting, annuals carpet empty spaces with lasting color and soon grow big enough to screen out the ripening of spring bulb foliage. The vivid zinnias and marigolds are so easy and so satisfying they're ideal for a child's garden. In dappled light, impatiens and coleus color well and grow more beautiful as summer advances; planted in complementary colors, they're stunning. Petunias, geraniums, and other tender (not winter hardy) perennials keep windowboxes and patio planters blooming all summer long. Some annuals self-sow and may spare you the trouble of replanting the next year. Rogue out those you don't want and transplant others for a late show.

Many annuals have a rewarding cut-and-come again habit: the more flowers you harvest, the more the plant produces. Many of the best cutting flowers are annuals. Knowing how to harvest—where to cut the stems—is the key to keeping them blooming. We've described the process below, and, where relevant, with each plant in this chapter. For a continuous supply of vivid zinnias, giant golden marigolds, and late summer bouquets of pastel cosmos scented with basil, establish a cutting garden where your pleasure in harvesting won't spoil the view. Or, plant cutting flowers in a kitchen garden with vegetables, herbs, and dwarf fruit trees.

PLANTING AND FERTILIZING

Annuals have modest root systems. To be all they can be, much like vegetables, they require sustained moisture and plenty of nutrients. The Introduction explains how to prepare beds for annuals in order to bring the soil to pH 5.5 to 7.0, the ideal range for most. The organic fertilizers release their nutrients slowly, so the plants should do well the first season without further fertilization. Then every year, in late winter or early spring, fertilize beds for annuals with applications of these same slow-release, long-feeding organic fertilizers. If your annuals seem to slow after periods of intense bloom, they may benefit from fertilization with one of the water-soluble organic fertilizers, such as seaweed or fish emulsion.

Nursery-grown seedlings of annuals are very tempting in mid-spring when you're looking for instant flowers. Those available at garden centers in spring are beautiful, already in bloom, healthy—and in everybody else's garden. Eventually you will want to try the alluring other varieties you see in garden magazines and catalogs. Then you will have to sow seeds—in the garden or, for a head start, indoors. (See Starting Seeds Indoors in the Appendix.) The time to sow seeds outdoors for annuals is well after the last frost for your area. Please don't rush the season! Most annuals just won't take off until the ground and the air warm up—seeds and seedlings that are set out too early will sulk. Flowers whose seed packets say they are "cold hardy" you can sow outdoors somewhat earlier than the others. Most annuals sown outdoors will come into bloom soonest when they are planted where they are to stay and flower.

Sow smaller seeds by "broadcasting," that is, sprinkling them thinly over the area. Larger seeds you can sow in "hills," groups of four to six, or three to five, equidistant from each other. Flowers for edging beds can be sown in "drills," that is, dribbled at spaced intervals along a shallow furrow, which is drilled in the soil by dragging the edge of a rake or hoe handle along the planting line. For planting depth, follow the instructions on the seed packet, or sow seeds at a depth that is about three times the seed's diameter, not its length. Seed packets usually suggest how much to thin seedlings to give the mature plants space to develop.

After sowing your seeds, give the planting bed a slow, thorough overhead soaking. (See Watering in the introduction.) Water often enough during the next two or three weeks to maintain soil moisture. Thin the seedlings to 3 to 5 inches apart and apply a 2-inch layer of mulch. In periods of drought, water gently and deeply every week or ten days, or when you see signs of wilting.

For windowbox, basket, and container plantings we recommend using a commercial potting mix. If you mix into the soil a polymer such as Soil Moist™ you'll find maintaining moisture much easier. It holds twenty times its weight in water, and releases the water (and dissolved soil nutrients) slowly.

ANNUALS CAN TAKE A LOT OF PINCHING

To be all they can be, some annuals need pinching at several junctures in the season. The pinching begins right at planting time. It's a fact that once an annual gets into flower production, the plant puts less strength into growing its root system. But the plant needs a big, healthy root system to get through hot summer days. The way to encourage the plant to grow its root system is to pinch out the flowering tips at planting time. If you are using the color of budded or opening flowers to decide where the plant goes, wait until it is in the ground to pinch out the flowers and buds. Then, at planting time, or very early in their careers, the branching tips of many, even most, annuals should be pinched out to encourage the production of side branches where flowers will develop. Again, at midseason, when the plants are fully matured, you can encourage new branching and more flowering in some long-branching annuals, such as petunias, by shearing all the stems back by a third or half. And some annuals bloom more fully and over a longer period if you deadhead them consistently and persistently. Pinch out the spent flowers between your thumb and forefinger—it's fast and easy. Frequent harvesting of most annuals has the same beneficial effect. Cut the stems for bouquets just above the next set of leaves: that's where the new flowering stems will arise.

NASTURTIUM CLOSE-UP

TO ENCOURAGE SELF-SOWERS

Annual flowers that sow their own seeds will naturalize—come back year after year—under favorable conditions. Volunteers self-sown by petunias, snapdragons, and little French marigolds pop up every year in our gardens. They'll come into bloom late, and for Zones 3 and 4—even 5—can't be counted on for late summer and fall bloom. But we often transplant them for the fun of seeing what will happen. Other self-sowers are so productive they become weeds—morning glory comes to mind—and should be rogued out as soon as you identify them.

You can encourage self-sowing by spreading a 1- or 2-inch layer of humusy soil around the crowns of the parent plants and allowing flowers to ripen seedheads toward the end of the growing season. Keep the soil damp, and gather the seeds as they ripen and scatter them over the soil. Or, wait until the seeds are dry and loose in their casings, then shake the seedheads vigorously over the soil.

THESE ANNUALS HAVE COLORFUL FOLIAGE

Alternantha (*Alternantha* cultivars)
Beefsteak Plant (*Acalypha wilkesiana*)
Burning Bush (*Bassia scoparia* forma *trichophylla*)
Coleus (*Coleus* × *hybridus*)
Coppertone Mallow (*Hibiscus acetosella*)
Dusty Miller (*Senecio cineraria*)
Jacob's Coat (*Acalypha wilkesiana*)
Joseph's Coat (*Amaranthus tricolor*)
New Guinea Impatiens (*Impatiens hawkeri* hybrids)
Polka Dot Plant (*Hypoestes phyllostacha*)
Snow on the Mountain (*Euphorbia marginata*)
Variegated Impatiens (*Impatiens wallerana* variety)
Variegated Wax Begonia (*Begonia semperflorens*
    Cultorum hybrids)
Variegated Zonal Geranium (*Pelargonium*
    'Ben Franklin')

THESE ANNUALS HAVE OUTSTANDING FRAGRANCE

Four-o-Clocks (*Mirabilis jalapa*)
Evening Stock (*Matthiola triscuspidata, M. bicornis*
    'Starlight Sensation')
Heliotrope (*Heliotropium arborescens*)
Large White Petunia (*Petunia axillaris, P.* F2 hybrids)

Mignonette (*Reseda odorata*)

Nicotiana hybrids (*N.* × *sanderae*)

Sweet Alyssum (*Lobularia maritima* 'Sweet White')

Sweet Pea (*Lathyrus odoratus* 'Cupani', 'Old Spice', 'Old Fashioned Scented Mixed')

Wallflower (*Cheiranthus cheirii*)

Woodland Tobacco (*Nicotiana sylvestris*)

HOW TO MAKE NEW PLANTS FROM STEM CUTTINGS

Cuttings and potted-up plants brought indoors last fall can provide you with new plants for this year's garden. Here's how you can multiply your holdings:

GERANIUMS: Cut off the top 4 inches of a sturdy, healthy stem just below a leaf node. Remove the leaves from the bottom 2 inches of the stem. Let the cuttings dry for a few hours or overnight. Then put them in a solution that is a gallon of water with a half to a teaspoon of bleach, and set them in a sunny window. When they have a grown a full set of roots—usually three or four weeks—transplant your cuttings to 3- to 4-inch pots filled with a gritty potting mix or nonclumping kitty litter. Or, root the cuttings in a rooting mixture. Grow your cuttings in a south-facing window.

You can also get cuttings to root by dipping the ends lightly in a rooting hormone and standing them in damp vermiculite or sand tented with plastic film. When the cuttings have developed enough roots to resist a slight tug, they're ready to transplant.

COLEUS AND WAX BEGONIAS: Cut off the top 6 inches of a leafy stem just below a leaf node. Remove the leaves from the bottom 3 inches, then place the cutting in water containing a few drops of bleach, and set it in a semi-sunny window to root. When it has grown roots, transplant it to an all-purpose potting mix. Grow it in an east- or west-facing sunny window.

HOW TO DRY FLOWERS FOR POTPOURRIS AND WINTER BOUQUETS

As flowers used in potpourris and dried bouquets come into bloom, harvest the best specimens. Summer's dry heat is a good time for drying flowers.

When harvesting for POTPOURRIS, pick the flower heads in a dry, hot moment of the day. Spread the petals over paper towels on screens. Set the screens to dry in a warm, airy, dry place—a high-ceilinged attic, for example, or a garage.

For DRIED BOUQUETS, harvest large, moist flowers like ZINNIAS when the blooms are fully open. Single varieties are better for drying than doubles. Harvest dryish flowers like the EVERLASTINGS and SALVIA just before the buds open. Cut fresh, healthy stems 12 to 14 inches long, and strip away all the lower leaves to prepare them for drying.

AIR DRYING. Tie the stems together in small, loose bunches, then enclose the heads in paper bags as they shed. Label the bags. Hang the bunches upsidedown for two to ten days, or until very dry, in a warm, dry, airy place. Direct sunlight fades the colors.

SILICA GEL. Use this light, grainy gel to dry delicate, moist flowers like COSMOS. Spread 2 or 3 inches of gel in a large box. Wire the flower stems, lay them on the gel, and cover them with more silica gel. In twenty-four hours, check a flower; if it is dry, remove the others from the gel, and leave them on top of it for another day. Then store them in layered tissue in air-tight, labeled boxes to which you have added a few tablespoons of silica gel. If gel clings to the petals, pour a little clean sand over them to remove it. With use, the gel's blue crystals turn pink. To restore it for later use, spread the gel over cookie sheets covered with paper towels and heat in a conventional oven on low, thirty minutes for a 1-pound can. The gel turns light blue when it is ready to use again. The gel gets hot, so let it cool in the oven five to ten minutes; then store it in air-tight containers.

OVEN-DRYING. Dryish flowers dry well in a conventional oven on a low setting, and a microwave oven at half-power can dry flowers in minutes. Dry a test flower for each batch to learn the length of time the others will need. Support the flower with paper towels before drying it. The outside petals will dry sooner than those inside. To avoid over-drying in either type of oven, check progress often through the oven window.

AFRICAN DAISY
Osteospermum spp.

Color(s)—Yellow, white, pink, lavender, purple

Bloom period—Most or all of the summer

Mature Size (H × W)—1 to 2 ft. × 2 to 4 ft.

Water needs—Although fairly drought-tolerant, they do need supplemental water during prolonged dry spells.

Planting/Care—These tough and perky daisies thrive in full sun, and average to poor soil is fine, so long as it is well-drained. Plant in spring after frost, and water regularly until established. As the summer progresses, you may pinch back the plants to encourage more compact, thicker growth.

Pests/Diseases—Fungal diseases or rot can occur if the plants are overwatered or water lingers on their foliage.

Landscaping Tips & Ideas—Because these daisies stretch and spread, give them plenty of room. They are ideal for embankments, slopes, and streetside plantings. They also do well in a hanging basket, planter box, or tucked into a mixed flower bed.

AGERATUM
Ageratum houstonianum

Color(s)—Blue, lavender-blue, pink, white

Bloom period—Late spring to mid-autumn

Mature Size (H × W)—6 to 12 in. × 6 to 12 in.

Water needs—For the first several weeks, keep the soil around the plants well-watered; then water plants often enough to make sure they don't go dry.

Planting/Care—Start seeds inside eight weeks before planting time, or direct-sow in mid-spring. Plant small plants after the weather becomes reliably warm. Best in well-drained, humusy soil. Provide a 2-inch mulch starting 3 inches from a plant. For fuller plants, pinch out the first set of flowering tips.

Pests/Diseases—None serious

Landscaping Tips & Ideas—Lovely with silver artemisia and mid-size pink-and-white snapdragons. It makes a pretty edging or a flower border when interplanted with white sweet alyssum and large-flowered pink wax begonias. Good varieties include 'Blue Danube', 'Adriatic', and 'Blue Surf'.

ANGELONIA
Angelonia angustifolia

Color(s)—Purple, white, pink, and bicolors

Bloom period—Late spring to fall

Mature Size (H × W)—1 to 2 ft. × 1 ft.

Water needs—Best in consistently moist soil

Planting/Care—Grow this easy, heat-tolerant, perky beauty in beds or containers, where it needs only plentiful sun and fertile, well-drained soil. It does not require deadheading to continue blooming.

Pests/Diseases—None serious

Landscaping Tips & Ideas—Its larger size and bushy, upright habit make it a fine choice for mixed flower beds, and the big, flower-laden stems are good in homegrown bouquets. Some varieties are more cascading or floppy in habit, which makes them suitable for pots or planter boxes. The Angel Mist series is excellent; deep plum 'Angel Face Dark Violet' is a standout. 'Catalina White Linen' is a good companion plant with any other hue.

BACHELOR'S BUTTON, CORNFLOWER
Centaurea cyanus

Color(s)—Purple, blue, white, pink, maroon

Bloom period—Spring to frost

Mature Size (H × W)—1 to 3 ft. × 4 to 8 in.

Water needs—Drought-tolerant once established

Planting/Care—These jaunty flowers, held aloft on wiry stems, prosper in full sun and average soil and need little care. Sow seed directly into the garden in early spring (or start them early indoors). Space plants about 8 to 12 inches apart. Mixes deserve a nice, open spot where they can reach their full potential and provide you with abundant color.

Pests/Diseases—None

Landscaping Tips & Ideas—Because the flowers are small, this plant should be grown in quantity for best impact, either in patches or sweeps in a sunny meadow-like setting or other open area. Curbside plantings are pretty. Mixes well with other small-flowered annuals and wildflowers. A wonderful bouquet flower, fresh or dried.

BEGONIA, WAX
Begonia Semperflorum-Cultorum hybrids

Color(s)—White, pale pink, rose, coral, deep pink, red, bicolors

Bloom period—Mid-spring to September

Mature Size (H × W)—6 to 9 in. × 12 to 18 in.

Water needs—Water often to get established; after that, maintain a moist soil.

Planting/Care—Start from seed in early January, or buy seedlings in April and May. Set out a few weeks after the last frost date, 6 to 8 inches apart. Water deeply when other flowers show signs of wilting; wax begonias are to remain crisp even in the first stages of water deprivation. Too much shade inhibits flowering.

Pests/Diseases—Slugs and snails may nibble the fleshy leaves; set out traps or bait.

Landscaping Tips & Ideas—Perfect edgers for semi-shaded flower borders. Look great when planted in clumps of three behind a ribbon of sweet alyssum. They're attractive in containers, and thrive in windowboxes.

CALIFORNIA POPPY
Eschscholtzia californica

Color(s)—Orange, red, pink, yellow, white, bicolors

Bloom period—Summer

Mature Size (H × W)—8 to 12 in. × 12 in.

Water needs—Drought-tolerant once established

Planting/Care—Very easy to grow from seed—this is also the best way to get some of the pretty non-orange cultivars. Needs full sun and decent-to-poor soil that drains well. The succulent ferny foliage helps it cope with dry weather. It can get a bit sprawling and raggedy late in the season, at which point you can pull out the plants and look forward to next year's show. Self-sows.

Pests/Diseases—None

Landscaping Tips & Ideas—A pretty sight in mixed flower beds as well as meadow-garden planting schemes. The pure orange species is wonderful in the company of any blue or purple flowers of your choice. The Thai Silk series has ruffled petals in red, pink, yellow, and orange.

CELOSIA, COCKSCOMB
Celosia argentea var. cristata

Color(s)—Red, pink, yellow, apricot, burgundy-red, gold, cream

Bloom period—Summer

Mature Size (H × W)—4 to 24 in. × 8 to 12 in.

Water needs—Water well after planting and maintain the moisture the first few weeks. Provide enough water so the plants don't dry out.

Planting/Care—Start seeds indoors in late winter. Or, as soon as the soil has warmed, sow the seeds in fertile, well-drained soil worked to a depth of 8 to 12 inches. Transplant or thin to 12 inches apart. The plants start well but sulk if roots are disturbed. Provide a 2-inch mulch, starting 3 inches from the plant.

Pests/Diseases—Susceptible to fungus if overwatered

Landscaping Tips & Ideas—Use to create solid splashes of color. A row makes a big statement in a kitchen garden, and the feathery varieties are graceful wherever situated.

COLEUS
Solenostemon scutellarioides

Color(s)—Foliage colors in combinations of red, mahogany, chartreuse, yellow, white, rose, near-black

Bloom period—Summer (not grown for flowers)

Mature Size (H × W)—14 to 24 in. × 12 to 18 in.

Water needs—Maintain moderate soil moisture.

Planting/Care—Grows quickly from seed sown in flats indoors. Or get seedlings in May from garden centers. Plant after last frost in rich, humusy soil. When the plants show signs of new growth, pinch out the top 3 to 4 inches of the lead stems. Encourage fuller growth by removing flower spikes as they start up, and pinch out the leggy tips of branches.

Pests/Diseases—None serious

Landscaping Tips & Ideas—The more red foliage there is, the more direct sun the plant can take. Containers full of coleus in mixed colors are breathtaking. Combine with contrasting hues of impatiens to brighten shady nooks.

CORN POPPY
Papaver rhoeas

Color(s)—Pink, red, salmon, white

Bloom period—Late May into June

Mature Size (H × W)—2 ft. × 1 ft.

Water needs—Water to establish, and thereafter if rain is scarce.

Planting/Care—Sow in March or early April, and again at two-week intervals for color all season. Early-spring soil is too wet to dig without harming it; just scratch its surface to make a shallow seedbed. Poppies take any well-drained soil, even alkaline soil. Because of their taproots, they are tricky to move later. After flowers fade, remove seedpods to encourage more flowering. Leave pods on from last flush of fall bloom to encourage self-sowing. You can naturalize by sowing seed randomly over mowed or bare-soil areas either after Thanksgiving or in early March.

Pests/Diseases—None serious

Landscaping Tips & Ideas—Use in informal settings alone or combined with ornamental grasses, bachelor's buttons, daisies, and other meadow-type flowers.

COSMOS
Cosmos bipinnatus

Color(s)—Crimson, orange, rose, yellow, white, pink, burgundy-red, and bicolors

Bloom period—Late summer to frost

Mature Size (H × W)—2 to 6 ft. × 2 ft. and more

Water needs—Water for the first two or three weeks, enough to sustain soil moisture. Once established, water only if wilting.

Planting/Care—Sow seeds indoors and transplant outdoors after the ground has warmed. Withstands drying winds but may need staking in an exposed location. Does well in well-drained soil of average fertility. When plants reach 24 inches, encourage branching by pinching out the top 3 to 4 inches of the lead stem. Repeat as the next set of branches develop.

Pests/Diseases—None serious

Landscaping Tips & Ideas—Essential in a cottage garden, great in a meadow garden, and makes a good follow-on for spring bulbs. Combines especially well with snapdragons, blue salvia, and Shasta daisies.

EDGING LOBELIA
Lobelia erinus

Color(s)—Light blue, deep blue, wine-red, spotted white, pure white

Bloom period—Spring into summer

Mature Size (H × W)—4 to 6 in. × 8 to 12 in.

Water needs—Water to sustain soil moisture for the first two or three weeks; maintain soil moisture throughout the growing season.

Planting/Care—Plant seedlings two to four weeks after the last frost in part sun; in cool regions, lobelia needs full sun. Prepare a well-drained, humusy bed and set 10 to 12 inches apart. Apply a 2-inch mulch between plants. After every flush of bloom, shear played-out stems to encourage a new round of flowering. Tends to die out in high heat.

Pests/Diseases—None serious

Landscaping Tips & Ideas—Carpet empty spaces between fading early-spring flowers. Lovely dripping from a basket or urn. Deep blue 'Crystal Palace' combines beautifully with zonal geraniums.

FAN FLOWER
Scaevola amemula

Color(s)—Lilac, purple, pink, white

Bloom period—Summer

Mature Size (H × W)—6 in. to 2 ft. × 4 to 5 ft.

Water needs—Water regularly, especially during hot spells or if in a pot or hanging basket.

Planting/Care—Get plants from garden centers in late spring or early summer, and plant in moderately fertile, well-drained soil. Fertilize occasionally for more robust, succulent growth and lush flowering.

Pests/Diseases—None

Landscaping Tips & Ideas—A hanging-basket and windowbox classic, thanks to its trailing habit and flower-laden stems. Also good in flower borders as an edging plant. Mixing several hues together makes a fine display. Full or dappled sunshine is recommended. Expect plenty of color for little effort. It's also easy to overwinter—just take cuttings or pot up plants and keep them barely moist.

FOUR-O-CLOCK
Mirabilis jalapa

Color(s)—Yellow, rose, white, red

Bloom period—Midsummer till frost

Mature Size (H × W)—2 to 3 ft. × 2 ft.

Water needs—Water to get established, and then only if there is a severe drought.

Planting/Care—These plant themselves by dropping seeds in the garden in the fall. To get started, direct-sow in the spring. Or plant or transplant seedlings. They like sun, but accept some shade. They will do fine in ordinary, well-drained soil. Space at least a foot apart to allow for their mature size.

Pests/Diseases—Japanese beetles can appear in July. Brush them off the foliage into a jar of soapy water several times daily. Cut back marred foliage.

Landscaping Tips & Ideas—Plant as edging along high walks, in flower borders, or in mixed borders where they can serve as temporary shrubs by late summer.

FOXGLOVE
Digitalis spp. and hybrids

Color(s)—White and assorted

Bloom period—Mid-spring to early summer

Mature Size (H × W)—30 in. × 30 in. or more

Water needs—Water to sustain soil moisture when getting established; after that, water deeply every week unless you get a soaking rain.

Planting/Care—In early fall or early spring, sow seeds. Or set seedlings out as soon as the soil becomes workable. Plant in sun in cooler areas, and in part shade where summers are warm. Cannot stand excessive heat, so avoid planting in hot, windless pockets. Taller cultivars may need staking. Space 12 to 15 inches apart.

Pests/Diseases—Slugs and snails can be a problem in shadier locations; trap or bait the culprits.

Landscaping Tips & Ideas—Foxglove is essential to the cottage garden's romantic tangle, absolutely striking when planted in clumps of three to five with columbines, poppies, and zinnias.

GERANIUM
Pelargonium hybrids

Color(s)—Red, salmon, fuchsia, pink, white, bicolors

Bloom period—Spring, summer, fall

Mature Size (H × W)—1 to 2 ft. × 1 to 2 ft.

Water needs—Allow the soil surface to dry out between deep waterings.

Planting/Care—Good morning light or a western exposure is ideal. Plant in well-drained garden or potting soil. Do not mulch. Encourage branching by pinching out the end of the lead stem and side branches. Repeat once more during the growing season. Deadhead consistently.

Pests/Diseases—Leaf spot and rots can occur when plants are overwatered or are crowded. Remove and discard marred leaves and blossoms.

Landscaping Tips & Ideas—Great container plants combined with one another or mixed with dusty miller, petunias, blue ageratum, and white sweet alyssum. For bedding schemes, use compact varieties like the Tango series; for landscaping, use the larger Rocky Mountain group.

IMPATIENS
Impatiens walleriana

Color(s)—White, red, orange, salmon, melon, lavender, orchid, spotted forms, and bicolors

Bloom period—Late spring to frost

Mature Size (H × W)—3 to 36 in. × 8 to 24 in.

Water needs—Keep newly planted seedlings nicely watered for the first few weeks. In high heat, flowering may slow and a light shower to cool them off can be a help. Otherwise, water only to keep from wilting.

Planting/Care—Plant in spring, in a spot of high or filtered shade in humusy, moist, well-drained ground. Set seedlings 8 to 10 inches apart, and apply a fine mulch.

Pests/Diseases—Slugs and snails can be a problem; bait or trap them.

Landscaping Tips & Ideas—Impatiens and coleus or caladiums in similar colors are beautiful together. Lovely with variegated hostas. Plants of the compact Sonic series are suited to containers; the larger Super Sonics are meant for landscaping.

LANTANA
Lantana camara

Color(s)—Orange, yellow, red, pink, lilac, purple, cream, bicolors

Bloom period—Summer

Mature Size (H × W)—2 to 4 ft. × 1 to 6 ft.

Water needs—Water to establish, and deeply thereafter when there are dry periods.

Planting/Care—Plant in spring after danger of frost is past. Poor to average, well-drained soil in a sunny spot is best. Pinch back the growing tips to encourage a bushier plant. By season's end, it could be quite shrubby. Fertilization is usually not needed, although container-grown ones may benefit.

Pests/Diseases—The most common problem is fungal diseases, usually caused by overwatering and/or crowding.

Landscaping Tips & Ideas—Because they are so bright and colorful, lantanas belong in prominent spots, in a sunny flower bed, in pots on a sunny deck or patio, even in windowboxes or planter boxes. Note that the foliage has a somewhat sharp fragrance, not unpleasant, but not sweet.

LARKSPUR
Consolida ambigua

Color(s)—Blue, pink, white, lilac

Bloom period—Midsummer to fall

Mature Size (H × W)—2 to 5 ft. × 2 to 3 ft.

Water needs—Water young plants regularly until they are established and then whenever rainfall is scarce.

Planting/Care—Larkspur does not like transplanting, so either plant very young plants in May, or sow seeds directly into the garden in late fall after frost or in very early spring. They do fine in well-drained garden soil of any type. Thin seedlings to 10 to 12 inches apart when they are a few inches tall. Mulch to discourage weeds. Deadhead often, and stake if needed. Larkspur tends to decline and die back after flowering.

Pests/Diseases—Crowding and humidity promote mildew. Note: all parts of larkspur are poisonous.

Landscaping Tips & Ideas—Use as filler in a flower border for a cottage-garden look, or add to a cutting garden.

LOVE-IN-A-MIST
Nigella damascena

Color(s)—Blue, purple, rose, pink, white

Bloom period—Summer

Mature Size (H × W)—1 to 2 ft. × 1 ft.

Water needs—Water transplants until established; water in dry spells.

Planting/Care—Grow in average soil that is well-drained, in a sunny spot, or try a few plants in a container with a lightweight potting mix. Be forewarned that these plants self-sow enthusiastically at season's end—to prevent or mitigate this, cut bouquets or harvest the ornamental, striped seedpods for use in flower arrangements or wreaths, or simply tear the plants out. Note that these plants are at their best in cooler weather—prolonged hot or humid weather can cause them to flag.

Pests/Diseases—None

Landscaping Tips & Ideas—These airy plants are a nice addition to sunny flower borders, where they will weave in and amongst other flowers. The Persian Jewels series is handsome and gets about 16 inches high.

MARIGOLD
Tagetes spp. and hybrids

Color(s)—Off-white, shades of gold, orange, yellow, mahogany, and bicolors

Bloom period—Summer until frost

Mature Size (H × W)—8 in. to 4 ft. × 10 in. to 3 ft.

Water needs—Water until the plants are a few inches high.

Planting/Care—Sow seeds in the garden after the soil has warmed up, or get a head start indoors four to six weeks earlier. Plant garden-center ones as soon as they are offered in the springtime. Best in well-drained, moderately fertile soil. Set small ones 6 to 8 inches apart, and tall ones 15 to 24 inches apart. Mulch. Deadhead or shear to keep blooms coming.

Pests/Diseases—None serious

Landscaping Tips & Ideas—Use to ornament dry, neglected corners. Also a great follow-on for spring bulbs. Vegetable gardeners like to use them for decoration as well as to repel some insect pests.

MELAMPODIUM
Melampodium spp.

Color(s)—Yellow, white

Bloom period—Spring through summer

Mature Size (H × W)—8 to 12 in. × 8 to 12 in.

Water needs—Though quite drought-tolerant, needs regular water when first getting established

Planting/Care—Plant after danger of frost is past in decent, well-drained soil in a sunny location. Once established, this plant needs little attention and will bloom its head off. Do water, however, if there is a prolonged dry spell.

Pests/Diseases—None serious

Landscaping Tips & Ideas—This perky plant forms low bushy mounds that are dense with handsome gray-green leaves and studded with flowers. It goes great with spring bulbs and perennials, out in the garden—particularly ones that are blue, purple, or bright red. It's also terrific in pots, planter boxes, and windowboxes, provided it gets the sun it loves.

MILLION BELLS
Calibrachoa hybrids

Color(s)—Violet, purple, pink, magenta, white, pale yellow

Bloom period—Summer

Mature Size (H × W)—6 to 8 in. × 1 to 2 ft.

Water needs—Drought-tolerant once established

Planting/Care—These incredibly floriferous petunia relatives (the flowers look like mini-petunias) will bloom all summer long for you if you give them a sunny spot with average, well-drained soil and occasional water. There is no need to deadhead.

Pests/Diseases—None serious

Landscaping Tips & Ideas—Their trailing habit makes them suitable for windowboxes and all sorts of pots, as well as hanging baskets. But they are also wonderful at weaving their glowing color in and among taller flowers in a mixed flower bed. They tolerate steamy weather and some neglect. Some recommended varieties include orange-red 'Terra Cotta' and bright pink 'Coral Pink'.

NASTURTIUM
Tropaeolum majus

Color(s)—Orange, yellow, red, cream, and bicolors

Bloom period—Summer

Mature Size (H × W)—12 to 15 in. × 20 to 24 in.

Water needs—Keep the bed watered until the plants are a few inches high.

Planting/Care—Sow seeds in full sun as soon as the weather warms, or start them indoors four or so weeks beforehand. This plant likes poor, well-drained soil and does best in full sun, though it can succeed in part sun in warmer areas.

Pests/Diseases—Worms, loopers, and aphids can attack your plants. If the infestation is bad, tear out the plants and try again.

Landscaping Tips & Ideas—They are wonderful in sweeps and beds, in pots, in planter boxes, at the front of flower borders, and near or among vegetables or herbs (for their flowers and leaves are edible—they have a peppery taste).

NICOTIANA
Nicotiana spp. and hybrids

Color(s)—Red, rose, pink, white, green

Bloom period—Summer to frost, sometimes beyond

Mature Size (H × W)—1 to 2 ft. × 1 ft.

Water needs—Water until plants are established, and thereafter when rainfall is sparse.

Planting/Care—Select plants that have no buds or blooms, if possible, and plant in May or as soon as the soil is workable. Site where they will receive full sun at least in the mornings; some afternoon shade is good and even enhances their colors. They like good garden soil that drains well. Cutting their flowers stimulates more flowering and provides blossoms for indoors.

Pests/Diseases—Vulnerable to mosaic virus and Colorado potato beetles

Landscaping Tips & Ideas—Use as their heights suggest—middle of borders, edging, containers, along fences, or in a cutting garden.

PANSY
Viola × wittrockiana

Color(s)—Shades and combinations of yellow, blue, white, orange, pink, rose, purple, black

Bloom period—Spring through cool summers

Mature Size (H × W)—8 to 10 in. × 8 to 18 in.

Water needs—Best when soil is kept evenly moist

Planting/Care—Plant in early spring, in partial or dappled shade. Well-drained, humusy soil is ideal. Space plants about 3 inches apart, then mulch. Fertilize with a liquid organic fertilizer. When the plants show vigorous growth, start deadheading. As spring advances, pansies become leggy.

Pests/Diseases—Sometimes rot is a problem if the plants are overwatered or the soil doesn't drain well.

Landscaping Tips & Ideas—For a showy spring display, plant mixed colors of large-flowered pansies, including lots of yellows, and interplant with early tulips. Handsome in windowboxes and containers. Delightful as accent plants or edgers in rock gardens, wild gardens, and woodsy places.

PENTAS, STAR-CLUSTER
Pentas lanceolata

Color(s)—Pink, red, purple, white

Bloom period—Summer

Mature Size (H × W)—1 to 2 ft. × 1 to 2 ft.

Water needs—Although established plants can be drought-tolerant, the plants look and flower best when watered regularly.

Planting/Care—Plant in the garden after danger of frost is past, in fertile, well-drained soil and plentiful sun. Encourage branching and bushier growth by pinching back the tips. Fertilizing is not necessary unless the plants are not vigorous; pot-grown ones appreciate a little food boost now and then.

Pests/Diseases—Aphids and spider mites can be a problem; the best prevention is a healthy plant.

Landscaping Tips & Ideas—Add this bright and exuberant bloomer to mixed flower borders or feature in containers. Though usually available in mixes, you can sometimes get it in individual colors or white, which helps if you have a special color theme in mind.

PETUNIA
Petunia × hybrida

Color(s)—White, yellow, orange, pink, red, blue, lavender, magenta, purple, bicolors

Bloom period—Summer

Mature Size (H × W)—6 in. to 2 ft. × 3 to 4 ft.

Water needs—Keep the soil evenly moist.

Planting/Care—Start seeds indoors ten to twelve weeks before the weather warms, or buy small plants at local garden centers in the spring. Grow where they will receive at least six hours of daily sunlight, in well-drained, humusy soil. You must deadhead to keep them in full bloom. Fertilizing is recommended for the Wave series.

Pests/Diseases—Fungal diseases can bother petunias that are too damp. Sucking and nibbling insects may attack both leaves and blooms.

Landscaping Tips & Ideas—Petunias make good follow-on plants for spring flowers. The sparkling whites of the cascading varieties harmonize mixed colors in baskets and containers. Petunias are versatile and reliable bedding plants.

PORTULACA, MOSS ROSE
Portulaca grandiflora

Color(s)—Pink, red, orange, yellow, white

Bloom period—Summer to frost

Mature Size (H × W)—6 to 10 in. × 6 to 12 in.

Water needs—Does fine on moisture provided by rain

Planting/Care—Plant young plants in late May. Needs heat and full sun to thrive. It actually prefers sandy, lean soil that drains well—plant it where nothing else will grow. Place seedlings 6 to 8 inches apart. A bit of weeding may be necessary until the plants really spread. Use no fertilizer or mulch.

Pests/Diseases—None

Landscaping Tips & Ideas—Use as a filler in sunny beds where other plants go dormant in midsummer, in rock gardens, between steppingstones, and in containers. Massed as a ground cover, it will obscure embarrassing bare spots in the yard.

POT MARIGOLD
Calendula officinalis

Color(s)—Orange, gold, lemon, apricot, white

Bloom period—Early summer to fall

Mature Size (H × W)—12 to 30 in. × 12 to 15 in.

Water needs—Pot marigold needs moisture in the soil, both during germination and as the seedlings grow. But it doesn't like to be soggy wet.

Planting/Care—Sow in the spring as soon as the garden soil can be worked, or start seeds early indoors, six to eight weeks before spring planting season begins. Needs full sun or very bright shade and rich, well-drained soil that contains enough humus to sustain moisture. Deadhead to prolong flowering. During the hottest weeks of summer, the plants may slow down. Be patient; they'll revive and bloom again when the weather freshens.

Pests/Diseases—None serious

Landscaping Tips & Ideas—These are great bedding plants. Try groups of six in flower beds. They are handsome in big tubs.

SALVIA
Salvia splendens

Color(s)—Red, lavender blue, many other colors

Bloom period—Midsummer till frost

Mature Size (H × W)—1 to 3 ft. × 1 to 1½ ft.

Water needs—Water to establish, and during prolonged dry spells.

Planting/Care—Start seeds indoors ten to twelve weeks before mid-spring, or sow seeds outdoors in well-drained, humusy soil. Space seedlings 6 to 8 inches apart. To encourage branching, pinch out the top 3 to 4 inches of the lead stem. Deadhead to promote more flowering.

Pests/Diseases—Mites, aphids, or whiteflies can attack stressed plants. If overwatered, rot can occur.

Landscaping Tips & Ideas—Full sun is best for scarlet sage, but blue sages flower moderately well with morning sun. Scarlet sage planted with coral New Guinea impatiens makes a striking show. The blue salvias are beautiful filler plants for shrub roses, and lovely with snapdragons or cosmos in complementary colors.

SNAPDRAGON
Antirrhinum majus

Color(s)—Red, pink, rose, yellow, and bicolors

Bloom period—Spring through early fall

Mature Size (H × W)—7 to 30 in. × 8 to 15 in.

Water needs—Water often when establishing, and then every week to ten days unless there is a soaking rain.

Planting/Care—Plant in mid-spring after the soil and air have warmed. (Seeds are easily started indoors ten to twelve weeks earlier.) Space seedlings 6 to 10 inches apart, then mulch the area. When they are 4 inches high, pinch out the tips of the lead stems and the next two sets of branches. Deadhead or harvest consistently. Stake if needed.

Pests/Diseases—Where rust is a problem, plant only rust-resistant varieties.

Landscaping Tips & Ideas—The tall ones in rosy colors are beautiful with tall ageratum and silver artemisia. For windy places, choose large-flowered tetraploids like 'Ruffled Super Tetra' for their strong stems.

SPIDER FLOWER
Cleome hassleriana

Color(s)—White and shades of pink, rose, lilac, purple

Bloom period—Midsummer till frost

Mature Size (H × W)—3 to 5 ft. × 1½ to 2 ft.

Water needs—Maintain soil moisture until seedlings are growing well, and deeply thereafter if plants show signs of wilting in a drought.

Planting/Care—Start seeds indoors eight to ten weeks early, or direct-sow or plant seedlings after last frost. Any well-worked, well-drained, light soil suits it, even sandy soil. Space seedlings 15 to 20 inches apart. Stake lead stems later in the season if the plants become shrub-size. Deadhead often to minimize self-sowing.

Pests/Diseases—None

Landscaping Tips & Ideas—A mass planting is handsome against a stone wall. An excellent background plant for a flower border. Also a lovely addition to a meadow garden.

STOCK
Matthiola incana

Color(s)—Red, purple, pink, white

Bloom period—Summer

Mature Size (H × W)—6 in. to 3 ft. × 1 ft.

Water needs—Do not let their soil dry out.

Planting/Care—Choose a site with some light shade, to preserve flower color and scent best. Average soil that is neutral to slightly alkaline is ideal. In those conditions, plants will grow quickly and generate lots of blooms.

Pests/Diseases—Minimal, if plants are in good health

Landscaping Tips & Ideas—Plant plenty, so you can enjoy them in your garden, mixed with other bloomers, and still harvest some for bouquets. To savor the spicy scent, grow some in containers on your porch or patio; remember to keep them well-watered. The Trysomic Mix has double flowers for extra impact and was bred to be weather-tough.

41

SUNFLOWER
Helianthus annuus

Color(s)—Yellow, orange, maroon, creamy white, bicolors; centers of green, maroon, or black

Bloom period—Summer to fall

Mature Size (H × W)—2 to 12 ft. × 2 to 2½ ft.

Water needs—Keep soil moist until established; drought-tolerant thereafter.

Planting/Care—Sow seeds directly in the garden once the soil is warm. Thin, or plant seedlings, up to 18 inches apart. The taller ones may need staking, especially as their seedheads become heavy. To save the seedheads from the birds, wrap the heads in gauze before the seeds ripen.

Pests/Diseases—Rust, mildew, and verticillium wilt can occur; plant resistant varieties.

Landscaping Tips & Ideas—The tall ones belong in a row of their own in the kitchen garden, or lining a fence or blank wall. The new dwarf forms look good in a flower border, or with vegetables and herbs in a kitchen garden.

SWEET ALYSSUM
Lobularia maritima

Color(s)—White, rosy-violet, purple

Bloom period—June till frosts

Mature Size (H × W)—4 to 8 in. × 12 to 18 in.

Water needs—Sustain soil moisture during establishment; water deeply in midsummer, especially during dry, hot weather.

Planting/Care—Seeds may be started indoors in early February, or get seedlings in the spring. Plant in well-drained, humusy soil. Needs four to six hours of daily sun to flower well. Sweet alyssum readily self-sows and often reverts to the original, less-interesting species, so discard volunteers.

Pests/Diseases—None serious

Landscaping Tips & Ideas—Makes a neat, fragrant edger for flowering borders and walks. Add some to hanging baskets, planters, and tubs so the stems will drip over the container edges as the plant fills out. It thrives tucked into moist planting pockets in a dry stone wall, and is very pretty with purplish ornamental peppers.

ZINNIA
Zinnia elegans and hybrids

Color(s)—Shades of red, pink, orange, magenta, yellow, white, and bicolors

Bloom period—Summer through early fall

Mature Size (H × W)—6 in. to 3 ft. × 1 to 3½ ft.

Water needs—Water every week to ten days during periods of drought.

Planting/Care—Sow seeds indoors about four weeks before planting time, which is when the soil has warmed. Set seedlings of miniatures 6 inches apart; space larger ones 18 inches apart. When the seedlings are 6 inches high, pinch out the tips of the lead stems to encourage branching. Deadhead consistently, and harvest flowers at will.

Pests/Diseases—Subject to leaf spot and mildew, so avoid mulch and crowding. Plant resistant cultivars.

Landscaping Tips & Ideas—Zinnias are ideal follow-on plants for gaps left by the passing of spring flowers. Dwarfs make good edgers. Bigger ones brighten flower beds and garden paths.

ANNUALS

USES OF ANNUALS

Colorful fillers: Summer-flowering annuals—sweet William, pinks, rocket larkspur, and garden balsam, for example—are your best bet for filler gaps in perennial beds to mask the oh-so-slow ripening of spring-flowering bulbs. Low-growing annuals are perfect fillers for empty spaces in new beds of perennials and shrubs. Annuals that are good cutting flowers are a kitchen garden's best friends.

Hedges and screening: Some annuals grow big enough that you can use them to plant a temporary hedge—giant marigolds ('Climax' marigolds) and burning bush (*Scoparia forma* [sic] *trichophylla,* for example.) Annual vines grow like weeds, making them perfect screening while a slow-growing vine gets going (see Chapter 10). They'll cover poles, trees stumps, and other garden eyesores in a matter of weeks.

Bedding plants: Long-blooming annuals (and flowering bulbs) are used for "bedding out," a practice used by municipalities to create flower beds that bloom all season. A typical sequence is a spring display of pansies, replaced when they fade by marigolds, replaced for fall by ornamental cabbages. Bedding out is a good way to deal with an area regularly scalped by winter snow removal. Ageratum, wax begonias, and sweet alyssum are also used to create ribbons of color to spell out municipal and business names and logos, a fun garden project to mark a very special anniversary.

Baskets and planters: Annuals have modest root systems, so lots can be fitted into a relatively small container. Cascade-type petunias are the stars, along with tiny, bright-as-sunshine creeping zinnias (*Sanvitalia procumbens,* a true annual) and the tender perennials *Scaevola aemula, Sutura cordata* 'Snowflake', and sweet potato vine. Spills of ivy and geraniums, helichrysum, and variegated vinca lend grace to flowery compositions.

Cutting flowers: Cut-and-come-again annuals are among the best cutting flowers. To have masses of blooms for bouquets, plant zinnias, snapdragons, cosmos, and China asters. Give them a bed of their own in an out-of-the-way place. or plant them in your kitchen garden—they'll make it beautiful!

Children's gardens: Annuals are a child's best garden friends. Quick popper-uppers, like zinnias, marigolds, and sunflowers, satisfy a youngster's need for early results. Seeing buried seeds grow, watching butterflies and bees seeking nectar, and sharing flowers and a garden's endless surprises give children proud stories to tell.

SEQUENCE OF BLOOM

Keeping color in the garden all season long requires that you know the sequence in which plants in the annuals group bloom. Garden literature, seed packets, and the annuals list in this book will tell you when each species peaks—spring, summer, or fall.

Some species come in varieties that bloom either early, midseason, or late. Where the growing season is very short, plant early-bloom varieties. To enjoy a long season, plant all three varieties, or sow seeds every two weeks until July.

If you want to have annuals in bloom in mid- to late spring, set out seedlings of those that peak in cool weather, like pansies and pot marigolds. To keep the summer garden blooming, sow a series of seeds of heat-tolerant annuals like marigolds and zinnias. For late summer color in semi-shade, plant impatiens seedlings. To have loads of flowers in summer and until frosts, sow seeds or plant seedlings of cosmos ('Sonata White' is lovely), China asters, and especially snapdragons. To keep your garden going into late fall, as space becomes available, set out pansy seedlings and ornamental cabbage and kale. In some areas, the pansies may still be good to go in spring.

To have a garden that's interesting in and out of bloom, include annuals with colorful foliage—they're long-distance runners. Dusty miller (*Senecio cineraria*) in varieties 'Silver Dust' and 'Cirrus' stay silver. Variegated geraniums and kaleidoscopic coleus grow and glow until the frosts begin.

STARTING ANNUALS FROM SEED

For mass "bedding" displays and effective garden design, you will need enough seeds or seedlings of annuals to plant them in groups of five, seven, ten, or more; the smaller the plant, the more you will need. Garden centers and mail-order catalogs sell seedlings of annuals, but growing your own saves money and provides a more interesting plant selection. Save even more—and avoid leftover seeds—by buying seeds with friends.

You'll find annuals are easy to grow outdoors from seed. To get a head start, you can sow seeds indoors in late March or April.

When to sow seeds indoors depends on how long the seeds take to germinate, how quickly the plants grow, and how soon they can be moved to your garden (which depends on how much cold they can stand). Seed packets label seeds "hardy," "half-hardy," or "tender," and most packets suggest when and where to sow the seeds in the garden and whether and when they can be started indoors.

Hardy: The seedlings of hardy annuals can take some frost. These can be started outdoors in early spring, even before the last frost. Seed packets indicate that some can even be sown in fall after freezing temperatures have come.

Half-hardy: These seedlings are harmed by frost, but they tolerate cool, wet weather and cold soil. You can sow these seeds outdoors a couple of weeks after the last frost.

Tender: These seeds grow fastest and do best when they are sown outdoors only after both the air and the soil have warmed. Indoors you can start these in late March or April, depending on your zone.

Sowing the seeds: The planting depth for seeds is usually given on the seed packet. The rule of thumb is to sow seeds at a depth of about three times the seed's diameter, not of its length.

Always sow seeds in moist soil, and always water them well after planting. If you can plant shortly after a rain or before, you won't have as much watering to do.

Larger seeds are sown in "hills," groups of four to six, or three to five, equidistant from each other. Flowers for edging are usually sown in "drills," dribbled at spaced intervals along a shallow furrow created by dragging the edge of a rake or hoe handle along the planting line.

Preparing the soil: Annuals depend on modest root systems to produce masses of flowers and foliage. So they need soil that is well supplied every year with nutrients as well as sustained moisture, especially the first several weeks in the garden.

To keep an established bed for annuals productive, it really is important to check and amend the pH every year.

Transplanting seedlings: The seedlings of hardy annuals will grow fastest transplanted after the air temperature has reached 55 degrees Fahrenheit during the day. The others will do best planted after the soil has warmed. Transplanting too early just leaves seedlings sulking and yellowing. But you can give seedlings of hardy annuals an early start under a cold frame or hot bed, or in the open garden under "hot caps," cloches, tenting, and other solar heat collectors. Before planting seedlings—your own or seedlings from the garden center—it's a good idea to let them "harden off" or acclimate a bit, either in a sheltered location protected from direct sun and wind or in a cold frame. Apply a two-inch layer of mulch after planting.

CARE ADVICE

Annuals do their best when they have a good head start and are deadheaded. Here's how:

1. Thin seedlings to space the plants as recommended on the seed packet.

2. Shortly after seedlings reach a height of 2 or 3 inches, pinch out the tips of cascading plants, like petunias, and branching annuals that have one, two, or three central stems, like cleome and snapdragons. Repeat during the growing season.

3. "Deadhead" (remove) fading blooms or harvest flowers to prevent the formation of seed-heads. Plants developing seeds generally stop blooming or are slow.

4. Snip off stems or plants crowding others in a container or bed; nasturtiums often do this.

5. Remove weeds as they appear. Some self-sowers are so productive they become weeds—love-in-a-mist comes to mind—so root them out as you would weeds.

WATERING

Seeds and seedlings need rain or watering not only before and right after planting, they also need enough water, especially during the early weeks, to maintain soil moisture so they can maintain constant growth. In periods of drought and any time you see signs of wilting, water deeply. Soil that has been plentifully supplied with humus and has a 2- to 3-inch mulch cover will need less watering.

FERTILIZING

If you are using an organic fertilizer such as Plant-Tone®, mix it into the top 3 inches of the soil at the rate of 5 pounds per 100 square feet, four to six weeks before planting. If you are using a chemical fertilizer, either granular or slow-release like Osmocote®, apply it just before planting. Annuals that slow after a first flush of bloom may benefit from a modest extra fertilization with a water-soluble fertilizer, either organic or chemical.

In addition, throughout the season, maintain a 2- to 3-inch mulch cover because the as the underside decomposes, it adds to the organic content of the soil. Every three to five years, mix in applications of rock phosphate, green sand, and gypsum, the soil additives recommended when preparing a planting bed.

PESTS

Annuals suffer from the pests and diseases common to other flowers. Aphids jam petunia tips, small green caterpillars bug geraniums, whiteflies love lantana, and spider mites spin tiny traps in marigolds and verbena. The plants withstand minor invasions when you prepare the soil well and fertilize annually. Space and prune the plants so that air keeps flowing through, and there will be fewer problems.

THESE ANNUALS ARE EASY TO START INDOORS

Start these seeds the designated number of weeks before planting season, and the seedlings will be ready to plant when the weather breaks.

- Ageratum, 8 to 10 weeks
- Cosmos, 4 to 6 weeks
- Celosia, 5 to 6 weeks
- China aster, 6 to 10 weeks
- Cleome, 6 to 10 weeks
- Flowering Tobacco, 9 to 11 weeks
- Mallow (*Lavatera trimestris*), 6 to 8 weeks
- Marigolds, dwarf, 8 to 10 weeks
- Marigolds, all, 5 to 6 weeks
- Petunia, 11 to 15 weeks
- Portulaca, 10 to 12 weeks
- Salvia, 8 to 10 weeks
- Snapdragons, dwarf, 12 to 14 weeks
- Snapdragons, tall, 7 to 10 weeks
- Verbena, 8 to 10 weeks
- Zinnias, dwarf, 6 to 8 weeks
- Zinnias, tall, 4 to 6 weeks

THESE ANNUALS ARE BEST FOR BASKETS

- Bacopa (*Sutera cordata* 'Snowflake')
- Basket Begonia (*Begonia* × *tuberhybrida* Pendula Group)
- Black-eyed Susan Vine (*Thunbergia alata*)
- Cascade Petunia (*Petunia* × *hybrida*)
- Cigar Flower (*Cuphea ignea*)
- Creeping Zinnia (*Santvitalia procumbens*)
- Edging Lobelia (*Lobelia erinus*)
- Fan Flower (*Scaevola aemula*)
- Impatiens, Busy Lizzy (*Impatiens walleriana*)
- Ivy-leaf and Balcon Geraniums (*Pelargonium peltatum*)
- Lady's-eardrops (*Fuchsia* × *hybrida*)
- Moss Rose (*Portulaca grandiflora*)
- Nasturtium (*Tropaeolum majus*)
- Painted Nettle (*Coleus blumei*)
- Sapphire Flower (*Browalia speciosa*)
- Tall Nasturtium (*Tropaeolum majus*)
- Trailing Coleus (*Coleus rehnelthiamus* 'Trailing Rose')
- Verbena (*Verbena* × *hybrida*)
- Water Hyssop (*Bacopa caroliniana*)
- Yellow Sage (*Lantana camara*)

THE IMPORTANCE OF DEADHEADING/HARVESTING

Removing fading blooms stops plants from developing seeds and stimulates the production of flowers. It's called "deadheading." If your garden is small, you can pinch out dying blossoms while you drink your morning cuppa. If the area is big, go to the garden in late afternoon and enjoy the sunset while you search out and remove spent blossoms.

"Pinching out" is the quick and easy way to deadhead large flowers on slender stems. Place your thumbnail and forefinger behind the bracts—the small scale-like leaves behind the petals—and squeeze the flower head off. To deadhead stems too thick to pinch out, use small pointed pruning shears, made especially for the purpose; they're as fine as embroidery scissors.

Shearing with hand-held shears is the easy way to deadhead plants that cover themselves with tiny florets, sweet alyssum for example.

Shearing may help plants attacked by mildew; cut them down to the ground. Diseased foliage goes into the garbage—not into the compost pile. Then apply sulfur, ultrafine horticultural oil, copper fungicide, Immunox, or Bayleton. Plant mildew-resistant varieties next year.

Harvesting most annuals has the same effect as deadheading. Cut the stems of zinnias and cosmos just above a pair of leaves, which is where the next set of flowering stems will develop.

JANUARY

- January is for dreaming. Use pages torn from garden catalogs to create your own album of annuals. Put a sticky note by each plant to remind yourself where it would fit in your garden and why you pulled the page.

- Maintain moderate moisture in pots of annuals and tropicals overwintering indoors.

- We gain almost a whole hour of extra daylight this month, so indoor plants are starting to grow again. Add a half-strength dose of houseplant fertilizer to the water for cuttings, plants, and tropicals.

- Starting seeds indoors can save you money, and it's also fun during the dreary days of winter. Shop for and gather the equipment you'll need, including the mix, the containers, and the seed packets.

- In Zones 6 and 7, during the January thaw there's enough warmth in the sun to heat up the interior of a south-facing coldframe. Monitor the interior temperature on sunny days and ventilate.

FEBRUARY

- Plan to attend one or more of the spring flower and garden shows for inspiration.

- Before finalizing catalog orders and buying your plants, make sure there is a suitable place and space for each plant chosen.

- Check your buying plans against your inventory of seeds that were left over or saved from last year, and take a look at the cuttings and potted plants you brought indoors last fall. List what you have, will order by mail, buy at the local garden center, and have to go looking for.

- In warm Zone 7, between the end of this month and mid-March, you can start seed indoors for hardy annuals like ageratum, alyssum, balsam, cleome, geraniums, pansies, annual phlox, stock, snapdragons, and slow-growers like petunias.

- Begin repotting plants brought indoors last fall, and pot up the strongest cuttings. Continue to fertilize them, at half-strength, every other time you water them.

MARCH

- Save your urge to plant hardy annuals outdoors until the mud season is over and the soil has drained enough to be workable.

- In your garden log, chronicle the progress of seeds started indoors and outdoors.

- In Zones 3 to 6, toward the middle of this month, you can start seeds indoors for slow-growing and hardy annuals. In a mild year in warm Zone 7, late this month you may be able to start some outdoors.

- As soon as the snow is gone and winter moisture has left the soil, you can begin readying beds for planting.

- Transplant seedlings as soon as they outgrow their planting pockets. Pinch out the growing tips of seedlings that are becoming leggy.

- Repot geraniums, lantana, mandevilla, and other tender perennials saved from last year. Discard poor performers.

- Clear the ground of last year's annuals, including ornamental cabbages and kale planted last fall.

APRIL

- Prepare containers for planting—even if they're too big to empty—by mixing a slow-release fertilizer and 2 inches of compost into the top 6 inches of the soil.

- Record the date of the last frost in your garden log. Also note when you planted what in your garden, and how the plants fared.

- Sow seeds indoors of annuals that need four to six weeks to mature before going outdoors.

- Wait until night temperatures are steady at or above 55 degrees F. to put seeds and seedlings of tender annuals and perennials outdoors.

- Transplant seedlings outgrowing their containers into larger pots.

- Deadhead early-spring annuals: pansies, sweet William, wallflowers.

- If the weather turns dry toward the end of the month, water your seedlings deeply.

- Spider mites can be a problem for seedlings growing indoors. Combat as soon as you notice them, before the infestation gets out of control.

MAY

- This month is a big planting season. When night temperatures are 55 to 60 degrees F., you can sow seeds of tender annuals outdoors, and set out seedlings of tender perennials grown as annuals.

- Where spring bulbs leave gaps, make successive sowings of zinnias and annual phlox.

- As spring gardens begin to peak, visit public and private gardens and record the plant combinations you wish were blooming in your own garden right now.

- Thin seedlings to 2 to 3 inches apart.

- Deadhead pansies and shear lobelia to prolong the flowering cycle.

- Unless the garden is moist from recent rain, before every planting gently and slowly water long enough to lay down 1 to 1 ½ inches. Use an empty can to measure the water.

- Begin a fertilizing program for hanging baskets and container plants. They'll benefit from bi-weekly applications of a water-soluble fertilizer or manure tea at half-strength.

JUNE

- It is far enough into the season now to evaluate the performance of transplants of rooted cuttings and plants saved from last year—geraniums, coleus, impatiens, wax begonias, and others—and decide whether this is something you want to do again in the fall.

- Be ruthless with weeds. They are easier to pull when the soil is damp.

- Remove hardy spring flowers that have gone by, to make space for seedlings of annuals that will bloom in the summer and fall—snapdragons, blue and white salvia, China asters, cosmos, and nasturtiums.

- Maintain a 2-inch mulch around your annuals, but try to keep it 2 or 3 inches away from the crowns of the plants.

- The tallest flowers may benefit from staking—tall snapdragons and zinnias, 'Climax' marigolds, and woodland tobacco. Set the stakes within 2 or 3 inches of the stem.

- Continue to pinch out the tips of petunias and other cascading plants and branching annuals.

JULY

- Before your vacation, arrange to have the container plantings watered, and group the containers in a semi-shaded spot.

- Weary of deadheading? Make a note to try annuals that self-clean next year: narrowleaf zinnias, wax begonias, impatiens, ageratum, pentas, New Guinea impatiens, and spider flower.

- Early this month, start seeds of hardy fall-flowering annuals such as pansies, calendula, ornamental cabbage, and kale.

- Remove crowded plants and poor performers from baskets and windowboxes. Replant with fresh seedlings if there is space, with six to eight weeks of growing weather ahead.

- Check the moisture in large plant containers every three to four days; check small pots and hanging baskets every day or two.

- In hot, airless corners, aphids, spider mites, and whiteflies are a threat. Spray with a Neem-based product to help.

- Plants that are blooming vigorously may benefit from a sidedressing of a handful of compost.

AUGUST

- Note the annuals that withstand August heat and drought best, and record those that go on blooming as summer cools. You'll want to plant those again next year.

- Toward the end of the month, replace spent annuals with seedlings of pansies, calendula, flowering cabbage, kale, and other fall annuals. If you didn't start them yourself earlier, you'll find seedlings at garden centers.

- Check and, if needed, replenish the mulch around your annuals. It decomposes in summer heat.

- Check the annuals you have staked. If needed, install taller stakes.

- Late summer annuals provide some of the year's loveliest bouquets, so harvest as the summer flowers peak!

- You will probably have to water the gardens twice this month. If you can, water in the early morning. If mildew is a threat, water the soil rather than the plants.

- Attics and garages are hot and dry in August, perfect for air-drying statice, blue salvia, and others.

SEPTEMBER

- Visit public and neighboring gardens, and keep notes on attractive combinations of fall bedding plants.

- Note the date of the first light frost, the one that blackens the tips of the impatiens, and report how each of the annuals withstood it, and how windowbox and basket plants fared as summer ended.

- Note where the self-sowers are likely to have dropped seed, so you will know to leave the soil undisturbed when preparing the garden beds for spring.

- When nighttime temperatures plunge toward 55 degrees F., get ready to move tender perennials and tropicals indoors. A week before the move, rinse the plants and clean the exterior of the containers, and when the plants are dry, spray them with an insecticide to protect them from whiteflies and spider mites.

- Apply a light foliar feeding to snapdragons, stock, and other annuals that bloom until frost.

- Deer are becoming very active. Set out or exchange deterrents.

OCTOBER

- This is an especially good time to start—or to change—the shape or size of a flower bed. Use a garden hose to outline potential changes, and live with them a few days before you start to dig.

- In your garden log, record the date of the first hard frost, the one that hits the salvias and snapdragons.

- Pull up and compost frost-blackened marigolds, impatiens, and the tender annuals still out in the garden and in containers.

- Continue to deadhead the pansies, calendula, and any other flowers still blooming.

- If the weather turns dry, water the pansies as well as the areas around self-sowing annuals.

- Watch out for whiteflies and spider mites on the plants brought indoors for the winter. If occasional showers and applications of insecticidal soap don't keep them away, apply an insecticide.

NOVEMBER

- From the public library, borrow garden books, such as Graham Rice's *Discovering Annuals* and *The Sweet Pea Book* (Timber Press), and videos or DVDs that can teach you more about using annuals in garden design.

- Empty, clean, and store hanging baskets, windowboxes, and other containers. Stack wire baskets, or hang them from a rafter in a garage or basement. Scrub plastic and terracotta containers with a scrub pad. Then dip them in a diluted bleach solution. Rinse and store upside-down out of the weather (they tend to crack if left outside).

- Spread the soil from hanging baskets, small and medium pots, planters, and windowboxes over your compost pile.

- Deadhead your indoor plants.

- Do not fertilize the plants you brought indoors, until they show signs of new growth in January.

- The annuals are all done for now. Focus on spring-flowering bulbs!

DECEMBER

- Do family and friends a favor by telling them about garden tools and accessories you'd enjoy receiving.

- Organize your supply of seeds—those purchased that weren't used and the seeds gathered in your garden. A convenient way to file and store them is in a spiral binder equipped with clear plastic sleeves. Place each variety of seed in its own small freezer bag, mark the date on the bag, and store each bag inside its own sleeve in the binder.

- Cuttings of geraniums, coleus, impatiens, and wax begonias growing in water should have masses of hair-like rootlets by now. Discard any that aren't rooting. If the water is growing murky, change it and add a few pieces of charcoal to keep it pure.

- After several heavy frosts, check the pansies, flowering cabbages, and kales—and discard those that are dead.

PERENNIALS
for New England

Perennial flower and foliage plants give our gardens continuity. Annuals live one season: some perennials come back for just a few years, but many live ten to fifteen, and peonies can go on for more than a hundred. When we're planning a garden, our first selections are a series of hardy perennial flowers whose sequence of bloom will carry color through the bed all season long. Within most species' stated bloom period, you can find varieties that come into flower early, midseason, or late. To avoid late spring frostbite in cool regions, choose late-blooming varieties of spring-flowering species; where frosts can come early in fall, choose early-blooming varieties of perennials that bloom in late summer. Most hardy perennials are resistant to surface frosts unless temperatures go below freezing (32 degrees Fahrenheit).

Once we've chosen the flowers for a garden, we look for foliage plants that will complement or contrast with the flowers. Colorful foliage—silver, blue, yellow, or red—placed to reinforce, or to be a foil for, the colors of nearby blooms, add depth to the design. Think of the effect of spiky globe thistle and furry lamb's ears. Two lovely blue-foliaged plants are the blue fescue and blue oat grass. Variegated foliage lightens the deep greens of summer. At a distance, white variegated foliage appears jade green or soft gray; yellow foliage looks like a splash of sunshine and fills the same role as flowers for color. We add ferns for the romance they lend to shaded spots, and ornamental grasses tall and small that dance, whisper, and bring sound and movement as well as contrasting texture to the garden.

In a large mixed border we include the big, dramatic leaves and striking architectural forms of a few bold-foliaged perennials, like the large hostas. In the shadow of tall perennials, these shade-lovers thrive even in a sunny border. Giant tropical foliage plants—dwarf canna and the hardy banana—add drama. These "tender perennials" won't winter over, but the effect they create is worthwhile. We also like to set two or three dwarf needled-evergreens in strategic places. Their solid forms and strong color anchor flower beds in early spring and, with the ornamental grasses, they maintain a sense of life when the garden falls asleep.

Finally, we look for places to tuck in a few aromatic herbs and very fragrant flowers. Low-growing, fuzzy, white-splashed pineapple mint and silver variegated thyme lighten the bed and release their fragrance as you brush by. Aggressive plants like the mints can be set out in buried containers. Some flowering bulbs and many important perennials have fragrant varieties. The most fragrant of the spring flowers are the hyacinths, in the Bulbs chapter, but there are fragrant varieties of many perennials not noted for scent. Two examples are 'Myrtle Gentry', a scented peony, and 'Fragrant Light', a scented daylily.

WHEN, WHERE, AND HOW TO PLANT

If you are interested in experimenting with a flowering meadow or a wild garden, you'll need hundreds of plants. Try your hand at starting the perennials indoors from seed. (See Starting Seeds Indoors in the Appendix.) Plants that are the species, rather than an improved or named variety, will come true from seed. But when you want named varieties, we strongly recommend you choose container-grown perennials grown from root divisions and rooted cuttings. Here's why: the named varieties (hybrids and cultivars) are superior plants selected from among thousands. Growers propagate them from cuttings or root divisions, and so they bloom true to the parent plants. Buy one plant, divide it into three plants, repeat for three years and you will have twenty-seven plants, in five years 243 plants, ad infinitum—so a perennial bed of the best can be inexpensive.

Perennials in 1-quart containers planted in the spring produce some blooms the first season: those sold in 2- to 3-gallon containers will make a bigger show. Most container-grown plants can be set out in spring, summer, or fall. In spring, growers ship some perennials bare root—astilbes, for instance.

These often flower fully only the second or third season. A perennial that blooms early in the spring—columbine, for example—gives the best show its first year when it is planted the preceding late summer or early fall.

The surest way to provide soil in which perennials will thrive for many years is to create a raised bed. In the Soil Preparation and Improvement section of the introduction, you'll find instructions for creating a raised bed and for bringing the soil to pH 5.5 to 7.0, the range for most flowers. Our recipe for a raised bed includes long-lasting, organic fertilizers.

The spacing of perennials depends on the size the mature plant will be: we've offered suggestions with each plant. Always provide a generous planting hole, one twice the width and twice as deep as the rootball. Before you plant, unwind roots that may be circling the rootball, or make shallow vertical slashes in the mass, and cut off the bottom ½ inch of soil and rootball. Soak the rootball in a big bucket containing starter solution. Half-fill the hole with improved soil. Then set the plant a little high in the hole, fill the hole with soil, and tamp firmly. Water slowly and deeply, then mulch around the planting following our suggestions in the Introduction. Staking protects very tall flowers in a storm. But most, if correctly fertilized and given plenty of space all around, won't need it. Tall, weak growth is often the result of force-feeding with non-organic fertilizers. Wide spacing also improves air circulation, reducing the risk of disease and mildew. Water a new planting, slowly and deeply, every week or ten days for a month or so unless you have soaking rains. Water any time the plants show signs of wilting.

CARE GUIDELINES

After summer, we like to leave in place seed-bearing perennials with woody upright structures, like black-eyed Susans, because they look interesting in winter and feed the birds. Some self-sow and will replenish the planting. In late fall we clear away collapsed foliage that will grow slimy after frost. When you remove dead foliage,

cut it off; don't pull it off because that may damage the crown beneath. In late winter or early spring, after the soil has dried somewhat, it is time to clear away the remains of last year's dead foliage: watch out for burgeoning stems while raking through perennials such as lilies. Every year in spring, and again in September to October, we fertilize established perennial beds, not individual plants, by broadcasting slow-release, organic fertilizer: an acid-type fertilizer at the rate of 4 pounds per 100 square feet for acid lovers, 6 pounds of a non-acid fertilizer for the others.

ARTEMISIA
Artemisia species and hybrids

Hardiness—Zones 3 to 7

Color(s)—Silver foliage, yellow blooms

Bloom period—August to October

Mature Size (H × W)—1 to 3 ft. × 1 to 3 ft.

Water needs—If rain is scarce, water new plants; once established, they will be quite drought-tolerant.

Planting/Care—Plant divisions in spring or fall in average, well-drained soil. Space plants 18 inches apart for good air circulation and to allow room to grow. Pinch stem tips to encourage bushier growth. Unless the flowers are useful, remove them. Stake tall varieties. Divide overlarge clumps in fall.

Pests/Diseases—None

Landscaping Tips & Ideas—The silver foliage punctuates green and sets off individual plants and their flowers. In spring, they obscure ripening bulb foliage, and they're still present to complement mums in fall. Do well in containers, especially the rampant 'Silver King'. For nice compact growth, drastically cut back by half in June.

ASTER
Aster spp., cultivars, and hybrids

Hardiness—Zones 3 to 8

Color(s)—Blue, dark purple, lavender, pink, rosy red, white

Bloom period—Fall

Mature Size (H × W)—1 ½ to 6 ft. × 3 to 5 ft.

Water needs—Water regularly to establish, then during dry spells.

Planting/Care—Sow seed in spring for bloom the following year; for bloom this year, set out root divisions. Soil should be moderately fertile, well-drained, and somewhat acidic. To keep plants stocky, pinch back shoot tips once in spring and again a month later. Taller ones will need support or staking.

Pests/Diseases—Avoid mildew by watering at the base of the plant. Plant resistant varieties.

Landscaping Tips & Ideas—Beautiful in naturalized plantings with ornamental grasses and Russian sage; good in mixed borders. Also lovely by a stone wall. Aptly named 'Purple Dome' is an excellent dwarf variety.

ASTILBE
Astilbe spp. and hybrids

Hardiness—Zones 4 to 8

Color(s)—Creamy white, pale pink, lilac, coral, red

Bloom period—Late spring and early summer

Mature Size (H × W)—1 to 5 ft. × 2 to 3 ft.

Water needs—Maintain a moist soil. Water deeply every week to ten days unless you have a soaking rain.

Planting/Care—Plant in mid-spring or late summer. Astilbe thrives in light shade in rich, moist, humusy soil with a slightly acid pH. Maintain a 2- to 3-inch mulch; replenish every spring. Fertilize once in early spring and again in early fall. Divide every three years if you wish, between early spring and August.

Pests/Diseases—Problems are rare.

Landscaping Tips & Ideas—Excellent fillers in the middle or back of shade borders. Lovely edging a woodland path, stream, or pond. Make a lovely tapestry when massed.

BABY'S BREATH
Gypsophila paniculata

Hardiness—Zones 3 to 9

Color(s)—White or pink

Bloom period—June to August

Mature Size (H × W)—2 to 3 ft. × 3 to 4 ft.

Water needs—Water when rainfall is scarce.

Planting/Care—Transplant potted plants anytime during the growing season. Likes average, well-drained soil that is not too rich in organic matter and is slightly alkaline. Choose the site well because they resent being moved later. Space plants 2 to 3 feet apart. Cut off branches when their flowers turn brown to stimulate renewed flowering and compactness. Stake as needed.

Pests/Diseases—Avoid possible crown, root, and stem rot problems with well-drained soil.

Landscaping Tips & Ideas—Use as a filler or as a foil to coarser, green-foliaged plants in a border or rock garden. Pink-flowered ones harmonize with silver-leaved artemisia and lamb's ears. Try it near the front of a border as a see-through plant.

BEEBALM
Monarda didyma

Hardiness—Zones 4 to 9

Color(s)—Scarlet, pink, cerise, red, white, violet

Bloom period—Late summer

Mature Size (H × W)—2 to 4 ft. × 2 to 4 ft.

Water needs—Water new plantings deeply for a month or so. Maintain soil moisture during dry spells.

Planting/Care—Set out container plants or divisions in spring, summer, or fall. It thrives in well-drained, moist, humusy soil that is slightly acid. Give it plenty of space and good air circulation—it will fill in quickly. Fertilize in early spring. Deadhead to extend bloom period. You may divide every two or three years in late summer.

Pests/Diseases—Prevent mildew by providing space and air circulation and choosing resistant varieties.

Landscaping Tips & Ideas—Makes an extraordinary statement, even from afar, when planted in a clump growing against a wall. Wonderful in perennial borders, meadows, wild gardens.

BELLFLOWER
Campanula spp.

Hardiness—Zones 3 to 8

Color(s)—Blue, white, lavender, pink

Bloom period—Late spring to early fall

Mature Size (H × W)—2 to 6 ft. × 2 to 3 ft.

Water needs—Water new plants deeply every week the first season, unless you have soaking rains.

Planting/Care—Seed sown indoors develops well and transplants readily. Springtime divisions and rooted cuttings also grow readily. Provide well-drained, fertile garden soil. Mulch well. Stake taller ones. Fertilize in early spring and early fall. Deadhead the taller forms only when all the buds on a stem have faded.

Pests/Diseases—Combat slugs and snails with traps and/or bait.

Landscaping Tips & Ideas—Taller ones are perfect for cottage gardens and lovely with Siberian iris. Attractive with gray artemisias and white- or pink-flowered plants. Height and habit varies with species and cultivar—shop around for ones that suit your garden plans.

BLACK-EYED SUSAN

*Rudbeckia fulgida var. sullivantii
'Goldsturm'*

Hardiness—Zones 3 to 9

Color(s)—Dark gold with a dark eye

Bloom period—Summer into fall

Mature Size (H × W)—1½ to 2½ ft. × 2 to 2½ ft.

Water needs—Water new plants weekly if there are no soaking rains; drought-tolerant once established.

Planting/Care—Plant from seedlings started indoors or as seed in the open garden once the soil can be worked in spring. Well-drained, light, fertile soil is best. Fertilize in early spring and early fall. Deadhead. Divide in early spring every four years to keep plants full and flowery.

Pests/Diseases—Powdery mildew is the biggest threat; prevent with good air circulation.

Landscaping Tips & Ideas—Excellent with ornamental grasses, in meadow gardens, and in sunny mixed flower borders. Leave some flowers on at season's end for the birds, for winter interest, and to reseed.

BLAZING STAR

Liatris spicata

Hardiness—Zones 3 to 9

Color(s)—Mauve, purple, white

Bloom period—Mid- to late summer

Mature Size (H × W)—2 to 3 ft. × 2 ft.

Water needs—Water during prolonged dry periods.

Planting/Care—Plant divisions in the spring in ordinary, moist, well-drained soil (they hate soggy winter soil). In good soil, they do not need routine fertilizing—in fact, a rich diet makes for floppy flower stems that need staking. Promote fall rebloom by cutting back the flower spikes to basal foliage after three-quarters of the florets have faded. Do not cut back foliage until it is brown. Dig and divide the corms in overlarge clumps every four years.

Pests/Diseases—None significant

Landscaping Tips & Ideas—The rose colors are most compatible with blue, lilac, or magenta flower companions, or yellow ones such as black-eyed Susan, goldenrod, beebalm, and Shasta daisy. Ornamental grasses make good neighbors as well.

BLEEDING HEART

Dicentra spectabilis

Hardiness—Zones 3 to 9

Color(s)—Pink, pink-and-white, white

Bloom period—Spring

Mature Size (H × W)—2 to 3 ft. × 2 to 3 ft.

Water needs—Maintain a moist soil; water deeply every week to ten days if there have been no soaking rains.

Planting/Care—Plant in early spring in well-drained, rich, moist, humusy soil. The key to a long bloom period is sustained moisture and mulch, especially in the warmer reaches of New England. Fertilize in early spring and early fall. Cut back to the ground when the foliage dies down. Established plants resent being disturbed, but with care you can divide them in early spring.

Pests/Diseases—Not common—though rot can occur in poorly drained sites.

Landscaping Tips & Ideas—Delightful in shady gardens, with wildflowers, and in rock gardens. Good companions include ferns, hostas, and Solomon's seal.

BLUE FALSE INDIGO
Baptisia australis

Hardiness—Zones 3 to 8

Color(s)—Indigo blue

Bloom period—Mid- to late spring

Mature Size (H × W)—3 to 4 ft. × 4 ft.

Water needs—Water new plants every week to ten days if there are no soaking rains; established plants are drought-tolerant.

Planting/Care—Plant seed in late summer and young plants in early spring where they will stay, as they resent moving later. Thrives in humusy, well-drained soil. Be patient—it is slow to establish itself. Mulch. You may fertilize in early spring. In partial shade, it may require support, such as a peony ring.

Pests/Diseases—None serious

Landscaping Tips & Ideas—Its medium-to-tall mound of foliage and handsome indigo flowers create strong vertical lines at the middle or back of a large flowering border. It's one of those substantial plants used to anchor other flowers. An excellent meadow plant.

CANDYTUFT
Iberis sempervirens

Hardiness—Zones 3 to 9

Color(s)—White

Bloom period—Late spring

Mature Size (H × W)—8 to 10 in. × spreading

Water needs—Water transplants if rainfall is sparse.

Planting/Care—Plant in spring or fall, in any well-drained soil. Choose the site carefully, because candytuft is not crazy about being moved. Space plants 1 foot apart. Fertilize at planting. After flowering, sheer back the stems to half their height. This limits their tendency to sprawl and get woody, and encourages repeat-bloom. Protect from winter cold with pine boughs, and clip off damaged or bare stems in early spring.

Pests/Diseases—Occasionally suffers from humidity and poor air circulation, which can cause fungal rot in the summer. Sometimes slugs bother it.

Landscaping Tips & Ideas—Although it makes a good groundcover, it does equally well in a flower border or rock garden. Or use it as edging or filler in container displays.

CATMINT
Nepeta × faassenii

Hardiness—Zones 3 to 8

Color(s)—Blue-purple

Bloom period—Late spring, early summer

Mature Size (H × W)—12 to 15 in. × 24 to 30 in.

Water needs—Water regularly when establishing; thereafter, it is drought-tolerant.

Planting/Care—Buy and plant container-grown plants in spring. If you are planning to use for edging, it's more cost-effective, and easy, to raise plants from seed. Light, moderately fertile, well-drained soil is ideal. Shear back by two-thirds after blooming, which keeps them from getting straggly and encourages rebloom. As plants mature, they tend to fall open in the middle—this is a sign that it's time to divide.

Pests/Diseases—None serious

Landscaping Tips & Ideas—Makes a lovely flowering mound useful for edging, among roses, to carpet sunny paths, and in sunny shrub borders. It is pretty alternating with 'Moonbeam' coreopsis.

CHRYSANTHEMUM
Dendranthema spp. and hybrids

Hardiness—Zones 3 to 9

Color(s)—Many colors

Bloom period—Fall

Mature Size (H × W)—12 to 15 in. × 1 to 3 ft.

Water needs—Unless you have a good soaking rain, water deeply every week to ten days, for the first month or so.

Planting/Care—Plant in early spring, summer, or early fall. A wide range of soils are suitable, but planting area must be well-drained. Hardy mums tolerate some drought but cannot stand soil that is soggy in winter. Fertilize between late winter and early spring, and again in early summer. Pinch the plants back in early summer for more compact, branched growth.

Pests/Diseases—Leaf spot and fungal diseases can be prevented by watering on the ground and allowing sufficient air circulation/elbow room.

Landscaping Tips & Ideas—For glorious fall color, interplant your hardy garden mums with perennials.

COLUMBINE
Aquilegia spp. and hybrids

Hardiness—Zones 3 to 8

Color(s)—White, yellow, blue, rusty pinks, lavender, purple, reddish-orange, red, bicolors

Bloom period—Spring

Mature Size (H × W)—1 to 3 ft. × 1½ ft.

Water needs—Water new plants deeply every week to ten days, unless there is a soaking rain.

Planting/Care—Easily raised from seed, or purchase small containerized plants in spring. Put in well-drained, rich, evenly moist ground. Provide noon shade in warmer areas. Fertilize in early spring and early fall. They generally only live four or five years, and need no dividing. They often self-sow.

Pests/Diseases—Leafminers may mar the foliage. After flowering, cut back affected plants almost to the crown; they will grow back and make a beautiful low foliage filler for the rest of the season.

Landscaping Tips & Ideas—Naturalize along sun-dappled woodland paths, add to partially shaded beds.

CONEFLOWER, PURPLE
Echinacea purpurea

Hardiness—Zones 3 to 8

Color(s)—Mauve, pink, purple, and newer cultivars in orange, orange-yellow, yellow

Bloom period—Late spring, early summer

Mature Size (H × W)—2 to 4 ft. × 2 ft.

Water needs—Water weekly to establish; thereafter, it should be drought-tolerant.

Planting/Care—Plant anytime after the soil can be worked in the spring in slightly acidic, reasonably fertile, well-drained soil. In warmer areas, a little shade is advisable; otherwise prefers full sun. Deadhead to prevent or reduce self-sowing, but leave some for the birds, who relish the seeds.

Pests/Diseases—Virtually pest- and disease-free

Landscaping Tips & Ideas—It's the backbone, the showpiece, the eye-catcher, of a meadow garden! It also makes a great summer-long show in groups of five or seven in the center or toward the back of a formal border.

57

CORAL BELLS
Heuchera spp. and hybrids

Hardiness—Zones 3 to 8

Color(s)—Foliage in shades of green to purple; flowers in coral, deep red, pink, white

Bloom period—Late spring, early summer

Mature Size (H × W)—15 to 20 in. × 18 to 20 in.

Water needs—Water deeply when establishing. Don't let the plants dry out.

Planting/Care—Plant after the ground can be worked in spring. Fertilize in early spring and early fall. Remove developing flower stalks if you prefer the foliage; otherwise, deadhead to prolong flowering. In colder areas, winter protection (pine boughs, mulch) is advised.

Pests/Diseases—If slugs and snails appear, use traps or bait.

Landscaping Tips & Ideas—Low enough for use to the front of a border or to edge a path. The newer cultivars with colorful leaves are a spectacular addition to mixed beds; the purplish ones tolerate more sun.

COREOPSIS
Coreopsis grandiflora

Hardiness—Zones 3 to 9

Color(s)—Yellow

Bloom period—Summer

Mature Size (H × W)—1 to 3 ft. × 1 to 3 ft.

Water needs—Water to establish; plants become drought-tolerant.

Planting/Care—Plant divisions in spring or fall in lean to ordinary, well-drained soil, and mulch lightly. If the soil is decent, fertilizing is not necessary. Cut dead stems to keep plants looking tidy and to inspire rebloom. Divide every three to four years.

Pests/Diseases—None serious; slugs can appear if plants are too heavily mulched.

Landscaping Tips & Ideas—A standout in informal or meadow-gardening schemes. Also a good, long-blooming contributor to mixed flower beds, with plants such as blazing star, purple coneflower, tithonia, black-eyed Susan, sneezeweed, and gaillardia. For a soft, creamy-yellow color on a smaller plant (12 to 18 inches), grow 'Moonbeam'. 'Early Sunshine' is one of several excellent bright-yellow cultivars.

DAYLILY
Hemerocallis spp. and hybrids

Hardiness—Zones 3 to 8

Color(s)—Near-white, creamy yellow, orange, gold, purple, pink, fiery red, lavender, bicolors

Bloom period—Summer

Mature Size (H × W)—2 to 4 ft. × 2 to 4 ft.

Water needs—Water deeply for the first two weeks. Once established, water deeply in droughts.

Planting/Care—The best planting time is spring. Adaptable to most any soil, they tolerate heat, cold, wind, and seashore conditions. Space about 2 feet apart. Maintain a mulch. Fertilize once in early spring and again in mid-fall. Divide every four or five years in mid-spring or early fall.

Pests/Diseases—None serious

Landscaping Tips & Ideas—Will bloom best in full sun as well as bright shade. Good with black-eyed Susan, heliopsis and helianthus, crocosmia, poppies, and ornamental grasses. Other good companions include fall-blooming asters and mums that will take over as daylilies begin to fade away.

GLOBE THISTLE
Echinops ritro

Hardiness—Zones 3 to 8

Color(s)—Steel blue

Bloom period—Summer

Mature Size (H × W)—3 to 4 ft. × 2 to 3 ft.

Water needs—Water new plants every week to ten days for the first month. Established plants are drought-tolerant.

Planting/Care—Plant in spring, in well-drained soil. It spreads in rich, moist soil, which may or may not be a blessing. Deadhead flowering stems by a third or a half to a pair of basal leaves. If cut back twice, will bloom a third time. In early spring, cut back to the crown. Fertilize then, and again in fall. Maintain a mulch.

Pests/Diseases—None serious

Landscaping Tips & Ideas—Handsome massed in a wild garden, and fronting tall shrubs. Nice with ferns, astilbes, and Japanese irises (alongside a water garden); in a border, mix with ornamental grasses, Siberian irises, peonies, yuccas, and coneflowers.

GOLDENROD
Solidago species and hybrids

Hardiness—Zones 2 to 8

Color(s)—Yellow

Bloom period—Midsummer to fall

Mature Size (H × W)—2 to 6 ft. × 2 to 4 ft.

Water needs—Water until established, then it is quite drought-tolerant.

Planting/Care—Plant in ordinary, well-drained soil. Fall planting allows plenty of time for transplants to develop strong root systems before they must put energy into foliage and flower production. For more compact plants and later bloom, cut stems back by half in early summer. Stake tall types, and those with softer stems growing in richer soils. Divide immediately after flowering in fall, or in spring, every three or four years.

Pests/Diseases—May suffer from downy mildew in stressed conditions.

Landscaping Tips & Ideas—Naturalize with asters and black-eyed Susans, or integrate tall types into the back of borders. Some of the named cultivars have improved flower plumes and more compact growth habits.

HARDY GERANIUM, CRANESBILL
Geranium spp. and hybrids

Hardiness—Zones 3 to 8

Color(s)—Magenta, pink, blue, violet, white

Bloom period—Late spring, early summer

Mature Size (H × W)—6 in. to 4 ft. × 1 to 2 ft.

Water needs—Water when rainfall is scarce for the first two seasons to fully establish them.

Planting/Care—Plant divisions in spring. They prefer morning sun and afternoon shade. Most accept average, reasonably moist, well-drained soil. Maintain a mulch. Fertilizing is not necessary. Cut back marred foliage at the end of July.

Pests/Diseases—Japanese beetles may appear in midsummer—handpick these pests. Sometimes mildew affects foliage in late spring but disappears later in the summer.

Landscaping Tips & Ideas—There is a hardy geranium to suit most any landscape situation; when choosing, match your site to the plant. Some do well in woodland settings, others in full sun as groundcovers.

HELLEBORE, LENTEN ROSE

Helleborus orientalis

Hardiness—Zones 3 or 4 to 8

Color(s)—Green-white, rose, maroon, pink, black-maroon

Bloom period—Early spring

Mature Size (H × W)—12 to 18 in. × 18 in. to 3 ft.

Water needs—During the first six weeks after planting, water often enough to keep the soil damp to the touch.

Planting/Care—Plant in early spring or early fall in a spot that gets morning sun or all-day dappled light. Thrive in well-drained, humusy, nearly neutral woodland soil. Fertilize in fall and remove spent foliage. Will self-sow. Divide in late summer to early fall.

Pests/Diseases—Blackspot, crown rot, and snails and slugs may occur in overly moist conditions.

Landscaping Tips & Ideas—Especially handsome under tall evergreen shrubs. Plant along well-used paths and where they can be admired from a window. Especially attractive with daffodils, skimmia, hostas, and lungwort.

HOSTA

Hosta spp. and hybrids

Hardiness—Zones 3 to 8

Color(s)—Foliage in green, chartreuse, blue, blue-green, gold, white, and variegated; flowers in white, lavender or purple

Bloom period—Varies with selection

Mature Size (H × W)—4 in. to 3 ft. × 7 in. to 4 ft. or more

Water needs—Keep new plantings watered for the first month or two; established plants (two to three years old) are drought-tolerant.

Planting/Care—Plant in spring in well-drained, moist, humusy, fertile soil. Maintain a mulch.

Pests/Diseases—Slugs may attack, especially in rainy spells. Trap or bait them. Clean beds of leaves in the fall, which can harbor these pests.

Landscaping Tips & Ideas—Mass in a woodland garden, or mix-and-match different ones to create exciting textures. Good companions for spring bulbs. Small, white-variegated ones are a neat edging for woodland paths.

JAPANESE ANEMONE

Anemone spp.

Hardiness—Zones 4 to 8

Color(s)—White, pink, deep rose

Bloom period—Late summer, early fall

Mature Size (H × W)—2 to 4 ft. × 2 ft.

Water needs—Water new plants every week to ten days, unless there is a soaking rain, for up to six weeks; water established plants during dry spells.

Planting/Care—Plant in spring after the ground has warmed. Best in morning sun or all-day bright shade. Needs well-drained soil. Stake taller cultivars. Deadhead to keep attractive. When the foliage dies down, cut the plant back to the ground. Provide winter protection such as a thick mulch. These plants need two or three seasons to get established and resent disturbance (so only divide every ten years).

Pests/Diseases—None serious

Landscaping Tips & Ideas—Lovely in woodland settings with ferns, hostas, and epimediums. Lovely backed by a tall ornamental grass.

LADY'S MANTLE
Alchemilla mollis

Hardiness—Zones 4 to 7

Color(s)—Chartreuse-yellow blooms

Bloom period—Summer

Mature Size (H × W)—12 to 18 in. × 2 ft.

Water needs—Maintain moist soil—water every week to ten days unless there's a soaking rain.

Planting/Care—Sow seed in late summer, or plant seedlings in early to mid-spring or fall. The ideal soil is well-drained, humusy, and rich. Remove fading flower stems. Cut back any browning leaves to keep the clump looking fresh. Divide in spring. Fertilize in early spring and again in early fall.

Pests/Diseases—None serious, although fungal diseases can occur in spells of heat and humidity.

Landscaping Tips & Ideas—Use to accent corners and curves of flower beds or edge walks and paths. Nice in a woodland garden. Good companions include fennel, rue, sage, and blue fescue ornamental grass. Lovely in pots or urns.

LAMB'S EARS
Stachys byzantina

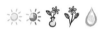

Hardiness—Zones 4 to 8

Color(s)—Silvery foliage; violet or white flower spikes

Bloom period—Summer

Mature Size (H × W)—12 to 15 in. × 12 to 18 in.

Water needs—Water new plants regularly, slowly, and deeply; established plants should be drought-tolerant.

Planting/Care—Plant in early spring or early fall. Requires a very well-drained site and light, fertile, humusy soil. Use a fine-textured mulch (such as cocoa hulls or pine needles) an inch deep, starting 3 inches from the outer leaves. Cut out marred or dried-up leaves. Remove the flower spikes; letting them open and go to seed will cause the foliage to deteriorate.

Pests/Diseases—Avoid wetting the foliage, which can lead to rot.

Landscaping Tips & Ideas—A good container plant. In the garden, it's a delight with 'Ruby Glow' or 'Vera Jameson' sedum. To make a show, plant in groups of at least three plants. The non-flowering, 8-inch-high 'Silver Carpet' spreads rapidly and is a good choice for cooler regions.

ORIENTAL POPPY
Papaver orientalis

Hardiness—Zones 3 to 7

Color(s)—Red, orange, salmon, pink, white, bicolors

Bloom period—Spring and early summer

Mature Size (H × W)—2 to 4 ft. × 2 ft.

Water needs—Water during the growing and flowering period; hold off, after.

Planting/Care—Plant in early spring. Best in well-drained, deeply dug, light but somewhat humusy soil. The big, decorative seedheads should be removed; it's better for the plant. When the foliage dies down, remove it from the crown. When the foliage begins to re-grow in the fall, fertilize. Thanks to a fleshy taproot, these plants are difficult to transplant.

Pests/Diseases—None serious

Landscaping Tips & Ideas—A spangle of these brilliant, beautiful blossoms lifts a garden from ordinary to extraordinary. Best in the back of a border because they're unsightly as they die down—disguise this with later-bloomers such as dahlias, asters, or mums.

PEONY
Paeonia hybrids

Hardiness—Zones 3 to 8

Color(s)—Shades of pink, rose, coral, deep crimson, bicolors

Bloom period—Late spring

Mature Size (H × W)—3 ft. × 3 ft.

Water needs—Water regularly to establish, then water during dry spells.

Planting/Care—Plant in early fall or early spring. They require a minimum of six hours of daily sun, and are most successful in well-drained, fertile, humusy, neutral to slightly alkaline soils. Space 3 feet apart. Do not mulch. Provide top-heavy ones with support. Fertilize in fall and early spring. Divide in fall or spring; divisions need a year or two to reestablish themselves. Cut the foliage to the ground in later fall.

Pests/Diseases—Leaf blight and stem wilt can occur; consult your local nursery for remedies.

Landscaping Tips & Ideas—Plant in groups of two or three to anchor large flower beds.

PHLOX
Phlox paniculata

Hardiness—Zones 3 to 8

Color(s)—White and shades of pink, rose, red, purple, and bicolors

Bloom period—Summer

Mature Size (H × W)—3 to 4 ft. × 1 to 2 ft.

Water needs—Maintain a consistently moist soil.

Planting/Care—Plant in early fall or spring. Soil should be well-drained, moist, and fertile (rich in compost and humus). Plant 2 feet apart. Mulch, starting 3 inches from the crown. Fertilize in early spring. Deadhead regularly. Cut down to the crown at the end of the season. Divide in spring every three years, discarding the crown's center.

Pests/Diseases—Mildew is the greatest threat. Plant resistant varieties, of which there are now quite a few. Provide good air circulation/don't crowd.

Landscaping Tips & Ideas—Fall-flowering asters, Japanese anemones, and mums are good companions, taking over as phlox starts to fade in late summer.

PINKS
Dianthus spp. and hybrids

Hardiness—Zones 3 to 9

Color(s)—Pink, red, salmon, white, yellow, often with contrasting eyes

Bloom period—Spring, summer, early fall

Mature Size (H × W)—6 to 24 in. × 8 to 12 in.

Water needs—Water to establish; plants are drought-resistant once established.

Planting/Care—Plant in early spring or early fall, in well-drained, even sandy, soil with a neutral to slightly alkaline pH. (Excellent drainage in winter is essential.) Mulch lightly. After the first flush of bloom, deadhead or shear off the faded flowers. If the plants show brown tips in August, cut them off, make sure the plants don't go dry, and wait for them to freshen and rebloom in fall.

Pests/Diseases—Rot and leaf rust can be problems.

Landscaping Tips & Ideas—Use as edgers, in pots, and anywhere their perky beauty and pleasant scents can be enjoyed.

RUSSIAN SAGE
Perouskia atriplicifolia

Hardiness—Zones 4 to 9

Color(s)—Light purple, powder blue

Bloom period—Midsummer to fall

Mature Size (H × W)—3 to 5 ft. × 3 to 4 ft.

Water needs—Water new plants regularly for their first two months; established plants are drought-tolerant.

Planting/Care—Plant in any well-drained, moderately fertile, sunny site. Cut stems back to about 6 inches in spring; it will regrow. In warm areas where it blooms early, try cutting back by two-thirds after flowering, and hope for a new flush of blooms. Rarely needs dividing.

Pests/Diseases—None serious

Landscaping Tips & Ideas—Nice at the back of a border, in groups of three or five or seven, backed by evergreens that show off their lovely color. Beautiful massed with boltonia, sedum, and ornamental grasses in naturalized settings, both in bloom and later, when the stems turn silvery. Also a great shore plant.

SALVIA
Salvia × sylvestris 'May Night'

Hardiness—Zones 4 to 7

Color(s)—Blue

Bloom period—Summer

Mature Size (H × W)—1½ to 3 ft. × 2 ft.

Water needs—Water new plants regularly for their first two months. After that, water only as needed.

Planting/Care—Plant in early to mid-spring or early fall, in a site that is well-drained in fertile and humusy soil. Place plants 24 to 30 inches apart. Keep mulched, and replenish the mulch each spring. Deadhead down to a pair of lateral leaves, and will rebloom. After blooming, you can cut down to the crown, water, fertilize, and watch for renewal and possibly rebloom.

Pests/Diseases—No serious diseases; scale and whitefly can trouble unhealthy plants.

Landscaping Tips & Ideas—A wonderful border perennial. Combine its rich, midnight violet-blue spires with dainty 'Moonbeam' coreopsis, chunky yarrow, and tall airy summer flowers like boltonia.

SCABIOSA
Scabiosa columbaria

Hardiness—Zones 3 to 7

Color(s)—Light blue, pink, white

Bloom period—Late spring to early fall

Mature Size (H × W)—12 to 18 in. × 12 in.

Water needs—Water young plants regularly until established; after that, water only as needed.

Planting/Care—Plant in early spring in very well-drained soil, with a pH close to 7.0. Excellent drainage in winter is essential. In cooler areas, it does best in full sun; in warmer parts of New England, it flowers well with some noon shade. Fertilize in early spring and again in early fall. Keep deadheaded. When it begins to put up just one central leader, cut it down to the basal foliage. Cut flowers last longer if harvested half-open.

Pests/Diseases—None serious

Landscaping Tips & Ideas—Plant in a perennial flower border with space all around. Also nice in tubs and other containers.

SEDUM
Sedum spp. and hybrids

Hardiness—Zones 3 to 10

Color(s)—Pink, red, white, yellow

Bloom period—Summer to fall

Mature Size (H × W)—2 to 24 in. × 1 to 2 ft.

Water needs—Water sparingly, and cut back when vigorous new growth appears. Withstands heat and drought well.

Planting/Care—Plant after the ground can be worked in spring, or in early fall. The ideal soil is pH 6.0 to 7.5, very well-drained, humusy, and fertile. Most seem to prefer dry soil, but tolerate moisture. Fertilize in early spring. Don't deadhead the taller sedums, like 'Autumn Joy'—the flowers change color as cold weather begins. In late winter, cut the stems off just above the basal foliage.

Pests/Diseases—None serious

Landscaping Tips & Ideas—Superb with ornamental grasses in naturalized plantings. Other good companions include 'Goldsturm' rudbeckia, purple coneflower, and Russian sage.

SHASTA DAISY
Leucanthemum × superbum

Hardiness—Zones 5 to 9

Color(s)—White with yellow centers

Bloom period—Early to midsummer

Mature Size (H × W)—1 to 3 ft. × 2 ft.

Water needs—Water new plants to establish, then water in the absence of rain, as these plants are shallow-rooted.

Planting/Care—Plant in spring, in moist, well-drained soil. Space 3 feet apart. Pinch back emerging flower stems to force branching. Maintain a mulch. Clumps are short-lived unless you divide every two or three years.

Pests/Diseases—Stems and leaves of stressed plants are sometimes bothered by aphids, but are easily pinched off and discarded.

Landscaping Tips & Ideas—Naturalize in informal meadow areas, or include them in the middle of a perennial border or cutting garden. Useful with foliage plants and ones with hot-colored flowers. Shorter plants in front will screen their ragged lower stems. Dwarf varieties can be used as edgings or displayed in pots.

SIBERIAN IRIS
Iris sibirica

Hardiness—Zones 3 to 8

Color(s)—Blue-purple, lavender, maroon, white, off-pink, yellowish tones

Bloom period—Late spring, early summer

Mature Size (H × W)—8 to 40 in. × 10 to 24 in.

Water needs—Water new plants weekly, for up to six weeks. Once established, they can stand some drought.

Planting/Care—Plant in early spring in well-drained, rich, evenly moist garden loam. Plant with the roots on the underside, and the tops just below the soil surface. Space 18 to 24 inches apart. Remove dead foliage in early spring, and fertilize. Divide in late summer or early fall, working quickly and keeping the rhizomes moist until they are back in the ground.

Pests/Diseases—None serious

Landscaping Tips & Ideas—Beautiful beside a water garden, lovely in a Japanese-style garden, and lovely massed in a large border. Recommended companions include sedum 'Autumn Joy' and coreopsis.

SOLOMON'S SEAL
Polygonatum spp.

Hardiness—Zones 4 to 8

Color(s)—Cream white

Bloom period—Late spring

Mature Size (H × W)—2 to 3 ft. × 18 to 20 in.

Water needs—Keep the soil moist while the plant is establishing itself, and water deeply during droughts.

Planting/Care—Plant in spring or fall. It thrives in well-drained, deeply dug, rich, somewhat acidic soil. Set the rhizomes 2 to 3 inches deep with the bud facing upward and pointing in the direction you want the plant to grow. Space plants 18 to 20 inches apart, and mulch. Fertilize in early spring.

Pests/Diseases—None serious

Landscaping Tips & Ideas—Magnificent in woodland and large wild gardens, and along paths. Good companions include ferns, columbines, lily-of-the-valley, primroses, trilliums, hostas, and lady's-slippers.

VERONICA
Veronica spicata

Hardiness—Zones 3 to 7

Color(s)—Blue, pink, or white

Bloom period—Early to midsummer

Mature Size (H × W)—18 in. to 3 ft. × 18 in. to 2 ft.

Water needs—Water well if rain is sparse until it establishes. After that, maintain soil moisture.

Planting/Care—Plant in spring or fall. It accepts any type of average, well-drained garden soil. Space plants 1 to 2 feet apart. Cut back stems of taller ones by 6 inches in June so the plants will be more compact; this delays bloom a bit, but the plants won't need staking. May bloom all summer with faithful deadheading.

Pests/Diseases—None serious. Sometimes foliage becomes coated with mildew during wet weather; cut back blackened stems and wait for dry weather.

Landscaping Tips & Ideas—Use as edging plants, filler in beds, as groundcovers, and in big container displays. Include them in cutting gardens.

YARROW
Achillea spp. and hybrids

Hardiness—Zones 3 to 7 or 8

Color(s)—Yellow, gold, off-pink, cerise, red, rust, salmon, off-white

Bloom period—Summer

Mature Size (H × W)—1 to 4 ft. × 2 to 3 ft.

Water needs—Water the first few weeks after planting. Once it shows signs of vigorous growth, it should do well with ordinary rainfall.

Planting/Care—Plant in spring or late fall. It thrives in very well-drained, sandy soils and even in poor soil. It is a wide-spreading plant, so space 18 to 24 inches apart. Mulch to keep weeds down and replenish every spring. Prune spent flowers down to the first pair of buds, and these will bloom.

Pests/Diseases—None serious

Landscaping Tips & Ideas—Yarrow's ferny foliage adds texture to perennial beds and is very attractive in naturalized plantings. The cut flowers are long-lasting, fresh as well as dried.

PERENNIALS

Cold tolerance and light needs are the first considerations when choosing perennials for our region. If frost threatens your garden through mid-spring, choose late-blooming varieties of spring-flowering species. If frosts come early in fall, choose early varieties—they'll have time to bloom before the frost gets there.

Most flowering perennials need a full sun location and six to eight hours of direct sun from 10 a.m. through mid-afternoon. Plants that can take shade need the bright shade under a tall tree or all-day dappled light under a tree with open branching. In Zones 3 and 4, perennials growing in full sun generally can stand a little more cold.

The ideal perennial garden includes

- Flowers that bloom in spring, summer, and fall. Our perennials list can help you locate those that are just right for your garden.

- Foliage plants for color and diversity, including ornamental grasses (see Chapter 5) and ferns.

- Small evergreens to anchor the composition and to keep it green in winter.

PLANNING

When will it bloom? Most perennials come into bloom their second season and grow fuller each year until they need dividing (see below). Only a few perennials will bloom the first year from seed. To be sure of a show of flowers the first season, buy big container-grown root divisions or second-year seedlings. Generally speaking, the larger the crown (and container and price), the fuller will be the floral display that year. If the perennial that you are interested in blooms in early or mid-spring—columbine, for example—you'll get more flowers the first spring if you set out a container-grown specimen the preceding late August or early September than if you plant it in early spring.

Some catalogs ship perennials in spring "bare root," with planting instructions—astilbes, for instance. In our experience, these often flower fully only in the second or even third season.

When you need lots of a particular perennial—catmint to edge a big bed, for example—seeds are the way to go. You can start seeds in flats indoors or in a cold frame, but most don't germinate as quickly as seeds for annuals. (See the January pages of the Annuals chapter.) Perennials can also be started from seed in the garden or in a cold frame, either in spring two weeks after the last frost date, or in early summer up to two months before the first frost date. When fall sowing is recommended on a seed packet, it usually means those seeds will benefit from a chilling period. The process, called "stratification," is described in November.

PLANTING ADVICE

Soil for perennials. The "good garden loam" that perennials thrive in is more often created than inherited. The solution to assorted soil problems, including rocky soil and poor drainage, is to grow perennials in raised beds enriched with organic additives.

Planting procedures. Whether you are planting in the soft soil of a new raised bed or preparing a planting hole in an established perennial border, make the hole three times the diameter of the rootball, and twice as deep.

If you are preparing a planting hole in an established bed, test and amend the soil pH as when preparing a raised bed (see Soil Preparation and Improvement in the Introduction to the book) and then mix in 3 to 4 inches of humus, enough so that a quarter of the soil is organic matter. Mix in a slow-release organic fertilizer, half-fill the hole with the amended soil, and tamp it down firmly.

Free the plant from matted roots circling the rootball. If you can't untangle them, make four shallow vertical slashes in the sides and slice off the bottom half inch. Dip the rootball in a bucket containing starter solution. Half-fill the hole with improved soil. Set the plant a little high in the hole. Fill the hole with improved soil, and tamp firmly. Water slowly and deeply, and then apply a 2- to 3-inch layer of mulch starting 3 inches from the crown.

The spacing between perennials depends on the size of the plant when mature. Edging plants under a foot tall need 12 to 18 inches all around. Intermediate sizes—1 to 1½ feet tall—which is most perennials—need 18 to 24 inches between plants. Larger plants need to be about 3 feet apart. Hostas and daylilies need 24 to 30 inches. Peonies need 3 to 4 feet. Cool climate gardeners find that close planting shades out weeds.

When summer is over, we like to leave in place healthy seed-bearing perennials with woody upright structures, like black-eyed Susans. They're interesting in the winter, and they provide seeds for the birds. Some self-sow and will refurnish your bed.

In the fall, clear away perennials' dead foliage; cut it off, don't pull it off because pulling may damage the crown beneath. Look before you leap; be careful not to damage burgeoning stems.

Maintenance. To sustain growth and satisfying bloom, your perennials need a continuous supply of nutrients. The fertilization schedule for established beds begins in late winter or early spring. After that, how often you fertilize depends on the type of fertilizer you are using.

Here's an overview of the annual maintenance needs of a perennial bed:

1. Before growth begins in late winter and early spring, clean up the beds, test and adjust the pH, fertilize and refurbish the soil.

2. Maintain a year-round mulch to protect plant roots from heat, cold, and drought. A winter mulch of pine boughs applied after the second hard frost in fall catches leaves and blown debris and saves some tricky raking in spring.

3. Deadhead and groom the plants during the growing season.

4. Every few years divide the crowns to keep plants producing and healthy.

5. Control the problems described in the section on pests and diseases.

6. Make a final application of fertilizer as growth slows at the end of the growing season: Zones 3 and 4, usually about August 15; Zone 5, early September; Zones 6 and 7, early September to early October.

7. Throughout the season, early spring to mid-fall, edge beds that are not protected by some form of barrier to prevent grasses and weeds from invading. Use an edger to create a trench 4 to 8 inches deep.

In addition to an annual check of the pH, every three to five years we recommend an application of rock phosphate, green sand, and where there is clay, gypsum. These are the granular soil additives recommended for preparing a new planting bed. Just measure the products into a bucket, mix them, and with your fingers scratch them into the soil a quarter-inch deep.

FERTILIZERS

If you are using organic fertilizers, such as Holly-Tone® or Plant-Tone®, then you will need to fertilize the first time about four to six weeks before growth is due to begin in spring, and then again as the growing season is ending.

If you are using time- or controlled-release chemical fertilizers, you will need to fertilize just before the plants start to grow and to repeat according to the formula inscribed on the fertilizer container. If you use a nine-month formula, that should carry you through the whole growth season.

If you are using granular chemical fertilizers, then you will need to fertilize just before growth begins in spring, and repeat every six weeks until the end of the growing season.

STAKING

Most tall perennials that are spaced properly, fertilized organically, and not stuck on a windy hill won't need staking. Wide spacing improves the plants' access to light and air, and that strengthens the stems. Weak growth is often the result of force-feeding with non-organic fertilizers. However, delphiniums, lilies, the tallest dahlias, and some other very big perennials usually do need staking.

When you set out a new plant that needs staking—or when an established plant that will be very tall starts to grow—insert a stake in the soil as close as possible to the crown and as tall as the plant will grow to be. Tie the main stem loosely to the stake with soft green wool, raffia, cotton string, wool yarn, or strips of pantyhose. As the plant grows, keep tying the main stem and branches onto the stake higher and higher.

PRUNING, SHEARING, AND DEADHEADING

You can improve the performance and health of some perennials by selective pruning, shearing, and deadheading. Our suggestions appear in the month-by-month pages that follow.

For some perennials, pruning or shearing early in the growth cycle keeps plants compact and encourages later and more, though usually smaller, blooms. Removing fading and dead blooms—deadheading—stops the development of seeds and, in most cases, results in more flowers.

Shearing is the way to deadhead plants with very small flowers—creeping phlox, miniature pinks, and baby's breath, for example. The quick and easy way to deadhead larger blooms is by pinching them out. Just place your thumbnail and forefinger in back of the bracts—the small scale-like leaves behind the petals—and squeeze the flower head off. If the flower stems are too thick to pinch out, snip them off with small pruning shears sold for that purpose.

Pruning and shearing also helps the health of some plants attacked by leafminer and mildew. Cut the diseased foliage to the ground and discard it. The new foliage should grow in clean.

WATERING AND MULCHING

Watering. Sustained moisture makes nutrients in the soil available and is essential to the unchecked growth and health of perennials.

When you plant a perennial, put down 1½ inches of water right after planting. New plants and established flower beds need 1½ inches of gentle rain or slow, deep, gentle watering every ten days to two weeks.

Between July and August, you will likely have to water perennials regularly. In fall, just before the ground freezes, water the perennials thoroughly.

Mulching. We recommend keeping a 2- to 3-inch layer of mulch around perennials. Deeper mulch may bury the crown and kill some perennials. (See Mulch in the Introduction to the book.) Start the mulch a few inches from the crown, and spread it out over an area wider than the plant's diameter. That is enough to minimize the loss of soil moisture—saving water and the time applying it—and to moderate soil temperatures. For year-round use, we recommend organic mulches such as shredded bark and pine needles (which can be piled a little deeper) because they add humus and nutrients to the soil as they decompose. Replenish the mulch after the late winter/early spring fertilization.

The need for a winter mulch depends on the severity of your climate, the hardiness of the plants, and the exposure of the beds. In Zone 6, the main purpose of winter mulch is to keep the perennials from heaving out of the ground as the ground freezes and thaws in winter and early spring. In Zone 7, a winter mulch can save perennials that are borderline hardy during especially severe winters. Apply a winter mulch only after the ground has frozen hard, and remove it when you first spot signs of active growth in the plants.

We recommend airy organics such as straw or pine boughs as a winter mulch. Apply the mulch so you can see the plant through it. For coastal dwellers, marsh hay and salt hay from the shore are excellent winter mulches as they are weed free, and they can be saved, covered in a pile, from year to year.

DIVIDING AND MOVING PERENNIALS

To remain productive and showy, most perennials should be divided and replanted every four or five years. Dividing also gives you plants for the development of new gardens and to give away as gifts. On the plant pages that follow, we explain when each is likely to need dividing. But the perennials themselves indicate when the time has come: the stems become crowded and leggy, the roots become matted, and there are fewer and smaller blooms.

You can help your perennials stay healthy and productive by dividing and replanting them every few years. Division forces the crowns to grow new roots, and replanting provides an opportunity to refurbish the soil. A new planting hole generally has freshly amended soil—and the plant benefits.

We divide when we need more of a plant, typically heuchera, catmint, and other edgers.

A plant needs dividing when it is producing fewer and smaller blooms or when the crown is pushing up and stems look crowded and leggy. Many perennials benefit from division every five or six years.

You can divide in early spring before growth begins. But the best time to divide most perennials is toward the end of the growing season—late summer, before and around Labor Day. The soil will be warm enough for several more weeks ahead to keep existing roots growing while new roots are developing. In Zones 3 and 4, divide around August 15. In Zone 5, divide about September 1. In Zone 6, most perennials can be divided September 1 to September 15. In Zone 7, divide September 1 to mid-October.

There's more than one way to divide a crown. For the gardener who wants to multiply his/her supply, the most profitable way is to lift the whole crown with a spading fork, and with a shovel or an edger, divide the crown into two or more pieces. While waiting to replant, keep the divisions moist and out of the sun. This method is best for perennials that have very hard crowns.

For the method that is easiest on the gardener, with a shovel, chop through the center of the crown and dig up one half. Amend and fertilize the soil around the section that is to remain where it is; it will grow on in lively fashion. Replant the other section in improved soil. We recommend this method for peonies and other perennials that are slow to recover from being moved. This method allows for reproduction without interrupting the blooming cycle of the garden.

PESTS AND DISEASES

Weeds. Keep weeds out of flower beds to eliminate competition for water and nutrients, to keep air moving in the garden, to avoid pests and diseases inherent to some perennials, and to keep the garden looking beautiful.

Deer and rodents. Deer prefer most all perennials, and especially hostas. So far they are snubbing ornamental grasses, ferns, and perennials with dainty foliage and tiny flowers, like baby's-breath. The deterrents we've tried keep deer away only until they realize smelly sprays and flashing lights are not hazardous to their health. Changing the deterrent every six weeks is some help. Dogs, electric fences, and deer fences work . . . up to a point.

To keep rabbits, woodchucks, and other rodents away from your flower beds, try chemical fungicide formulations such as Thiram (Arasan) and hot pepper wax.

If you see signs of vole or mole activity, bait the main runway with a rodenticide.

Insects and diseases. Pests, such as aphids, caterpillars, beetles, and mealybugs, and diseases, such as powdery mildew, root and stem rot, rust disease, and spider mites, can afflict perennials. Keep an eye out for these problems.

PERENNIALS THRIVE IN CONTAINERS

You can outwit limitations imposed by light, wind, and some pests by planting perennials in containers. Deer bait, the gorgeous perfumed 'Casa Blanca' lily for example, is safer in pots on your terrace than in the garden.

Soil:
  ¼ good garden soil or bagged topsoil
  ¼ compost
  ⅜ commercial soilless mix
  ⅛ PermaTill® or perlite
  water-holding polymer

Light: Set large containers (too big to move) where they will receive some sun on all sides over the course of the day. Turn small pots often so all sides receive some direct light.

Containers: Hardy perennials can survive Zones 6 and 7 winters outdoors if in containers big enough to buffer the cold, 14 to 16 inches wide and deep. Grow tender perennials in big tubs, and move them for the winter to a frost-free shed or attached garage. Equipment on casters makes moving easy.

Insulation: Wrap very large containers remaining outdoors for the winter with a double row of large bubble wrap before filling them with soil. You can also pack bags of leaves around them to keep the cold out.

PRUNING ENCOURAGES REBLOOMING

Deadheading—removing fading and dead blooms—encourages almost all flowering perennials to bloom on. To keep the plant shapely, cut off the stem of the spent bloom just above the next node on the stem. That's where the next flowering stem will arise.

In some plants, cutting out-of-bloom stems to the ground and reducing deteriorating foliage by 4 to 6 inches or more will encourage regrowth and reblooming. Some perennials that respond to this treatment are catmint, *Campanula carpatica*, *Centranthus*, *Echinops*, *Chrysanthemum* 'May Queen', and cultivars of the Shasta daisies, daylilies that are rebloomers, delphiniums, *Salvia nemerosa*, *Scabiosa*, *Stokesia*, *Tradescantia*, *Verbena*, *Veronica*, and yarrow.

Shearing tall fall-blooming perennials by half their height June 1 and again by July 15, or no later than eight weeks before their scheduled bloom time, results in more attractive plants and better blooms. Some that benefit from this treatment are asters, boltonia, chrysopsis, helianthus, heliopsis, mums, Russian sage, *Salvia grandiflora*, and *Saponaria officinalis*.

Shearing spring bloomers soon after they finish blooming keeps them from getting leggy and promotes fuller bloom next season. Some that benefit from this treatment are candytuft, creeping phlox, and sweet alyssum.

WHEN YOUR PERENNIALS NEED WATERING

Climates and microclimates and the weather patterns from year to year affect the size, color, and health of perennials, their bloom time, their hardiness, and their seasonal performance.

Understanding how heat and humidity affect your perennials helps you to water correctly.

- The hotter and drier the air, and the windier the weather, the more water your plants need. Don't water by rote; water when the soil feels dry.

- The sandier the soil, the more often your garden will need watering. You can offset sandy soil by incorporating plenty of humus in the soil before planting new plants. The windier the exposure, the sooner container and plants and garden soil will dry out.

- The higher the heat, the drier the air will be, and the more likely you are to encounter spider mites infesting your plantings. Overhead watering humidifies the air and can help. Perennials growing in moist humusy soil and mulched 2 to 3 inches deep can stand considerably more heat, sun, and drought than plants without mulch.

- The wetter the season, the higher the humidity, and the more likely the soil is to become waterlogged, especially in beds that don't drain well. Humidity encourages mildew and other negative conditions.

The first line of defense against disease in areas of high heat and humidty is to plant perennials advertised as disease-resistant. Equally important is provide your plants with very well-drained soil, a must for most perennials. Uncrowded, well-spaced plants have better drainage and good air circulation. The solution to finding a wet spot right where you want to put your flower bed is to create a raised bed.

JANUARY

- If you have in mind moving some plants this spring, spend some time now with your garden books and catalogs and make a spring-planting and moving plan. If you will be adding plants, try for ones that have more than one asset.

- It's too early to plant anything, but not too early to decide whether you want to try starting seeds indoors. Seed packets and the blurbs in many garden catalogs tell you whether and when the seeds can be started early indoors.

- If you are without snow cover, make the rounds of your perennial beds to see if there are crowns that have been heaved. If yes, gently heel them in, and cover them with a winter mulch of evergreen boughs to keep the ground cold until winter ends.

- Prune back ornamental grasses that are looking weatherbeaten. Use shears, and cut back to within a few inches of the crown.

FEBRUARY

- While the cold keeps you housebound, look through garden catalogs for summer-flowering bulbs, tender tropicals, aromatic herbs, dwarf evergreens, and flowering trees that enhance the seasonal color, structure, and texture of your perennial borders. Decide what to order. It's time.

- You can start some perennials indoors from seed this month and next. Some to try are garden mums, delphiniums, catmint, sweet rocket, hollyhocks, and phlox.

- Check snow-free flower beds for plants heaved by thaw-and-freeze cycles, and press the crowns back into place. Add a light winter mulch to plants that have been heaved and those that retain green foliage over the winter—for example, garden mums, candytuft, and basket-of-gold.

- Cut off battered hellebore foliage to make space for new growth and flowering.

- Seedlings started indoors that are crowded or lack good drainage may show symptoms of damping off, which rots stems near the soil surface. Discard affected plants, and increase light and fresh air.

MARCH

- Take advantage of early sales this month to buy fertilizers, other soil additives, and mulch. But be cautious. If the price is a steal, make sure the bag is unbroken. Moisture that gets into bags of cocoa hulls, for example, encourages mildew.

- If bare-root perennials arrive too soon for planting, store them in their packages in a dark, cool, but frost-free place.

- As soon as you can, rake up the perennial borders to get them ready for their first annual application of fertilizer.

- Adjust or repair barriers that are edging beds. Edge beds that are not protected with some form of barrier.

- When the snow leaves the garden beds, take a set of markers to the garden and reserve space for the plants you have ordered. Plant row markers indicating the flowers you plan to put there.

- Transplant seedlings as they outgrow their planting pockets. Pinch out the growing tips of leggy seedlings.

APRIL

- As your perennials come into bloom, record the dates in a garden log. It will help you plan your garden next year.

- As soon as mud season is over and the earth has dried some and warmed, move plants around in the beds and add new perennials when available. Start planting those that are most cold-hardy when the forsythia start to bloom toward the end of this month or early next month. That includes moving peonies.

- Plant astilbe crowns and other bare-root perennials shipped by mail order as soon as possible after they arrive.

- The best time to divide perennials is before growth begins. Fast-growing ones—asters, eupatorium, helianthus, heliopsis, and monarda, for example—need dividing every four to six years.

- Experiment with pinching back branching-perennials by half an inch or so to encourage shorter, bushier growth and more (though smaller) flowers. Perennials that benefit from this include pink turtlehead, veronica, and 'Autumn Joy' sedum.

MAY

- Maintain the moisture in newly planted seeds and seedlings. Unchecked growth is essential to the development of root systems, so they'll be strong enough to withstand summer heat.

- This month and early next month are excellent for planting container-grown perennials and root divisions. Replace perennials whose performance isn't satisfying with new container-grown plants mature enough to bloom this year.

- When the air warms, move seedlings of perennials started indoors to a sheltered corner outside to harden them off in preparation for planting in the open garden.

- If you are using chemical fertilizers, apply to the garden and container plants every six weeks. If you are using an organic fertilizer and haven't yet applied it, do it now.

- Prevent slug and snail damage before it starts. Diatomaceous earth, a natural control, works in dry soil but isn't effective on moist spring soil. Various traps and baits may be worth a try.

JUNE

- When the spring flowers have peaked, areas where more summer color is needed will begin to show up. Make a planting plan showing those areas with potential solutions to try when fall-planting season comes around.

- This is not a good time to move most perennials. Those that have already bloomed are preparing for next year's show, and those that haven't bloomed yet are getting ready to do so.

- Every few weeks, adjust the ties on the tall flowers you have staked.

- Deadhead flowers on your perennials as they fade. This may encourage a second round of flowers.

- As the weather warms and dries, maintain moisture in all new plantings.

- Watch out for aphids and spider mites.

- Every two weeks, add a half-dose of fertilizer to the water for small containers. Use compost or potting soil to top off large containers of perennials whose soil level seems to be shrinking.

JULY

- Before your vacation, arrange to have containers of perennials watered. Ease the chore by grouping the containers in a semi-shaded spot and providing smaller containers with saucers.

- Tie tall perennials to the upper third of their stakes.

- Replenish the mulch in the perennial beds to keep roots cool and to maintain moisture now that the year's driest season is about here.

- Go through your garden with hand-held shears and deadhead spent flowers. Do this daily if you enjoy it, or every two weeks.

- If there's no rain for a week or ten days, slowly and gently apply 1½ inches of water to the garden.

- Keep an eye on asters, beebalm, phlox, dahlias, and other flowers susceptible to powdery mildew. If you see a smoky film forming, thin the interior growth to improve airflow. Spray if needed with a diluted solution of baking soda and horticultural oil (1 tbsp each to a gallon of water).

AUGUST

- Evaluate the light reaching your flower beds. If some flowers are flopping forward, they may be short of light. Tree branches may have grown out and be casting shade on beds that were once in full sun. Prune culprits now, the sooner the better.

- Container-grown perennials and root divisions can be planted successfully this month as long as you water them every week or so; hose them down gently if they show signs of wilting on especially hot days.

- In New England's cool Zones 3 and 4, divide and replant perennials that need it around mid-month. Warmer areas can wait till later.

- Continue to harvest or deadhead phlox, perennial salvia, scabiosa, purple coneflower, and other summer-flowering perennials.

- High humidity and heat encourage powdery mildew. Drought weakens plants and makes them more vulnerable to diseases such as rust. Apply sulfur, ultra-fine horticultural oil, copper fungicide, or other recommended remedies to afflicted plants.

SEPTEMBER

- September rains should keep the garden well-watered, but check and, when needed, water small pots and baskets still outdoors.

- In Zone 5, around September 1 is a good time to plant, divide, and transplant perennials. In Zone 6, do this work from September 1 to 15. In Zone 7, all the way through mid-October is fine. This timing gives crowns time to develop roots before the soil cools and growth stops.

- In Zones 3 and 4, move big containers of hardy perennials to sheltered locations for the winter. Add insulation by packing bags filled with dry leaves around them.

- Cut peonies to the ground before the first frost and discard the debris.

- In Zones 5-7, if you are using organic blend fertilizers, make a final application now. If you are using granular chemical fertilizers, use for the last time just as the growing season ends, sometime between early September and early October.

OCTOBER

- Let perennials that are attractive in winter remain. Even old flower stalks can be interesting.

- This is an excellent month to start new beds for next spring—doing it now gives the soil and its amendments fall and winter to settle in.

- In Zone 7, you can plant, divide, and transplant perennials until mid-month.

- In Zones 6 and 7, move hardy perennials in containers to a sheltered location. Add insulation by packing bags filled with dry leaves around them.

- Clear dead leaves from flower beds, and do not compost them. They may shelter pests and diseases that will flourish in spring.

- The most important preparation for winter is a deep and thorough watering of new, established, inground and container perennials before the soil freezes. If the sky doesn't do it, then you must compensate.

- Apply or change whatever deer deterrents you are using.

- Continue to root out weeds.

NOVEMBER

- After the first hard frost, protect perennials that are borderline hardy in your zone, and those that have just been planted, by applying a winter mulch of pine boughs or straw.

- There is still time to sow seeds that require stratification (this information, and planting instructions, may be found on the seed packets). For more control of the process, you can start the seeds in containers.

- To encourage garden mums to perennialize, let the old stems stand as insulation for the new growth emerging from the base of the plants.

- If you see signs of vole activity, bait the main runway with a rodenticide.

- During this gray month, take the time to enlarge your horticultural knowledge. Invest in some good books on perennial plants as well as garden design, if you haven't already, and spend some time reading these and taking notes.

DECEMBER

- Tools that make gardening easier become dearly held companions. You get attached. Good tools are expensive, but they last well and make welcome gifts. Share your wish list with friends and relatives!

- Seeds that need stratification can be planted as long as the soil can be worked.

- Use only snowmelt products that don't harm plants, turf, and concrete.

- Clear away and discard perennials that frost has reduced to mush. Leave plants with interesting structures and seedheads for the birds to browse—coneflowers, for example.

- Maintain soil moisture in containers stored indoors, and also in containers of hardy perennials outdoors if there's neither snow nor rain. The soil needs just enough moisture to keep the roots from drying out.

- Fertilizer is not needed now because the growing season is over.

BULBS
for New England

The earliest flowers come from bulbs, corms, and tubers planted September and October the fall before. The little bulbs open first, in March in our gardens that are in Zones 4 and 5. We plant these early risers under shrubs and trees that are tall enough to allow them dappled light. We edge flower beds with them, and woodland paths, and set them adrift in rock gardens. We plant lots of them near entrances where they keep us aware of the progress spring is making in New England. Each small bulb adds just a scrap of color to the winter landscape, so we plant them in drifts of twenty to one hundred. Many of these small bulbs thrive and perennialize even in lawns.

The next wave of color comes in late April and May from large bulbs planted in fall—depending on the severity of the winter and on how much heat early spring brings. Spring temperatures can be unpredictable: now and then in March and April, heat waves throw everything off. The earliest of the big bulbs to bloom are the perfumed hyacinths, which we plant near entrances. Then come the daffodils and the tulips. We plant dozens in flower borders accompanied by perennials (and annuals) that will grow up and hide the fading bulb foliage that must be allowed to ripen before it is removed. That's the major drawback of the big bulb flowers—for the larger bulb flowers to bloom well the following year, the foliage must be allowed to ripen (yellow) before it is removed. That takes weeks, and the process is unsightly.

The large spring bulbs are most effective planted in groups of ten in flower borders and naturalized in drifts of twenty or more.

The summer-flowering bulbs provide excellent screening for the fading foliage of the spring-flowering bulbs. They come into bloom when the nights turn warm—mid- to late June—and some go on until mid-September. Those that are winter hardy can be planted the fall before, while the tender bulbs are set out in the spring. To be effective these big bulbs need to be planted in sets of five or ten. In the flower borders, we like to add a few real tropicals, including canna and the ornamental banana, for their exotic foliage.

They're available pot-grown in late spring, and some gardeners have luck wintering canna and other tropicals in their containers in a cool basement. We've tried wintering canna and bougainvillea in our root cellar, which theoretically stays at 42 degrees Fahrenheit year-round, but the bulbs rotted. Our bloom sequence list includes our favorite tropicals and a few exquisite bulbs that don't live through our winters and have to be lifted and stored. Some tender bulbs that shouldn't survive New England winters in the ground, do. We think it has to do with how much insulation is provided by deep snow cover. Tuberose, which was first discovered in Mexico, wintered over in Jacqui's first big garden, which was in Plainfield, in northern Vermont. Or was it a tender jonquil? Either way, that's an almost unthinkable thought, but the unpredictable and almost impossible are part of what makes gardening so fascinating in New England.

Bulbs that bloom in fall when all other flowers have gone by have a special place in the gardener's heart. The silky petals and tender colors look so fragile, but they endure cold rain and windstorms. The fall-flowering bulbs can be planted in summer—as soon as they're available. These small bulbs are most effective planted in groups of twenty and fifty.

WHEN, WHERE, AND HOW TO PLANT

Spring-flowering bulbs in waiting can be stored in the crisper or a cool garage or cellar. Do not store them with apples, which put out vapors that encourage ripening. If you can, plant them after the very first frost. Planted late they have shorter stems and bloom late. Most bulbs bloom earliest growing in full sun; in part shade they open later. Their first year, spring-flowering bulbs will bloom planted in some shade. But to perennialize and bloom fully they need at least bright or dappled light under deciduous trees, or bright shade under a tall evergreen. Ideal is a sunny, sheltered location whose soil is dryish in summer and in winter. The small fall-flowering bulbs can be planted as soon as you have them.

The ideal soil for bulbs is light, very well drained, and improved by additions of organic matter such as peat moss, compost, or aged pine bark, along with an organic 4-10-6 fertilizer at the rate of 5 to 10 pounds per 100 square feet. The ideal pH range for most is 6.0 to 7.0.

Set bulbs so the pointed tips are upright; set corms and tubers with the roots facing down. For bulbs under 2 inches in size, provide holes at least 5 inches deep and 1 inch wide. Or, prepare a planting bed 5 to 6 inches deep. Set the small bulbs 2 inches apart. Plant bulbs 2 inches or larger in holes 8 inches deep and 3 inches wide. Or prepare a planting bed 8 to 10 inches deep. Set the bulbs 4 to 6 inches apart. To create drifts for naturalizing, dig an irregularly shaped planting bed, throw the bulbs out by the handful, and plant where they fall. Avoid leaving bits of bulb casings around the planting—squirrels notice.

Before planting bulbs, inventory the vole population. For voles your bulbs are the local gourmet counter. Squirrels shop there, too, and store their catch for later use. When they forget where they stored your bulbs, the flowers bloom in totally unexpected, sometimes delightful, places. To foil the sweet dears, plant your bulbs in pockets of VoleBloc™ or PermaTill®. Either one improves drainage, by the way. Place 2 inches of VoleBloc™ or PermaTill® in the bottom of the hole. Set the bulb on top of it, and fill in all around with VoleBloc™ or PermaTill®, leaving just the tip exposed. Fill the hole with a mix of 50 percent VoleBloc™ or PermaTill® and improved soil from the hole. Mulch with 2 inches of pine needles, oak leaves, composted wood chips, or with shredded bark. Daffodils don't need protection from voles, or, so far, from deer because they are toxic to wildlife.

CARE GUIDELINES

Most of the bulbs we recommend come back, at least for a season or two. Daffodils and some of the small bulbs are likely to return and to multiply indefinitely. Allow the stems and foliage of the other bulbs to ripen six to seven weeks before removing them. The foliage of the bulbs you plan to lift and store for winter also should be allowed to ripen before being removed. Tulip foliage may be cut when it yellows halfway down. If well fertilized, some tulips perennialize, but the following year many just put up puny foliage and fail to bloom. We dig and discard those. Most bulbs require ample moisture during the season of active growth, from the moment the first tip breaks ground. Once the foliage disappears, the bulbs are dormant, and excess watering isn't good for them. After flowering, but before the foliage disappears, spread an organic, slow-release fertilizer over the bulb plantings at the rate of 4 to 6 pounds to 100 square feet. Large bulbs benefit from deadheading. Remove only the flower itself. Allowing the flower stem as well as the foliage to ripen adds nourishment to the bulb, which enhances next year's flowering.

More complete details are provided later, starting on page 123.

BLOOM SEQUENCE OF FLOWERING BULBS

LATE WINTER/EARLY SPRING BULBS:

Early Crocus. *Crocus* spp.
Dwarf Beardless Iris, *Iris reticulata*
Glory-of-the-Snow, *Chionodoxa luciliae*
Grape Hyacinth, *Muscari* spp. and hybrids
Miniature Cyclamen, *Cyclamen coum*
Miniature Daffodils, Narcissus 'Tete-a-Tete' and
    other early daffodils
Snowdrops, *Galanthus nivalis*
Species Tulips, *Tulipa saxatilis, T. tarda, T. turkestanica,*
    and others
Squill, *Scilla mischtschenkoana*
Striped Squill, *Pushkinia schilloides*
Windflower, *Anemone blanda*
Winter Aconite, *Eranthus hymenalis*

EARLY/MID-SPRING BULBS:

Bearded Iris, *Iris* hybrids
Daffodils, *Narcissus,* early and midseason
Fritillaria, *Fritillaria imperialis* 'Rubra Maxima'
Hyacinth, *Hyacinthus* hybrids
Late Crocus, *Crocus* spp.
Lily-of-the-Valley, *Convallaria majalis*
Mid- and Late-Season Tulips, *Tulipa* spp. and hybrids
Silver Bells, *Ornithogalum nutans*

Starflower, *Ipheion uniflorum* 'Wisley Blue'
Wild Hyacinth, Wood Hyacinth, *Hyacinthoides*
    hispanica (syn. *Scilla campanulatus*)
Wood Sorrel, *Oxalis adenophylla*

SUMMER BULBS:

Crocosmia, *Crocosmia* spp. and hybrids
Dahlia, *Dahlia* hybrids
Dwarf Canna, *Canna* × *hybrida*
Flowering Onion, *Allium giganteum*
Gladiola, *Gladiolus* hybrids
Lilies, *Lilium* spp. and hybrids
Peacock Orchid, *Acidanthema bicolor*
Peruvian Daffodil, *Hymenocallis narcissiflora*
    (syn. *Ismene calathina*)
Poppy Anemones, *Anemone coronaria*
Rain Lily, *Zephranthes* spp.
Spider Lily, *Lycoris* spp.
Summer Hyacinth, *Galtonia* spp.
Tuberose, *Polianthes tuberosa*

FALL/WINTER BULBS:

Colchicum, *Colchicum autumnale*
Hardy Cyclamen, *Cyclamen hederifolium*
Fall Crocus, Saffron Crocus, *Crocus sativus,*
    C. kotschyanus (syn. *C. zonatus*), *C. speciosus*
Lily-of-the-Field, *Sternbergia lutea*
Winter Daffodil, including Tenby Daffodils,
    Narcissus asturiensis, and 'Grand Soleil d'Or'

LATE BLOOMING BULBS AND TROPICALS:

Autumn Zephyr Lily, *Zeprhranthes candidum*
    (Zones 6 to 9)
Canna, *Canna* × *generalis* (tropical)
Hardy Cyclamen, *Cyclamen hederifolium*
    (Zones 5 to 9)
Ornamental Banana, *Musa velutina* (tropical)
Peacock Orchid, *Acidanthera bicolor* (tropical)
Peruvian Daffodil, *Hymenocallis narcissiflora*
    (syn. *Ismeme calathina*) (tropical)
Spider Lily, *Lycoris squamigera*
    (Zones 5 to 8)
Summer Hyacinth, *Galtonia candicans*
    (Zones 6 to 11)
Tuberose, *Polianthes tuberosa*
    (Zones 8 to 11)

AUTUMN CROCUS
Colchicum autumnale

Hardiness—Zones 4 to 8

Color(s)—Lavender, rose, white

Bloom period—Mid-autumn

Mature Size (H × W)—4 to 6 in. × 6 to 12 in.

Water needs—Maintain a moist soil if rainfall is sparse.

Planting/Care—Plant in late summer in well-drained soil, burying the little corms a few inches below the soil surface. Don't crowd them, because the leaves—which appear in spring—need sufficient room. In ensuing years, they'll add to their numbers by producing offsets. You can separate these off in summer once the foliage has died down and replant in other areas if you wish.

Pests/Diseases—None serious

Landscaping Tips & Ideas—Because both foliage and flower are a bit informal, the best place to grow autumn crocuses is scattered among low perennials or groundcovers, or under trees. Also a nice way to get some color and interest in a rock garden in the fall.

BEARDED IRIS
Iris spp. and hybrids

Hardiness—Zones 3 to 8

Color(s)—Shades of white, yellow, apricot, rose, maroon, blue, lavender, purple, and bicolors

Bloom period—Spring to early summer

Mature Size (H × W)—15 to 40 in. × 20 to 40 in.

Water needs—Keep a new planting slightly damp. Bearded irises do not like "wet feet."

Planting/Care—Best planted or transplanted in late summer to early fall. Prefer light, sandy, well-drained soil. Bury the rhizome with the top just barely beneath the soil surface but with the roots firmly anchored. Heavy feeders—be sure to fertilize regularly. Keep deadheaded, and cut stalks back to the crown when blooming ends. Divide every two or three years.

Pests/Diseases—The iris borer is best combated with regular spraying with an insecticide labeled for its control.

Landscaping Tips & Ideas—Beautiful in groups—mix and match the colors.

BUTTERCUP
Ranunculus asiaticus

Hardiness—Zones 8 to 11; grow as an annual

Color(s)—Yellow, orange, pink, red, white

Bloom period—Late spring to early summer

Mature Size (H × W)—8 to 18 in. × 12 to 24 in.

Water needs—Don't water much until they start to poke their heads up above the soil, then keep the soil evenly moist. Do not overwater.

Planting/Care—Plant the tubers in the spring, in the ground or in containers. Fertile soil that drains well is a must. Feed each time you water with a diluted general-purpose fertilizer. They are not cold-hardy and must be considered annuals in New England gardens.

Pests/Diseases—None serious

Landscaping Tips & Ideas—These are stunning in pots, arrayed in sunny spots, including a patio or porch steps. In the garden, they offer glorious early summer color after other spring-flowering bulbs have faded away.

CALADIUM
Caladium bicolor

Hardiness—Zones 9 to 11; grow as an annual

Color(s)—Green foliage overlaid with patterns in white, pink, rose, salmon, crimson

Bloom period—Not applicable

Mature Size (H × W)—20 to 30 in. × 12 to 18 in.

Water needs—Keep the soil evenly moist.

Planting/Care—Start the tubers indoors in peat moss or sterile soilless mix, about eight weeks before frost-free weather. Display outdoors in pots, or plant in well-drained soil that is rich in humus or peat moss. Best in semi-sun or light shade.

Pests/Diseases—Deer love caladiums! If slugs and snails trouble your plantings, use traps and/or bait.

Landscaping Tips & Ideas—These are superb bedding and pot plants, glorious growing with impatiens whose colors complement the leaves (white impatiens with white-and-green caladium, red impatiens with red-and-green). For best impact, plant in groups of four to six.

CANNA
Canna × generalis

Hardiness—Zones 8 to 10; treat as an annual

Color(s)—Pink, salmon, yellow, orange, red

Bloom period—Mid- to late summer

Mature Size (H × W)—3 to 6 ft. × as permitted

Water needs—Cannas prefer fairly damp soil; water during drought periods.

Planting/Care—Plant in spring after the soil has warmed up to about 65 F. Or start them in pots indoors four weeks before the last expected frost. Give them fairly rich, slightly acidic, well-drained soil. Plant 3 to 4 inches deep and 18 to 23 inches apart. Add slow-release fertilizer. Deadhead promptly. Stake tall types.

Pests/Diseases—Japanese beetles may be a problem. Handpick, or treat with an insecticide.

Landscaping Tips & Ideas—Other tropicals are good companions, including elephant ears and ornamental bananas. Relegate tall, stately ones to the back of a border or use along a fence. Use smaller ones in mixed flower beds.

CROCOSMIA
Crocosmia spp. and hybrids

Hardiness—Zones 6 to 10

Color(s)—Orange-red, red, yellow, apricot

Bloom period—Mid- to late summer

Mature Size (H × W)—18 to 24 in. × 18 to 24 in.

Water needs—Keep the soil nicely moist.

Planting/Care—Hardiness is borderline in most of New England, so plant in a protected area, cut back in late fall and mulch well for winter, or lift and store the plants each fall. Plant in mid-spring, in well-drained, humusy, fertile soil. Set the corms 3 inches deep and 5 inches apart.

Pests/Diseases—Spider mites can be a problem.

Landscaping Tips & Ideas—Use as a screen for the dying-back foliage of spring bulbs. Add to the center of a flower border in groups of five or ten—note that it needs a lot of space all around.

CROCUS
Crocus spp. and hybrids

Hardiness—Zones 3 to 8

Color(s)—White, pink, lavender, purple, yellow, orange, often with contrasting stripes or streaks

Bloom period—Late winter to early spring

Mature Size (H × W)—4 to 6 in. × 2 to 4 in.

Water needs—Natural rainfall is usually sufficient, but water if the weather is unseasonably dry.

Planting/Care—Plant in the fall in light, well-drained soil that has been improved with organic matter. Plant 5 to 6 inches deep, and space 2 inches apart. Avoid leaving bits of bulb casings around; squirrels notice. Mulch the area. After flowering but before the foliage dies down, apply a slow-release bulb fertilizer according to label directions.

Pests/Diseases—Except for hungry rodents, none serious

Landscaping Tips & Ideas—Plant in drifts of twenty to one hundred, near house entrances, at the edge of flower beds, fronting shrub borders, and along woodland paths.

CROWN IMPERIAL
Fritillaria imperialis

Hardiness—Zones 5 to 8

Color(s)—Orange, yellow, red

Bloom period—Mid-spring

Mature Size (H × W)—2 to 4 feet × 1 to 2 feet

Water needs—Maintain a moist soil.

Planting/Care—Plant in late summer in good, fertile soil—good drainage is a must. Plant fairly deeply, 6 to 12 inches down. Come spring, a stout stem will emerge, soon decorated with leaves lower down and topped with a whorl of four to six bell-like, downward-facing flowers with a tuft of leaves above. Keep the area mulched. Can thrive for years without requiring division.

Pests/Diseases—No serious pests. Rot is a danger in poorly drained sites and during very wet springs.

Landscaping Tips & Ideas—The flowers exude a pungent scent, so place where you can enjoy the color but not be assailed by the smell. Spectacular in combination with other hot-colored spring bulbs such as orange or yellow tulips.

DAFFODIL
Narcissus spp. and hybrids

Hardiness—Zones 3 to 8

Color(s)—White, yellow, gold, orange, bicolors

Bloom period—Spring

Mature Size (H × W)—4 to 20 in. × 3 to 5 in.

Water needs—Water when rainfall is sparse.

Planting/Care—Plant bulbs in the fall, in well-worked fertile loam with excellent drainage, about 8 inches deep and about 3 to 6 inches apart. Mulch. Deadheading isn't essential. Allow the foliage to yellow about six weeks before cutting back. Fertilize the area after blooming.

Pests/Diseases—None serious

Landscaping Tips & Ideas—Plant in irregular drifts of ten, twenty, or more. Large types are breathtaking naturalized in woods, fronting evergreens, edging meadows, and along the banks of streams or ponds. The smaller ones are exquisite in rock gardens, containers, or in rocky nooks. Choose an array of early-, mid-, and late-season varieties for a prolonged show.

DAHLIA
Dahlia cultivars and hybrids

Hardiness—Zones 5 to 9

Color(s)—Pastels and jewel tones of pink, salmon, white, cream, lemon, mauve, red, and bicolors

Bloom period—Late summer, early fall

Mature Size (H × W)—1½ to 5 ft. × 1 to 2½ ft.

Water needs—Unless there's a good soaking rain, provide water every week to ten days.

Planting/Care—Plant tubers or container-grown dahlias in spring, when the lilacs bloom. Provide an open, sunny site and light, fertile, humusy, well-drained soil. Cover tubers with 2 or 3 inches of soil, and space 18 to 24 inches apart. Provide tall, sturdy stakes. Rhizome clumps may be dug up in fall after blooming and stored indoors for the winter.

Pests/Diseases—None serious; however, rot can occur in soggy ground.

Landscaping Tips & Ideas—Add to cutting and vegetable gardens. Edge or include in perennial beds.

FLOWERING ONION
Alliums spp. and cultivars

Hardiness—Zones 3 or 4 to 8

Color(s)—Blue, purple, pink, white, yellow

Bloom period—Late spring and late summer

Mature Size (H × W)—6 to 48 in. × 10 to 15 in.; flower heads are 1 to 12 in. across

Water needs—Maintain soil moisture during the growing season; after that, the soil can be average to dry.

Planting/Care—Plant in late fall, in well-drained, humusy, fertile soil. Depending on their size, set the bulbs 3 to 5 or 8 inches deep, and 3 to 6 or 8 inches apart. Mulch. Tall ones might need staking. Keep deadheaded. Allow the foliage do die down naturally before removing it.

Pests/Diseases—None serious

Landscaping Tips & Ideas—Add to mixed flower beds for drama. Plant where the foliage of other flowers can serve as filler or as a screen for when the leaves are dying back.

GLADIOLUS
Gladiolus hybrids

Hardiness—Treat as an annual

Color(s)—All colors, including green and bicolors

Bloom period—Summer

Mature Size (H × W)—3 to 4 ft. × 8 to 10 in.

Water needs—Water at planting time, and maintain soil moisture as the plants grow.

Planting/Care—Plant in mid-spring in well-drained, rich soil with lots of peat moss, about 5 inches deep, 4 inches apart. Stake taller ones, especially in windy spots. Mulch. For a continuous supply, stagger planting dates at two-week intervals through early summer. Fertilize annually. After flowering, allow the foliage to die down, then dig up and store the corms indoors for the winter.

Pests/Diseases—Dust stored corms with a fungicide powder to prevent rot.

Landscaping Tips & Ideas—Ideal in a cutting garden, or plant them along a fenceline; include them in mixed flower beds, or incorporate into a kitchen garden.

GLORY-OF-THE-SNOW
Chionodoxa luciliae

Hardiness—Zones 3 to 9

Color(s)—Blue, pink, white, bicolors

Bloom period—Early spring

Mature Size (H × W)—4 to 6 in. × 4 to 6 in.

Water needs—Water well if rain is sparse.

Planting/Care—Plant in the fall, in the same sort of soil or location where you plant daffodils or tulips—well-drained ground is important. Set the bulbs about 3 inches deep. Fertilize yearly. After flowering, allow the foliage to die down naturally. It isn't very tall, so it shouldn't be much of an eyesore.

Pests/Diseases—None serious

Landscaping Tips & Ideas—Because this is a smaller plant, get great impact by planting plenty in large drifts or sweeps under deciduous trees and shrubs or throughout a semi-wild area. It mixes well with other spring bulbs in flower beds. This is an easy-going plant, blooming well every spring and increasing its numbers from one year to the next.

GRAPE HYACINTH
Muscari spp.

Hardiness—Zones 3 to 7

Color(s)—Many shades of blue, yellow, and white

Bloom period—Early to mid-spring

Mature Size (H × W)—6 to 8 in. × 4 to 6 in.

Water needs—Maintain a moist soil during the growing season, watering if rainfall is sparse.

Planting/Care—Plant in the fall in light, well-drained soil that has been improved with organic matter. Plant the bulbs 5 to 6 inches deep, 2 inches apart. Deadheading is not necessary. Will multiply if well-fertilized after blooming each year.

Pests/Diseases—Voles and squirrels can be a problem.

Landscaping Tips & Ideas—Plant in large groups or drifts of twenty to a hundred. White ones stand out more, so fewer can be effective. It can be grown in good soil in open, sunny woodland areas and will eventually carpet the earth with an extraordinary "river" of blue.

HYACINTH
Hyacinthus orientalis

Hardiness—Zones 4 to 8

Color(s)—White, yellow, coral, pink, rose, shades of blue and purple

Bloom period—Early to mid-spring

Mature Size (H × W)—8 to 12 in. × 4 to 6 in.

Water needs—Maintain moisture in spring, but avoid it in summer and winter.

Planting/Care—Plant in fall. Provide well-worked fertile loam with excellent drainage. Set 8 inches deep, about 3 to 4 inches apart, and mulch the area. After flowering but before the foliage disappears, fertilize to encourage them to return.

Pests/Diseases—None serious

Landscaping Tips & Ideas—Plant in groups along paths, and in pockets near patios and entrances. In flower beds, plant in groups of five to fifteen. In containers, plant in sets of three to five. For bedding, choose slightly smaller bulbs; they'll have outstanding blooms the first year and a looser cluster the second.

LILY
Lilium spp. and hybrids

Hardiness—Zones 4 to 9

Color(s)—Every color but blue, also bicolors

Bloom period—Summer—exact time varies with type

Mature Size (H × W)—1 ½ to 6 ft. × 1 ½ to 2 ft.

Water needs—Needs evenly moist soil, but tolerates a dry period after flowering

Planting/Care—Provide perfect drainage and very fertile soil. Mulch to keep the roots cool. Most need rather acidic soil. Four to six hours of full sun, plus partial sun the rest of the day is ideal. When flowering is over, cut the stalks to just above the leaves. Let the leaves yellow, then cut them to the ground and mark the spot.

Pests/Diseases—In some areas, the lily beetle is devastating.

Landscaping Tips & Ideas—For best impact, plant lilies in groups. Short annuals help keep the roots cool and hide the lily's "bare knees."

LYCORIS
Lycoris spp.

Hardiness—Marginally hardy in most of New England; overwinter indoors or treat as an annual

Color(s)—Pink, red, white

Bloom period—Late summer, fall

Mature Size (H × W)—18 to 30 in. × 12 to 24 in.

Water needs—Best in evenly moist ground

Planting/Care—Provide good, rich soil and even moisture. The straplike foliage appears in spring. The flowers don't appear till late summer or fall, when they deliver welcome, striking color. You may fertilize after the flowers fade.

Pests/Diseases—None serious

Landscaping Tips & Ideas—Best in groups. Provide some companions, both to mark the spot (when the plants are not evident) and to flatter the flowers, such as ferns, hostas, low-growing asters, and colorful annuals. Also nice displayed in pots (you can overwinter these indoors, still in their container, in a cool, dry spot).

SNOWDROPS
Galanthus nivalis

Hardiness—Zones 3 to 9

Color(s)—White

Bloom period—Early spring

Mature Size (H × W)—12 in. × 12 in.

Water needs—Maintain moist soil if weather is dry.

Planting/Care—Plant in good, humusy, well-drained soil in partial shade. It should be moist but not damp. Plant in the fall, setting the bulbs about 3 inches deep and 3 inches apart (they will self-sow on their own to form a substantial colony over the years). If a planting becomes congested, bulbs will push up to the soil surface—these are easily replanted or moved to another spot.

Pests/Diseases—None serious

Landscaping Tips & Ideas—Wonderful at the base of deciduous trees or shrubs, where they offer a delightful show at the beginning of spring every year. Easy to naturalize in woodsy areas and shade gardens. Note that "giant" snowdrops are *Galanthus elwesii,* and bloom up to two weeks earlier.

TUBEROUS BEGONIA
Begonia × tuberhybrida

Hardiness—Not cold hardy; treat as an annual

Color(s)—Red, pink, orange, yellow, white

Bloom period—Summer to fall

Mature Size (H × W)—8 in. × 12 in.

Water needs—These begonias need moisture alternated with short dry periods to avoid crown rot.

Planting/Care—Plant in spring after danger of frost is past. Avoid full sun; these are shade-lovers. Best in humusy soil, in a spot with good air circulation. Pick off spent flowers to stimulate reblooming. Pinch to keep plants compact. Provide support for taller or floppy plants.

Pests/Diseases—Prevent fungal disease by keeping water off the leaves. Watch for the occasional aphid blitz, and pinch off stem tips where they tend to gather. Keep pots off the ground to avoid slug invasions.

Landscaping Tips & Ideas—Use pots or hanging baskets to decorate shady areas and porches. Combine different colors or mix with compatible-hued shade-tolerant annuals.

TULIP
Tulipa spp. and hybrids

Hardiness—Zones 3 to 7

Color(s)—Every color but blue

Bloom period—Spring

Mature Size (H × W)—4 to 24 in. × 6 to 8 in.

Water needs—Maintain an evenly moist soil if rainfall is sparse.

Planting/Care—Plant in the fall in slightly acidic, well-drained soil enriched with compost and humus. Set large tulips 4 to 6 inches apart, 8 inches deep; set small bulbs 3 to 4 inches apart, 4 to 5 inches deep. Mulch. Even in the best conditions, many do not perennialize, though deadheading, feeding after bloom, and letting foliage die down naturally helps.

Pests/Diseases—Keep away voles and squirrels by planting bulbs in buried wire cages.

Landscaping Tips & Ideas—Plant a series of early, midseason, and late tulips for a long season of bloom. Big annuals—tall snapdragons, big marigolds, and zinnias—make fine screening for ripening tulip foliage.

BULBS

Asked when a bulb is a bulb and not a corm or a rhizome or a tuberous something, Dr. August A. de Hertogh, horticulturist with the University of North Carolina famed for his work with tulips, responded by saying, "Plant materials with underground storage organs can all correctly be called 'bulbs.' But the agreed-upon technical name for bulbous and tuberous plants is 'ornamental geophyte.'"

The term, coined by Danish plant geographer Christian Raunkiaer in 1933, has been shortened to "geophytes." What geophytes have in common is that they are all large storage organs ready to produce a plant—like seeds, but on a much larger scale.

Dr. de Hertogh predicts geophytes will be the name our children and our children's children will know. For now, we refer to the group as bulbs; our children can take it from there.

PLANNING

You can count on bulb flowers to bloom the first year planted. Under the right circumstances, you can expect many species and varieties, but not all, to come back year after year. To have the large bulb flowers perennialize, you must allow the foliage to ripen at least six weeks before removing it.

There are bulb flowers that bloom in every season. In spring daffodils and bluebells spread carpets of color in our woodlands. Summer gardens are sweet with the perfume of the majestic lilies. Autumn crocus come up when the trees start to shed, and fragrant paper-white narcissus and hyacinths, golden daffodils, cheery amaryllis, and a host of others can create a sequence of bloom in your home all winter long.

Spring-flowering bulbs. The year's first flowers, these bulbs are planted the preceding fall. They all tolerate our winters. All but the narcissus/daffodil group need protection from creatures that think of them as food. If you plant tulips, which are favorites of the squirrels, plant them 8 inches down, for a safeguard. Where snow cover is not certain, covering bulb plantings with a winter mulch will limit the depth of the freeze line and protect the bulbs beneath. Mulch just before or right after the ground starts to harden, not earlier.

We mentioned the group's only drawback before: the foliage must be allowed to "ripen" (patience is a virtue; possess it if you can!) for many weeks after the blooms fade. The larger bulbs, like tulips and daffodils, take forever, so plan to place them where the growth of summer-flowering bulbs like the big lilies, perennials, or annuals will screen the fading leaves. Another option is to have a garden of flowering bulbs interplanted with annuals.

Summer-flowering bulbs. The lilies start up as the daffodils fade. Others begin to grow when the weather becomes milder. Early and late varieties bring color to mixed borders and container gardens when they need it most, mid- and late summer. The summer-flowering bulbs whose winter hardiness rating is north of Zone 6 may be planted in mid-fall (or mid-spring) without special protection for winter. Those that are at the upper edge of their cold tolerance in Zone 6 are safest in a protected spot and provided with a winter mulch. Examples are crocosmia and wood sorrel (*Oxalis adenophylla*).

Summer-flowering bulbs rated as "tender" in our area, canna, caladiums, colocasia, dahlias, gladiolus, and the perfumed tuberose, for example, must be lifted in fall, dried, and stored for winter indoors in a cool, dry place. Most need cool storage temperatures—between 35 to 50 degrees for bulbs such as canna, dahlias, and tigridia. Others can be stored at room temperatures—caladiums and calocasia, for example. Except for Zones 6 and 7, these tender bulbs are best started indoors early and set out in the garden when it's warm enough to plant tomato seedlings.

Fall-flowering bulbs. These bulbs usually are planted in summer for fall blooming. If you haven't grown the lovely late bloomers, try a few this fall. Colchicum, fall crocus, and winter daffodil open showy blooms just above ground in early September; in spring large glossy leaves rise and, after many weeks, disappear for the summer. The beautiful resurrection lily (*Lycoris squamigera*) produces exotic, fragrant, trumpet-shaped blooms from bulbs planted in mid-summer; north of Zone 5 it must be brought in to winter in a frost-free place.

Bulbs for winter. In New England, these bulbs bloom indoors. In early fall, plan to pot up spring-flowering bulbs—we especially recommend tulips, daffodils, and perfumed hyacinths—for forcing into bloom indoors in winter. A few cold-tender bulb flowers can also be forced into bloom indoors in winter, notably amaryllis (*Hippeastrum*) and perfumed paper-whites.

PLANTING

Light. Crocus, daffodils, bluebells (Squill, *Scilla*), and the lovely wood hyacinth bloom in partial shade, as do some of the smaller bulbs. But most big bulb flowers do their best in full sun and need at least six hours of sun daily to come into flower a second year. That said, daffodils and other early flowering spring bulbs growing under deciduous trees bloom well because the trees don't leaf out until the bulb foliage has ripened.

Soil for bulbs. The garden and container soil in which bulbs do best is light and very well drained. Repeat: *very well drained*. Ideally, a raised bed on a slope. There are always exceptions to the rule; a few summer-bloomers tolerate moist spots— canna, bog iris, summer snowflake, crinum, rain lily, and spider lily.

The pH range most bulbs prefer is 6.0 to 7.0. There are exceptions to that rule, too. The most popular lilies prefer a somewhat acidic soil.

When you are planting bulbs in an existing bed, the soil needs the same careful preparation as for a raised bed for bulbs. (See Soil Preparation and Improvement in the Introduction to the book.) Outline the area, then cover it with 3 to 4 inches of humus, enough so that one quarter of the content of the soil from the hole will be organic matter. The humus can be decomposed bark, compost, partially decomposed leaves or seaweed, sphagnum peat moss, black peat humus, decomposed animal manures, or other decomposed organic material. Adding humus is particularly important if your soil has high clay content. Mix the humus into the soil as you dig it out of the hole along with the amendments for a raised bed.

Planting. About bulb planters—these tools work well only if the soil has been well prepared. We recommend the Dutch method of planting bulbs, which is to use a spading fork to dig a generous hole or a bed, remove the soil, and mix it thoroughly with the soil amendments mentioned above. Then, return 2 or 3 inches of improved soil to the hole, tamp it down, and plant the bulbs on top at the depth recommended.

When you aren't sure of the planting depth, set the bulbs at a depth that is about three times the height of the bulb itself.

Set true bulbs so the pointed tips are upright; set corms and tubers with the roots facing down. Set rhizomes horizontally in the soil with the roots down.

If voles, chipmunks, and squirrels hang around, plant all but the daffodils with a deterrent such as VoleBloc™ or PermaTill®, small sharp chips of expanded natural slate. Using it is easy. Line the planting hole or bed with 2 inches of either product. Set the bulbs on top, and fill in around them with VoleBloc™ or PermaTill® leaving just the bulb's tip exposed.

Cover with an inch of VoleBloc™ or PermaTill®, then fill the rest of the hole with a mixture of 30 percent VoleBloc™ or PermaTill® and improved soil from the hole. Mulch with 2 inches of pine needles, oak leaves, composted wood chips, or shredded bark.

CARE AND MULCHING

Fall care. Clear away dead leaves and the remains of annuals and perennials over bulb areas to prevent raking over tender new bulb foliage in spring. A light winter mulch of pine boughs helps keep leaves off.

Mulch. Most bulbs do not tolerate wet feet, especially when their blooming period is over. Two or 3 inches of a light mulch is all you need to give the garden a nice finish, keep weeds down, retain soil moisture, and moderate soil temperature. Never cover bulbs with more than 2 or 3 inches of mulch.

PERENNIALIZING AND MULTIPLYING YOUR BULBS

Most hardy bulbs planted in the garden will perennialize. Tulips are iffy. Growers identify those likely to come back year after year. Darwin hybrids and the little species tulips almost always return. Fertilize tulips generously after they finish blooming, and you have a better chance of having them repeat and even multiply.

Smaller bulbs and naturalized daffodils don't need deadheading, but deadheading the larger bulbs helps them to store up the energy needed for a fine flower show the following year. Even more important than deadheading is that you allow the foliage of the large bulb flowers six to seven weeks to ripen (yellow) before removing it. Tulip foliage may be cut when it is yellow halfway down. The leaves of the smaller bulbs tend to disappear on their own.

Once small bulb flowers are established in a garden, they send up clumps of grass-like foliage—in spring for bulbs that flower in fall, and in late summer for bulbs that bloom in spring. Those grassy clumps aren't weeds! If you happen to dig up small bulbs when you are planting in the area, just push them back into the soil, and they likely will survive.

Dividing bulbs, rhizomes, and tubers. You can multiply your holdings and, in some species, improve their performance by periodically dividing your bulbs. True bulbs growing well produce offsets that in three to four years may crowd the planting and cause the flowers to be smaller and diminish.

The best time to divide bulbs is after the foliage has withered, and it's easy to do. Use a spading fork to dig and lift the bulb clump. Then you can either pull the bulbs gently apart or halve the clump, and replant. Bulblets (baby bulbs) need years to become mature enough to bloom, so plant these in an out-of-the-way place. You don't have to divide naturalized daffodil bulbs to keep them gorgeous . . . just fertilize them. Lilies, on the other hand, do best when the big bulbs are moved or divided every four years.

You may divide rhizomes and tubers either before the growing cycle begins (easier since there is no foliage to contend with) or when it is over. Dig the rhizomes or tubers, and cut them into sections that each contain at least one growth bud or eye.

Tuberous roots, such as dahlias, do best when they are separated shortly before growth begins.

Transplanting. It once was the custom to lift bulbs intended for transplanting after they had bloomed in spring, store them for the summer, and replant in the fall. But now Dutch growers assure us the best place for winter-hardy bulbs at every season is in the ground. Lifted and stored they are susceptible to fungus and disease. But growers do recommend lifting and storing bulbs that can't survive winters in your garden.

Spring-flowering bulbs can be transplanted successfully in spring, summer, or fall. You can move daffodils in bloom. Or wait until the flowers have faded, then cut off the flower heads, leaving the green leaves. Dig the plants with care so as not to damage the roots, and move the whole clump to the desired location. Allow the foliage to ripen naturally, just as it would have in its original spot. You can also dig the bulbs in summer or very early fall. However, after the foliage dies they're not easy to locate, and digging blind may damage the bulbs; so before the foliage fades, mark the positions of bulbs you want to move.

Summer-flowering bulbs that are hardy enough to be left in the ground in New England's warm coastal regions, Zone 6 (-10° F winter lows) or Zone 7 (0° F winter lows), may be transplanted either in fall after the foliage has yellowed or in spring just as growth begins.

Fall-flowering bulbs may be moved after the blooms fade. Those with foliage that comes up in spring, like the fall-blooming crocus, can be moved then.

Winter-flowering bulbs that have been forced into bloom indoors are weakened. They won't be good for forcing a second year. Tulips and the smaller bulb flowers are best discarded. Some other spring-flowering bulbs, notably daffodils, and often hyacinths, forced into bloom indoors and then replanted out in the garden, sometimes come back the next year. If you plan to try them out in the garden, keep forced daffodils and hyacinths in a sunny window and continue to water and fertilize them while the foliage ripens and dies down. Keep them in a cool spot during the summer, then plant them in the garden in early fall. Many will eventually bloom in their outdoor locations.

A DAFFODIL BY ANY OTHER NAME

The immense variety of *Narcissus*, their easy ways, and their imperviousness even to deer make them spring's favorite bulb. Daffodil is used as a common name for the entire genus Narcissus but is most often associated with the large trumpet type. Jonquils are varieties of *Narcissus jonquilla*, late-bloomers that bear clusters of fragrant flowers on each stem.

Plant open woodlands with big, yellow daffodils in irregular drifts of twenty, fifty, or one hundred bulbs, and they will carpet it with gold. A dusting of wood ashes in early September is enough to keep naturalized daffs blooming.

Plant early daffs, like 8-inch 'Jack Snipe', to edge flower beds and in rock gardens, containers, in the shelter of boulders, and along fences.

For bouquets, grow show-stoppers like 12-inch orange-cupped 'Jetfire', and 18-inch pink-cupped 'Chinese Coral'. Bouquets of daffodils are long-lasting, but before combining just-cut daffodils with tulips or other flowers, be sure to place the daffodil stems in water overnight to detoxify.

For fragrance, in addition to jonquils, plant polyanthus daffodils. A favorite is 'Geranium', which has crisp white petals surrounding frilled orange cups. The perfumed paper-whites, so easy to force, belong to this group; they're not winter hardy here. Pot up paper-whites, a variety of tazetta narcissus, in late fall, and they will bloom and perfume your house in just a few weeks.

Planting daffodils. Plant daffodils in the fall after the first hard frost. They thrive in full sun or partial shade in well-drained, slightly acidic soil. Set large bulbs 8 inches deep, 3 to 6 inches apart; small bulbs 3 to 5 inches deep, 1 to 3 inches apart. Add a handful of 5-10-20 slow-release fertilizer as topdressing after planting. Deadhead the show daffs; naturalized daffs don't need it.

Perennializing daffodils. Most daffodils and jonquils perennialize. Allow the foliage to remain undisturbed until it has withered away. Binding the foliage while the leaves ripen cuts off the light and oxygen the bulbs need to nourish the next year's flowers, so we advise against it.

Watering. It's not necessary to water the soil after planting bulbs. But you do have to keep the soil moderately damp for bulbs growing in containers.

On the rare occasion when spring runs dry, provide spring-flowering bulbs with ample moisture from the moment the tips first break ground and during the season of active growth. Once the foliage disappears, the bulbs are dormant and excess watering can be detrimental. Underground automatic sprinkling systems spell death to most bulbs unless adjusted to water deeply and only when moisture is needed—not every day, not every other day, not even every third day.

Fertilizing. All bulbs need continuing fertilization if they are to thrive and multiply.

There are two schools of thought on fertilizing spring-flowering bulbs:

In their book *Daffodils*, daffodil gurus Brent and Becky Heath recommend applying a diluted organic fertilizer to spring-flowering bulb plantings from the time the tips show in spring until the bulbs bloom. They suggest fertilizing again in early fall with a slow-release product (5-10-12 or 5-12-20) such as Bulb Mate.

André Viette, the nurseryman's nurseryman, recommends fertilizing spring- flowering bulbs as soon as they finish blooming with Bulb-Tone® at the rate of 4 to 6 pounds to every 100 square feet, and again in early September. André also recommends fertilizing established summer-flowering bulbs in early spring before growth begins and again in mid-fall.

Pests. Squirrels, chipmunks, and voles truly believe you plant all bulbs except daffodils (which are toxic) just for their delight—in the ground, planters, windowboxes, and hanging baskets. The solution is to plant bulbs in VoleBloc™ or PermaTill®, as recommended in Planting earlier. Deer love tulips, crocus, lilies, too! Spraying is no deterrent, but a temporary chickenwire enclosure (see Pests, Diseases, & Controls in the Appendix) or bird netting may save them.

JANUARY

- A pleasant way to satisfy the hunger for spring flowers is to take out favorite bulb catalogs, tear out garden pages that show bulbs you would like to try or add, and then organize them into an album.

- Move indoor-potted bulbs that have finished chilling into a warmer room, and begin to water and fertilize them as you do houseplants. In two weeks or so, the shoots will grow tall and initiate flower buds. Place them in good light but out of direct sun. Feed a half-dose of liquid fertilizer at every watering.

- When all the blooms are dead on amaryllis and other forced bulbs, cut the flower heads off and move the plants to a bright, sunny window to grow. Do not save the paper-whites; discard them.

- Don't allow the soil of tender tropical bulbs overwintering indoors to dry out completely; they are semi-dormant.

FEBRUARY

- This year, take the dahlia plunge! They come in an exciting variety of shapes and colors. The 6-footers rival sunflowers in size and are real showstoppers at the back of a mixed border. Massed in the front of the bed, the smaller, bushier cactus-flowered varieties like pink 'Park Princess' are sensational. Place your orders early to be sure of getting the exact varieties you want.

- There's still time to force paper-whites, and many garden centers carry them this time of year.

HORTICULTURIST JOHN ELSLEY'S PICK OF COMPANION PLANTS FOR EARLY SPRING BULBS

If you can't find the bulb mentioned, try to match the color and the time of bloom.

- Daffodils with perennials for all-season color

- Daffodils, with garden mums, in front of daylilies, backed by peonies, backed by willowleaf sunflowers (*Helianthus salicifolius*), then ornamental grasses

- Giant snowdrop with shrubs and ground covers; giant snowdrop (*Galanthus*) 'Atkinsii', and Bergenia 'Sunningdale' or 'Appleblossom', under blood-twig dogwood (*Cornus sanguinea*) 'Winter Beauty' or *C. stolonifera* 'Cardinal', or with red-stem *Salix* 'Erythroflexuosa'

Good Together:

- Bluebell (*Hyacinthoides non-scripta*) with white wake-robin (*Trillium grandiflorum*) and *Rodgersia podophylla*

- Flowering onion (*Allium* 'Purple Sensation' with 'Miss Kim' lilac; or *Allium* 'Mount Everest') with violets or violet-red cranesbill (*Geranium sanguineum*), or iris 'Batik' or blue false indigo (*Baptisia australis*), or peony 'Red Red Rose'

- Glory-of-the-snow (*Chionodoxa luciliae*) with *Magnolia* x *loebneri* 'Merrill'

- Grape hyacinth (*Muscari armeniacum*) 'Blue Spike' with hostas and *Weigela* 'Wine and Roses'

- *Narcissus* 'Delibes' with tree peony (*Paeonia suffruticosa*); *Narcissus* 'Scarlet O'Hara' with 'Crimson Pygmy' barberry

- Giant snowdrop and narcissus 'Jet Fire' with hellebore hybrids

- Species tulip (*Tulipa saxatilis*), with bleeding heart (*Dicentra spectabilis*) 'Gold Heart'; tulip 'Maureen' with dogwood (*Cornus alba* 'Aurea'); tulip 'Candy Club' with Solomon's seal (*Polygonatum falcatum*); tulip 'Golden Parade' with 'Red Jade' crabapple; tulip 'Monte Carlo' with Colorado blue spruce (*Picea pungens* 'Glauca'); tulips with American arborvitae (*Thuja occidentalis* 'Degroots Emerald Spire'); *Tulipa tarda* with azalea 'Staccato'

Shrubs That Complement Early Spring Bulbs

- Azalea 'Tri-lights'; cornelian cherry (*Cornus mas*) 'Golden Glory'; crabapple 'Louisa'; dwarf witch alder (*Fothergilla gardenii*) 'Beaver Creek'; eastern ninebark (*Physocarpus opulifoliu*) 'Diabolo'; eastern redbud (*Cercis canadensis*) 'Appalachian Red'; giant arborvitae (*Thuja plicata*) 'Deerproof'; *Magnolia* × *soulangiana* 'San Jose', magnolia 'Butterflies'; and Turkish filbert (*Corylus avellana* var. *contorta*)

- When forced bulbs finish blooming, discard any you suspect of insect infestation.

- Maintain some moisture in pots of bulbs that are being, or have been, forced and that you plan to replant later.

- Assuming the ground isn't frozen, as soon as the tips of early bulbs show, start watering them weekly with a diluted organic fertilizer. Continue this until they bloom.

MARCH

- Clear leaves and remains of annuals and perennials from garden areas planted in bulbs, as soon as you can work outdoors. Raking beds once the bulbs are up can damage the emerging tips and even tear the little bulbs up by the roots.

- Protect tulips and crocus from deer with a repellent and change it every six weeks.

- Now that the small, early spring-flowering bulbs are showing their colors and the daffodils are inching up, consider where you'd like to see more or different colors and plants next spring. Make notes.

- Start tender summer-flowering bulbs and tropicals indoors late this month.

- Transplant forced daffodils and other forced bulbs that look healthy to an out-of-the-way place in the garden. Do not remove the foliage.

- Deadhead early daffodils, tulips, and other large bulb flowers that have finished blooming. Allow the foliage to remain. The small-bulb flowers are self-cleaning.

APRIL

- You can move spring-flowering bulbs around in the garden after the plants go out of bloom. Do it while the foliage is still green; once the foliage dies, the bulbs are hard to locate.

- Daffodils and forsythias come into full bloom this month—and light up the day! If you haven't made this pairing before, remedy that by planting a forsythia now.

- When temperatures reach 60 degrees F. during the day, you can get ready to repot summer-flowering bulbs that wintered indoors—ornamental banana, canna, ginger lilies, lily-of-the-Nile. Set them in a sheltered spot and begin weekly watering and fertilization.

- You can lift and transplant the small fall-flowering bulbs, autumn crocus for example, whose grass-like foliage comes up now.

- After the foliage has died down, but while you can still see it, is the best time to divide clumps of spring-flowering bulbs. If you plan to move them later, mark their positions now.

MAY

- Unhappy with bare spots where the spring-flowering bulbs have gone by? When the air warms, hide them with pots of the big tropical-leafed canna and ornamental banana plants.

- When the air warms, in Zones 6 and 7, gardeners can plant dahlia tubers outdoors. Set them 18 to 24 inches apart, in well-worked, fertile soil. Be prepared to stake them.

- You can start planting glads when you plant sweet corn—ideal soil temperature is 50 degrees F. Plant sets of six to twelve for cutting, and repeat every ten days until the end of June. Set the corms 5 inches deep, 5 inches apart.

- If you hope to perennialize tulips, fertilize them now with bulb fertilizer. Darwin hybrids and species tulips should be encouraged.

- Japanese beetles can ruin the foliage of canna, dahlias, and other bulb flowers. Pick them off by hand.

JUNE

- Cut the yellowed foliage of the spring-flowering bulbs off at the base. If there are some you wanted to move but didn't get to, mark the spot with a plant marker or a golf tee so you'll know where to dig.

- Mail-order catalogs for spring-flowering bulbs start arriving now. They offer discount prices on early orders for fall- and spring-flowering bulbs. They offer a wide selection and ship at planting time.

- Continue to plant gladiolus corms at ten-day intervals so you'll have plenty for cutting.

- Move tuberous begonias, dahlias, caladiums, and other tender bulbs to their permanent place in the garden. They need some protection from noon and late-afternoon sun.

- Check the soil moisture of small containers of summer-flowering bulbs and tuberous begonias every two days. Don't neglect pots of amaryllis summering in the garden.

- Fertilize spring-flowering bulbs as soon as they finish blooming. This inspires bigger and more plentiful blooms next year.

JULY

- Take advantage of the mail-order bulbs suppliers' discounts for early orders. They start shipping as early as mid-August and can run out of popular varieties.

- To have a showing from the little bulbs, order enough of each variety to plant drifts of twenty, fifty, or one hundred. For the mid-sized bulbs to be effective, you'll need ten, twenty, or more of each.

- Plant the little bulbs that bloom in the fall in a sunny spot in the shelter of a stone wall or a big rock. Most will perennialize.

- Tie tall dahlias and lilies to the upper third of their stakes.

- Hill the soil around glads as they gain height, and stake the tallest ones.

- Mulch around summer-flowering bulbs to keep their roots cool and to maintain moisture.

- Add a half-dose of water-soluble fertilizer to the water for bulbs growing in baskets and pots, at every second watering.

AUGUST

- Weed faithfully. A swing-head hoe works well. It's a push-pull oscillating hoe that cuts through weeds and cultivates the soil without disturbing the mulch.

- Some mail-order houses start shipping spring-flowering bulbs for fall planting as early as mid-August. Some can be forced into winter bloom indoors; these you can start next month. It's best to wait until after a hard frost to start planting the spring-blooming bulbs out in the garden. Store bulbs-in-waiting in a cool cellar, a crisper, or a cool garage.

- Late this month you can begin to transplant established spring-flowering bulbs that you marked in spring for moving. Use a pitchfork to lift them. Pick out the largest bulbs and replant them in their new spot.

- Dahlias need deadheading and are good for cut flowers, so don't skimp on bouquets.

- If tall bearded iris foliage is browning at the tips, cut the tips back to healthy tissue.

SEPTEMBER

- Keep bulbs waiting to be planted in a refrigerator crisper, away from fruits and vegetables, or in a cool garage or cellar.

- Spread bulb fertilizer or fine wood ashes over established beds of spring-flowering bulbs at the rate of 4 to 6 pounds to 100 square feet.

- When tuberous begonias begin to yellow, bring them indoors, let the soil dry to barely damp over five or six weeks. Then remove dead foliage and store the tubers in a cool, dark place.

- Bring in pots of amaryllis that summered in the garden. You can let the soil dry, or keep them growing in a window. Either way, they need 55 degrees F. temperatures for eight to ten weeks.

- Before real frosts arrive in Zones 3 to 6, harvest gladiolus corms, remove the stalks, and cure on screens for three or four weeks at room temperature before storing.

OCTOBER

- As temperatures drop into the 50s, organize the planting of the spring-flowering bulbs. The best time is six weeks before the ground freezes hard. The daffodils go in first, after the first hard frost. The tulips and other large bulbs go next, after two hard frosts. The small bulbs—muscari, crocus—go in after the tulips.

- When you are planting groups of bulbs, prepare planting beds rather than individual holes.

- For a lasting show, plant a three-tier bulb garden. Plant big bulbs on the lowest level, cover with a few inches of soil, then plant medium bulbs, add a few inches more of soil, and plant small bulbs on top.

- Cut down the foliage of the tall bearded iris and Dutch irises down to 2 inches.

- Clear dying foliage and dig up weeds from established beds of fall- and summer-flowering bulbs. Then fertilize with bulb fertilizer according to the label directions.

NOVEMBER

- If you haven't already, fertilize established beds of bulbs now.

- Save and store wood ashes to use to fertilize naturalized plantings of spring-flowering bulbs in early March.

- If you mulch in areas planted with spring-flowering bulbs, it may discourage squirrels.

- Cut down any remaining stems of lilies, irises, and other summer-flowering bulbs.

- Continue to monitor the moisture in pots of bulbs being forced. Do not allow them to dry out.

- Maintain a little moisture in pots of tender perennials and tropicals wintering indoors; they are only semi-dormant.

- Kits of amaryllis bulbs for indoor blooming are sold this time of year, along with paper-whites. Both species take a few weeks to come into bloom.

DECEMBER

- If you have unplanted spring-flowering bulbs, plant them if the ground remains soft enough!

- When amaryllis finish blooming, cut the blossoms off and continue to grow the plants in a bright, sunny window.

- Mid-month, check bulbs being forced. Bring those that are showing roots and shoots into a warmer room and indirect light. Water and fertilize them lightly when you water houseplants.

- When they are growing well, move them to good light and out of direct sun. Keep the soil barely damp while they are blooming.

- Mold sometimes appears on pots of bulbs being forced when the growing medium is too wet. Move the bulbs to a location with good air circulation and allow the soil to dry down to barely damp.

GROUND
COVERS
for New England

Groundcovers create a unified field that harmonizes and pulls together the various elements of the landscape—shrub borders, flower beds, and specimen trees. A groundcover can be any height: even daylilies can be a groundcover. Those we recommend here are low-growing, need almost no maintenance once established, can do what lawn grasses do where mowers can't go, and can replace lawns you are weary of mowing. The most attractive and enduring groundcovers for New England landscapes are the plants on the pages that follow, but not every one of these is perfect for every site. They are designated as groundcovers because, like weeds, most of them spread rapidly: so think twice about planting any of these where they might later invade stands of native plants or woodlands we are trying to preserve.

The toughest evergreen groundcovers are ajuga, vinca, ivy, and creeping juniper. Ajuga and vinca bear sweet little flowers in early spring and can be walked on—with discretion. Ivy can take months to expand, but once started spreads irrepressibly. Creeping juniper withstands sun, heat, drought, and salt, and it's a good bank holder.

A beautiful plant that lightens shaded places is dead nettle, which produces masses of small hooded flowers in spring. Leadwort has handsome glossy foliage, and in late summer bears long-lasting gentian-blue flowers. For cooler regions, dappled light, and a formal look, pachysandra is the perfect choice. The ferns we recommend also do well in dappled light and are lovely in transitional areas edging woodlands.

Combining several compatible groundcovers adds texture to an area and is a safeguard should one of the plants run into difficulties. For a richly varied lawn substitute, we like drifts of small winter-flowering bulbs, over-planted with aromatic Greek oregano and thyme, ajuga in the sunny places, vinca in part-sun, and dead nettle under the trees.

PLANTING GROUNDCOVERS

We recommend starting a groundcover with flats or pots of rooted cuttings. If you will be planting in an area covered by turf or unwanted weeds, in early spring or fall when the soil is dry, spray the area with herbicide, or remove the top layer. Top the area with 2 or 3 inches of compost or decomposed leaves, and broadcast over it slow-release fertilizers, along with greensand (with its thirty-two micro-nutrients) and rock phosphate. Follow the rates recommended on the packages. Rototill all this 8 inches deep, three times over a two-week period. If you are installing an invasive groundcover such as ivy or ajuga, bury a 6-inch metal barrier to keep it from overrunning neighboring plantings.

At planting time, cover the area with 3 inches of mulch and plant the groundcover seedlings through it. Working in even rows and starting at the widest end, dig a row of evenly spaced planting pockets 8 to 14 inches apart. Set the plants into the pockets and firm them into place. If you are planting on a slope, set the plants so their backs are a little lower than their fronts. Position the second row plants zigzag style between those of the first row. For row three, repeat row one, and for row four repeat row two. Maintain the mulch until the groundcover has grown so dense that it shades out weeds. Plan on at least two years for the plants to grow enough to cover well.

If weeding won't be possible, plant your groundcover through a porous landscape fabric. Push the edges of the fabric sheet into the ground and weight them with rocks, or use your heel to push them in. Make rows of X-shaped slits in the fabric, and insert the plants through the slits with a trowel. Landscape fabric slows the rooting of the aboveground branches, so plant densely.

In fall, clear your groundcover of the thickest drifts of fallen leaves with a blow-vac. Certain groundcovers when fully mature benefit from shearing every year or two in early spring before growth begins.

OTHER GOOD OPTIONS

The plants on the following pages are the best of the best, but we have other favorites:

GROUNDCOVERS:

- Bloody Cranesbill, *Geranium sanguineum*
- Golden Star, *Chrysogonum virginianum*
- Mountain Pink, *Phlox subulata*
- Soapwort, *Saponaria officinalis* 'Rosea Plena'
- Snow-in-Summer, *Cerastium tomentosum*

FERNS:

- Beech Fern, *Thelypteris hexagonoptera*
- Cinnamon Fern, *Osmuda cinnamonomea*
- Deer Fern, *Blechnum spicant*
- Japanese Shield Fern, *Dryoptera erythrosora*
- Maidenhair Fern, *Adiatum pedatum*
- Marsh Fern, *Thelypteris palustris puffense*
- Massachusetts Fern, *Thelypteris simulata*
- New York Fern, *Thelypteris novaborensis*
- Royal Fern, *Osmuda regalis*

GROUNDCOVERS FOR PROBLEM SITES

If you find turfgrass high-maintenance or have a problem with growing it under trees, consider these solutions:

Lawn substitute. Four groundcovers are commonly used as substitutes for turf lawns. They are evergreen and can be walked on occasionally without being damaged.

- English Ivy (*Hedera helix*). An evergreen with tough glossy dark-green leaves on woody vines. There are lovely small-leaved and also variegated forms.

- Pachysandra, Japanese Spurge (*Pachysandra terminalis*). Low-growing, wide-spreading, formal groundcover. Short green-white flower spikes in early spring.

- Vinca, Periwinkle (*Vinca minor*). Small, dainty, shiny dark-green leaves on slim trailing stems 2 to 3 feet long. Lavender-blue flowers in early spring.

- Wintergreen, Checkerberry (*Gaultheria procumbens*). Evergreen shrubby ground-hugging mat with aromatic foliage and bright berries.

Under trees. Tree shade and root competition are hard on turfgrass. These groundcovers do well under trees.

- Bugleweed (*Ajuga reptans*). Semievergreen rosettes of leaves and flowering spikes in blue or white in spring.

- Hosta (*Hosta*). Small colorful hostas like 8-inch 'Gold Edger'; 3-inch 'Venusta'; and 7-inch *H. helemoides*.

- Golden Moneywort (*Lysimachia nummularia*) 'Aurea'. Deciduous, lime-green, low-growing, and spreads rapidly in moist soil. In early summer, it bears masses of small cup-shaped yellow flowers.

- Lilyturf (*Liriope muscari*). Grasslike, and 12 to 18 inches high. Flowering spikes in blue, purple, lavender, or white in late summer.

- Lily-of-the-valley (*Convallaria majalis*). Deciduous, lovely 6- to 8-inch high groundcover ideal for open woodlands. The flowers are exquisitely fragrant.

- Spotted Deadnettle (*Lamium maculatum*). Semievergreen, low-growing, silver-white-green variegated foliage lightens the shadows. Pink or white florets in May and June.

MAKING MORE GROUNDCOVERS

You can save money and learn some valuable new gardening skills by propagating your own to fill gaps, empty spots, or start new beds.

Some groundcovers can be started from seed, including common myrtle (*Vinca minor*). When seeds are available, starting the plants yourself from seed is the most cost-efficient way, but remember that named varieties may not come true from seed gathered in your garden.

Most groundcovers root easily from cuttings or root division. Those that multiply by means of aboveground runners, like ajuga and vinca, you can divide by simply cutting the plantlet from the parent and digging it up and transplanting.

Ivy is easy. You can divide a densely-rooted clump in spring, but cuttings taken in late summer or early fall root more quickly. Lamium cuttings root easily in spring; divisions of the plant root easily in spring or early fall. Rampant growers like creeping Jenny (*Lysimachia nummularia*) can be grown from cuttings taken in spring or divisions planted in fall. Pachysandra will root from cuttings almost all year round, but we find the easiest is to dig clumps in very early spring before the plants start to grow, or in early fall. Dig the clumps by shovel and include as much of the roots and the soil clump as you can get.

Ferns are usually propagated by root division in spring. Plants that clump, like liriope, are multiplied by dividing a mature crown; use a spading fork to lift and gently break the clump apart, or use a spade to cut the clump apart.

COMPANION PLANTS FOR YOUR GROUNDCOVER—TRY BULBS!

These large-flowering bulbs are attractive planted here and there among groundcovers, adding color when it is most welcome, as well as appealing contrast.

- Yellow daffodils

- Lily-Flowered tulips

- Red Parrot tulips

- Fosteriana tulips ('White Emperor', 'Orange Emperor', 'Red Emperor')

- *Tulipa greigii* ('Sweet Lady', 'Goldwest', 'Oriental Splendor')

- Foxtail lily (*Eremurus stenophyllus*)

- Giant onion (*Allium giganteum*)

- Indian lily (*Camassia quamash*)

BEARBERRY
Arctostaphylos uva-ursi

Hardiness—Zones 2 to 7

Color(s)—Pink, white

Bloom period—Spring

Mature Size (H × W)—6 to 12 in. × 2 to 4 ft.

Water needs—For the first season, water every week or two; thereafter, only during prolonged dry spells.

Planting/Care—Plant in very early spring. It prefers well-drained, infertile soil with an acid pH of 4.5 to 5.5. It is difficult to transplant and fairly costly, so put the effort necessary into soil preparation. Space plants 12 to 24 inches apart. Mulch with pine needles or rotted leaf mold; replenish every spring. In cold weather, the glossy leaves turn bronze-red. Birds love the red berries.

Pests/Diseases—None serious

Landscaping Tips & Ideas—It is especially attractive as a groundcover for hillside terraces or rambling over stony slopes. It tolerates sandy soil and makes an excellent groundcover for seashore gardens.

BELLFLOWER
Campanula porscharskyana

Hardiness—Zones 3 to 8

Color(s)—Lavender-blue or pale blue

Bloom period—Late spring, early summer

Mature Size (H × W)—4 to 6 in. × up to 12 in.

Water needs—Water if rains are scarce.

Planting/Care—Plant young potted plants in sandy or other thin, well-drained soil. Add a slow-release fertilizer. Set plants 8 to 10 inches apart. Mulch to discourage competing weeds and maintain soil moisture. After they bloom, clip or pinch them back. Intermittent repeat bloom over the summer is fairly common.

Pests/Diseases—None serious

Landscaping Tips & Ideas—Use at the front of a flower bed as an edging to set off minor bulbs, or blend with other groundcovers such as rock cress. Plant along stone walls, between steppingstones, and along paved walks. Looks good under yellow daylilies.

BUGLEWEED
Ajuga reptans

Hardiness—Zones 4 to 9

Color(s)—White, shades of purple, pink, rose

Bloom period—Spring

Mature Size (H × W)—4 to 8 in. × 12 to 14 in.

Water needs—Water new plantings every week to ten days unless it rains.

Planting/Care—Plant in early spring or early fall. Does best in well-drained ordinary garden soil. Space plants 3 inches apart, and be prepared to divide, or prune them back, the following summer. Mulch. Fertilize lightly once a year.

Pests/Diseases—Prevent crown rot by clearing out fallen autumn leaves. If a fungal problem develops, ask your local garden center to recommend a fungicide.

Landscaping Tips & Ideas—It will cover a small area with a low, dense mat. Avoid growing it close to flower beds or other areas easily invaded. The colored varieties are showiest if they get some direct sun.

95

CHRISTMAS FERN
Polystichum acrostichoides

Hardiness—Zones 3 to 8

Color(s)—Evergreen foliage

Bloom period—Not applicable

Mature Size (H × W)—12 to 18 in. × 18 to 24 in.

Water needs—Maintain soil moisture. Provide some overhead watering or misting in high heat or drought.

Planting/Care—Plant in spring after the last frost, in moist, humusy soil. Since the fern is long-lived and multiplies, dig wide planting holes 20 to 25 inches apart. Set the rootball just a little higher than it was growing in the pot. Mulch with pine needles, shredded leaves, or leaf compost. In the second season, apply a slow-release fertilizer for acid-loving plants under the foliage. Avoid cultivating next to the crown; hand-pull weeds.

Pests/Diseases—None serious

Landscaping Tips & Ideas—Lovely in a glade with hostas and astilbes. Because it is shallow-rooted, it competes successfully with tree roots and does well in rock gardens.

CREEPING JUNIPER
Juniperus horizontalis

Hardiness—Zones 3 to 9

Color(s)—Evergreen foliage may deepen or change color in the fall, depending on the variety

Bloom period—Not applicable

Mature Size (H × W)—6 to 12 in. × 5 to 8 ft.

Water needs—The first season, water every week or two; drought-tolerant thereafter.

Planting/Care—Plant practically anytime, in well-drained soil in six hours or more of direct sun (those grown in shade get thin and ratty). Set about 3 feet apart. Mulch; replenish every spring. Do not fertilize unless the soil is extremely poor. Where branches overlap, you may prune in midsummer.

Pests/Diseases—If the branches brown here and there, chances are spider mites are at work.

Landscaping Tips & Ideas—A fine bank-holder, as a groundcover in neglected areas, among rocks, and edging masonry walls. Nice with early daffodils and other medium-height spring-flowering bulbs.

CREEPING PHLOX
Phlox stolonifera

Hardiness—Zones 4 to 9

Color(s)—White, blue, purple, pink

Bloom period—Late spring

Mature Size (H × W)—2 in. × spreading

Water needs—Water regularly until established; thereafter, provide water in dry spells.

Planting/Care—Plant in spring or fall. Does best in woodsy soil—moist, acidic, rich in organic matter, and well-drained. Set plants 8 to 10 inches apart. Mulch to discourage weeds until the plants knit together. Clip faded flowers back to the foliage after bloom. Cut off injured or dead runners anytime during the growing season. You may divide overcrowded clumps after flowering.

Pests/Diseases—None serious. However, too much summer sun may cause stress, reducing plant vigor and causing foliage to become pale.

Landscaping Tips & Ideas—Ideal for edging walks and beds, and for transition areas between shade and sunny sites. Also does well between steppingstones.

ENGLISH IVY
Hedera helix

Hardiness—Zones 5 to 9

Color(s)—Evergreen foliage

Bloom period—Spring flowers are insignificant.

Mature Size (H × W)—6 to 8 in. × 25 to 50 ft., or more

Water needs—The first season, water the plants deeply every week in hot and dry weather. The second year, keep the soil moderately damp.

Planting/Care—Plant in early spring or early fall, in rich, fairly humusy, well-drained ground. Set the plantlets 6 inches apart. Mulch. Do not fertilize established beds unless the foliage yellows. Keep it well-groomed, and shear it back every three or four years to maintain dense foliage.

Pests/Diseases—Combat slugs and snails with traps and/or bait.

Landscaping Tips & Ideas—Thickly planted, it makes a dense "lawn." Also a great edger between strips of pavement. Handsome in urns and containers. Discourage it from climbing walls or tree trunks with yearly pruning.

EPIMEDIUM
Epimedium spp. and hybrids

Hardiness—Zones 4 to 9

Color(s)—Yellow, pink, orange, rose, lavender, white, bicolors

Bloom period—Spring

Mature Size (H × W)—6 to 10 in. × 12 to 18 in.

Water needs—Water well the first two months, and weekly thereafter unless there is a soaking rain. Established plants can handle some drought.

Planting/Care—Plant in well-drained, rich soil with an acidic pH 4.5 to 5.5. Place the plants, which are slow to establish, about 12 inches apart. Maintain a mulch as needed for the first year or two. The plants do best in bright shade. In early spring, shear old foliage and fertilize. You may divide in very early spring or toward the end of summer.

Pests/Diseases—None serious

Landscaping Tips & Ideas—A beautiful groundcover under trees, shrubs, and in woodlands. Use to border a woodland path. Handsome growing with hellebores in the shade of a tall shrub border.

EUROPEAN GINGER
Asarum europaeum

Hardiness—Zones 4 to 7

Color(s)—Evergreen foliage; insignificant brownish flowers

Bloom period—Spring

Mature Size (H × W)—6 to 8 in. × spreading

Water needs—Water to establish; after that, water during dry spells.

Planting/Care—Plant divisions in spring or early fall. Happiest in classic woodsy soil—rich in humus, acidic, moist, and well-drained. Set plants 6 to 8 inches apart, and do not plant too deeply. Fertilize at planting time and probably not again. Because it spreads so slowly, plants rarely need dividing unless they are restricted to a small space. There is no need to shear it for extensive renewal. Just pick off ratty leaves as needed during the season.

Pests/Diseases—None serious

Landscaping Tips & Ideas—The foliage beautifully sets off the colorful flowers of small spring bulbs. It then obscures their dying foliage over several weeks.

FOAMFLOWER
Tiarella cordifolia

Hardiness—Zones 3 to 9

Color(s)—White

Bloom period—Spring

Mature Size (H × W)—6 in. × 2 ft.

Water needs—Maintain soil moisture for the first season. Mature plants tolerate brief periods of drought.

Planting/Care—Plant root divisions or runners in early spring. It thrives in damp, shady places where the soil is rich in humus. Set 8 to 12 inches apart, and mulch. Scatter a light application of organic acid fertilizer under the foliage each spring. Control its growth by chopping off runners.

Pests/Diseases—None serious

Landscaping Tips & Ideas—Along with ferns, it makes a lovely living mulch for clematis vines. Use as an underplanting for drifts of bleeding heart along woodland paths and in sun-dappled glades. In shaded corners, it's pretty with hellebore, creeping phlox, and ferns. Some of the newer cultivars have pink or pinkish flowers.

GOLDEN MONEYWORT, CREEPING JENNY
Lysimachia nummularia 'Aurea'

Hardiness—Zones 3 to 8

Color(s)—Yellow blooms, chartreuse to yellow foliage

Bloom period—Early summer

Mature Size (H × W)—1 to 2 in. × indefinite spread

Water needs—Water a new planting every week unless the ground is naturally moist.

Planting/Care—Plant after the last spring frost or before the first fall frost, in somewhat neutral, humusy soil. Set the plants 12 to 18 inches apart. Maintain a mulch while the plants are establishing. Fertilize once in early spring. Prune back the plants if they become matted. Can spread aggressively in moist conditions.

Pests/Diseases—None serious; however, the plants will suffer if the soil surface is dry for days at a time.

Landscaping Tips & Ideas—This is an excellent groundcover for wet, difficult places. Lovely in rock gardens, between paving stones, and edging patio containers. Attractive with golden-leaves coleus.

JAPANESE PAINTED FERN
Athyrium nipponicum 'Pictum'

Hardiness—Zones 3 to 8

Color(s)—Blended silver-green and maroon fronds

Bloom period—Not applicable

Mature Size (H × W)—14 to 24 in. × 18 to 30 in.

Water needs—Maintain soil moisture for the first season. A little overhead watering in drought and high heat is helpful.

Planting/Care—Set out root divisions in late spring after frost. Thrives in moist, humusy soil. It lives long and multiplies all around, so dig wide planting holes 25 to 30 inches apart. Set the rootball a little higher than it was growing before. Mulch with shredded leaves, leaf compost, or peat moss. Fertilize lightly each spring. Hand-pull encroaching weeds. Protect it from winter cold and late frosts.

Pests/Diseases—None serious

Landscaping Tips & Ideas—Lovely with white impatiens, wild ginger, and creeping thyme. Other good companions include astilbes, white bleeding heart, and Japanese irises.

LAMIUM
Lamium maculatum

Hardiness—Zones 4 to 8

Color(s)—Pink, lavender-pink, white

Bloom period—Spring

Mature Size (H × W)—8 to 12 in. × 12 to 16 in.

Water needs—Water regularly when establishing, if rainfall is sparse.

Planting/Care—Plant root divisions in early spring. They do well in almost any soil, but spread rapidly in light, well-drained loam. Set the plants 12 to 18 inches apart, water well, and apply a mulch (replenish the mulch every spring, especially to keep weeds at bay). If the plants become straggly toward midsummer, renew them by cutting back to 6 or 8 inches high. In fall, remove dead stems and clear out fallen autumn leaves.

Pests/Diseases—None serious

Landscaping Tips & Ideas—Lamium brightens dark corners and makes a nice contrast when planted with dark-foliaged groundcovers such as wild ginger.

LEADWORT
Ceratostigma plumbaginoides

Hardiness—Zones 5 to 9

Color(s)—Blue

Bloom period—Summer, early fall

Mature Size (H × W)—8 to 12 in. × 12 to 18 in.

Water needs—Maintain soil moisture during establishment.

Planting/Care—In early spring, plant in full sun or moderate shade. Needs a well-drained site. Does best in rich, acidic loam, but will tolerate other soils. Set the divisions 9 to 15 inches apart. Mulch to keep weeds at bay until the plants fill in—this can take two or three seasons. In fall, after frost, cut back. Plumbago blooms on new growth, so if you do not cut it back, you will get lots of foliage but miss out on the beautiful flowers. It gets matted in time and benefits from division every three or four years.

Pests/Diseases—None serious

Landscaping Tips & Ideas—Mixes well with other flowering groundcovers, including periwinkle and lamium.

LILY-OF-THE-VALLEY
Convallaria majalis

Hardiness—Zones 2 to 7

Color(s)—White, pink cultivars

Bloom period—Spring

Mature Size (H × W)—10 to 12 in. × spreading

Water needs—During the first six weeks after planting, water often enough to keep the soil damp to the touch.

Planting/Care—Best planted in early spring or early fall. It thrives in somewhat acidic soil that is well-drained, humusy, and moist. Set plants 6 to 8 inches apart. Provide a mulch. Fertilize lightly in fall. Fall is also the time to divide crowded clumps.

Pests/Diseases—If the foliage browns in late summer, it means spider mites are at work; apply a miticide according to label directions.

Landscaping Tips & Ideas—Charming with wildflowers. Delightful in a woodland garden with columbines, primroses, Solomon's seal, trilliums, and lady's slippers. Keep it out of any flower bed where its aggressive nature will become a problem.

LILYTURF
Liriope muscari

Hardiness—Zones 5 to 9

Color(s)—Blue, lavender, purple, white

Bloom period—Late summer, early fall

Mature Size (H × W)—1 to 1 ½ ft. × 1 to 2 ft.

Water needs—Keep plants watered during dry spells the first summer and beyond.

Planting/Care—In early spring or early fall, set out container-grown root divisions. It is not particular about soil pH, tolerates high-alkaline soils, and succeeds in hot, dry locations, though it is best in moderately fertile, well-drained ground. Set the plants 12 inches apart. Mulch. In early spring, trim the foliage down to the crown to allow for fresh growth, and replenish the mulch. May be divided in early spring before growth begins.

Pests/Diseases—Fight slugs and snails by waiting till the soil dries, then sprinkling diatomaceous earth around the plants.

Landscaping Tips & Ideas—Use as filler or edging in flower beds.

PACHYSANDRA
Pachysandra terminalis

Hardiness—Zones 4 to 8

Color(s)—Evergreen foliage, insignificant white flowers

Bloom period—Spring

Mature Size (H × W)—8 to 10 in. × spreading

Water needs—Water transplants weekly during establishment; drought-tolerant thereafter.

Planting/Care—Plant rooted cuttings in early spring or early fall. Humusy, well-drained, acidic soil is best. Set the cuttings 4 to 6 inches apart, and mulch to conserve soil moisture and keep weeds at bay. Remove fallen autumn leaves and fertilize in late fall. Keep the bed airy and cool by thinning and cutting. In winter, a cover of snow is definitely a benefit.

Pests/Diseases—Susceptible to a stem blight (especially in more sun) and to scale and mites; treat with appropriate controls.

Landscaping Tips & Ideas—Perfect groundcover for formal plantings. Beautiful under rhododendrons, azaleas, tall trees, and in open woodlands.

PERIWINKLE
Vinca minor

Hardiness—Zones 4 to 9

Color(s)—Periwinkle blue, white

Bloom period—Spring

Mature Size (H × W)—3 to 6 in. × 2 to 3 ft.

Water needs—Do not allow to dry out the first season; water during extended droughts.

Planting/Care—Set out flats of rooted cuttings in early spring or fall, in well-drained, fertile, loamy soil. Space 8 inches apart. Mulch. In early spring, mow or shear to keep the bed thick. Scratch in a slow-release fertilizer. You may divide and replant in early spring or during wet weather in late summer and fall.

Pests/Diseases—None serious

Landscaping Tips & Ideas—Some shade is advisable in hotter areas. Doesn't tolerate much foot traffic. Thrives in bright shade under tall trees or in the partial shade created by a building. Nice with other groundcovers that like the same growing conditions (ferns, pachysandra, plumbago).

SWEET WOODRUFF
Galium odoratum

Hardiness—Zones 4 to 8

Color(s)—White

Bloom period—Late spring

Mature Size (H × W)—6 to 8 in. × spreading

Water needs—Water new patches regularly if rainfall is scarce; keep moist well into summer to delay decline.

Planting/Care—Plant in spring before the weather becomes hot and dry. Prefers moist, well-drained soil rich in organic matter. Space plants 6 to 10 inches apart. As the summer progresses, stems elongate and flop. Shear back to 2 or 3 inches high to extend its attractiveness. Rake up dead foliage in the fall and spread a winter mulch.

Pests/Diseases—None serious

Landscaping Tips & Ideas—Use it under shallow-rooted shrubs such as rhododendrons and azaleas. Its foliage provides a wonderful backdrop for spring-flowering bulbs, and it gets along well with ferns and hostas, which like the same growing conditions.

WINTERCREEPER
Euonymus fortunei

Hardiness—Zones 3 to 8

Color(s)—Evergreen foliage, sometimes variegated

Bloom period—Not applicable

Mature Size (H × W)—8 to 12 in. × spreading

Water needs—Water regularly when establishing if rainfall is sparse; drought-tolerant thereafter.

Planting/Care—Plant rooted cuttings in spring, in almost any soil that is not soggy. Set each transplant so its crown is at or slightly above soil level. Set plants 2 feet apart. In decent soil, there is no need to fertilize once plants are established. Prune back unruly stems to keep plants in bounds. Every few years, shear back with a lawn mower in spring. Mulch or erect a low burlap screen to protect it over the winter.

Pests/Diseases—Vulnerable to scale; spray with horticultural oil according to label directions.

Landscaping Tips & Ideas—Successfully obscures utility boxes, rocks, and stumps. Variegated versions brighten dark areas under trees and building eaves.

GROUNDCOVERS

Groundcovers are low-maintenance plants used to carpet the earth where lawn turf and ornamental plants are impractical or undesirable. Any fast-growing plant that spreads and grows without much attention can be used as groundcover—daylilies in the sun, hostas in shade. Many vines also fit the job description. But the plants specifically designated as groundcovers spread rapidly and grow so thickly that they keep out weeds, even when they die down in winter; for example, the foliage of lily-of-the-valley vanishes in the fall, but the rhizomes remain so densely packed, few weeds can get in.

PLANTING A GROUNDCOVER

A new groundcover takes off and fills out most rapidly when you start with rooted cuttings and plant in fertile, improved soil.

1. If you will be replacing turf, in early spring or in fall when the soil is dry, spray the bed with Round-Up®, or remove the top layer of turf.

2. Cover the area with the amendments recommended in the Introduction to the book under Soil Preparation and Improvement, including 2 or 3 inches of compost, decomposed leaves, or peat moss.

3. Rototill three times over a two-week period, each time 8 inches deep. If you are installing an invasive groundcover such as ivy or ajuga, bury a 6-inch metal barrier along the border.

4. To keep weeds out, plant through a cover of 3 inches of mulch. If even minimum weeding will be difficult, plant through a porous landscape fabric; push the edges of the fabric sheet into the ground, and weight them with rocks or heel them in. Make rows of X-shaped slits in the fabric, and insert the plants through the slits with a trowel. Landscape fabric slows the rooting of the above-ground branches, so plant densely.

5. Working in even rows and starting at the widest end, scoop out a row of evenly spaced planting pockets 8 to 14 inches apart. If you are planting on a slope, dig the holes so the uphill side is lower to keep water from escaping down the slope. Set the cuttings in the hole, and firm them into place.

6. Position the second row of plants zig-zagged, between those of the row above. Row three repeats row one; row four repeats row two.

7. Put down 1½ inches of water right after planting. Newly-planted groundcovers need 1½ inches of gentle rain or watering every ten days to two weeks.

8. Weed faithfully, and keep the mulch topped up until the groundcover has grown dense—at least two years.

9. Fertilize the bed as and when you do perennials.

If you like a garden that has a serene look, use just one type of plant as groundcover. Like a turf lawn, it will unify the various elements in view—shrub borders, flower beds, specimen plantings, and trees. On the other hand, combining several compatible groundcovers adds extra texture to the area, makes it more interesting. Using several also is a safeguard should one type of plant fail. For a richly varied carpet, plant drifts of small winter-flowering bulbs in sunny places here and there, over-planted with aromatic Greek oregano, thyme, and ajuga. In areas that have part sun, plant myrtle (*Vinca minor*) or pachysandra. In the dappled shade under trees, the luminous foliage of lamium is lovely.

Caution: The plants designated as groundcovers, like weeds, spread rapidly.

The toughest evergreen groundcovers are ajuga, pachysandra, myrtle, and ivy. All four can be walked on some and can be used as replacement for a lawn. Ajuga and myrtle bear sweet little flowers in early spring. Ivy can take a few years to get going, but once started it spreads irresistibly. All four are seen by environmentalists as a potential threat to native plants, so use them responsibly. Don't plant a groundcover where it might invade stands of native plants or woodlands.

PLANTING AND MAINTENANCE

The easy way to carpet an area with a groundcover is by planting rooted cuttings. Starting with seed is economical and generally successful if you start the plants indoors in flats and grow them to a size that fills a 3-inch pot before putting them outdoors.

ABOUT PRUNING GROUNDCOVERS

It isn't necessary to prune groundcovers every year. Even so, when a groundcover like pachysandra matures, it gets straggly. When that happens, prune it before growth begins in order to encourage compact new growth. Do not remove more than a third of the top growth at one time.

Use hand shears to thin low groundcovers like pachysandra, ivy, and vinca.

• Use hand shears to deadhead ajuga, myrtle, and other spring-blooming groundcovers immediately after they have bloomed.

• Use head shears to shear euonymus, juniper, liriope, and ophiopogon.

• Use a string trimmer to cut back tall meadow plants.

• Use a hedge trimmer to trim ferns when they brown in fall.

• Use a lawn mower (if you can raise it sufficiently—at least 4 inches off the ground) to trim and renew low-growing groundcovers such as ivy and myrtle.

HOW TO CALCULATE THE AMOUNT OF A GROUNDCOVER NEEDED

To know how many plants you will need to fill an area with a groundcover, divide the square footage of the bed by the amount of space each plant will need. Here's the drill:

Start by measuring the area to be planted. Outline the bed with shrub and tree marking paint or a hose, and then measure the length and the width. Multiply the length by the width, and that gives you the square footage. To get the approximate size of a free-form shape, outline the area with a hose, and then shape the hose into a square or a rectangle that encompasses the area, measure, and multiply the length by the width.

Next, divide the spacing required for the plant you have chosen into the square footage of the area to be planted. The answer is the number of plants you will need. Most plant tags recommend spacing between or around plants. Typical spacing for crowns of Japanese painted fern is 24 inches apart; for 'Munstead' lavender, 15 inches; for dusty miller, 8 inches apart. The number of inches "apart" means "all around." To get the square inches needed for one dusty miller plant, multiply 8 times 8, which gives you 64 square inches. Divide 64 into the square footage of the area multiplied by 12, the number of inches in a foot. That tells you how many plants you will need.

Some growers' tags indicate how many plants to set out per square yard; Blooms of Bressingham tags recommend for the barren strawberry (*Waldsteinea ternate*) 'Red Ruby Strawberry' three to four plants per square yard. A square yard is 9 square feet. Dividing 9 (square feet) by four (plants) yields 2.2—one plant for every 2.2 square feet.

Small groundcovers that spread are planted one to four per square foot—four for upright plants like pachysandra; one to two for vining plants like vinca—two plants if it is rooted in a small pot, one if it is rooted in a large pot.

The more closely spaced these groundcovers are, the sooner they fill in the area. Widely spaced plants will need two or three years to fill in.

Often enough you will find you have friends willing to share, provided you do the work!

To get a groundcover off to a fast, successful start, provide a well-prepared bed with humusy fertile soil. Dig the whole area to be planted, and improve the soil just as completely and carefully as you do a bed for perennials. If you are installing an invasive groundcover such as ivy, vinca, or ajuga, plan to edge it with a 6-inch metal barrier to prevent it from overrunning neighboring plantings.

Planting through a mulch cover will minimize weeding chores, which can be burdensome in the year or two it will take for the groundcover to thicken enough to keep invaders out.

Watering. The first season of growth, a newly installed groundcover will need watering any time the perennial bed needs watering, which is weekly or every ten days unless you have a soaking rain. Water the soil slowly, gently, and thoroughly with a sprinkler, a soaker hose, a bubbler, or by hand. In the following years it should need watering only if the leaf tips are wilting; then water thoroughly as you would a perennial bed.

Pruning. An occasional pruning keeps a groundcover neater and stimulates branching and new growth. Pachysandra, plumbago (*Ceratostigma plumbaginoides*), and ivy when fully mature will benefit from shearing every few years.

Fertilizing. You fertilize a bed of groundcovers when you fertilize the perennials. In fall, clear groundcover(s) of fallen leaves only if they have matted down. Leaves that slip through the foliage decompose on the ground, and that nourishes the soil.

Like perennials, groundcovers don't fill out until the second or third season, but once they are flourishing, you can divide them to make new plants to fill gaps or enlarge the beds.

JANUARY

- Snow protects low-growing groundcovers, such as pachysandra, from winter cold, so let it be.

- Avoid using salt on walks and drives that are near your groundcover plantings. If too much leaches into or lingers in that area, the plants will be damaged, "burned," or even killed.

- During a January thaw, take a walk out and look over your groundcover areas and embankments. If it looks necessary, toss on additional mulch or evergreen boughs, to stabilize the temperature of the soil.

- Browse the incoming nursery and seed catalogs, noting groundcovers that catch your eye. If you are planning a larger planting, you can save money by raising the plants from seed indoors ahead of time. Alternatively, consider ordering a quantity of smaller-sized or bare-root plants.

- Seed packets will supply you with the necessary information regarding when and how to get started with indoor sowing.

FEBRUARY

- Place your order for mail-order catalog plants this month.

- If there is a thaw towards the middle or end of this month, you may be able to get outside and start cleaning up your groundcover areas. A light raking will do, just enough to get rid of soggy patches of leaves, twigs, and such.

- After warm spells, check new plantings for signs of heaving. Gently press the crowns back into the ground.

- Maintain moisture for seedlings started indoors or in a cold frame or hot bed.

- Every two weeks, fertilize all seedlings that will remain indoors another six weeks or more, with a soluble houseplant fertilizer at half-strength.

- Seedlings started indoors that are crowded and lack good drainage and air may show symptoms of damping off, which rots stems near the soil surface. Discard affected plants, and increase the light and fresh air. If the problem reappears, try misting the seedlings with a fungicide.

MARCH

- For your indoor-raised seedlings, pinch out the growing tips of ones that are becoming leggy.

- Shear overgrown groundcovers before growth begins, among them pachysandra and myrtle.

- Continue watering seedlings started indoors. You may fertilize them when the second or third set of leaves appears.

- Continue to keep a lookout for damping-off on your indoor plants. Always discard affected plants. Then reduce watering and increase light and air circulation.

- If you are contemplating a new groundcover area, it is probably still too soon to start digging—the soil is still too cold and wet. However, you can go out and mark the corners of the bed in preparation. This also allows you to observe whether you think the area is too large or too small, and also gauge how much sun and foot traffic it receives.

APRIL

- The ground is usually ready for planting in early April in warm Zone 7, toward the end of April in Zone 6, and in May in cooler gardens.

- Groundcovers are vulnerable to curious pets. To keep cats out, apply diatomaceous earth. It doesn't bother dogs, but some of the animal deterrents offered by garden centers do. Train dogs to stay away because their urine will burn plants.

- If you are installing an invasive or aggressive groundcover such as ivy or ajuga, bury a 6-inch metal barrier along the border.

- To keep weeds out, plant through a cover of 3 inches of mulch. If even minimum weeding will be difficult, plant through a porous landscape fabric. Push the edges of the fabric sheet into the ground, and weight them with rocks or heel them in. Make rows of X-shaped slits in the fabric and insert the plants through the slits with a trowel.

MAY

- Root out seedlings of groundcovers that are stepping out of bounds. If you need new plants, pot up the rogues and coddle until they are growing lustily; then transplant them to bare spots.

- When the weather warms, move seedlings started indoors to a protected, shaded spot outdoors to harden off for a week or so, and then transplant them to the garden.

- Keep track of the moisture in the soil for seedlings and newly planted groundcovers. Unchecked growth is the name of the growing game, and that requires sustained moisture.

- Weeds are flourishing this month; get them gone.

- If you are using granular chemical fertilizers, fertilize every six weeks.

- If you've combined groundcovers with spring-flowering bulbs, hopefully they help disguise or distract from the dying-down bulb foliage. If you would like to try this practical and attractive idea in the future, peek in other gardens or look in gardening magazines for successful combinations.

JUNE

- Good-sized container-grown groundcovers may be on sale this month, so if you are in the market for new plants, make a point of visiting the garden centers.

- Run control patrol in established groundcovers, and root out and pot up or discard stragglers headed for forbidden pastures.

- If you are using chemical fertilizers, fertilize every six weeks. If you have already applied an organic fertilizer, you won't need to repeat until September. Vigorously growing groundcovers really don't need to be fed.

- Keep the beds clear of weeds. Weeds that mature and go to seed will be followed by an army of offspring.

- Slugs and snails may invade. Diatomaceous earth, a natural control, works in dry soil but isn't effective on moist soil. If June is wet, do pests in with slug and snail bait and/or traps. You can make your own by pouring a little beer into shallow aliminum pie plates or empty tuna cans.

JULY

- Assess the summer condition of your groundcovers, and make notes in your garden journal suggesting care and improvements to make this fall.

- Check garden centers for bargain plants to fill gaps and replace plants lost to winter weather. For ideas, get out your garden catalogs, magazines, and books.

- Rust loves lily-of-the-valley and ferns. Control by avoiding overhead watering and by cutting out and disposing of infected foliage. Twice a month, spray with a fungicide—see your local retailer for advice and information on how to properly apply.

- This month can be dry and hot. Even groundcovers growing in shady areas can begin to wilt, especially ones that you put in this spring. Maintain a moist soil by watering with a sprinkler or soaker hoses, and maintain or replenish a moisture-conserving mulch.

- Keep after weeds in your groundcover beds. If they take off, they can be hard to eradicate, plus they spoil the area's appearance.

AUGUST

- Summer heat and drought reveal the vulnerabilities of plants, sites, and your annual soil maintenance program. Patches of groundcover that are wilting when others do not may need you to add more humus when you fertilize and refurbish the soil early next year.

- In spite of heat and drought, container-grown groundcovers can be planted successfully this month—as long as you water them every week or so and hose them down with a gentle spray if they wilt on hot days.

- This month is usually dry, so expect to compensate for the missing rain by watering your groundcovers two or three times this month, that is, every week to ten days.

- Patches of pachysandra that are browning, wilting, and dying may be getting too much sun in winter or they may be suffering from leaf and stem blight. Consult with your local garden center and get advice about control products as needed.

SEPTEMBER

- If you would like to reduce the need to hand-trim grasses around deciduous trees, plan to underplant them with low-maintenance, all-season groundcovers like ajuga, lamium, or vinca—plants that can take shade in summer and sun in winter. Indian summer is a good time for the project.

- Now and as the first leaves begin to fall is an excellent planting time for groundcovers. Warm Zone 7 gardeners can plant into October and even November some years.

- You can divide-to-multiply groundcovers early this month.

- If you are using organic fertilizer, then you will need to fertilize one last time this month. If you are using chemical fertilizers, it can be a little later—by the end of this month or early next month.

- Give groundcovers a radical weeding.

- Check and remove groundcovers that are creeping outside their boundaries.

OCTOBER

- Continue to divide, move, and transplant groundcovers this month in most areas of New England.

- Now is the time to clear your groundcover plantings of fallen leaves. To avoid damaging the plants or inadvertently dislodging them, try using a leaf-blower.

- If you are using organic fertilizers and didn't feed your groundcover areas one last time last month, do it early this month.

- Give groundcover beds one last slow, thorough soaking if rainfall is sparse, thus sending them into the colder months in the best possible condition.

- Some areas of groundcover plantings may be scraggly or damaged, or simply didn't prosper. Assess the situation now that the season is ending, and don't be afraid to yank out part or all of a failed project. You can always replant with something more suitable next spring.

NOVEMBER

- If you didn't do so last month, before the first anticipated hard freeze, water your groundcovers slowly, deeply, and thoroughly.

- Rake away leaves creating mats over patches of groundcovers.

- When bringing in outdoor furniture, bicycles, and the like, avoid trekking or dragging these items across groundcover areas.

- Add a winter mulch of evergreen boughs, and your groundcovers should be good to go in late winter.

- There is no fertilization this month.

DECEMBER

- If you are considering planting a slope with a groundcover, think outside the box. Consider, for example, a low-growing forsythia such as 'Arnold Dwarf', which roots where it touches, can withstand drought, needs only periodic trimming, and is not attractive to deer. To bloom at the same time as your forsythia hill, naturalize bulbs—daffodils, daylilies—between the shrubs. They'll help cover the slope and maintain the soil there.

- Planting is over for this year. Take the time to assess what did and did not grow well last year, and consider whether to move or replace plants.

- Use evergreen boughs to provide winter protection for European ginger and other evergreen groundcovers that suffer in cold weather. A discarded Christmas tree may work well.

- There is nothing to fertilize this month. Be sure any leftover fertilizers are tightly sealed and stored away from children and pets.

LAWNS &
ORNAMENTAL
GRASSES
for New England

There is a grass for every purpose, whether you are looking for a better turfgrass for your front lawn, hoping to repair or revive a tired lawn, wanting to create a ribbon of attractive ornamental grasses, or simply choosing a few low-maintenance accents to enhance your flower beds. No matter what type of grass you grow, there are unique care and design issues, which we have outlined below.

LAWN GRASSES

Like teenagers, turfgrasses grow fast and need unchecked access to food, drink, and air to do well. They also need protection from weeds and diseases. Aerating every two or three years and de-thatching now and then are the other major chores. But fertilizing comes first. The type of fertilizer you use decrees how often you need to do it.

ORGANIC FERTILIZERS. Organics release their nutrients slowly; two applications a year are enough. A Cornell University study found that using organic fertilizers may suppress some diseases, including brown patch, snow mold, dollar spot, and red thread. With organic fertilizers, any herbicides, pesticides, and fungicides you use are usually applied separately.

CHEMICAL FERTILIZERS. Balanced granular chemical fertilizers green the lawn overnight and are soon depleted, so you need to apply them four or five times a year. "Fertilizer-plus" products that include pre-emergent or post-emergent herbicides can be used to control crabgrass and broadleaf weeds. Insect and disease controls are usually applied separately.

Herbicides, pesticides, and fungicides are applied only when needed. Granular products applied with a drop-spreader are safest for the garden.

To know how much fertilizer you need to follow these steps: Measure the areas planted in the lawn, multiplying the width by the length to get the number of square feet in each, then add them all up for the total number of square feet you need to cover. Fertilizer bags tell you how many square feet the contents will cover.

SOIL PH. If the pH of the soil is between pH 6.0 and 7.0, the lawn should do well. The ideal pH for turfgrass is 6.5. Heavily cropped lawn soils eventually become acidic and have a lower pH reading. However, do not lime by rote to raise the pH. Check the pH of your soil annually, but adjust it only when adjustment is needed. Sandy soil whose pH has been corrected is good for two years, clay soil for three. A pH check can be made any month.

Grass thrives on a good soaking every week to ten days. Soak it more often and it will grow, use up the nutrients in the soil, and need mowing almost twice as fast. If you make the mistake of watering the lawn frequently and shallowly—every one to three days—the roots will grow near the surface of the soil, which warms and dries out when the weather does and is a bad place for roots to be. The watering advice the July section is easy on your time, effort, pocketbook, and lawn. Only your patience will suffer.

ORNAMENTAL GRASSES

Windblown, untamed, graceful, 1 to 12 feet tall and more, the ornamental grasses are the signature plants of today's naturalistic landscaping, and they need little maintenance. The sight and sound of wind whispering through tall grasses is refreshing on a hot summer day—a country sound very welcome in a city garden. Airy, luminous seedheads develop late in the season and remain lovely through fall and early winter.

The low-growing ornamental grasses add texture to the front of flower beds and to pockets of wild gardens. Those reaching 6 feet and more can replace a high-maintenance espalier fronting a masonry wall. Planted among native trees and shrubs, grasses become part of a handsome low-maintenance screen. The mid-height ornamental grasses are the natural transition plants to woodland or water, and, in combination with native wildflowers, make a beautiful flowering meadow. The recommended ratio for a meadow garden is one-third flowers to two-thirds ornamental grasses for sunny places, and one-third grasses to two-thirds flowers for shade.

LAWNS: GENERAL INFORMATION ON FERTILIZING AND FERTILIZERS

Save money by leaving grass clippings on the lawn. Reduced to their elemental forms by microorganisms in the soil, clippings can lower the amount of fertilizer needed by as much as 30 percent. Clippings from a 1,000 square foot lawn contribute ½ to 2 pounds of nitrogen depending on how much the lawn was fertilized.

When to Fertilize. Avoid fertilizing when temperatures are over 90 degrees.

Organic fertilizers. Organic fertilizers are applied twice a year. They can be applied in any season without danger of burning. Organics do not include herbicides, pesticides, or fungicides; these are applied separately and only when needed.

The first fertilization is best made before grass starts into growth in early spring. For Zones 6 and 7 that could be as early as late March, but for most of New England it will be in well into April.

The second fertilization is best applied in early September. A third fertilization can help lawns doing poorly and can be made in late fall or even late winter.

Chemical fertilizers. Granular chemical fertilizers are applied four times a year.

Formulations are available that include pre-emergent or post-emergent controls for crabgrass and broadleaf weeds. For a new lawn, choose a fertilizer with an NPK of 1-1-1, or 1-2-2. For an established lawn, choose a fertilizer whose NPK ratio is 3-1-2 or 4-1-2.

The first fertilization is best made as grass starts into growth in early spring. For warm Zones 6 and 7 that can be as early as March, but for most of us it is during the month of April.

The second fertilization is May to June; the third is made in July or August; the fourth in August or September. The fifth fertilization is optional and can be made October or November.

The first consideration in choosing a grass, after you have checked its hardiness in your zone, is how the end-of-season height and width of the plant will fit the site. The very tall grasses must be featured as specimens and nearby plantings chosen to complement them. Next consider the overall form. Some grasses clump, some mound, some fountain. The texture of the leaves and their color is important—fine, coarse, bold, bluish, greenish, reddish, gold, striped, or variegated. For contrast, combine both fine- and coarse-textured grasses. When you have thought all that through, then you

can consider which of the flower heads you are going to fall in love with. Grouping many plants of a few varieties is more effective than planting a few of many.

Writer Carole Ottesen classes the grasses into cool-season and warm-season plants, and it's a useful concept. The cool-season grasses shoot up in the spring, so they're cut back in early spring. Their early growth makes them the best choice when you want a grass that will be highly visible—the main show all year round. The warm-season grasses begin to grow later, so you can wait until mid-spring to cut them back. A warm-season grass is a good choice when you're considering combining grasses and flowers: interplant them with big, early spring-flowering bulbs that will bloom after the grasses' annual haircut and hide the bare crowns while the grass is growing up. The grass will soon grow tall enough to hide the ripening bulb foliage.

WHEN, WHERE, AND HOW TO PLANT ORNAMENTAL GRASSES

Like the perennial flowers, the ornamental grasses begin to fill out the second year. They may be planted in early spring, summer, or early fall. At garden centers they are sold in containers. Mail-order suppliers may ship some ornamental grasses bare root; these plants must be soaked thoroughly before planting. Most of the ornamental grasses thrive in acidic to neutral soil that is one-half to one-quarter humus, and most need a well-drained site.

Set the crowns ½ to 1 inch higher than the soil surface. Surround the plants with 1 to 2 inches of mulch.

The annual haircut is just a matter of shearing for the low-growing grasses. When a big grass matures, before cutting it back use sisal twine to rope the leaves together all the way to the top so that it ends up looking like a telephone pole; then saw the top off a few inches above the crown. If you use a chain saw take care not to catch the twine in the teeth!

Most ornamental grasses need annual fertilization. The time for it is when new growth appears. Apply a slow-release organic fertilizer. In prolonged droughts, water slowly and deeply.

More complete information on their care is provided starting on page 175.

ORNAMENTAL GRASSES: SUGGESTED COMPANION PLANTS

Ornamental grasses can stand alone as specimen plants. But to achieve a naturalistic effect, plan to include foliage, bark, and stem plants—that's the way nature designs her wild gardens.

For structure and contrast, include small- and medium-sized deciduous treessuch as:

*   Chinese dogwood (*Cornus kousa* var. *chinensis*)
*   Franklin tree (*Franklinia alatamaha*)
*   Fringe tree (*Chionanthus retusus*)
*   Serviceberry, Shadblow (*Amelanchier* species)
*   Witchhazel (*Hamamelis* × *intermedia* hybrids)

For change and as foils to the dramatic effects of the dried seedheads and foliage in the winter landscape, include shrubs and some evergreens:

*   Azaleas and Rhododendrons
*   Cotoneaster (*Cotoneaster* hybrids)
*   Fountain Buddleia (*Buddleia alternifolia*)
*   Rugosa rose (*Rosa rugosa* 'Sir Thomas Lipton')
*   Siebold Viburnum (*Viburnum sieboldii*)
*   Winterberry (*Ilex verticillata* 'Sparkleberry')

For contrast with the grasses' buff and tan, sea green and green, gold and pale gold colors, plant colorful, carefree perennials:

*   Asters (*Aster* species and cvs.)
*   Astilbe (*Astilbe* × *arendsii*)
*   Black-eyed Susan (*Rudbeckia fulgida* var. *sullivantii* 'Goldsturm')
*   Catmint (*Nepeta faassenii*)
*   Daylilies (*Hemerocallis* hybrids)
*   Joe-pye Weed (*Eupatorium purpureum*)
*   Purple Coneflower (*Echinacea purpurea* and cvs.)
*   Russian Sage (*Perouskia atriplicifolia*)
*   Sedum, Stonecrop (*Sedum spectabile* 'Autumn Joy' and cvs.)
*   Tickseed (*Coreopsis verticillata* 'Golden Showers')
*   Yellow Loosestrife (*Lysimachia punctata*)
*   Fern-leaved Yarrow (*Achillea filipendula* 'Coronation Gold')

Many of the spring-flowering bulbs that catalogs discount for early orders are excellent companion plants for ornamental grasses. The bulbs carpet the earth with color while the grasses are waking up. They also show up well against the emerging growth of the grasses, which later masks their ripening foliage.

These small spring bulb flowers are very effective planted in front of the taller ornamental grasses—they bloom in about this order in full sun, later in part shade.

*   Early Crocus (*Crocus* spp. and cvs.)
*   Snowdrops (*Galanthus*)
*   Winter Aconite (*Eranthis*)
*   Squill (*Scilla tubergeniana*)
*   Daffodils (*Narcissus* Miniatures and Early varieties)
*   Glory-of-the-Snow (*Chinodoxa luciliae*)
*   Bluebell (*Hyacinthoides non-scripta*)
*   Grape Hyacinth (*Muscari* spp. and hybrids)
*   Botanical/Species Tulips (*Tulipa turkestanica*)
*   Giant Snowflake, Summer Snowflake (*Leucojum aestivum*)

AMERICAN BEACH GRASS
Ammophila brevigulata

Hardiness—Zones 4 to 8

Color(s)—Rust-colored leaves in fall

Bloom period—Summer

Mature Size (H × W)—2 to 3½ ft. × 10 ft. annually

Water needs—Keep the planting area moist if you can until there are signs of new growth.

Planting/Care—Set out container-grown plants in early fall or early spring. The spacing between rows should be 18 inches, or 12 inches where erosion is severe. Every year in early spring, fertilize with an organic, long-lasting lawn fertilizer.

Pests/Diseases—None serious

Landscaping Tips & Ideas—The most common use of this native grass is as groundcover in dry, sandy soils. It is often used to stabilize or even create sand dunes; if you have beach property and want to try this, please do not rip up dunes without first seeking advice. This grass will be offered at local conservation-minded nurseries.

BLUE FESCUE
Festuca glauca

Hardiness—Zones 4 to 8

Color(s)—Blue foliage; tan flower heads

Bloom period—Mid- to late spring

Mature Size (H × W)—8 to 12 in. × 8 to 10 in.

Water needs—Water a new planting every week or two for the first season. After that, local rainfall should suffice.

Planting/Care—Set out container-grown plants as soon as the soil can be worked. It grows best in soils that are not especially fertile and on the dry side. Set an inch above soil level about 2 feet apart. Mulch. Do not try to force growth by watering or fertilizing. Toward early spring, prune the plant back to the crown. Divide every few years.

Pests/Diseases—None serious

Landscaping Tips & Ideas—Attractive as an edging for beds or shrubbery, walks, naturalized areas, and grass gardens. It looks nice, and grows well with lavender, salvia, and Russian sage.

BLUE OAT GRASS
Helichtotrichon sempervirens

Hardiness—Zones 4 to 8

Color(s)—Metallic blue leaves, blue-gray inflorescences turn tan

Bloom period—Summer

Mature Size (H × W)—2 to 3 ft. × 25 in.

Water needs—Water a new planting every week or two for the first season; once established, supply water only during droughts.

Planting/Care—As soon as the ground can be worked in spring, set out plants or rooted divisions. Avoid damp spots. Thrives in rich soil and is not particular about soil pH. Set the plants an inch above ground level and about 2 feet apart. In early spring, prune back to the crown. You can divide in fall.

Pests/Diseases—None serious

Landscaping Tips & Ideas—Makes a colorful neutral accent in a mixed perennial border. Beautiful massed and naturalized. Combines effectively in wild gardens with silvery plants such as artemisia, catmint, and lamb's ears.

CHINESE SILVER GRASS
Miscanthus sinensis

Hardiness—Zones 5 to 9

Color(s)—Pale pink flower clusters

Bloom period—Late summer

Mature Size (H × W)—6 to 8 ft. × 3 to 5 ft.

Water needs—Water a new planting every week or two the first season.

Planting/Care—Set out container-grown plants in spring as soon as the ground warms. While it thrives with a constant supply of moisture, established plantings sustain modest growth with less—the leaves roll if they need more. Wait till mid-spring to cut it back to the crown. Maintain the mulch to thwart weeds. In northern New England, varieties don't attain the heights common in warmer areas.

Pests/Diseases—None serious

Landscaping Tips & Ideas—Some are planted as specimens, others as transitional plants near water. Beautiful growing in groups, or massed. Shop from among many attractive cultivars, including striped ones.

CREEPING RED FESCUE
Festuca rubra

Type/Hardiness—Cool-season grass; hardy throughout New England

Color(s)—Glossy, deep green

Texture—Extremely fine

Recommended Mowing Height—2 to 2½ inches

Water needs—Drought-tolerant once established

Planting/Care—Fall or early spring planting is best; start as seed. Sow 3 to 4 lbs per 1,000 square feet. Needs less fertilizer. Tends to lie flat and cause uneven mowing.

Pests/Diseases—Disease-prone unless well-drained

Landscaping Tips & Ideas—Foot-traffic tolerant. Its creeping growth habit helps in establishment and filling bare areas. Often mixed with Kentucky bluegrass and perennial rye for genetic diversity and disease tolerance.

FEATHER REED GRASS
Calamagrostis × acutiflora 'Karl Foerster'

Hardiness—Zones 5 to 9

Color(s)—Purple-tinted flower heads that change to tan

Bloom period—Spring

Mature Size (H × W)—5 to 6 ft. × 20 in.

Water needs—If the plants are in dry soil, water every week or two the first month, or until you see signs of vigorous growth.

Planting/Care—Set out container-grown plants in spring, an inch above ground level and about 2 feet apart. Cut back to the crown early every spring. Do not try to force growth by watering or fertilizing.

Pests/Diseases—None serious

Landscaping Tips & Ideas—Grows rapidly during cool weather and may sulk in hot, dry periods. Beautiful as a specimen or hedge against a masonry wall. Lovely among shrubs and evergreens. Its meadowy autumn golds are beautiful backing black-eyed Susan, 'Autumn Joy' sedum, purple asters, and boltonia.

HAKONE GRASS
Hakonechloa macra 'Aureola'

Hardiness—Zones 6 to 9

Color(s)—Variegated gold-and-green foliage

Bloom period—Not applicable

Mature Size (H × W)—18 to 24 in. × 24 in.

Water needs—Water new plantings well, especially during hot weather.

Planting/Care—Plant or divide overlarge clumps either in spring or fall; plant containerized ones any time. Site in moist, well-drained soil rich in organic matter. Set each plant so that it is at soil level or slightly above; space 2 feet apart. Mulch to discourage weeds and conserve soil moisture. Fertilization is unnecessary if soil is organically rich. Cut back each spring to make way for new growth.

Pests/Diseases—None serious

Landscaping Tips & Ideas—Not at all invasive. Effective as an edging, groundcover, or under trees where lawn grass will not grow. Prefers the partial shade of woodland settings, where it provides interesting contrast with other woodland plants. Likes some morning sun.

HARD FESCUE
Festuca longiflora

Type/Hardiness—Cool-season grass; hardy throughout New England

Color(s)—Deep green

Texture—Extremely fine

Recommended Mowing Height—3 or more inches

Water needs—Tolerates drought

Planting/Care—Sow seed in spring or fall, at three or four pounds per 1,000 square feet. Needs little or no mowing. It is slow to establish and spread. A tough, low-growing, bunch-type grass that tolerates shade, cold, salt, and poor soil.

Pests/Diseases—Few, if any, problems. Disease-tolerant mixes are available.

Landscaping Tips & Ideas—Often used for erosion control. It is slow to recover from wear. It tolerates heat and shade better than other fine fescues.

KENTUCKY BLUEGRASS
Poa pratensis

Type/Hardiness—Cool-season grass; hardy throughout New England

Color(s)—Rich blue-green

Texture—Fine

Recommended Mowing Height—3 inches

Water needs—Continue to water seedlings into winter if rainfall is sparse. Once grass plants are established, water only when grass looks limp. In poor or compacted soils, water more often.

Planting/Care—Sow seed in fall; lay sod or patch lawns with seed in either spring or fall. Best in an organically rich soil that is neutral or slightly acidic. Generally needs lots of water and fertilizer during the growing season.

Pests/Diseases—Prone to fungal diseases in hot, humid weather. You may see powdery mildew, fusarium, pythium, or red thread. To treat chronic problems, overseed with disease-resistant varieties or other types of turfgrass.

Landscaping Tips & Ideas—Widely valued for lawns in most parts of New England for its good color, even texture, and uniform spread.

NORTHERN SEA OATS
Chasmanthium latifolium

Hardiness—Zones 4 to 8

Color(s)—Green in summer, gradually changing to pink and copper

Bloom period—Summer

Mature Size (H × W)—3 to 4 ft. × 2 to 3 ft.

Water needs—Water a new planting weekly the first season. Once established, local rainfall should be sufficient.

Planting/Care—Set out container-grown plants in spring when the ground warms. Thrives in at least six hours of full sun daily. Thrives where the soil has sustained moisture without being soggy. Set the plants about an inch above ground level and apply a mulch. Cut back the plant to its crown early every spring. If it self-sows, you may have to pull out volunteers.

Pests/Diseases—None serious

Landscaping Tips & Ideas—Looks best when massed. Especially lovely growing on a slope where the seedheads will be backlit. Good companions include Japanese anemone, lobelia, and toad lily.

PERENNIAL RYE GRASS
Lolium perenne

Type/Hardiness—Cool-season grass; hardy throughout New England

Color(s)—Medium green

Texture—Medium

Recommended Mowing Height—3 inches

Water needs—Water seedlings into winter if there is no rain; water established grass only when there has been no rainfall for more than two weeks and it looks limp.

Planting/Care—Plant anytime during the growing season. Lay sod or patch lawns with seed in either spring or fall. Rich organic soil that is neutral to slightly acidic is ideal. Fertilize in spring or fall.

Pests/Diseases—Hot, humid weather can lead to outbreaks of fungal diseases, including pythium, brown patch, and red thread. Treat chronic problems by overseeding with disease-resistant varieties.

Landscaping Tips & Ideas—This is a good-looking, fast-germinating grass, valued as an important component of fall-sown mixtures. As a "nurse" grass, it quickly provides some green. Good for patching bare spots in summer so weeds won't move in.

PURPLE FOUNTAINGRASS
Pennisetum setaceum 'Rubrum'

Hardiness—Grown as an annual in New England

Color(s)—Burgundy to bronze-red

Bloom period—Summer

Mature Size (H × W)—2 to 3 ft. × 2 to 3 ft.

Water needs—Water regularly when establishing and then during dry spells. Water container-grown specimens regularly.

Planting/Care—Plant in spring when the soil has warmed up. Does best in full sun in any well-drained soil, including clay. It likes moist soil and can even tolerate an inch or two of water over its roots. Set plants 3 to 4 feet apart to allow for their gradual spread, closer for a mass planting. Not cold hardy; tear out when it dies back or overwinter in pots indoors.

Pests/Diseases—None serious

Landscaping Tips & Ideas—A good color accent for yards with limited space. Looks great with 'Autumn Joy' sedum, purple coneflower, or with conifers in the background. Does very well in containers. Does well on pond banks and near streams.

SWITCH GRASS
Panicum virgatum 'Heavy Metal'

Hardiness—Zones 3 to 8

Color(s)—Pink inflorescences; flowers and foliage are gold in fall and winter

Bloom period—Summer

Mature Size (H × W)—5 ft. × 2 to 3 ft.

Water needs—Water a new planting every week or two the first season. Thereafter, water during dry spells.

Planting/Care—Set out container-grown plants or root divisions in mid-spring or fall. Any well-worked soil will do, and it is tolerant of sandy soils. Maintain a mulch. Each spring, cut the plant back to 4 or 5 inches above the crown, and fertilize lightly. Once established, it is deeply rooted and withstands drought, high heat, and bitter cold. Divide in spring before new growth begins.

Pests/Diseases—None serious

Landscaping Tips & Ideas—Attractive planted as a specimen, set out in large sweeps in transitional areas near water, and added to a wild garden.

TALL FESCUE
Festuca eliator

Type/Hardiness—Cool-season grass; hardy throughout New England

Color(s)—Dark green

Texture—Slightly coarse

Recommended Mowing Height—3 inches

Water needs—Water seedlings if rainfall is undependable. Established in good soil, this grass has legendary drought-tolerance.

Planting/Care—Choose a premium-quality seed. Sow in early fall. Lay sod in spring or fall. It prefers neutral or slightly acidic, organically rich soil. Fertilize when seeding or later in the fall. Every few years, mow close and overseed with premium tall fescue to maintain turf density.

Pests/Diseases—In areas with hot, humid summers, this grass is prone to pythium and brown patch.

Landscaping Tips & Ideas—Cut when it approaches 4 inches tall. Maintain at 3 inches until it goes dormant in the fall, then cut to 2 inches to overwinter. It can be used alone or as a welcome addition to mixes.

TUFTED HAIR GRASS
Deschampsia caespitosa

Hardiness—Zones 4 to 9

Color(s)—Yellow and gold

Bloom period—Late spring, early summer

Mature Size (H × W)—2 to 3 ft. × 2 ft.

Water needs—Water a new planting every week or two the first season. Thereafter, maintain soil moisture at the roots.

Planting/Care—Set out container-grown plants or root divisions in early spring. Thrives in part shade and prefers rich, moist, well-worked, somewhat acidic soil. Space the plants 2 to 3 ft. apart. In late summer or early fall, shear the whole clump back to the crown. If grown in rich soil, it shouldn't need fertilizer. May need dividing every three or four years.

Pests/Diseases—None serious

Landscaping Tips & Ideas—Looks best in groups or massed. Add clumps to a perennial bed. Good companions include low-growing bergenia, epimediums, hostas, and ligularia.

LAWN GRASS PROJECTS

Aeration (coring). Compacted soil has no space for water or air, nor does it have growing room for roots. The solution is to aerate the soil by cutting out core plugs of sod so that water, air, and fertilizer can get down to where they are needed. If the lawn is well used and beginning to bald or show a thatch buildup, then aerate. If all is well, every two or three years aerate to keep it that way. You can do it by hand, and you also can rent power equipment to aerate and de-thatch.

Thatch and de-thatching. Grass clippings landing on the lawn are decomposed by the microorganisms there, and that adds nutrients to the soil. That layer of clippings is called thatch, and it's a good thing as long as the clippings are less than ¼ inch deep. However, if the lawn gets too much fast-acting high-nitrogen fertilizer and water, it may grow quickly and the clippings may fall so thick and so fast the microorganisms can't keep up; that's when a layer of thatch a couple of inches deep accumulates, which is harmful. A lawn that feels spongy when you walk on it probably has thatch building to unhealthy levels. You can fix it by aerating and de-thatching. You can also prevent thatch buildup.

Repair. The rule of thumb is that if 50 percent of a lawn needs fixing, then you need a new lawn. If 30 percent or less is in trouble, it can be patched or restored. From 30 to 50 percent, you must renovate. For lawn patching or restoration to succeed, you must mix humus and fertilizers into the soil before you seed or sod the area.

You can repair a small area with sod, new or stripped from somewhere else in the lawn, or by seeding the area. Lawn patching products include mulch and nutrients and are easy to apply.

Restoration. This involves sowing seed into an existing lawn after vigorously cultivating the ground with rented power equipment.

Starting a new lawn. To seed or to sod, that is the question. It is not nobler to seed, just less costly. Sodding is faster, but the soil needs the same deep preparation and patient watering until it is established. Also, sod won't keep weeds out forever, and sod varieties are limited. Seeding saves money. The bigger the lawn, the greater the savings. To seed 1,000 square feet costs about $10, not including the humus, fertilizer, and other soil amendments the soil will need to get a good start. If you seed, you can choose from among the varieties of grasses in our turfgrass table. Sod if you enjoy making magic. It's the way to have an instant lawn. The cost for a 1,000 square foot area is about $200, if you do the work yourself. Your choice of grasses will be limited.

Timing for a new lawn. Cool-season grasses peak in spring, go semi-dormant in mid-summer, and peak again in fall. They're best started around Labor Day. Early spring is second best. Most seeds germinate when daytime temperatures are 68 to 95 degrees Fahrenheit.

MAINTAINING & TROUBLESHOOTING LAWN GRASSES

The rule of thumb is to mow every five to seven days during the peak season, and as needed at other times. Keep the mower blades sharpened, cut the grass high, and don't let the mowing get away from you. Mow at the right height for the grass and the season.

About mowers. There are many sizes and types of mowers, but only two ways of cutting—reel or rotary. The reel mower does a slightly better job but is slower. The rotary mower does a fine job and is faster. The most important thing to know about a mower is that it must be sharpened throughout the mowing season. Dull blades tear and damage the grass, and that shows up in the appearance of the lawn and the health of the grass plants.

Leaves and your lawn. If there's just a scattering of leaves on your lawn, they'll dry and crumble into bits that the microorganisms in the soil will reduce to nutrients. The residue will blow away with winter winds and weather. But, matted accumulations of leaves rob the grass of the sunlight it needs as growth continues through fall. Crunch the leaves under the lawn mower, rake, and bag them—or grind them, and distribute the bits over the garden with a blower-vacuum.

CONTROLLING WEEDS, PESTS, AND DISEASES

Weeds, pests, and diseases attack lawns made vulnerable by lack of fertilizer and poor garden practices. There are ways to control them.

Cultural practices. Feed, mow, and water your lawn wisely.

Biological methods. Apply agents such as beneficial nematodes, bacteria, and other organisms. A biological control becoming more available is endophytes—fungi bred to live within grasses and stop insect pests.

Chemical controls. Pre-emergent and post-emergent herbicides, and pesticides and fungicides—some natural, some man-made—are used to control weeds, pests, and diseases. Many now on the market are considered environmentally sound. Once again we caution you to apply these only if really needed.

WEEDS

All post-emergent liquid weed killers work best when the dose called for on the label is combined with 1 teaspoon of liquid dish detergent to each gallon of water.

Broadleaf weed seeds. These weeds, including dandelions, can be controlled by applications of a pre-emergent broadleaf weed killer when the forsythia petals drop. Repeat in fall.

Broadleaf weed plants. If a variety of weeds leaf out in May and June, apply a post-emergent broad-spectrum herbicide.

Chickweed, bindweed, violets, sorrel, and clover plants. Kill these weeds by applications of a post-emergent control such as 2,4-D+TurflonD, Dicamba 2,4-D+BanvelD, or Gordon's Trimec Broadleaf Herbicide. Repeat in the fall.

Crabgrass seeds. When the forsythia petals drop, stop the weed seeds by applying pre-emergent weed killers such as Betasan, Tupersan, Balan, Dacthal, Team, or Sidriron.

Dandelion, plantain, and other broadleaf weed plants. Control them by individual applications in April and May of 2,4-D and 2,4-D combinations.

Wild onion (garlic). Apply a post-emergent control such as 2,4-D+ Dicamba (Banvel D) or 2,4-D+TurflonD in early spring when the onions first emerge, and repeat two weeks later.

PESTS

November through April, pests and diseases appear to be on vacation. They're with you the rest of the year, though.

Grubs. To control the larvae that become rose chafer or Asiatic beetle, in May and June and again in August and September, apply biological controls such as beneficial nematodes. Or apply chemical controls such as Merit or Marathon.

Ants. Use Permethrin.

Chinch bugs. Apply Sevin, Permethrin, or Baygon in April and May, and again in August and September.

Cutworms. Use beneficial nematodes, Sevin, or Safer soap in spring.

Japanese beetles. Apply rotenone, Neem, or Sevin. For Japanese beetle grubs, use milky spore disease.

Moles. Runs of heaved sod ending in mounds of dirt are signs that moles are shopping for grubs. Apply a grub control such as Merit or Marathon to kill off the grubs, and chances are the moles will find another supermarket.

Sod webworms. In late June and again in late August and early September, apply Bt, Sevin, Permethrin, or Baygon.

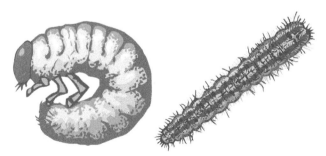

White Grub   Sod Webworm

Helminthosporum leaf spot

DISEASES

To control a variety of diseases at one time, apply a broad-spectrum fungicide or, better yet, a broad-spectrum systemic fungicide such as Daconil, Mancozeb, Chipco, Clearys 3336, and Bayleton. Make the applications when the disease appears and twice a month in May, June, July, and August.

Fusarium blight (now called necrotic ring spot), copper spot, and dollar spot. They show up as a circle of dead grass with some green tufts in the middle. The disease will likely run its course. The controls are fungicidal copper, sulfur, Bayleton, or Cleary 3336.

Helminthosporum leaf spot and melting out. These diseases cause brown and black spots on the blades, and the grass dies in irregular patches. Treat with a fungicide labeled for use on turf and melting out diseases, such as Fore or Heritage, every two weeks from the first appearance of the problem until it is gone.

Powdery mildew. It looks as though the leaves have been powdered. Powdery mildew turns up in shady spots, so try to get more light to the area. Or control with applications of fungicidal copper or sulfur, or a systemic fungicide such as Bayleton or Banner Maxx, applied twice a month from June through September.

Red thread and pink patch. Patches of grass turn light tan to pink, and pink threads bind the blades. As soon as it appears, treat the lawn with a contact fungicide twice, seven to ten days apart.

Rust-infected leaves. These leaves are spotted yellow, orange, or brown. Rust is common in new lawns with a high percentage of ryegrass. It generally fades as other grass varieties take over from the rye. Control with applications twice a month of sulfur, mancozeb, or manzate, or a systemic fungicide such as Bayleton and Banner Maxx, from the time it appears—usually May through September.

Snow mold. This causes small to large gray or white matted patches of grass. Rake the lawn in early spring, and avoid over-use of nitrogen fertilizers.

WORKING WITH ORNAMENTAL GRASSES

Ornamental grasses are lovely in perennial beds, and since many grow aggressively, they also make excellent ground covers. On hot summer days the foliage sways and whispers in the slightest breeze, and late summer when most flowers have peaked, the airy dancing flower heads (inflorescences) are a delight. The seedheads and drying foliage remain beautiful fall and winter, anchoring the garden's fourth season.

The ornamental grasses have another great virtue: deer don't eat them.

DESIGNING WITH GRASSES

You can learn much about the use of grasses from a visit to the two-acre Friendship Garden at the U.S. National Arboretum in Washington, D.C. They, and other botanic gardens, are showing us how to use grasses in low- maintenance naturalized plantings that include a healthy diversity of flowering perennials, bulbs, small trees, and shrubs. There are no straight paths. The heights, mixtures, and widths of the flower beds vary to avoid any formal sense. Medium-sized grasses are islands with curved borders.

Fruiting and berry-producing plants promote a healthy ecological balance by encouraging birds and beneficial insects.

Size. When you are choosing a grass, the first consideration is its size. Sizes are judged by the end-of-season height and width of the foliage. The large landscaping grasses are used boldly, in big spaces. They're excellent plants for transitional areas and screening. Some thrive in moist situations. Massed, medium-tall grasses make good bank-holders and ground covers. A few patches of medium-tall grasses woven through a perennial border add beauty and interest. Some we like are maiden and silver grasses (*Miscanthus* species and varieties), bold plants with broad, grassy, gracefully arching leaves. We also favor switchgrass (*Panicum virgatum*) and beautiful 3- to 4-foot (but, alas, cold tender) fountain grass (*Pennisetum alopecuroides*), with arching foliage that ends summer topped by flower spikelets.

The little grasses, those under 2 feet, are generally used as ground cover for small areas and to add variety to the front of a flower border. Our favorites are the little sedges (*Carex* species), mosquito grass (*Bouteloua gracilis*), and blue sheep's fescue (*Festuca amethystina* var. *superba*).

Form and texture. Once you have decided on a size, consider the plant's structure and textural effect. Chinese silver grass is very erect, and maiden grass arches, while the foliage of the fountain grasses, well . . . fountains. The texture of the leaves and their color impact the garden design—fine, coarse, bold, bluish, greenish, reddish, gold, striped, variegated. We like contrast, so we recommend combining both upright and fountain-like forms, fine and coarse-textured grasses, green and variegated forms.

Think all this through before you fall in love with the seedheads, the "flowers" of the ornamental grasses. They are almost all irresistible!

Finally, when planning a grass garden, we recommend grouping several plants of a few varieties rather than setting out a few plants of many varieties.

PLANTING AND MAINTENANCE

Like the perennial flowers, newly-planted ornamental grasses begin to fill out the second year. Starting them indoors from seed saves money, but the seedlings will take two years to gain any size. Planting root divisions is more satisfactory unless you need lots and lots.

Like perennials, ornamental grasses are available as seed, container grown, and bare root. They are best started in spring, not fall. Follow the planting procedures for perennials, and provide improved soil and generous planting holes. Set the crowns ½ to 1 inch higher than the soil surface. Don't "drown" the grasses in mulch—2 to 3 inches of mulch is enough.

Maintenance. Ornamental grasses develop throughout the year without pruning, staking, spraying, or deadheading. Let the seedheads ripen and stand through fall and winter. In late winter or early spring, just before new foliage emerges, give them their annual haircut. Cool-season grasses begin to grow in cool weather and need their haircut earlier than warm-season grasses. Our plant list tells you which.

Most ornamental grasses need annual fertilization. The time for it is when signs of new growth appear. With grasses, be sure to use a slow-release organic fertilizer such as Holly-Tone® or Espoma Organic Lawn Food. In prolonged droughts, water slowly and deeply.

Once installed, ornamental grasses are not expected to require division for at least five to ten years.

JANUARY

- If you didn't get your lawn mower serviced when mowing ended last year, take care of it now.

- Walking on frozen grass damages it, especially if there is no snow cover.

- Shovel walkways and driveways before applying snowmelt salts. Otherwise you risk damaging the lawn.

- Save wood ashes to use as fertilizer for the lawn. They make lime and potash quickly available and can be applied over a few inches of snow.

- If snow mold appears, just rake the patches clear and avoid overuse of nitrogen fertilizers.

- Dream a grass garden. Low-growing species add texture and movement to the front of flower beds. Mid-height ones are the natural transition plants to a woodland or water garden. The tall grasses make excellent summer screening.

FEBRUARY

- If your lawn mower needs servicing, take it to the dealer now, during his quiet season. Keeping the blades sharp is essential to giving the lawn a good cut.

- You can overseed thin areas in late winter or early spring. It's okay to sow seed on a few inches of snow.

- In warm Zone 7, the first application of an organic fertilizer can be made between now and April. If you are using a chemical fertilizer, wait until shortly before the grass begins to grow.

- Thinking of adding some ornamental grasses this year? Browse the mail-order catalogs and place your order this month.

- After warm spells, check on existing ornamental grass plantings for signs of heaving. Gently press the crowns back into the ground.

- If you plan to plant lots of ornamental grasses, consider starting your own from seed.

MARCH

- Decide on a lawn feeding and weeding program.

- When the snow has gone, check the lawn over for areas that need repair and overseed them. You can begin repairs when the soil stops being squishy.

- When the snow has gone, clear fallen branches from the lawn.

- Reposition pavers, keeping groundcovers from invading grass areas.

- Organic fertilizers can be applied as early as the end of this month. If you are using chemicals, wait until closer to the time the grass begins to grow

- For your cool-season ornamental grasses, now is the time to cut them to a few inches above the crown. New growth will appear soon.

- When the snow goes, the ground around your ornamental grasses is bare, but it doesn't have to be. Plan next fall to plant the area with some spring-flowering bulbs.

APRIL

- When the grass begins to grow, keep an eye on emerging weed and pest populations. If mole runs appear, apply a grub control to send them elsewhere for food.

- Repair areas in the lawn that have been damaged over the winter.

- When the soil has warmed and dried, check the soil pH; lime it if needed.

- If you have a sodded or seeded area, maintain soil moisture.

- The first of two annual applications of organic lawn fertilizer is best made a few weeks before the grass begins to grow. Make applications of chemical fertilizers just before the lawn begins to grow.

- Now through May is an excellent time to plant ornamental grasses.

- Before you buy new ornamental grasses, do your homework, not just on looks and dimensions but on cold hardiness. Not all the popular ones can survive winters in Zones 3, 4, and 5.

MAY

- If you want to reduce the amount of water you use on the lawn, consider replacing outlying areas with a drought-tolerant groundcover.

- May is the time to aerate and de-thatch your lawn.

- Begin to mow this month in most areas. Mow often so you never have to cut off more than a third of the grass to maintain its recommended height.

- If dandelions, plantain, chickweed, bindweed, sorrel, clover plants, or other broadleaf weeds appear, apply post-emergent controls before they go to seed.

- For ornamental-grass seedlings that you started indoors, this is the month to move them to a shaded spot outdoors to harden them off. Then you can transplant them into the garden.

- If you are using chemical fertilizers on your ornamental grasses, fertilize every six weeks.

JUNE

- Time to assess your mowing equipment and perhaps take advantage of sales to upgrade.

- Sod installed from now on will likely need watering daily until it begins to root and grow again.

- Keep your mower blades sharpened!

- If you spot broadleaf weeds in the lawn, apply a post-emergent broad-spectrum herbicide. Follow the label instructions exactly.

- Good-sized container-grown ornamental grasses may be on sale this month, so if you are in the market for new plants, make a point of visiting the local garden centers.

- If you are thinking of planting a large transitional area in ornamental grasses, consider starting seeds now for transplanting in September or early October. If the grasses you are interested in are named varieties—'Heavy Metal' blue switchgrass, for example, not just the original blue switchgrass species, then it's best to plant divisions, as cultivars do not reliably come true from seeds.

JULY

- As summer reveals the pests and diseases that love your lawn best, plan fall and spring strategies for reducing their numbers.

- You can repair with sod now, but wait until September for any serious seeding project.

- When you will be away for more than a week, arrange to have the lawn mowed. The growth rate of grasses is slowing, but if on your return you have to cut more than a week's worth of lawn, the lawn will suffer.

- The lawn needs a good soaking every week, especially in very hot weather . . . by rain or by you.

- Assess the summer condition of your ornamental grasses, and make a memo in your garden log suggesting care and improvements to make this fall.

- Once established, most ornamental grasses are pretty well drought-tolerant. They only need watering in prolonged droughts. You can tell they need water because the edges of the leaves curl up. Water slowly and deeply.

AUGUST

- A lawn that is consistently and deeply watered has deep roots and will be just fine in spite of heat and drought.

- If you have a coastal home and lawn, you can offset the damage potential of exceptionally high tides by flooding the lawn until the soil is so saturated it can't absorb much of the salt water.

- Mow high—mowing high is especially important during the hot, dry months.

- If you haven't applied your third chemical fertilization yet, do it now.

- Smaller ornamental grasses can be planted successfully this month as long as you water them every week or so and hose them down with a gentle spray if they wilt on hot days.

- This month is usually dry, so expect to compensate for the missing rain by watering your ornamental grasses every week to ten days.

SEPTEMBER

- If you wanted to aerate the lawn this spring but didn't get around to it, plan to do it mid-fall, after the grass stops actively growing.

- Labor Day is the beginning of the best season for lawn repair and renovation, as well as for starting a new one.

- Expect the lawn to slow its growth, but keep the mower blades sharpened anyway.

- Make your second application of organic fertilizer now.

- Controls for various lawn pests and fungal diseases must be applied in September.

- Now and as the first leaves begin to fall is an excellent planting season for ornamental grasses.

- You can divide-to-multiply established stands of blue fescue, blue oat grass, feather reed grass, and many others early this month.

OCTOBER

- The soil still has warmth, though the air is cooling, a happy time for our lawns, which are cool-season grasses. You can still seed or sod, repair, overseed, or renovate early this month.

- The best time to aerate a lawn may be now; aerate when the grass isn't actively growing.

- Rake up or use a blower vacuum to clear leaves accumulated on the lawn. Leaving a few to decompose is okay.

- October should be wet, but if it isn't, water. For new lawns, water if you haven't had rain for seven or eight days.

- Ornamental grass gardens peak this month. Plan to visit nearby public and botanic gardens to learn more about keeping your garden beautiful in the fall, to learn about suitable varieties for your area, and to get inspiration about how to place or highlight them in a landscape.

- You may continue to divide, move, and transplant ornamental grasses this month.

NOVEMBER

- If your winters include heavy snow, lay in a supply of sand or environmentally friendly de-icing products that will enable you to have skid-proof paths and walks without harming the surrounding lawn.

- Put away your supply of herbicides, pesticides, and fungicides for the winter—far out of reach of pets and children.

- Mow the late-late leaves and let the wind blow the chaff away.

- Keep areas recently seeded or sodded watered if early November runs dry.

- Gather armfuls of the most beautiful grasses and their seedheads, tie them loosely in bunches, and hang them upside down to dry in a dark, dry, warm place. Keep them from shedding or shattering by spraying them with hair spray or a spray varnish. When they are done, display them in tall vases or use as table decorations for the holiday season.

- Before the first anticipated hard freeze, water your ornamental grass plantings slowly, deeply, and thoroughly.

DECEMBER

- The giving time is near; draw up a lawn wish list.

- Get all your lawn gear together and in good shape before you store it.

- Shovel snow away before spreading de-icing products, and you will use less. Use snowmelt products safe for grass and plants.

- Hose season is over. Drain and store the hoses before freezing weather.

- Enjoy the seedheads of ornamental grasses out in your yard over the winter months, often attractively capped with a bit of snow.

- Now that planting and caretaking is over for the year, take the time to assess what did well for you, and what did not. Consider whether to replace or move your ornamental grasses.

ROSES
for New England

The rose was designated the nation's floral emblem in 1987. Gardeners fall in love with the beautiful form and seductive fragrance of varieties like the green-eyed, white, old garden rose 'Madame Hardy', and David Austin's English rose 'Graham Thomas'. Do fall in love, but confine your passion to roses billed as "disease-resistant." We count on roses that hold awards from the All-America Rose Selections and the American Rose Society to be disease-resistant.

PLANTING AND CARE GUIDELINES

For roses to produce a dazzle of flowers and fragrance, nearly all need eight hours of morning sun, or six hours of afternoon sun. They need a well-drained site, and for most a pH of between 5.5 and 7.0. (See Soil Preparation in the introduction.) The key to success is thorough and deep soil preparation—deeply dug planting holes 24 inches wide and 24 inches deep, and humusy, fertile soil. Apply an organic fertilizer three times a year: in late winter or early spring, in early midsummer, and in early fall.

You can plant a container-grown rose in early or late spring, and in summer or fall before Indian summer. If the rootball is encircled by roots, untangle them gently. If they can't be unwound, make four shallow vertical cuts in the wall of roots and slice off the matted roots on the bottom. Half-fill the planting hole with improved soil, and pack it down very firmly. Set the rootball into the hole so that it's about 1 inch above ground level. For hybrid roses, position the plant so that the bud union is 2 to 3 inches above ground level. Half-fill the remainder of the hole with improved soil, and pack that down firmly. Finish filling the hole with improved soil and pack it down firmly again. Make a saucer around the plant, and water it slowly and deeply. You plant bare-root roses the same way, but soak the roots in water for twelve hours before planting, and drape them over a firm mound in the center of the hole.

Deadheading and harvesting big-flowered show roses keeps them blooming. When cutting roses for bouquets, leave a five-leaf sprig on each shoot as a base for new flowering shoots. Make all pruning cuts ½ inch above an outside bud eye or sprig. Do not prune roses after the wood has hardened for the winter. Before growth begins in early spring, cut out diseased and damaged canes. Prune roses that bloom on new wood to the desired shape in early spring. Prune roses that bloom on wood from the previous season—some shrub and climbing roses—after they have flowered. Cut the oldest canes of recurrent bloomers back to two or three bud eyes, and remove twiggy ends. As new canes grow, tie them to fencing or trellising. To encourage growth of flowering laterals, cut side branches back to short spurs.

Winter protection for roses is a necessity in Zone 3 and even 4, unless the grower has certified the rose for those zones. Even with that promise, if snow cover fails, your rose will suffer. Roses whose winter hardiness is doubtful in our zone we plant facing south, with the house behind them blocking the north wind. A house creates a microclimate that can be a zone or two warmer than the prevailing climate. Hybrid teas and miniatures are especially likely to require winter protection. Cover the plants with pine boughs or hill soil over the lower stems. Don't mulch with leaves or anything that creates a cozy habitat for field mice (voles): they'll girdle the roses and kill them.

Additional and more detailed information on rose care appears starting on page 197.

COMMON ROSE PROBLEMS

Here in New England, if you run into the big three problems with Rosa—Japanese beetles, blackspot, and powdery mildew—what we have learned may help.

One approach with Japanese beetles is to spray plants under attack with rotenone, an okay spray. Another is to apply milky disease spores to the gardens and the lawn. Effective the second year, this natural deterrent kills the larvae.

Also, in early morning the beetles are sluggish, and you can knock them into a pot of soapy water. Letting loose native parasitic wasps and flies that go for the beetles helps, too. Do not crush the beetles as that releases pheromones that will draw more Japanese beetles to the garden.

For blackspot, which loves hybrid teas, floribundas, and grandifloras, try the spray recommended by Cornell University research: 1 tablespoon of baking soda (bicarbonate) and 1 tablespoon of ultrafine horticultural oil to 1 quart of water. And, remove infected vegetation from the plant and the ground.

Spraying with the Cornell University research solution may also minimize powdery mildew. Ask your garden center about new, environmentally safe controls.

Concerning deer—well, sprays may keep deer away for a time. But the only sure protection is to erect a fence, or screen the bushes with chicken wire, which isn't noticeable at a distance.

ABOUT ARS AND AARS RATINGS FOR ROSES

Two major influences on the world of roses in the United States are the non-profit American Rose Society (ARS) and the All-America Rose Selections (AARS). The ratings given roses are national ratings based on how the roses perform nationwide. Some do better or worse regionally than the national rating. Local rose societies and growers will know which winners work, if you'd like to do some follow-up research.

The ARS is an association of rosarians who rate rose introductions on a scale of 1 (worst) to 10 (best). The ratings average individual ratings given by beginners as well as experienced rose growers. They are printed yearly in the "Handbook for Selecting Roses" available from the ARS. The highest rating given even the enduringly popular roses, 'New Dawn', 'Double Delight', 'Iceberg', 'The Fairy', and 'Bonica', reach no higher than 8.7.

The rose gardens near the ARS headquarters in Shreveport, Louisiana, are open to the public during the growing season. Their Web site, www.ars.org, can help you locate local rose societies.

The AARS (www.rose.org) is a nonprofit association of rose growers and rose producers that introduces and promotes roses judged exceptional in their trial programs. They are headquartered in Chicago. The roses go through a two-year field trial. The AARS seal of approval has influenced rosarians since 1938.

HOW TO GROW ROSES IN CONTAINERS

Smaller roses do well in containers. Miniatures, rose trees, smaller Meidilands, floribundas, and some hybrid teas are all candidates.

- Light. The roses will need six, or even better, eight hours of sun each day. Be prepared to turn the pot often to keep the bush growing evenly all around. A movable container makes it easy to take advantage of shifting light. Garden centers offer plant saucers and containers equipped with casters.

- Container size. For a miniature rose, a 6-inch pot that's 5 inches deep is sufficient. For standard roses, provide a tub that is at least 18 inches in diameter and 14 inches deep. Save watering time by planting in a container with a built-in water reservoir or water ring that lets the plant soak up the water from the bottom.

- Preparation. Soak porous containers—clay, wood—before adding soil, or they will take moisture from the soil you put into them. For winter protection, wrap the interior with a double row of large bubble wrap or Styrofoam™.

- Soil. Line the bottom with PermaTill®, then fill with this mix: ¼ good garden soil or bagged top soil, ¼ commercial soil-less mix, ¼ compost, and ¼ sand, or ⅛ perlite and ⅛ PermaTill®. Add a modest application of Osmocote® slow-release fertilizer and a water-holding polymer such as Soil Moist to help maintain moisture. Soak the growing medium before you plant.

- Watering. After planting, water well and maintain soil moisture thereafter.

- Fertilizing. Liquid feed every two weeks with a half-strength dose of a good rose or container plant fertilizer.

- Winter care. Before freezing cold temperatures, store the container in a detached, unheated garage, shed, or cool basement. A potted rose needs to be cold enough to go dormant but must not freeze. Water lightly once a month.

YOU CAN GROW MINIATURE ROSES INDOORS

Given the sort of winters we have here in New England, it is good news indeed that you can continue to enjoy roses when the weather turns cold. Ones available out of season were raised in a greenhouse and will appreciate some pampering when you bring them home or receive them as a gift plant. But they can also be enjoyed indoors any time of year, given proper care.

Some favorites for this purpose are 'Rise'n'Shine', 'Little Jackie', 'Red Beauty', and 'Starina'.

To grow a mini indoors:

- Repot it in a clay pot lined with pebbles or PermaTill and filled with a potting mix that includes a water-holding polymer.
- Grow it on a south-facing windowsill, under grow lights, or in a window greenhouse.
- Keep the plant cool at night.
- Water when the surface feels dry to the touch.
- Fertilize at every watering with a half-dose of a water-soluble fertilizer.
- Deadhead back to the first five leaflet set.
- Prune out crowded and crossing stems to keep the center open.
- Remove infected foliage and stems at once.
- Cleanse the plant with a shower every two weeks.
- In May, move the plant outdoors to a semi-sunny spot for a summer vacation.

BEST ROSES FOR HEDGES

A rose hedge is a pleasure and an effective barrier. The height you want to achieve indicates the variety to plant. As always—make sure your choice is winter hardy, not just almost, but completely!

LOW BORDERS. Miniature roses make pretty borders for rose gardens, and they bloom all season. 'China Doll' tops out at about 18 inches, and covers itself with clusters of 1½-inch light pink, semi-double blooms.

LOW HEDGES. The rose most often advertised as the "living fence" hedge is 'The Fairy', a polyantha under 30 inches that blooms all season. It is borderline hardy in my garden, Zone 5. 'The Fairy' and other polyanthas grow into brambly hedges covered with clusters of roses under 2 inches.

MEDIUM HEDGES. The vigorous floribundas, which are cluster-flowered bush roses that bloom all season, make fine hedges 4 to 5 feet tall. Our favorite is 'Betty Prior' whose vivid pink flowers and emerald green foliage stay beautiful all summer. The Meidiland group of roses develops into wide-spreading naturalized hedges that bloom all season with little care. 'Bonica', an upright 4- to 5-foot bush, bears 3-inch, fully double, shell pink flowers set off by rich deep green glossy leaves.

TALL HEDGES. The rugosa roses grow into tall, very thorny hedges that withstand strong winds and sea spray. Very hardy, they do not appeal to deer. The only pruning they need is the removal in early spring of older canes to encourage vigorous new growth. The flowers of the modern cultivars are quite beautiful, and many produce spectacular rose hips.

CORNELL UNIVERSITY'S REMEDY FOR BLACKSPOT AND MILDEW

From Cornell University came this control for mildew that may also help with blackspot and some other rose problems; many New England rose gardeners have had good luck with it.

Combine 1 tablespoon baking soda and 1 tablespoon of ultra-fine horticultural oil in a gallon of water. Apply to your plants using a spray bottle.

ANGEL FACE
Rosa cultivar

Type—Floribunda

Color/Bloom Size—Dark lavender, 3½ to 4 in.

Fragrance—Intense, citrusy

Bloom period—Midseason, repeats

Mature Height—2½ to 3 ft.

Water needs—Water regularly throughout the growing season.

Planting/Care—Plant in spring in deeply prepared soil, in full sun. Mulch well and fertilize to boost health and performance.

Disease-resistance—Good

Landscaping Tips & Ideas—This low-growing rose is ideal for mixed borders, where it settles in, spreads out a bit, and dependably produces those enchanting flowers throughout the summer. The coppery, dark-green foliage is also attractive in such a setting. Combine with white flowers such as Shasta daisies or white campanulas, or silver-leaved favorites like lamb's ears and artemisia.

BLAZE
Rosa cultivar

Type—Climber/Rambler

Color/Bloom Size—Cherry red, 2 to 3 in.

Fragrance—Mild, fruity

Bloom period—All season

Mature Height—10 to 15 ft.

Water needs—Water regularly throughout the growing season.

Planting/Care—Plant in spring in deeply prepared soil, in full sun. Mulch well and fertilize to boost health and performance.

Disease-resistance—Good; 'Improved Blaze' is touted as even more disease-resistant.

Landscaping Tips & Ideas—Unlike some other climbers, 'Blaze' produces blooms along its entire length, which makes it especially suitable for high-traffic areas where it can be admired close at hand. A healthy, vigorous plant with easy-to-manipulate stems. Well-suited to adorning wooden fences or draping over stone walls. Also a fine choice for backing a mixed flower border with bold, season-long color.

BONICA
Rosa cultivar

Type—Shrub

Color/Bloom Size—Pink, 1 to 2½ in.

Fragrance—None

Bloom period—All season

Mature Height—2 to 4 ft.

Water needs—Water regularly throughout the growing season.

Planting/Care—Plant in spring in deeply prepared soil, in full sun. Mulch well and fertilize to boost health and performance.

Disease-resistance—Good to excellent

Landscaping Tips & Ideas—Borne in generous sprays, the flowers are prettier and fuller than those of some other hedge or landscaping roses. Though well-suited to screen, hedge, and foundation plantings, individual plants are a lovely, no-nonsense addition to a flower border.

DOUBLE DELIGHT
Rosa cultivar

Type—Hybrid Tea

Color/Bloom Size—Red-pink-yellow-cream blend, 5½ in.

Fragrance—Spicy, strong

Bloom period—All season

Mature Height—3½ to 4 ft.

Water needs—Water regularly throughout the growing season.

Planting/Care—Plant in spring in deeply prepared soil, in full sun. Mulch well and fertilize to boost health and performance.

Disease-resistance—Unfortunately, this beauty is susceptible to mildew in cool, damp areas, but it's a great performer elsewhere.

Landscaping Tips & Ideas—Site this unusually colored, richly-scented rose where it can be the star of the show—in the front of a border, in an entryway, along a walkway, beside a patio or deck. It forms a medium-sized, irregularly bushy plant.

FOURTH OF JULY
Rosa cultivar

Type—Climber/Rambler

Color/Bloom Size—Ruby red-and-bright-white, 4½ in.

Fragrance—Strong sweet apple

Bloom period—All season

Mature Height—10 to 14 ft.

Water needs—Water regularly throughout the growing season.

Planting/Care—Plant in spring in deeply prepared soil, in full sun. Mulch well and fertilize to boost health and performance.

Disease-resistance—Excellent

Landscaping Tips & Ideas—Looks splendid mounting a pergola, arch, or trellis. If the support is painted white, to match the white petal markings, the show is even more dazzling.

FRAU DAGMAR HASTRUP
Rosa cultivar

Type—Shrub

Color/Bloom Size—Pink, 3 to 3½ in.

Fragrance—Intense, clove

Bloom period—All season

Mature Height—3 to 4 ft.

Water needs—Water regularly throughout the growing season.

Planting/Care—Plant in spring in deeply prepared soil, in full sun. Mulch well and fertilize to boost health and performance.

Disease-resistance—Excellent

Landscaping Tips & Ideas—The simple but deliciously fragrant flowers cover the plant all summer, and big, bright-red hips decorate the bush in the fall. With a tidier, better-mannered habit than some other rugosas, this rose is ideal for low hedge or property-line plantings. Just be warned—it's very thorny.

GOLD MEDAL
Rosa cultivar

Type—Grandiflora

Color/Bloom Size—Golden yellow, 3½ to 4½ in.

Fragrance—Moderate, fruit-and-spice

Bloom period—All season

Mature Height—4 ft.

Water needs—Water regularly throughout the growing season.

Planting/Care—Plant in spring in deeply prepared soil, in full sun. Mulch well and fertilize to boost health and performance. More cold-sensitive than other grandifloras, so provide winter protection in chillier areas.

Disease-resistance—Good

Landscaping Tips & Ideas—Abundant blossoms cloak a tough, handsome bush in clusters and singles, making for an impressive show. Thorns are sparse on the long stems, which makes them easy for cutting bouquets. A fine addition to a flower bed that features bright colors.

GOLDEN CELEBRATION
Rosa cultivar

Type—English/Austin

Color/Bloom Size—Golden sunny yellow, 5 in.

Fragrance—Sweet honey

Bloom period—Midseason, repeats

Mature Height—5 ft.

Water needs—Water regularly throughout the growing season.

Planting/Care—Plant in spring in deeply prepared soil, in full sun. Mulch well and fertilize to boost health and performance.

Disease-resistance—Good; vulnerable to blackspot in hot, humid weather.

Landscaping Tips & Ideas—A handsome plant with big, glorious scented blooms and dark green foliage, it is well-suited to a cottage-garden or a large mixed flower border.

HERITAGE
Rosa cultivar

Type—English/Austin

Color/Bloom Size—Pink, 4½ to 5 in.

Fragrance—Intense, citrusy

Bloom period—Midseason, repeats

Mature Height—5 to 6 ft.

Water needs—Water regularly throughout the growing season.

Planting/Care—Plant in spring in deeply prepared soil, in full sun. Mulch well and fertilize to boost health and performance.

Disease-resistance—Blackspot can mar the leaves in some areas; treat by spraying.

Landscaping Tips & Ideas—Classic loveliness—breeder David Austin has declared this one to be his most beautiful. A standout as a specimen plant, pretty with pastel-hued perennials, and a fine choice for a shrub border. Just be sure to locate it where you can appreciate it often and easily harvest sensational bouquets.

ICEBERG
Rosa cultivar

Type—Floribunda

Color/Bloom Size—White, 3 in.

Fragrance—Moderate, honey-sweet

Bloom period—Midseason, repeats

Mature Height—3 to 4 ft.

Water needs—Water regularly throughout the growing season.

Planting/Care—Plant in spring in deeply prepared soil, in full sun. Mulch well and fertilize to boost health and performance.

Disease-resistance—Good

Landscaping Tips & Ideas—Because it is an easygoing shrub, it is most popular as a hedge rose or in mass plantings. But the flowers, which appear a bit later than some other roses, are lovely in the garden and in bouquets. If you keep the bushes pruned low, they stay in bounds and provide you with loads of blooms on long cutting stems. If you let the bush grow taller, you'll get a great show but the flowers will be carried on shorter stems. Either way, it's hard to find a better landscape rose. Beautiful in combination with purple-flowered perennials.

JEAN KENNEALLY
Rosa cultivar

Type—Miniature

Color/Bloom Size—Pink-apricot, 1½ in.

Fragrance—Soft, mild

Bloom period—Midseason, repeats well

Mature Height—1½ to 2 ft.

Water needs—Water regularly throughout the growing season.

Planting/Care—Plant in spring in deeply prepared soil, in full sun. Mulch well and fertilize to boost health and performance.

Disease-resistance—Very good

Landscaping Tips & Ideas—In a pot, this is the perfect little plant. In the ground, it may grow a bit taller and wider than other minis, with abundant flowers. Tuck some into a pastel-themed perennial border, where they will be a constant source of pretty color.

JOSEPH'S COAT
Rosa cultivar

Type—Climber/Rambler

Color/Bloom Size—Hot-colored pink-orange blend, 3 to 4 in.

Fragrance—Mild, fruity

Bloom period—Midseason, repeats

Mature Height—8 to 10 ft.

Water needs—Water regularly throughout the growing season.

Planting/Care—Plant in spring in deeply prepared soil, in full sun. Mulch well and fertilize to boost health and performance.

Disease-resistance—Susceptible to mildew

Landscaping Tips & Ideas—This old favorite has jazzy, distinctive blooms in bright hues of orange, red, yellow, and pink, sometimes all of these in one cluster. This is not an easy plant to mix with others, but on the other hand, it is a showstopper in the right spot, such as a garden entrance, or a pergola. It's also a dashing choice for a boundary or property-line planting.

KNOCK OUT
Rosa cultivar

Type—Shrub

Color/Bloom Size—Ruby-red, 3 to 3½ in

Fragrance—Light, sweet

Bloom period—All season

Mature Height—3 ft.

Water needs—Water regularly throughout the growing season.

Planting/Care—Plant in spring in deeply prepared soil, in full sun. Mulch well and fertilize to boost health and performance.

Disease-resistance—Exceptional

Landscaping Tips & Ideas—The sensational ruby-red, single-form blossoms are abundant. These are followed in fall by big, bright orange hips that attract migrating birds to your garden. A great addition to a low-maintenance flower bed, or massed along a pathway, poolside, or sunny patio or deck. Also available in other colors—browse the choices at your local nursery, they're all good plants.

NEW DAWN
Rosa cultivar

Type—Climber/Rambler

Color/Bloom Size—Pink, 3 to 3½ in.

Fragrance—Moderate, fruity (reminiscent of ripe peaches)

Bloom period—All season

Mature Height—12 to 20 ft.

Water needs—Water regularly throughout the growing season.

Planting/Care—Plant in spring in deeply prepared soil, in full sun. Mulch well and fertilize to boost health and performance. It is especially cold hardy, all the way up to Zone 4.

Disease-resistance—Good resistance to blackspot

Landscaping Tips & Ideas—This rose looks beautiful on an arch, cascading over a tall fence, or draping a front-porch railing. Thanks to its long, pliable canes, it is easy to train (though look out for its big, plentiful thorns).

OLYMPIAD
Rosa cultivar

Type—Hybrid tea

Color/Bloom Size—Ruby red, 4½ to 5 in.

Fragrance—Slight, sweet

Bloom period—All season

Mature Height—4 to 5 ft.

Water needs—Water regularly throughout the growing season.

Planting/Care—Plant in spring in deeply prepared soil, in full sun. Mulch well and fertilize to boost health and performance.

Disease-resistance—Exceptional mildew-resistance, so a good choice for damp climate

Landscaping Tips & Ideas—The strong, weather-tough bush is upright and vase-shaped, like other hybrid teas, but more compact than some, so it's a nice choice for solo plantings where you want a show-off rose. It's also good in a mixed border with other strong colors.

QUEEN ELIZABETH
Rosa cultivar

Type—Grandiflora

Color/Bloom Size—Pink, 3½ to 4 in.

Fragrance—Mild tea rose

Bloom period—Midseason, repeats

Mature Height—5 to 7 ft.

Water needs—Water regularly throughout the growing season.

Planting/Care—Plant in spring in deeply prepared soil, in full sun. Mulch well and fertilize to boost health and performance. Cold hardy in most of New England.

Disease-resistance—Good to excellent

Landscaping Tips & Ideas—Owing to her tall, impressive profile and large-size flowers, 'Queen Elizabeth' needs to be appropriately placed. She looks regal flanking a doorway or garden entrance, or grown against the side of a house or other building in need of spectacular, reliable color.

ROSE DE RESCHT
Rosa cultivar

Type—Old Garden/Antique

Color/Bloom Size—Fuchsia-purple, 3 in.

Fragrance—Rich, ravishing rose perfume

Bloom period—Midseason, repeats well

Mature Height—2½ to 3½ ft.

Water needs—Water regularly throughout the growing season.

Planting/Care—Plant in spring in deeply prepared soil, in full sun. Mulch well and fertilize to boost health and performance.

Disease-resistance—Good

Landscaping Tips & Ideas—This is a fine rose for modern gardens, thanks to its compact size. Fall brings a nice display of distinctive, tubular hips. The rich blossom color and full, old-fashioned flower is an inspired contribution to a cottage-garden scheme. It also mixes beautifully with perennials and annuals in white or yellow, including Shasta daisies.

SUNSPRITE
Rosa cultivar

Type—Floribunda

Color/Bloom Size—Yellow, 3 in.

Fragrance—Strong, sweet licorice

Bloom period—Midseason, repeats

Mature Height—2½ to 3 ft.

Water needs—Water regularly throughout the growing season.

Planting/Care—Plant in spring in deeply prepared soil, in full sun. Mulch well and fertilize to boost health and performance. Does better in cooler temperatures.

Disease-resistance—Good

Landscaping Tips & Ideas—Medium-sized 'Sunsprite' has such excellent and dependable color, it is often used as a hedge plant. But single plants make a cheerful addition to a mixed flower bed. And because it is so productive, you can harvest bouquets for the house and still continue to enjoy a good show in the garden.

THE FAIRY
Rosa cultivar

Type—Shrub

Color/Bloom Size—Pink, 1 ½ to 2 in.

Fragrance—None

Bloom period—Midsummer, repeats

Mature Height—2 to 3 ft.

Water needs—Water regularly throughout the growing season.

Planting/Care—Plant in spring in deeply prepared soil, in full sun. Mulch well and fertilize to boost health and performance. It's hardier than many larger roses, surviving well into Zone 4.

Disease-resistance—Good

Landscaping Tips & Ideas—Because its growth habit is compact and its profusion of flowers so little, 'The Fairy' is a popular choice for perennial gardens. It's low-growing and spreading enough to be used as groundcover or embankment rose—just be sure it gets full sun. It also makes a good show as an entryway plant in a large container, such as a half whiskey barrel.

WINSOME
Rosa cultivar

Type—Miniature

Color/Bloom Size—Magenta-red, 2 in.

Fragrance—None

Bloom period—Midseason, repeats

Mature Height—16 to 22 in.

Water needs—Water regularly throughout the growing season.

Planting/Care—Plant in spring in deeply prepared soil, in full sun. Mulch well and fertilize to boost health and performance.

Disease-resistance—Excellent

Landscaping Tips & Ideas—The plant is quite bushy and grows vigorously, so it is a good mini for growing in the ground rather than in a container. Its good health and sweetheart blossoms would be a welcome addition to a mixed flower border or cutting garden.

ROSES

In full bloom a rosebush rewards you with the heart-stopping beauty of its flowers. The very best have a rich perfume that makes everything else go right out of your head.

Like other great beauties, roses can be demanding. Pruning is a must; fertilizing too. But when the right rose is planted in the right place, it will perform beyond all expectations.

COLD HARDINESS IS ESSENTIAL

The hardiness of a rose variety depends on the hardiness of its understock (the roots). Multiflora rose roots (which do well in acidic soils) are very hardy, so a rose budded (grafted) on a multiflora understock is very hardy. Hardy rose varieties growing on their own roots are also very hardy. The most widely used understock, 'Dr. Huey', is not very hardy, so even hardy rose varieties budded on Dr. Huey understock are not very hardy. The species roses, the wild roses from around the world that are the parents of all garden hybrids and many once-blooming old garden roses, are generally cold hardy. Of the repeat bloomers, rugosas are very hardy. Miniatures and the modern roses, including hybrid teas whose tags say they are growing on their own roots and are hardy in your zone, will most likely succeed. Own-root roses are the best bet for New England because if one of our exceptionally nasty winters kills the top, the rose that regrows from the rootstock will be the one you fell in love with and planted. Winter protection is wise no matter how hardy the rose. You'll find suggestions in Winter Care for Roses.

PLANTING ADVICE

The humidity present in spring and fall is kinder to new roses, but they'll succeed planted even in hot dry summer months if given adequate care. For a rose to bloom up to its potential, it must be placed where it has full sun, air all around it, well-drained top quality soil to grow in, and adequate fertilizer and water.

Roses are sold bare root, container-grown, and in plantable containers.

Bare-root roses are available when it's time to plant them, early spring before growth begins. Follow exactly the suppliers' instructions for planting.

- Container-grown roses are available throughout the season, and in most of New England you can plant them late April up to October.

- Roses in plantable containers are easy to plant, but they are available only in spring and early summer.

Light and spacing. Roses need at least six hours of direct sun, and eight is better. Morning light is especially valuable because it dries the leaves, and that helps prevent disease. The most shade-tolerant roses are hybrids of the musk rose, albas, rugosa roses, and the lovely floribunda 'Iceberg' (which may die back but likely will regrow in spring).

In addition to full sun, roses need air. Be sure to give your roses enough space all around for good air circulation. The rule of thumb is, compact roses need to be 2 to 4 feet apart. Climbing and heirloom roses need 5 to 10 feet between them. Miniature roses do well with just 18 to 24 inches all around.

Soil. The ideal soil for roses has good drainage, has lots of water-holding humus, and is very, very fertile. The soil pH that favors roses is between pH 5.8 and 6.8

The hole for a bush rose needs to be at least 24 inches deep. If your soil is less than wonderful or if you have difficulty digging deeply enough, create a raised bed for roses.

FERTILIZERS FOR ROSES

Rose soil needs refurbishing in early spring every year.

1. Check and adjust the soil pH.

2. Fertilize:

   - If you are using an organic fertilizer, apply it four to six weeks before growth begins.

   - If you are using a granular chemical fertilizer, apply it just before growth begins.

   - If you are using a time-release fertilizer, just before growth begins apply an eight-month formulation.

3. Renew the mulch. This organic blanket will stabilize soil temperature and renew the humus content of the soil.

4. Every three to five years improve the soil by applying rock phosphate, green sand, and if your soil has a lot of clay, gypsum. These are the granular soil additives used in preparing a new bed for roses. Measure it all into a pail, mix it, and scratch the mixture into the soil around the rose. Rain will do the rest.

When you use them depends on the type of fertilizer you are using—organic, chemical, slow- or time-release.

Organic blend fertilizers. Every six weeks spread Rose-Tone®, Plant-Tone®, or your favorite organic fertilizer blend over the inside perimeter of the watering basin at the rate of 10 pounds per 100 square feet.

1. Make the first application four to six weeks before growth begins;

2. Second application six weeks later, in early summer;

3. Third application six weeks later, in midsummer;

4. Last application, when growth slows, somewhere between mid-August in the colder zones and late September.

Chemical fertilizers. If you are using granular chemical fertilizers, apply these every six weeks beginning just before the roses come into bloom and ending with a final application of an organic, not chemical, fertilizer when growth slows.

Time-release fertilizer. Just before growth begins, apply an eight-month formulation.

In addition, roses that have been producing masses of blooms benefit from an occasional foliar feeding with a solution containing a liquid fertilizer. You'll find soluble organics such as fish emulsion, liquid seaweed, compost, and manure teas available at garden centers, as well as water-soluble chemical fertilizers.

PRUNING, DEADHEADING, AND HARVESTING

Roses must be pruned to remain shapely and stay healthy and productive. The best time is late in their dormant period before the buds begin to swell and new leaves appear—April and May. But late is better than not at all. The exception: one-time bloomers are pruned after they have finished blooming because next year's flowers develop on this year's new growth.

Prune to remove any cane thinner than a pencil and all damaged, weak, and non-productive canes. That allows the plant's energy to go into flower production and larger, healthier canes. Hybrid teas and exhibition roses are pruned hard when the goal is to encourage a few large blooms. The cluster-flower roses and compact roses are pruned lightly to encourage growth and maintain their shape.

Deadheading and harvesting. Removeing spent blooms will encourage the bushes to produce. Harvesting roses for bouquets is a form of deadheading—so indulge!! If you don't, blooms that were pollinated may begin to form seedpods (hips), which takes away energy needed for growth and flower production. Miniatures, small polyanthas, species, carpet roses, and 'Knock Out' series generally do not need deadheading.

Let the last roses stay on to produce hips. That causes the plant to undergo chemical changes that slow growth, inhibit blooming, and generally prepare for dormancy by focusing on "hardening" the canes. The formation of hips tells the plant that it's done its job and can now rest.

WATERING AND MULCHING

What roses need—what all plants need—is deep watering because that encourages the roots to grow deep into the soil. A deep root system survives dry spells and winter freezes. By "deep watering" we mean a slow, gentle, and thorough watering with a sprinkler, a soaker hose, a bubbler, or by hand. Water deeply after planting, then every week for the next eight weeks unless you have a soaking rain.

In good soil in average summer weather, both new and established roses need 1 to 1½ inches of water each week, by rain or by you. During a hot summer, each established bush needs a 5-gallon bucket of water each week. Roses growing in sandy soil need more frequent watering than roses in clay soil. One of the most important winter preparations is a deep and thorough watering before the ground freezes.

We favor installing a drip irrigation system or soaker hoses for roses. These two methods release water directly to the plant roots and not to the foliage, which helps avoid some diseases, and you don't waste water in runoff.

Mulch. After planting or transplanting a rose, spread mulch 2 to 3 inches deep, starting 3 inches from the main stem and out to a point wider than the plant's diameter. Replenish the mulch in later winter after fertilizing, in early summer, and in late fall.

WINTER CARE FOR ROSES

To help roses harden off and mature for winter, about six weeks before the first frost we recommend making a last fertilization of a slow-release, organic product such as Espoma Rose-Tone® or Plant-Tone®. It will work slowly over winter without promoting top growth that can be harmed by fall frosts.

Remember when cold weather threatens to stop deadheading and allow the flowers to go to seed and form rose hips. When the bush is bare of leaves, to prevent disease and fungus from overwintering, remove the petals and leaves and other debris on the ground. Spray with dormant oil to kill insects and diseases on the bush and on the ground. Water the plant thoroughly before the ground freezes hard.

Winter mulch. Once the ground has thoroughly frozen, in Zones 3, 4, 5, and 6, we recommend adding about a foot to the mulch to stabilize the soil temperature and prevent heaving. Use straw, salt hay, leaves, compost, or pine bark mulch. If the site is windy, encase the plant in a cage of wire and straw, or wrap it with burlap and straw and tie together.

You can also use Styrofoam™ rose cones as a protection. First, trim and defoliate the bush and mound it up with 12 inches of soil and mulch. Tie up the canes, place the protective cone over it, and weight the cone down.

When the forsythias bloom, remove the mulch and other protection.

PEST PATROL

Weeds. Rake away weeds, including grass and dandelions, early and often.

Deer and voles. For controls, try rodenticides or seek help locally.

Insects and diseases. The first line of defense is to plant pest- and disease-resistant roses, to give your roses lots of air all around, to fertilize, and to water well. When you encounter an infestation, treat it, and immediately remove every scrap of infected vegetation from the plant and the ground.

Blackspot and powdery mildew. Blackspot causes black spots about ¹⁄₁₆ to ½ inches in diameter on the leaves and sometimes the stems. The infected leaves later turn yellow around the spots and fall off. It is promoted by wet foliage, splashing water, and warm temperatures. The new 'Knock Out' shrub roses seem impervious, but most others are not.

Powdery mildew covers buds, stems, and leaves with a white-gray powdery substance. It cannot reproduce in water. It thrives during high humidity but forms on dry leaves.

You may succeed in warding off these two diseases if you:

- Spray with a combination of 1½ tablespoons of baking soda and either 2 tablespoons of horticultural oil or a few drops of dishwashing liquid in 1 gallon of water. The first application is made before foliage appears. It must be reapplied after rain.

- Remove leaves close to the ground (the first 6 to 8 inches), which are likely to be wetted. Mulch well to minimize water splashing onto the leaves.

- Remove all diseased leaves from the plant or ground immediately to prevent spreading the disease. Prune infected canes all the way back to healthy tissue in late winter.

- Prune to open the center of the bush to allow sunlight and air to reach all the plant.

- Remove the old mulch in early spring of plants that had a lot of problems the previous year. Allow the area to dry, and spread clean new mulch.

MOST SUCCESSFUL ROSES IN ZONE 3 TRIALS

Rachel Kane, of the Perennial Pleasures Nursery in East Hardwick, Vermont, recommends these for Vermont's Zone 3 and cold climates. They were the most enduring roses in trials conducted at Rogers Farm, University of Maine, in the years 2001-2003.

1. Rosa rugosa 'Hanse', reddish purple flowers, sweetly scented, makes a good hedge

2. 'Blanc Double de Coubert', 4 feet, white double that blooms all summer

3. 'Therese Bugnet', an almost thornless, double rugosa rose, 5 to 6 feet tall that repeat blooms in soft pink flowers

4. 'Harrison's Yellow', a late spring floriferous bloomer; rather scraggly plant but a good yellow

5. The Explorer series, 6 to 8 feet, repeat bloomers: Red 'John Cabot'; deep pink 'William Baffin'; medium pink 'John Davis'

6. Pale pink 'Grootendorst'; deep pink 'Grootendorst Supreme'; shrubs about 5 feet tall that bear clusters of small flowers with pinked edges

7. 'Iceberg' white; pure white floribunda blooms twice a season; it dies back but regrows in spring to 30 inches

- Keep the plant well watered. A weak or stressed plant is more susceptible to disease.

- Apply chemical fungicides to prevent blackspot and mildew. Spray every seven to fourteen days—especially the undersides of the leaves. Follow the label directions exactly.

Remember: Using a single fungicide over and over may cause the fungus to build a resistance to it. Alternate between two fungicides, Triforine (Funginex) and Daconil for example, to keep resistant fungi from building up. Fungicides generally can prevent blackspot, but do not cure an existing case of blackspot.

Japanese beetles, aphids, spider mites. These busy bees cut semi-circle shaped holes in the leaves of roses. They pose no real threat to rose health, but they drive exhibitors crazy.

Viral diseases. Symptoms are a mottling or mosaic discoloration of the leaf or ring spots. In most cases, removing the infected plant is the only control. Another suggestion is to buy roses from growers who are committed to producing resistant plants. These growers, including Jackson & Perkins, make cuttings from "indexed" blocks of mother plants. An "indexed" block is a group of plants that has been tested and has a high likelihood of not being infected with a virus.

THE WHEN AND HOW OF PRUNING ROSES

Wear thick leather gloves, and use sharp, clean pruning shears for small canes, and a small pruning saw for large canes.

Pruning can begin before or as the buds swell:
- Zone 7: in March
- Zone 6: mid- to late March
- Zones 3, 4, 5: early to late April

Basics

- Place pruning cuts so the center of the bush remains open for maximum air circulation.

- Make cuts ¼ inch above an outward-facing bud or leafset. Cut at a 45-degree angle with the high side on the side the bud or leafset is on—the outward facing side.

- Squeeze a drop of white glue over the cut ends of larger canes to keep borers out.

- Scrub the woody surface of the bud union with a brass wire brush (sold by hardware stores) to clear dead tissue and stimulate growth.

Pruning Established Roses

- **All but one-time bloomers.** Before or as the buds swell, remove dead canes, growth skinnier than a pencil, and canes crossing the center that are growing in the wrong direction and crowding others. Cut winter-damaged canes back to healthy green wood. Leave enough stem above the bud union

for new growth to develop. The exception to this rule: one-time bloomers are pruned after the roses have faded.

- **All roses.** Saw off old woody canes as close to the bud union as possible.

- **All grafted/budded roses.** Remove suckers growing from below the bud union of hybrid teas, grandifloras, and other grafted roses, or they will take over.

- **Hybrid teas, grandifloras.** Cut hybrid teas back to six well-placed canes and grandifloras back to eight canes. Reduce the canes a third, to 14 to 18 inches long.

- **Floribundas, polyanthas.** Cut three-year-old canes off at the bud union or to the crown. Cut two-year-old stems back by half. Cut back new canes by a third, or to just below where they bloomed last year.

- **Modern bush roses, 'Bonica', the Meidiland family.** Trim branch tips back to shape the plant.

- **Cluster-flowered bush roses, heirloom, and species roses.** Prune lightly to shape the plant.

- **Miniatures.** Remove all but the best four or five canes, and cut those back by a third.

- **Climbers.** For the first two years, prune to remove unproductive canes. After that, prune out the oldest canes, leaving five or six healthy ones, and shorten their side shoots by two-thirds.

- **Carpet roses.** Prune the canes back to 6 inches.

- **Rugosa roses.** Cut unproductive older canes back to the ground.

HOW TO PLANT ROSES

Preparing a New Rose Bed

Any airy, sunny, well-drained soil site can be made into a fine bed for roses. Start three to four weeks before planting season so the soil amendments will settle in before you plant.

1. Choose a site with full sun—at least six to eight hours.

2. Lay out the bed.

3. Check and adjust the pH.

4. Thoroughly water the turf.

5. Spray with Round Up™ Weed and Grass Killer. The turf will be completely dead in about two weeks. Or, remove the turf (and compost it).

6. Cover the bed with 3 to 5 inches of organic material— any combination of decomposed bark, compost, partially decomposed leaves, sphagnum peat moss, black peat humus, and well-rotted animal manure.

7. For every 100 square feet of garden bed, spread on these long-lasting organic fertilizers and amendments:
   Rose-Tone® or Plant-Tone®: 5 to 10 pounds
   Rock phosphate: 5 to 10 pounds
   Green sand: 5 to 10 pounds
   Clay soils: gypsum, 5 to 10 pounds

8. With a rear-tine rototiller, which you can rent from a garden center, mix all this as deeply as the rototiller will go.

9. Rake the bed smooth, and discard rocks, lumps, and bumps.

Preparing a New Planting Hole for a Rosebush

1. Outline a hole at least 20 inches wide. Dig a hole twice as deep as the rootball.

2. Test the pH of the soil. Bring to the site the products needed to adjust the pH, along with the fertilizers and amendments recommended for a new 100-square-foot bed, above. If the area you are planting measures only 10 square feet, combine one-tenth of the amount of each supplement given for a bed over 100 square feet.

3. As you dig, every 4 or 5 inches mix a portion of the fertilizer and amendments into the soil from the hole. The soil by the side of the hole is now "improved" and ready for the next step.

4. Pack in enough improved soil to place the graft (bud union—a thickened node at the base of the stem), if there is one, or the crown at the right depth.

Planting A Rosebush

1. **Depth.** The right depth depends on your plant-hardiness zone. In Zone 6 and north, grafted/budded roses do best planted if the graft lies 2 to 3 inches below the soil surface. In Zone 7, the bud union can be at soil level.

2. **Arranging the roots.** *Bare-root rose.* Firm a cone in the center of the mound, drape the roots over it, and spread them out in the hole. *Container rose.* Settle the rootball on packed improved soil. *Plantable container rose.* Set the container on firmly packed improved soil. Make sure the plant is sitting straight and its crown is level with the sur-rounding soil, fill the hole half way with improved soil, and pack it down. Water. Finish filling with improved soil, pack it down, and water again.

3. **Watering.** Shape the soil around the crown into a wide saucer (water basin), and create a rim around it that will keep rain or hose water from running off. Water the soil slowly, gently, and thoroughly with a sprinkler, a soaker hose, a bubbler, or by hand. You need to put down 1½ inches of water. Or, slowly and gently pour on 10 to 15 gallons of water from a bucket.

4. **Mulching.** Mulch 2 to 3 inches deep, starting 3 inches from the main stem.

JANUARY

- Take this respite from the garden to learn more about roses. Mail-order catalogs from the rose specialists are great teachers. Make an album of catalog pages of roses you would like to try. Go out to the garden and find likely places to plant them.

- If there is no snow, you could go out now and lay out a new rose bed, but you won't be able to dig till the soil dries.

- If miniature roses growing indoors aren't blooming, add grow lights for the evening.

- If spider-mite webs show up on miniature roses growing indoors, rinse the plants every two weeks. Air the room daily. Segregate infected plants.

- Where there is no snow cover, check and adjust winter mulch and other forms of protection for inground roses.

- Maintain the soil moisture of roses in containers overwintering in a frost-free shed or garage.

FEBRUARY

- When ordering roses, make sure they withstand your winters. Be wary of roses that have no hardiness rating; growers don't always know how new roses will perform. If you want to try a hybrid tea or other rose whose hardiness is iffy in your zone, grow it in a container and plan to overwinter it indoors in a frost-free shed or garage.

- Check your rosebushes for signs of heaving; it can happen in our milder zones during January and February thaws. Gently press the crowns back into the ground and add a light mulch.

- During warm spells, gauge the pruning job ahead for your roses. Wait until the last of the really cold weather to prune away dead or damaged branches.

- When mud season is over, remove the mulch layer under roses that were troubled by blackspot and mildew last year. Wait until you have tested the pH and fertilized to spread a fresh mulch.

MARCH

- Maintain the soil moisture of miniature roses growing indoors and roses in containers overwintering in a frost-free shed or garage.

- Look over your roses and determine which survived winter. That may impact your order for new rosebushes. If you have lost a lot of roses, order early because the weather that killed your roses may cause a run on the most desirable plants.

- Adjust winter protection for roses before the last storms hit.

- Roses are best pruned before the buds swell. If winter was mild, gardeners in Zones 6 and 7 had best keep an eye on their progress.

- As soon as mud season is over and before you fertilize or mulch, remove and discard old mulch under plants that had blackspot or mildew last year. Apply an ultrafine (dormant) horticultural oil spray to smother overwintering insect eggs. There are temperatures for its effectiveness, so read the label.

APRIL

- As roses begin to wake up, record in your garden log which ones did what and when. That information will be helpful next year when you are getting ready to prepare the bed and prune your roses.

- If you have not yet pruned your inground roses, do so now. The goal is to prune before the buds break. But late is better than not at all. Prune first-year plants only lightly to allow them to concentrate on establishing a strong root system.

- If you have a sunny, sheltered porch or patio, you may soon be able to plant a few container roses. The miniatures thrive in moss-lined baskets, planters, and clay or cement containers.

- Weeds are popping. Rake them away.

- Before growth begins, fertilize the soil around inground and container roses. Mark the date in your garden log, and note on your calendar when the next application is due.

MAY

- This is a fine month for planting new roses.

- To keep specimen roses looking good and producing flowers, deadhead religiously—that is, remove spent blooms—hybrid teas and grandifloras especially.

- To deadhead, make the cut a 45-degree angle just above the next five- or seven-segment leaf down the stem. The first year, cut back to the first three- or five-segment leafset.

- Make sure inground roses receive 1 ½ inches of water every week—that's two or three five-gallon buckets.

- Liquid-feed your roses growing in containers every two weeks with a half-strength dose of a soluble rose fertilizer.

- For inground roses, six weeks after your first application of fertilizer, repeat. The usual timing is early summer, but it depends on when you made your first application.

- Aphids cluster on rosebuds and cane tips. Use a strong spray of water or bloom them away in the early morning. If they persist, spray with Neem or insecticidal soap.

JUNE

- Check budded/grafted roses, and remove new canes coming from the rootstock below the bud union.

- Prune one-time bloomers when they finish blooming.

- The roses that didn't sell this spring may be on sale now—or soon. Be tempted, but be wise. Check out the rootball, and go for plants whose leaves are shiny, green, and plentiful, with no yellowing or stippling, or little spider webs.

- Top up the mulch around the roses before the heat gets intense.

- Attach the new growth of the climbers and ramblers to their supports.

- Deadhead hybrid teas, grandifloras, and other show-time roses.

- Growing in good soil, new and established roses need 1 to 1½ inches of water each week, which you must supply if the sky does not.

- Continue to root out weeds, and look out for aphids, spider mites, thrips, blackspot, and powdery mildew. If you have already sprayed without effect, switch to another control.

JULY

- This month and next, check the soil moisture daily in pots and baskets. Those roses may need a good soaking almost every day.

- Visit public gardens noted for roses—and smell the roses. Note the names of those that are really fragrant, and plan to try them.

- Heat is here. Check and replenish the mulch under the roses.

- Harvest—and deadhead—hybrid teas and grandifloras. The everblooming roses generally don't need deadheading, but if they aren't producing well, give it a try, then apply liquid fertilizer.

- Keep roses that suffer from powdery mildew well-watered. Warm dry days and cool dry nights are ideal for powdery mildew. A weak or stressed plant is more susceptible to disease.

- Mites attack roses stressed by hot weather and drought. Hose off the leaves, especially the undersides, every day or two for a week. If there are signs of webs on twigs and leaf stems, apply Neem or an insecticidal soap.

AUGUST

- Late afternoons in August, the scent of perfumed roses is heady because the fragrant oils have been volatized by a whole day of hot sun. Oils drawn from the scented florals were once our only source of fragrance. Harvest and dry petals for making homemade potpourri.

- If roses go on sale and you haven't the inclination to plant your purchases in August's high heat, grow them in their containers until September brings cooler conditions. The larger roses will do better if repotted into a larger container.

- If the foliage of hybrid teas wilts in high temperatures, help them recover by misting the leaves with a mild solution of liquid seaweed. Apply it in early morning before the sun starts to climb.

- Remove suckers growing up from under the bud union of your grafted hybrid roses, along with any diseased or damaged canes.

- Make sure inground roses receive 1 ½ inches of water every week.

SEPTEMBER

- If you did not check and adjust the pH of the soil in your rose beds in March or April, you can do it now. Roses prefer a slightly acidic soil, pH 5.8 to 6.8.

- September is a fine month for planting as well as transplanting roses, so take advantage of end-of-season sales to complete your rose collection.

- To help roses harden off and mature for winter, stop the use of high-nitrogen fertilizers about six weeks before the first frost.

- Continue to check soil moisture daily in roses growing outdoors in containers as well as the inground ones.

- If you are using organic or water-soluble chemical fertilizers, make the last application between the first of this month and early October.

- Rake away and destroy mulch under roses that have had blackspot, mildew, and other problems. Let the soil air out and dry, then apply fresh mulch.

OCTOBER

- As the weather cools, allow the last of the roses to form rose hips. That encourages the plant to slow growth and blooming and to harden the canes, all in preparation for dormancy.

- If you lose roses when winter temperatures fall to 10 degrees, plan to cover them for the winter. The time to do this is just before or just after the ground begins to freeze. Be wary of covering roses before the temperatures fall to 28 degrees F. as that may keep the rose from hardening properly and will slow the onset of dormancy, leaving the plants vulnerable to frost.

- This month, apply potassium to the soil to help winterize your roses.

- Begin to prepare your climbers, roses growing in containers, and tree roses for winter. Spray the canes of your climbers with a rose fungicide or dormant oil, and use an antidesiccant to help them withstand winter dryness.

NOVEMBER

- Now that the leafy season is over and the garden bare, evaluate the setting you've given your roses and consider which might do and look better moved to another spot.

- In Zone 7, you can plant and transplant roses as long as the weather stays comfortable.

- Save the pruning of long canes for late winter and early spring as branch tips generally have some winter dieback, and you'll have to prune them anyway.

- A major danger to roses in winter is a lack of water before the plant is completely dormant. Be sure before the ground freezes to give your roses a deep and thorough watering.

- To prevent disease spores of infected roses from infecting new growth when it comes along in spring, before protecting roses for the winter, strip off the leaves and pick up fallen leaves. Remove the mulch below diseased plants and replace it with fresh.

DECEMBER

- Bring your garden log up to date.

- If vole runs appear around your roses, bait the main runway with a rodenticide.

- Don't let the containers of hardy roses sheltering in a cold garage or shed dry out. As long as the ground isn't frozen, water roses in containers that are under eaves or pergolas.

- If miniature roses growing indoors aren't flowering, increase the light by adding grow lights after dusk and putting them under fluorescents in a light garden until they begin to bud.

- Dry air invites spider mites to adopt miniature roses. Air the room every day. When you water container roses, water the soil, not the foliage.

VEGETABLES
& HERBS
for New England

Our very first kitchen garden, a vegetable garden my father planted for us near the Canadian border, taught us to appreciate the excellence of home-grown foods. It was also a source of luxury items that were not easy to find elsewhere—sweet baby peas, just-picked corn, shallots, asparagus. We discovered there's deep satisfaction in harvesting home-grown lettuces and tomatoes warm from the sun, fresh flowers for the house, and fragrant herbs to use for cooking. In time we learned to make our kitchen garden beautiful. The flower-filled kitchen garden we share now in Connecticut is a favorite destination—even when there's weeding to be done!

PLANNING

The first step in making a kitchen garden appealing is to set it off handsomely. A picket fence adds charm. If deer and other four-footers love your food, you can install a six-foot high chickenwire fence inside the pickets—it will be almost invisible from a few feet away.

Make the entrance special with an antique gate or a gated pergola supporting one of the fragrant climbing roses recommended in Chapter 7; we love 'New Dawn'. Plan to train a grape vine over the fence and an espaliered pear if there's space. Gussy it up with ornate birdhouses, an antique sundial, and a water basin with a bubbler.

Make it exciting. Wake up your appetite. Grow lemon cucumbers, heirloom vegetables and fruits, exotic perfumed Galia melons from Israel, and pungent Oriental tat-soi greens. Pick baby head lettuce and tiny squash, or plant a giant variety of pumpkin and aim for 600 pounds! Serve real haricots verts, true petits pois without concern for the price. Grow your own asparagus, rhubarb, and strawberries.

Make it colorful. Plant bronze fennel, globe and purple basil as well as the sweet varieties, and variegated mint. Plant red, not green, romaine, Bibb, and oakleaf lettuce; red scallions, not white; yellow, purple, and orange sweet peppers along with red and green; scarlet, yellow, and purple runner beans; and violet broccoli (which cooks up green).

Make it interesting. Plant summer squashes with different shapes and colors—round 'Gourmet Globe', yellow 'Gold Rush' and 'Butterstick', and pattypan 'Sunburst'. Add curly Russian kale for texture; arugula, radicchio, and mache for fall salads. Be tempted by little white and mauve eggplants, wildly colorful hot peppers, red new potatoes, yellow watermelons, golden beets.

Make it beautiful and fragrant. Plant rhubarb, and allow the magnificent flower heads to grow up. Edge the garden with aromatic perennial herbs— chives, variegated thymes, colorful sages, golden oregano, and fragrant English lavender. The flowers as well as the foliage of the culinary herbs are edible. Center the beds on a dwarf apple or a plum tree, and the air will be sweet when you arrive to plant the mid-spring crops.

Choose flowers whose colors and texture will enhance the beauty of the vegetables. Edge plain green vegetables such as spinach with brilliant 'Copper Sunset' mounding nasturtiums, whose flowers and foliage are edible. Grow red-stemmed rhubarb chard with deep red 'Empress of India' nasturtiums. Back bush beans with pink or lavender powder puff asters, and edge the row with blue ageratum or dwarf purple gomphrena and purple basil. Plant late tulips in the fall, and overseed the row in early spring with leaf lettuce and Johnny-jump-up violas. For fragrant summer bouquets, plant aromatic basils with cosmos, snapdragons, and dahlias.

Intertwine snap beans with morning glories, and edge the row with blue salvia, white cosmos Sensation Strain 'Purity', and blue ageratum. Back the solid structures of the earth-hugging lettuces, beets, and cabbages with airy bronze fennel, tall snapdragons, caraway, or cosmos. These gardens can be prettier than flower gardens.

Caution: Don't combine edibles with poisonous plants—for example, larkspur, foxgloves, and sweet peas are toxic.

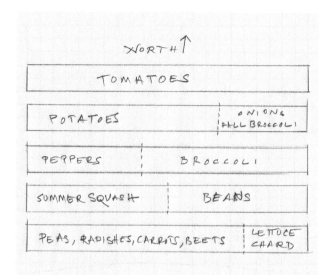

START WITH A PLANTING PLAN

A planting plan is the first step in planning a kitchen garden. To put together herbs, vegetables, and flowers that will enhance each other, you need to partner varieties that mature at about the same time. The information you need is in garden literature and in mail-order herb, vegetable, and flower catalogs. Match the early, midseason, and late species and varieties of annual flowers (see the introduction to annuals) to the cool-season, warm-season, and hot-season vegetables.

Cool-season vegetables are offered in early and late varieties. Where the growing season is short, seedlings of the early varieties are started indoors, set out in spring fairly early, and matured before high summer heat. Seeds of the late, or long-standing, varieties are sown in the garden in late spring or early summer, and mature crops are planted in cooling fall weather.

Warm-season vegetables are available in early and late varieties. Tiny cherry tomatoes and small Early Girl tomatoes mature before the Big Boy and long-keeper types. Most New England gardeners set out seedlings.

Hot-season vegetables need a long season to mature. Examples are shell beans and eggplant. Some varieties are available in smaller, earlier varieties—watermelons and cantaloupes, for example—that have time to mature even in the frost-belt. These also are set out as seedlings.

INTENSIVE CROPPING

When you know what you want to plant, the next step is to see how much of it will actually fit your space. With careful timing, you can get more than one crop from the same row. It's called "intensive cropping." Here's how to do it:

1. Clear out early crops as soon as they have been harvested, and replant the rows with mid- and late-season varieties.

PREPARING THE KITCHEN GARDEN FOR PLANTING

As soon as the snow is gone and winter moisture has left the soil, you can begin readying beds for planting. The earth is ready to be worked when a ball of earth packed between your hands crumbles easily; if it sticks together, the soil is still too wet.

A new bed needs careful preparation. Established beds for the annual vegetables and herbs must be reworked every year.

* If you didn't do it last fall, clear away the remains of last year's crops.

* Check the pH and apply whatever is needed to adjust the pH to between 6.0 and 7.0, the range suited to most food plants. The main exceptions are basil (5.5 to 6.5), blueberries (4.5 to 5.5), dill (5.5 to 6.7), eggplant and melon (5.5 to 6.5), potatoes (4.5 to 6.0), and sorrel (5.5 to 6.0). Vegetable gardens produce multiple crops, and over time the soil tends to become acidic, so testing and adjusting the pH annually is important. Try a dusting of wood ashes over the rows to add lime, which sweetens the soil, and potash (potassium), which strengths stems and keeps growth healthy. Many garden soils have a potash deficiency. Retest, and if the pH still is off, follow the instructions for adjusting pH in Soil Preparation and Improvement in the Introduction to the book.

* Turn and loosen the soil, by hand or with a rototiller, and at the same time work into the soil whatever amendments you are adding.

* Fertilize the top 3 to 6 inches of the planting rows with a generous helping of nutrients (except for nasturtiums). If you are using an organic fertilizer such as Plant-tone, apply it four to six weeks before planting begins. If you are using a chemical fertilizer—granular or coated eight-month slow release—apply it just before planting.

You must also fertilize the soil around the perennials—strawberries, orchard and bramble fruits. For asparagus, use an organic fertilizer high in nitrogen.

2. Combine sowings of cold-resistant, quickie vegetables such as radishes and lettuce, with taller, slow-to-mature species such as Brussels sprouts.

3. Plant together tall and short crops that mature at about the same time, such as corn or sunflowers, with long-standing, late-season, ground-hugging pumpkins or winter squash. The rambling vines of the pumpkins and winter squash shade out weeds.

PLANTING HERBS AND VEGETABLES

Because we are eager for early harvests, we start many vegetables and herbs indoors. The seedlings

CHOOSING AND PLANTING TOMATOES

Tomatoes are warm-season vegetables that flourish when nights reach 65 degrees Fahrenheit. The blossoms fall when days are above 90 and nights above 76 degrees Fahrenheit.

Determinate tomatoes are okay without staking, reach about 3 feet, and ripen a big crop in a short time. They bear all at once, not continuously. If you have a very short growing season—plant several determinate varieties.

Indeterminate tomatoes need staking or caging and produce continuously until stopped by cold. If you have a fairly long growing season and little space, choose indeterminate varieties.

The letters VFNA appear on the labels of plants resistant to the common insects and diseases that assail tomatoes.

Planting. In most of New England, it is safe to start tomato seeds indoors six to seven weeks before the last frost is anticipated.

Set seedlings out only after all danger of frost is past, early to late May depending on your zone. They do best when temperatures are 65 degrees Fahrenheit. When buying tomato seedlings, bypass small containers with tall plants already fruiting and choose stocky, leafy, dark-green plants just budding.

Two weeks before planting time, dig an organic or timed-release 5-10-10 fertilizer into the soil along with hydrated lime to prevent blossomend rot. Add a handful of gypsum for each plant to provide calcium without changing the soil pH. Set stocky transplants so the first leaves are just above soil level; lay leggy plants in the ground horizontally with most of the stem buried and the head upright.

We set tomato seedlings so they have 4 feet all around.

When the plants start to set fruit, apply a water-soluble organic fertilizer.

of cool-season vegetables usually can be moved out to the garden within four to six weeks—cabbage and broccoli, for example. They're transplanted as quite young seedlings directly from the flats they were sown in.

Warm- and hot-season vegetables and herbs benefit from being transplanted from the flats they were started in and planted in individual 2- to 4-inch peat pots before being moved out to the garden. In cold regions, the bigger varieties of tomato may do best transplanted a couple of times to ever-larger containers. After transplanting vegetable and herb seedlings to larger pots, wait to fertilize until the appearance of two or three new leaves tells you the root system is growing again. At that stage, provide very good natural light all day in a cold frame, on a windowsill, or in a glassed-in porch. Or grow the seedlings under fluorescent light about sixteen hours a day and set about 3 inches above the seedlings. As the seedlings grow, raise the light to 4 to 6 inches overhead. Once the seedlings show strong growth, reduce the lights to twelve hours a day.

Complete details on care of your crops start on page 236.

ASPARAGUS
Asparagus officinalis

When to plant—Plant crowns as soon as the ground can be worked in spring.

Where to plant—Prepare a bed in full sun away from encroaching tree or shrub roots. Any well-drained ground will suffice, but sandy soil is best.

How to plant—Plant in trenches 6 inches deep and 15 inches wide. Set the plants about a foot apart with the buds pointing up, and cover with 2 inches of soil.

Water needs—Water to provide about an inch of water a week, if rainfall is sparse.

Care/Maintenance—Remove weeds diligently, taking care not to harm the developing asparagus plants. Fertilize after harvest.

Pests/Diseases—No significant diseases, but asparagus beetles can wreak havoc. Control by handpicking or with an insecticide labeled for their control.

Days to maturity—This is a perennial plant, and you need to be patient. Spears are not ready for harvesting until the third year.

Recommended varieties—'Jersey Knight', 'Jersey Supreme', 'Purple Passion'

BASIL
Ocimum basilicum

When to plant—Plant seeds in spring after the last frost, or start indoors about two months early.

Where to plant—In full sun, in well-drained, moist soil. If in a pot, use a light soil mix.

How to plant—Space plants or thin seedlings 12 inches apart in all directions.

Water needs—Maintain a moist soil; do not let soil dry out.

Care/Maintenance—When plants are about 6 inches tall and growing vigorously, pinch out the growing tips to stimulate branching.

Pests/Diseases—Aphids and mites can occur. Pinch off affected shoots or spray with an insecticidal soap (remember to wash off the leaves well at harvest). Rot can occur if the soil is too soggy.

Days to maturity—60 to 80, depending on the variety

Recommended varieties—'Genovese', 'Magical Michael', 'Purple Ruffles'

BEAN
Phaseolus vulgaris

When to plant—Sow two weeks before last frost.

Where to plant—Full sun is best (8 to 10 hours a day), in well-drained soil.

How to plant—Sow bush beans 2 to 3 in. apart, pole beans 6 in. apart, then cover with an inch of soil. Add beneficial bacteria (legume inoculants), available from garden stores or catalogs, if needed.

Water needs—Provide about an inch per week.

Care/Maintenance—Help pole beans get onto their supports (they twine counterclockwise). Weed and water regularly.

Pests/Diseases—Don't work in the beans when they are wet. Diseases include bean mosaic virus and bacterial blight. Leaf bean beetles may eat holes in the leaves.

Days to maturity—50-70 days, depending on the type and variety

Recommended varieties—Bush beans: 'E-Z Pick', 'Jade', 'Provider'

Pole beans: 'Fortex', 'Garden of Eden', 'Northeaster'

BEETS
Beta vulgaris

When to plant—Sow one month before the frost-free date.

Where to plant—In well-prepared loamy, neutral-to-alkaline soil. Full sun and good drainage are key.

How to plant—Fertilize the area, then work the soil into a fine seedbed. Sow seeds 1 in. apart and allow them 12 to 15 in. between rows. Cover with a half-inch of fine soil.

Water needs—If no rain falls for 7 to 10 days, apply an inch of water.

Care/Maintenance—These plants require little care. Hoe or pull any weeds.

Pests/Diseases—Keep some out by covering the plants with netting or row covers. Leafminers, soilborne maggots, and leaf-spot diseases are all potential problems that may be controlled with garden chemicals specifically labeled for this use.

Days to maturity—48 to 60 days, depending on the variety

Recommended varieties—'Chiogga', 'Golden Beet', 'Red Ace'

BROCCOLI
Brassica oleracea var. *botrytis*

When to plant—Sow seed as early as the soil can be worked. Or sow seeds indoors, 8 weeks before the last frost date.

Where to plant—Full sun (8 to 10 hours per day) is best.

How to plant—Plant in prepared, fertilized soil. Space transplants about 18 inches apart, with 36 inches between rows. In a bed, space plants 16 to 18 inches apart.

Water needs—Water as necessary to keep the plants vigorous and growing—about an inch a week.

Care/Maintenance—When the plants are about half-grown, side-dress them with a complete fertilizer.

Pests/Diseases—Plant disease-resistant varieties, and practice crop rotation. Root maggots, cabbage worms, or sparrows can bother your crop—if they do, get advice and appropriate garden chemicals from your local garden center.

Days to maturity—65 to 85 days, depending on the variety

Recommended varieties—'De Cicco', 'Marathon', 'Packman'

BRUSSELS SPROUTS
Brassica oleracea var. *gemmifera*

When to plant—Transplants can go into the garden in June. Start seed indoors about a month before your frost-free date; remember to harden them off.

Where to plant—In full sun, in well-drained garden soil. (Plants grown in shade will be weak and may fall over.)

How to plant—Plants 18 inches apart. Space rows 36 inches apart. Set plants at the same depth they were growing.

Water needs—Water regularly; do not let soil dry out.

Care/Maintenance—Side-dress when they are a about a foot tall. Healthy, full-sized leaves must be left at the top of the stem to provide nutrients for the plant. Pick or cut the sprouts as they attain full size, 1 ½ to 2 inches in diameter. The plants are very cold hardy.

Pests/Diseases—Root maggots, cabbage worms, leaf-spot disease, and rots can occur. Plant disease-resistant varieties, practice crop rotation, and keep your plants healthy.

Days to maturity—90 to 110, depending on the variety

Recommended varieties—'Diablo', 'Oliver', 'Rubine'

CABBAGE
Brassica oleracea var. *capitata*

When to plant—Sow indoors 8 weeks before last frost date, and set out about 6 weeks later.

Where to plant—Full sun (a minimum of 8 hours per day) or partial shade (filtered sun all day or shade part of the day), in well-prepared soil with good drainage.

How to plant—Space 12 to 18 inches apart, with 24 inches between rows.

Water needs—They need about an inch of water a week; dry weather ruins them (causes cracking).

Care/Maintenance—Side-dress with a complete fertilizer when they are about half-grown.

Pests/Diseases—Cabbage are susceptible to various problems, which you can prevent or should treat quickly (get advice from your local garden center): root maggots, cabbage worms, and various leaf-spot diseases.

Days to maturity—55 to 82 days, depending on the variety

Recommended varieties—'Gonzales', 'Rubicon', 'Tendersweet',

CARROTS
Daucus carota var. *sativus*

When to plant—Sow seeds as soon as the soil is workable in the spring; a freeze will not harm them. For successive crops, sow every two or three weeks.

Where to plant—In full sun, in well-drained soil that is deeply prepared so it is free of rocks and other obstructions.

How to plant—Sow three per inch, later thinning to one plant every 2 inches. Space rows 12 to 15 inches apart. Cover with ¼ inch of fine soil.

Water needs—Water regularly; do not let soil dry out. Carrots that develop in dry weather are fibrous and woody.

Care/Maintenance—A little hoeing or pulling of weeds, especially while the seedlings are small, will prevent weeds from competing with the carrots for water and nutrients.

Pests/Diseases—Soilborne maggots can damage the roots.

Days to maturity—56 to 68, depending on the variety

Recommended varieties—'Napoli', 'Nelson', 'Scarlet Nantes'

CAULIFLOWER
Brassica oleracea var. *botrytis*

When to plant—Grow as a spring or fall crop to avoid heat, cold, and dry weather. Start plants 8 weeks before your last frost, and set out 6 weeks later.

Where to plant—Deeply prepared, well-drained soil, in full sun.

How to plant—Space transplants about 18 inches apart, 36 inches between rows. Water them in with a high-soluble phosphorus fertilizer.

Water needs—Provide an inch per week as needed.

Care/Maintenance—When they are about half-grown, provide a dose of high-nitrogen fertilizer. Heads exposed to light will be off-color; blanch them by securing leaves around the heads when they are about 3 inches in diameter.

Pests/Diseases—Root maggots, cabbage worms, leaf-spot diseases, black rot and blackleg diseases, clubroot. Grow resistant varieties and/or take quick action (get control advice from a local garden center).

Days to maturity—50 to 62 days, depending on the variety

Recommended varieties—'Fremont', 'Snow Crown', 'Violet Queen'

CHIVES
Allium schoenoprasum

When to plant—Sow seeds in early spring. Plant transplants when they become available in spring.

Where to plant—For best growth, give them full sun (though they will tolerate some shade). Choose an undisturbed garden spot or grow in pots, so their spreading nature will not be a problem.

How to plant—Sow seeds about 12 inches apart, cover lightly. Put started plants into well-prepared soil, about 12 inches apart.

Water needs—Provide water if there is no rainfall.

Care/Maintenance—Little, if any, care is needed. Keep the plants clipped, both for harvesting and to prevent flowering, which affects the flavor and leads to often unwelcome self-sowing.

Pests/Diseases—Thrips and root maggots are possible. Seek local advice for combating, and remember to wash off insecticides after harvesting.

Days to maturity—80 to 100 days

Recommended varieties—The larger, related garlic chives, *Allium tuberosum*, yields a tasty harvest.

CORN, SWEET
Zea mays var. *rugosa*

When to plant—Around the frost-free date in your area. Plant additional seedlings until early July if you want a staggered harvest.

Where to plant—Needs full sun (8 to 10 hours), good drainage, and lots of room.

How to plant—Sow seeds in rich soil, 9 inches apart in rows, 24 to 36 inches between rows. Plant two or more rows of each variety side-by-side to assure pollination.

Water needs—Water regularly, especially when the plants are tasseling, making silk, and during kernel development. Soaker hoses are a good idea.

Care/Maintenance—Control weeds. Side-dress with a complete fertilizer (such as 10-10-10) when they are about 1½ feet tall.

Pests/Diseases—Plant disease-resistant varieties. Corn earworm, corn borers, and smut disease are potential problems; combat with advice from a local garden center.

Days to maturity—50 to 70 days, depending on variety

Recommended varieties—'Delectable', 'Silver Queen', 'Xtra Tender'

CUCUMBER
Cucumis sativus

When to plant—Sow directly in the garden or set out transplants only after all danger of frost is past.

Where to plant—Full sun and good drainage are key.

How to plant—Bush types can go in the garden or in containers; train vining types on supports such as trellises. Plant in prepared soil, 36 inches apart, two or three per hill, and thin later.

Water needs—Provide an inch of water a week.

Care/Maintenance—Protect plants from pests with row covers and/or insecticides. Keep area well-weeded.

Pests/Diseases—Cucumber beetles are a serious threat. A virus disease, cucumber mosaic, may cause misshapen, lumpy cucumbers. Grow resistant varieties.

Days to maturity—50 to 63 days, depending on the variety

Recommended varieties—'Diva', 'Marketmore 76', 'Olympian'

DILL
Anthemum graveolens

When to plant—Sow seeds or set out started plants in early spring. Make successive sowings throughout the summer.

Where to plant—Anywhere there is well-prepared, moist soil. Either full sun or partial shade is fine.

How to plant—Sow seeds an inch apart in rows 1 foot apart. Thin the seedlings when they are about 6 inches tall (and use the discarded seedlings in salad). Transplants may be set 1 foot apart in beds or 2 feet apart in rows.

Water needs—Water when the weather is dry, providing an inch a week.

Care/Maintenance—Dill requires little care once it has started to grow.

Pests/Diseases—None serious. You may instead observe the larvae of the black swallowtail butterfly on your plants. These large black-and-yellow-striped caterpillars do not eat much and make spectacular butterflies.

Days to maturity—50 to 70 days, depending on variety

Recommended varieties—'Bouquet', 'Fernleaf', 'Super Dukat'

EGGPLANT
Solanum melongena var. *esculentum*

When to plant—Sow seeds indoors only two weeks before your last frost; set out in the garden six to eight weeks later, when soil and air have warmed up.

Where to plant—Full sun (8 to 10 hours a day), in warm, well-drained, organically rich soil.

How to plant—Sow seeds in hills 12 inches apart, with 24 to 30 inches between rows or even closer for small-fruited varieties; thin later to one per hill. Plant leggy transplants on their sides, and cover the long stems lightly with soil. The tips will turn up and the buried stems will sprout new roots.

Water needs—They need an inch of water a week.

Care/Maintenance—Side-dress them with high-nitrogen fertilizer at one foot tall. Mulch to conserve soil warmth.

Pests/Diseases—Plant resistant varieties. Typical problems are flea beetles and verticillium wilt.

Days to maturity—65 to 75 days, depending on the variety

Recommended varieties—'Fairy Tale', 'Nadia', 'Rosa Bianca'

ENDIVE
Chicorium endivia

When to plant—Sow indoors eight weeks before last frost, or sow directly into the garden as soon as the soil can be worked. For a fall crop, start seeds around mid-July and set plants out in the garden in late summer.

Where to plant—In full sun, in well-drained soil.

How to plant—Plant eight to ten per foot in rows 18 inches apart. Thin seedlings to one plant every 10 inches.

Water needs—Keep the soil slightly on the dry side, but do not let the plants wilt.

Care/Maintenance—Fertilize at planting time. Control weeds. Blanch the leaves before harvest: tie the outer leaves over the developing heads, harvest two or three weeks later, discarding the outer leaves. The plants bolt in hot weather.

Pests/Diseases—Earwigs and slugs can be troublesome because they get into the heads while the plants are small, so control these pests early.

Days to maturity—33 to 45, depending on the variety

Recommended varieties—'Clodia', 'Keystone', 'Rhodos'

KALE

Brassica oleracea var. acephala

When to plant—For a fall crop, sow in midsummer and set out six weeks later. For a spring crop, start seeds indoors eight weeks before the last frost, and set out six weeks later.

Where to plant—Well-drained soil in full sun is best.

How to plant—Space 12 inches apart, with 18 to 24 inches between rows. In a bed, space 12 inches apart. Fertilize.

Water needs—Provide about an inch of water a week.

Care/Maintenance—Crop rotation and choosing disease-resistant varieties will make raising a good crop easier. Prevent cabbage worms with Bt. In the fall, wait till a frost before harvesting—the flavor is much better.

Pests/Diseases—Root maggots and cabbage worms are potential pests. Leaf spot, yellows, black rot and blackleg diseases can occur. Take preventative steps or seek local advice about controls.

Days to maturity—50 to 60 days, depending on the variety

Recommended varieties—'Champion', 'Red Russian', 'Winterbor'

LEEKS

Allium ampeloprasum

When to plant—Start seeds in mid-February and transplant outdoors three weeks before last frost or as early as the soil is workable. Or direct-sow as early as the soil is workable.

Where to plant—Plant in deeply prepared, well-drained soil. Full sun is preferred.

How to plant—Prepare the bed deeply, adding organic matter and fertilizer. Space 4 inches apart, with 12 to 18 inches between rows. Set the plants somewhat deeper than they were growing.

Water needs—Provide an inch of water a week.

Care/Maintenance—Leeks are heavy feeders, so side-dress them with nitrogen six weeks after transplanting. Blanch the lower parts of the stems by gradually hilling up soil around their bases.

Pests/Diseases—Use appropriate garden chemicals to combat onion maggots or thrips.

Days to maturity—75 to 120 days, depending on the variety

Recommended varieties—'Bandit', 'King Richard', 'Upton'

LETTUCE

Latuca sativa

When to plant—Plant early, in spring, before hot weather. Head lettuce should be started indoors earlier than leaf lettuce; consult seed packets for full information. Stagger plants to assure a continuous harvest.

Where to plant—Excellent drainage is important. Site in full sun or part shade.

How to plant—Space larger types (head lettuce) a foot apart, leaf types 4 to 6 inches apart.

Water needs—Provide about an inch a week.

Care/Maintenance—Control weeds carefully with a hoe or hand-pulling, taking care not to uproot shallow-rooted plants. When plants are large enough, harvest every other one, leaving more room for the remaining ones.

Pests/Diseases—Earwigs and aphids are possible problems. Proper spacing and insecticidal soap can help.

Days to maturity—46 to 90 days, depending on type and variety

Recommended varieties—'Black Seeded Simpson', 'Red Sails', 'Simpson Elite'

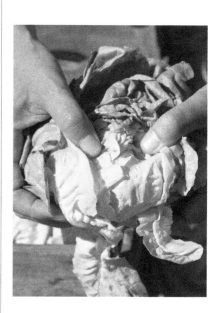

MINT
Mentha spp.

When to plant—Set out started plants in spring.

Where to plant—Most will thrive in full sun or partial shade. Plant where you can control them.

How to plant—Plant in well-drained soil, separating various types by barriers. Contain plants with concrete blocks, timbers, and 12-inch clay drain tiles. Space plants 2 feet apart in beds.

Water needs—Keep the soil constantly moist but not wet.

Care/Maintenance—Control weeds and watch that growth doesn't get out of hand. Mulch with straw in areas with cold winters and the plants will be protected; remove before they begin to grow the following spring.

Pests/Diseases—Verticillium wilt is the most damaging disease; do not plant mint where solanaceous crops (tomatoes, potatoes, etc.) have been grown because they all carry the disease and infect the soil.

Days to maturity—Approximately 60 days

Recommended varieties—Peppermint, *Mentha* × *piperita*; apple mint, *Mentha saureolens*; pineapple mint, *Mentha saureolens* var. *variegata*

MUSKMELON
Cucumis melo var. *reticulatus*

When to plant—Sow seeds in peat pots a week before last frost. Direct-sow or set out transplants once the soil is warmed up and all danger of frost is past.

Where to plant—Put in a full-sun location with well-drained soil, and plenty of space.

How to plant—Sow seeds an inch deep in hills 36 inches apart. In a bed, space them 36 inches apart down the middle.

Water needs—They need at least an inch of water a week.

Care/Maintenance—Cover plants with row covers, for warmth as well as pest protection, until they begin to vine and to allow bees to pollinate the flowers. A trellis or fence must be strong enough; tie a little net or cloth parachute under each melon.

Pests/Diseases—Row covers and insecticides will fight off cucumber beetles.

Days to maturity—70 to 96 days, depending on type and variety

Recommended varieties—'Halona', 'Jenny Lind', 'Sweet Granite'

ONION
Allium cepa

When to plant—Put them out as soon as the soil can be worked in the spring.

Where to plant—Plant in full sun in well-prepared, well-drained soil.

How to plant—In rows, space stick-outs 3 inches apart, with 12 to 15 inches between rows. Set transplants about an inch deeper than they were growing.

Water needs—Apply an inch of water a week if the weather is dry.

Care/Maintenance—Control weeds carefully with hoeing or hand-pulling, to avoid disturbing the shallow roots. Try to get as much top growth as possible by the first day of summer; the size of the dry onions is determined by the tops. Side-dress when the plants reach 12 inches.

Pests/Diseases—Onion maggots and thrips may become troublesome; get control advice locally.

Days to maturity—85 to 110 days, depending on the type and variety

Recommended varieties—'Olympic', 'Prince', 'Super Star'

153

OREGANO
Origanum heracleoticum

When to plant—Set out plants in early spring; they can stand a freeze. Divide them in the spring or fall.

Where to plant—Locate in full sun in reasonably good garden soil—it should drain well and should not be puddled or compacted.

How to plant—Put transplants in the garden 18 inches apart in 18-inch rows.

Water needs—It needs little water—about an inch a week at most.

Care/Maintenance—True oregano is not invasive, though it is vigorous enough to squeeze out most weeds. Cut off flowers as they appear to stimulate more production. Only the newer leaves are tender and flavorful. If the plant goes to seed, growth of new leaves stops. In cold-winter areas, it should survive the winter if you mulch it.

Pests/Diseases—None serious.

Days to maturity—60 to 90 days

Recommended varieties—Pot marjoram (*Origanum onites*) is actually an oregano that has a bite to it.

HERB

GREEK OREGANO

PARSLEY
Petroselinum crispum

When to plant—Sow seed indoors in midwinter, or direct-sow or plant seedlings when the soil outside can be worked.

Where to plant—Site in deeply prepared soil, in full sun or partial shade. They only reach about a foot, so plant them wherever they fit.

How to plant—Sow seeds an inch apart in rows a foot apart, and be patient, as germination sometimes takes four or more weeks. Then thin seedlings to a 5- or 6-inch spacing. Transplants can be spaced a foot apart in each direction in beds, or a foot apart in rows 2 feet apart.

Water needs—If rainfall is not sufficient, provide an inch a week.

Care/Maintenance—Parsley takes little care in the garden. Hoe or pull weeds as they appear.

Pests/Diseases—If mites occur, spray with insecticidal soap; rinse the treated leaves before use.

Days to maturity—75 to 84 days, depending on the variety

Recommended varieties—'Banquet', 'Forest Green', 'Titan'

PARSNIP
Pastinaca sativa

When to plant—Sow seed as soon as the soil can be worked in spring.

Where to plant—This crop will be in the ground for a long time, so grow where it will not be disturbed. Give it a spot in deeply prepared, well-drained soil in full sun.

How to plant—Work the soil surface into a fine seedbed, and sow seeds 2 inches apart with 12 inches between rows, then cover with ½ inch of fine soil.

Water needs—Water regularly; do not let soil dry out. It needs about an inch per week.

Care/Maintenance—Fertilize at planting time, and again when the tops are 8 to 10 inches tall. Weed diligently. Harvest only after they have been exposed to freezing temperatures; cold changes the starch in the roots to sugar. You can leave in the ground all winter in many areas, harvesting as needed.

Pests/Diseases—Canker can be a problem; grow resistant varieties.

Days to maturity—110 to 120, depending on the variety

Recommended varieties—'Andover', 'Javelin', 'Lancer'

PEA
Pisum sativum var. sativum

When to plant—Only in cool weather! Sow as soon as the soil can be worked in spring. For a fall crop, use heat-tolerant varieties, and sow in midsummer so they mature in the cool weather.

Where to plant—Plant in a part of the garden that drains well and dries out early in the spring. Partial shade shields the plants from intense heat and may prolong the season.

How to plant—Sow seeds an inch apart and an inch deep into prepared, raked ground. Rows should be 12 to 18 inches apart. Thin seedlings to 8 to 10 inches apart.

Water needs—Provide about an inch of water every 10 days if rainfall doesn't.

Care/Maintenance—Bush peas are self-supporting, but vining types need support such as short, slender branches ("pea sticks").

Pests/Diseases—Avert problems by choosing resistant varieties.

Days to maturity—57 to 74 days, depending on type and variety

Recommended varieties—'Feisty', 'Oregon Giant', 'Sugar Ann'

PEPPER, HOT
Capsicum spp.

When to plant—Start seeds indoors 2 weeks before last frost, and plant in the garden after danger of frost is past.

Where to plant—Full sun (8 to 10 hours per day) and prepared, well-drained soil is best.

How to plant—In rows, space them 10 inches apart, 18 to 24 inches between rows. In beds, space plants 15 inches apart in all directions.

Water needs—Provide an inch of water a week if rainfall doesn't.

Care/Maintenance—When the plants set fruit, sidedress with a complete fertilizer.

Pests/Diseases—Avoid common problems by planting disease-resistant varieties. If diseases or pests (such as aphids or caterpillars) appear, get advice locally on effective controls.

Days to maturity—68 to 87 days or more, depending on variety

Recommended varieties—'Cherry Bomb', 'Habanero', 'Jalapeno'

PEPPER, SWEET OR BELL
Capiscum annuum

When to plant—Start seeds indoors about two weeks before last frost. Set transplants out after all danger of frost is past.

Where to plant—Site in a well-drained part of the garden that receives full sun.

How to plant—In rows, space plants 10 inches apart, with 18 to 24 inches between rows. In beds, space 15 inches apart in all directions. Plant leggy ones on their sides, covering the long stems lightly with soil; the tips will turn upwards and the buried stems will sprout new roots.

Water needs—Provide an inch of water a week if nature does not cooperate.

Care/Maintenance—Side-dress the plants with a complete fertilizer when they have set fruit.

Pests/Diseases—Aphids, mites, and whiteflies occur, and tobacco mosaic virus can be a problem. Insecticidal soaps and good garden hygiene can help.

Days to maturity—65 to 90 days, depending on the variety

Recommended varieties—'Ace', 'Sweet Chocolate', 'Yankee Bell'

POTATO
Solanum tuberosum

When to plant—Plant about 3 weeks before last frost.

Where to plant—Well-drained, well-tilled soil in full sun is ideal.

How to plant—Potatoes are started from seed pieces, not from actual seeds. Use certified seed potatoes from a reliable outlet. Space 12 to 15 inches apart, with 24 inches between rows. Plant 2 to 3 inches deep with the eyes up.

Water needs—Even, consistent moisture is key—provide an inch of water a week.

Care/Maintenance—When sprouts are 6 inches high, begin (carefully) hilling soil around them. The hills eventually should be about 6 inches high and a foot wide.

Pests/Diseases—Floating row covers can protect your crop from various pests, including leaf hoppers, potato beetles, and flea beetles. Scab disease affects potatoes grown in alkaline soil; buy resistant varieties.

Days to maturity—100 to 130 days, depending on the variety

Recommended varieties—'Dark Red Norland', 'Kennebec', 'Yukon Gold'

PUMPKIN
Cucurbita pepo

When to plant—Sow seeds indoors one month before last frost, in peat pots. Set plants in the garden after danger of frost is past.

Where to plant—A sunny spot with well-drained soil is best (light shade may be tolerated). Room to spread out is important!

How to plant—Start out by sowing six seeds or two or three seedlings in hills about 5 feet apart, with rows 10 feet apart. The tiny roots are easily damaged, so work with care. Thin to two or three seedlings per hill when they are big enough to handle.

Water needs—Provide an inch of water per week.

Care/Maintenance—After they set fruit, pumpkins need lots of water and fertilizer.

Pests/Diseases—The worst pest is squash-vine borers. Cucumber beetles and squash bugs can also occur. Control with appropriate insecticides.

Days to maturity—100 to 120 days, depending on the variety

Recommended varieties—'Connecticut Field', 'Baby Pam', 'Jack Be Little'

RADISH
Raphanus sativus

When to plant—In spring, sow seeds as soon as the soil is dry enough to work. For a fall or winter crop, sow in late summer or fall.

Where to plant—Choose a well-drained site in full sun or partial shade.

How to plant—Work the soil into a fine seedbed. Sow about three per inch in rows 8 to 10 inches apart, and cover with ¼ inch of fine soil. Thin spring radishes to 1 inch; thin winter radishes to 3 or 4 inches. In beds, broadcast, then thin to 2 or 3 inches.

Water needs—Apply an inch of water a week when rainfall does not.

Care/Maintenance—Hoe or pull weeds so they don't compete.

Pests/Diseases—Soilborne maggots may damage the roots; treat with an insecticide.

Days to maturity—22 to 28 days, depending on the variety

Recommended varieties—'Cherriette', 'Crunchy Royale', 'Easter Egg'

RHUBARB
Rheum rhabarbarum

When to plant—Plant root divisions as early in the spring as the ground can be worked.

Where to plant—In full sun, in well-drained soil. Pick a site where it will not be disturbed or interfere with other garden activities, such as at one end, or along the side.

How to plant—Set the roots with the buds about an inch below the soil surface. Space them 3 feet apart in rows 4 feet apart.

Water needs—Water regularly, especially when rain is sparse.

Care/Maintenance—Keep weeds under control as the plants develop. Fertilize at planting time and every spring.

Pests/Diseases—Rot and fungal diseases can occur where humidity is high or soil is too wet.

Days to maturity—Do not harvest the first season after planting. When you do finally harvest, wait until the leaves reach full size, removing no more than a third at any time. Pull them with a twist to release them from the crown.

Recommended varieties—'Canada Red', 'MacDonald Strain', 'Valentine'

SAGE
Salvia officinalis

When to plant—Start seed indoors in peat pots in late winter. Seedlings may go in the ground as soon as the soil can be worked in spring; they can withstand a frost.

Where to plant—Well-drained soil and full sun is important. Also, because the plants will eventually become quite big, place them where they will shade or interfere with other plants or foot traffic.

How to plant—Prepare the soil deeply and well. Set out the started plants 15 to 18 inches apart so they have room to develop.

Water needs—If there is no rain for one or two weeks, apply an inch of water.

Care/Maintenance—Sage is low-maintenance, requiring only a bit of weeding and pruning. Keep weeds under control.

Pests/Diseases—Use insecticides to control pesky mites. Wet weather and damp soil can lead to rot.

Days to maturity—80 to 90 days, depending on the variety

Recommended varieties—Pineapple sage, *Salvia elegans*

SPINACH
Spinacia oleracea

When to plant—Plant early and harvest before hot weather arrives. Direct-sow as early as the soil can be worked. Or start seedlings indoors early, sowing three to four weeks before the last frost.

Where to plant—In full sun, in well-drained soil. To extend production into the warmer summer months, plant in part-day shade.

How to plant—Space transplants 6 to 8 inches apart, with 12 inches between rows.

Water needs—Need lots of water for vigorous growth—the roots cannot stand soggy soil.

Care/Maintenance—Fertilize at planting time. Because spinach is shallow-rooted, weed carefully and attack weeds while they are still small. Protect the plants from cold as well as pests with row covers. Harvest by snipping off outer leaves as soon as they are large enough to use.

Pests/Diseases—Various pests and diseases may attack, notably aphids (control with insecticidal soap) and leafminers (row covers work).

Days to maturity—30 to 40, depending on the variety

Recommended varieties—'Giant Noble', 'Space', 'Tyee'

SQUASH, SUMMER
Cucurbita maxima, C. pepo

When to plant—Set out started plants (in peat pots, because they don't tolerate root injuries well) or sow seeds directly after last frost.

Where to plant—In full sun, in well-drained soil.

How to plant—Place 5 feet apart, in rows 10 feet apart. Provide vining types with a trellis or other strong support.

Water needs—Requires plentiful and consistent moisture, especially after it sets fruit.

Care/Maintenance—Feed at planting time and again when the vines have almost covered the grown (rinse the fertilizer off the leaves). Bees will pollinate, so avoid insecticides or apply them in the evening hours.

Pests/Diseases—Squash-vine borers can be fought with insecticide and/or by slitting affected stems and burying the damaged section so it can form new roots. Other insects and mildew can also be problems—seek advice from your local garden center.

Days to maturity—52 to 58, depending on the variety

Recommended varieties—'Multipik', 'Sunray', 'Yellow Crookneck'

SQUASH, WINTER
Cucurbita maxima, C. pepo

When to plant—Set out started plants (in peat pots, because they don't tolerate root injuries well) or sow seeds directly after last frost.

Where to plant—In full sun, in well-drained soil.

How to plant—Place 5 feet apart, in rows 10 feet apart. Provide vining types with a trellis or other strong support.

Water needs—Requires plentiful and consistent moisture, especially after it sets fruit.

Care/Maintenance—Feed at planting time and again when the vines have almost covered the grown fruit (rinse the fertilizer off the leaves). Bees will pollinate, so avoid insecticides or apply them in the evening hours. Harvest when the rinds are hardened.

Pests/Diseases—Squash-vine borers can be fought with insecticide and/or by slitting affected stems and burying the damaged section so it can form new roots. Other insects and mildew can also be problems— seek advice from your local garden center.

Days to maturity—88 to 100, depending on type and variety

Recommended varieties—'Blue Hubbard', 'Buttercup', 'Spaghetti Squash'

SWISS CHARD
Beta vulgaris var. cicla

When to plant—Start seeds indoors about 6 weeks before last frost, sow directly into the garden, or set out transplants after the frost-free date.

Where to plant—Good drainage and well-drained soil are important. A location with 8 to 10 hours of sun is best.

How to plant—Seeds are actually dried-up fruits containing two or more seeds, so don't plant too close together, and thin to 4 to 6 inches apart. Final spacing should be 8 to 10 inches apart, allowing 18 inches between rows.

Water needs—Provide an inch of water a week.

Care/Maintenance—Cover plantings with cheesecloth or commercial row covers. Try to keep the foliage dry when watering.

Pests/Diseases—Very susceptible to leafminer damage, as well as beet leaf spot. Cover the plants as suggested above and/or get control advice locally.

Days to maturity—About 40 days, depending on the variety

Recommended varieties—'Bright Lights', 'Fordhook Giant', 'Ruby Red'

TARRAGON
Artemisia dracunculus

When to plant—Set out started plants in early spring (they can stand a freeze).

Where to plant—In full sun, in fertile, well-drained soil. Set it to one side of the garden where it will not be disturbed by other gardening activities. May be grown in a pot as well.

How to plant—Space 1-foot in all directions in beds or rows.

Water needs—Water to keep from wilting.

Care/Maintenance—Pinch newly started plants to encourage branching. Avoid fertilizing, which can lead to rank, floppy plants. Harvest often, which encourages the development of fresh, new leaves. Divide plants every three or four years.

Pests/Diseases—Mites may become troublesome. Spray with insecticidal soap, and remember to rinse off the leaves before using. Root rot and mildew occur if soil doesn't drain well.

Days to maturity—Start harvesting six to eight weeks after setting out.

Recommended varieties—Not applicable. The species may be sold as "French tarragon."

THYME
Thymus vulgaris

When to plant—Spring. Use plants that have been grown in containers, or divide existing plants.

Where to plant—Grow in well-drained but not overly fertile soil. Full sun is best, partial sun is tolerated. Thyme also grows well in containers and makes an attractive porch, patio, or windowbox plant.

How to plant—Set plants on 12-inch centers in rows or beds. Erect barriers if you want to distinguish between varieties or control rampant growth.

Water needs—Excess moisture easily damages thyme, so water only if rain has not fallen for several weeks.

Care/Maintenance—Trim thyme to keep it in bounds. When plants become overgrown and woody, take cuttings.

Pests/Diseases—Mites can occur on indoor plants, and are best treated with insecticidal soap (wash them thoroughly before use).

Days to maturity—70 to 90, depending on the variety

Recommended varieties—English thyme, French thyme, Lemon thyme

TOMATO
Lycopersicon lycopersicum

When to plant—Sow or set out transplants at the frost-free date.

Where to plant—Well-prepared, well-drained soil, in full sun, is ideal.

How to plant—Sow seeds of smaller ones in hills 2 feet apart; for larger staked and caged ones, sow 36 to 42 inches apart (put support in place at planting time). Thin to one plant per hill.

Water needs—Supply an inch of water a week.

Care/Maintenance—Row covers will protect from cold weather and some pests. Maintain even soil moisture and mulch. Feed when fruit is the size of golf balls, and repeat every three or four weeks.

Pests/Diseases—Foliar diseases may be prevented by good garden hygiene and watering on the ground; if they occur, combat with recommended garden chemicals. Aphids and mites can be combated with insecticidal soap.

Days to maturity—62 to 78 days, depending on variety

Recommended varieties—'Big Beef', 'Brandywine', 'New Girl'

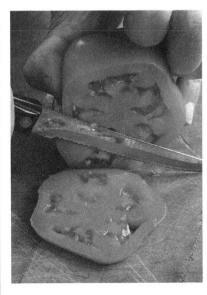

TURNIP
Brassica rapa var. *rapifera*

When to plant—For a spring crop, sow seeds in mid-spring; for a fall crop, sow in midsummer.

Where to plant—In full sun, in fertile, well-drained, well-prepared soil (no rocks or other obstructions).

How to plant—Plant eight to ten per foot, in rows 10 to 12 inches apart. Cover with ½ inch of soil.

Water needs—Turnips do best with regular, consistent watering.

Care/Maintenance—Fertilize at planting, and keep the bed moist. Note that rapid growth leads to best quality. Harvest greens about five weeks, and roots when they are 2 to 3 inches in diameter (roots will become sweeter with the cold; mulch to extend the harvest into winter).

Pests/Diseases—Root maggots can be a problem.

Days to maturity—38 to 50, depending on the variety

Recommended varieties—'Hakurei', 'Purple Top White Globe', 'Scarlet Queen'

WATERMELON
Citrullus lanatus

When to plant—Sow seeds indoors in peat pots a month before last frost. Direct-sow or set out transplants after danger of frost is past.

Where to plant—Site in full sun, in well-drained soil, with ample room to spread.

How to plant—Set two or three plants to a hill, 26 inches apart. Bush types may be grown in large containers. Black plastic mulch is a good idea since it traps soil warmth.

Water needs—Supply an inch of water a week.

Care/Maintenance—Use floating row covers to warm the plants and keep out pests. Remove when flowers appear so bees can pollinate. Support rampant vines.

Pests/Diseases—The main enemy is cucumber beetles—fight them with covers and/or insecticides.

Days to maturity—76 to 89 days, depending on the variety

Recommended varieties—'Bush Sugar Baby', 'Crimson Sweet', 'Sweet Favorite'

ZUCCHINI SQUASH
Cucurbita pepo

When to plant—Set out started plants (in peat pots, because they don't tolerate root injuries well) or sow seeds directly after last frost.

Where to plant—In full sun, in well-drained soil.

How to plant—Place 5 feet apart, in rows 10 feet apart. Provide vining types with a trellis or other strong support.

Water needs—Requires plentiful and consistent moisture, especially after it sets fruit.

Care/Maintenance—Feed at planting time and again when the vines have almost covered the grown fruit (rinse the fertilizer off the leaves). Bees will pollinate, so avoid insecticides or apply them in the evening hours.

Pests/Diseases—Squash-vine borers can be fought with insecticide and/or by slitting affected stems and burying the damaged section so it can form new roots. Other insects and mildew can also be problems—seek advice from your local garden center.

Days to maturity—48 to 50, depending on the variety

Recommended varieties—'Bush Baby', 'Cashflow', 'Raven'

GROWING HERBS AND VEGETABLES

Here's an overview of the year in a kitchen garden:

1. In October or November, or in early spring as soon as the cold and moisture have left the earth, turn the rows by hand or with a rototiller.

2. Then check and adjust the soil pH, and work in fertilizer and soil amendments.

3. Plant hardy and half-hardy vegetables and herbs early to mid-spring (late March and April).

4. Plant warm- and hot-season vegetables and herbs in May and June.

5. As crops mature, harvest the rows; when a row is finished, clear it, fertilize, turn the soil, and replant the rows.

6. In September, October, or November, clear the rows.

LIGHT

Most herbs and vegetables do best in full sun. To provide as much sun as possible, arrange the planting rows in your kitchen garden to run east to west. At the north end, set tall plants, like staked tomatoes, sunflowers, and corn (planted in groups to assure pollination). At the south end, set low-growing things so they won't be shaded by the taller plants. Some cool-season vegetables that bolt with heat—lettuce, peas, and spinach, for example—may produce longer if planted where the shade of taller plants cuts the heat of the late spring sun.

SPACING

If you are starting a new kitchen garden, we recommend creating raised beds.

Raised beds or rows, about 36 inches wide and 24 to 36 inches apart, give you room to work from both sides comfortably and enough width to plant low-growing crops like lettuce and beets in the same row with flowers. When the vegetable seedlings are up, thin them out around the strongest flower seedlings. As the early vegetables are harvested, the flowers will fill out.

Big, rapid growers like eggplants, tomatoes, and summer squash need 24 to 36 inches around each plant. To create a living mulch for these vegetables, plant spreading flowers like sweet alyssum, nasturtiums, and multiflora petunias about 12 inches away. Where mildew is a problem, avoid dense plantings, which cut down on air circulation.

SOIL AND FERTILIZING

To support the lavish productivity of an established kitchen garden, every year before planting season begins it's a good idea to check and adjust the soil pH.

In addition, before planting, work into the top 6 to 8 inches of the soil a generous helping of nutrients. (The exception is nasturtiums.) Use an organic fertilizer such as Plant-Tone®, or an eight-month formulation of a controlled-release chemical fertilizer for vegetables and annuals. (See Understanding Fertilizers in the Introduction to the book.) That will carry the plants through the whole growing season. In early spring before growth begins, scratch fertilizer into the soil around the kitchen garden perennials—asparagus, the strawberry patch, rhubarb, bramble fruits, and the others.

The long-season hot-weather crops, including tomatoes, benefit from a modest additional fertilization during the growing season. Use a water-soluble organic fertilizer such as fish emulsion or liquid seaweed. Prompts for fertilizing are given in the month-by-month pages that follow. In addition, before replanting a row that has already produced a crop, renew the fertilizer.

Planting a cover crop at the end of the growing season renews the organic content and fertility of the soil.

WATERING

Seeds need consistent moisture to germinate and grow. Before sowing seeds, unless the garden is moist from recent rain, water the soil slowly and thoroughly. Use a sprinkler or a hose to lay down 1 to 2 inches of water. Set a coffee tin or other container under the watering equipment to measure the time it takes to lay down that much water, and record it in your garden log. After the seeds are planted, water the area for half an hour or so.

Maintaining soil moisture keeps root systems growing, and big root systems deliver lots of produce and withstand summer drought and heat. Your kitchen garden needs a good soaking rain every week to ten days, or enough hose water to lay down 1 or 2 inches.

In addition, water any time seedlings show signs of wilting.

PEST CONTROL

Integrated Pest Management is the scientific and commercial approach to handling pests, and it includes some old-fashioned controls that many gardeners swear by. Some gardeners report greater success planting tall crops when the moon is rising and root crops when the moon is diminishing, but that's not proven, whereas IPM methods are.

Organic gardeners also report some success with these plant combinations for combating pests:

Asparagus beetles. Try basil, parsley, and tomato plants nearby.

Aphids. Try garlic and nasturtiums nearby.

Beetles. Try nasturtiums near your radishes, beans, cucumbers, eggplant, squash, and tomatoes.

Colorado potato beetle. Try marigolds nearby.

Mexican bean beetles. Try potatoes near beans.

Mites. Try radishes near beans, cucumbers, eggplant, squash, and tomatoes.

Nematodes. Try marigolds nearby.

CROP ROTATION EQUALS BETTER HEALTH

You can avoid encouraging pests and diseases by rotating your crops annually. The rotation rule applies not only to individual species but also to members of that species' plant family.

These six plant families benefit from crop rotation:

- **Cabbage group.** Broccoli, Brussels sprouts, cabbage, cauliflower, Chinese cabbage, collards, kale, kohlrabi, radishes, turnips

- **Carrot and parsley group.** Carrots, celery, coriander, dill, fennel, parsley, parsnips

- **Cucumber group.** Cucumbers, gourds, melons, squash, pumpkins, watermelons

- **Legumes.** Beans, peas

- **Onion group.** Chives, onions, garlic

- **Tomato group.** Eggplant, peppers, potatoes, tomatoes

HOW TO HARVEST AND KEEP CULINARY HERBS

Herbs are most flavorful harvested in the early morning before the sun dissipates the essential oils that give them flavor. Herb foliage stays fresh for a week or so in the crisper sealed in a vegetable bag lined with damp paper towels.

We renew our winter supply of herbs at the end of the growing season by drying or freezing. We use just-picked herbs. We rinse herbs only if they're muddy. Mulched herbs stay clean.

FREEZING HERBS

Pick the leafy tops of parsley and parsley-like leaves (cilantro, for instance), and chop them fine in a food processor. Turn them loosely into a plastic bag, seal, and freeze.

STORING IN OIL

Basil, oregano, tarragon, and the larger leafy herbs tend to darken when frozen. Pick the tiny tender leaves at the tips of the stems, pack them into a wide-mouthed jar, cover completely with good olive oil, seal, and store in the refrigerator. Both leaves and oil are good for cooking, and the oil makes an excellent salad dressing.

AIR-DRYING LEAVES

It's easy to do. Here's how:

1. Pick fresh, healthy branch tips 12 to 14 inches long. Strip the coarse lower leaves and discard. Gather the stems in loose bunches, and hang them upside down in an airy, dry, preferably dark place.

2. When the stems are crackling dry, strip the leaves off the stems by rubbing the stems between your palms.

3. Pour the leaves into glass jars and cap tightly. After a few days, check to see whether moisture has appeared inside the glass. If yes, oven-dry the herbs for two hours at 150 degrees Fahrenheit.

4. Store the herbs in small jars, and write the date and the name on the label.

OVEN DRYING

Spread the leaves out over paper towels, and heat them on Low until crackling dry. The length of time depends on the thickness of the herb and on your oven.

MICROWAVE DRYING

Dryish herbs, like thyme, dry well in a microwave oven at half-power. Experiment with timing when you can afford to ruin a batch or two. Drying moist herbs such as basil in a microwave keeps the color and the flavor, but it's time-consuming. Prop several leaves on crumpled paper towel, and microwave 1 or 1½ minutes on High. A whole branch in our oven dries in three to four minutes.

DRYING SEEDS

Spread seedheads and seeds on screens (try second-hand shops) lined with newspaper, and set them to dry in a dry, warm room until the seed envelopes are crackling dry, about five days. Separate the seeds from the chaff by rubbing the seedheads between your palms over a bowl. Gently blow away the chaff. Spread the seeds out to dry for another ten days.

ABOUT THINNING VEGETABLES

When you sow seeds by broadcasting them, the seedlings come up too closely-spaced to mature individual plants. You must thin the sowings until each seedling has space enough all around to grow well. Seed packets indicate suitable spacing.

Thinnings of the root vegetables such as beets and turnips, and leafy vegetables such as lettuce and spinach, are good raw in salads, and they add nutrients to stews, sauces, and soups. So think of thinning as early harvests of the rows.

We use the thinnings of many vegetables in the kitchen. Here are some examples of our approach to thinning:

Carrots, like most root crops, don't transplant well. We broadcast the seeds over well-worked soil, and cover them ½-inch deep. Germination takes several weeks. Then we thin the plants repeatedly until they stand about 3 inches apart. We use the thinnings in salads, stews, and soups.

Kale thinnings are excellent steamed. We scatter the seeds in a 4-inch band, then thin the seedlings several times until they are 8 to 12 inches apart.

We thin beet seedlings until the plants are 2 inches apart. Baby thinnings are good in salads, but we leave some of the thinning until the extra plants are large enough to cook up as beet greens, which we like even better than fresh spinach.

YOU CAN GROW HERBS AND VEGETABLES IN CONTAINERS

Herbs and vertical vegetables make great container plants. Tidy herbs, like parsley, globe basil, and thyme suit a windowbox and make pretty edgers for tall or short potted flowers. Tomato seedlings perform beautifully growing in pots, planters, and even paper garbage bags.

Shell beans and eggplant climb from a container as readily as from the soil. Small summer squash, gourds, or cucumbers can be trained to a teepee (three or four long poles tied together at the top like a Native American tent). Melons and even pumpkins work, too, but their fruits will need the support of a sling made of a mesh bag or a section of pantyhose tied to the teepee when the fruits get big. Varieties with medium- to small-sized fruits carried high on the plant are more attractive for container growing than are the low-growing, heavy-fruited types.

Some of the perennial kitchen garden plants do well in big tubs and planters—artichokes, rhubarbs, strawberries, dwarf peaches, and columnar apple trees.

For windowbox, basket, and container plantings, we recommend a humusy commercial potting mix enriched with slow-release fertilizer. Mix a polymer such as Soil Moist into the soil, and you'll find maintaining moisture much easier. Where summers are cool, place containers in warm microclimates, in the reflected heat from a south wall, for example.

JANUARY

- Gather your favorite mail-order catalogs for herbs, vegetables, and annuals, and sketch a planting plan. Plan to maximize your garden's productivity by closely spacing the plants and by interplanting and succession cropping.

- If you plan to start seeds indoors, begin to gather the equipment and the seeds you will need.

- Save wood ashes to use as a pH modifier for the kitchen garden. They make lime and potash quickly available to plants.

- Harvest and groom herbs such as parsley you brought indoors last fall. Discard plants that are failing.

- Maintain the soil moisture in herbs growing indoors.

- Add five drops of houseplant fertilizer to the water for herbs growing indoors.

- If you are overwintering herbs not quite hardy in your area in a cold frame, as they days grow longer and the sun grows warmer during spells of thawing weather, monitor temperatures and ventilate to keep the interior moderately cool.

FEBRUARY

- Check your buying plans against your inventory of vegetable seeds left over or saved last year. List what you have, will order by mail, or plan to buy at a garden center.

- When your plan is final, prepare catalog orders and mail them.

- If you plan to set vegetable seedlings out in the garden very early, best gather protective covers now (hot caps, "walls of water," and the like).

- Late this month or early next month, Zone 7 and warm Zone 6 can start the perennial herbs that are slow to germinate or that must be fairly large before they can succeed in the open garden—lavender and thyme, for example.

- Groom, prune, and repot herbs brought indoors last fall.

- If you planted a cover crop in your garden in the fall, turn it under as soon as mud season ends and cold and moisture have left the earth.

MARCH

- In Zones 3 to 5 late this month and next, depending on your climate and the year, start seeds indoors for early beets and turnips. In late March, you can start eggplant and kale.

- You can save seedlings from an occasional night frost by covering them with newspaper, coffee cans, dry-cleaner plastic bags, old sheets, blankets, bedspread, or burlap.

- Cut back by half thyme, chives, sage, tarragon, oregano, and other perennial herbs.

- Maintain the moisture for seeds and transplants—those indoors and those in a cold frame.

- You can start fertilizing transplanted seedlings started indoors when the appearance of two or three new pairs of leaves indicates the root system is growing.

- Protect plantings from rabbits and other pests with row covers or bird netting. A chickenwire fence is one sure way to keep rabbits out. If there are woodchucks, leave the wire loose between posts because they can climb taut chickenwire.

APRIL

- Keep an eye on the rows where you have sown vegetables. When the seedlings start to come up thick and fast, thin the rows as instructed by the seed packet.

- When danger of frost is over, you can set out seedlings of cabbage, cauliflower, chives, onion sets (late April to early May), fennel, sage, and thyme.

- Plant peas as soon as the ground can be worked.

- Plant broccoli and lettuce seedlings or seeds now through early May.

- Before transplanting vegetable and herb seedlings to the open garden, set them in a sheltered spot outdoors to harden off for a few days.

- Keep weed seedlings raked up when very young, then as the good plants grow up, they'll shade out the weeds.

- If rain fails, be sure to water seeds and seedlings deeply.

- Weekly, include a half-dose of water-soluble organic fertilizer in the water for vegetables growing in containers.

MAY

- The classic way to sow vegetable seeds is in shallow furrows (drills) created by dragging the edge of a rake or hoe handle along the planting line. Then you can dribble the seeds into the drills at spaced intervals.

- Harvest asparagus, lettuce, radish, mesclun, and other early crops.

- When cool-season crops are over, peas and spinach, for example, pull them out and compost them. Before replanting the rows, work an application of an organic or slow-release fertilizer into the soil.

- When temperatures head over 65 degrees F., you can set out seedlings of tomatoes, eggplant, peanuts, hot and sweet peppers, and melons. You can also sow seeds (Zone 7) or set out seedlings of lima and shell beans in the month of May.

- Seeds or seedlings of vining plants like cucumbers and winter squash may be sown around a supporting teepee in groups of four to six, or three to five.

JUNE

- Wishing for more space in your kitchen garden? Free up planting space by training your vining vegetables to grow with their heads in the air. Just provide a support, and leave the first stems of eggplant, pole beans, and small squash varieties to it—the plants will do the rest.

- When the weather heats up, the cool-season crops will play out. Peas are over now, lettuces and spinach begin to "bolt;" that is, they grow tall, produce seedheads, and taste bitter. So pull them all up and compost them.

- To encourage your herbs to bush out and be more productive, early on pinch out the tips of the main stems.

- Continue to thin vegetable seedlings.

- Later this month, keep an eye on your corn patch. When the silk is beginning to show, provide a deep watering.

- Weed control is essential! Weeds allowed to mature take water and nutrients from the vegetables they are invading.

JULY

- Prepare to harvest each species as it reaches peak flavor. Some vegetables maturing now must be kept picked to maintain productivity—something to consider when planning your vacation.

- A vegetable garden needs at least an inch of water per week in the summer. The water from a hose hit by July sun is as hot as hot tap water, so run the hose until the water is tepid before you turn it on the garden.

- When tomato plants start to set fruit, drench the foliage and the soil with a water-soluble organic fertilizer, and repeat every four weeks until the fruits near mature size.

- With summer's high heat and muggy air, vegetables become more susceptible to invasions of pests and diseases just as plants are crowding their rows. Thin to let in more air.

- Since many fungal diseases thrive in a wet garden, water in the early morning so the rising sun will dry the foliage.

AUGUST

- It's hot out! Remember that a vegetable garden needs an inch of water per week, by sky or by you.

- In a drought, before pulling up roots of vegetables that are finished, water the garden and then tug the plants gently but firmly. Shake the soil clinging to the roots back into the garden and compost the plants.

- Pinch out basil flowers to keep the plants producing foliage.

- Keep maturing tomatoes, beans, and summer squashes picked to keep the plants producing.

- As the weather freshens mid-month, begin to harvest the herbs you wish to freeze or dry. You can strip basil and other annual herbs, but take no more than a third of the perennials.

- If the stems of your cucumbers and summer and winter squash are rotting and the leaves yellowing, the culprit is the squash-vine borer. Beneficial nematodes and Bt are controls. Next year, plant resistant varieties.

SEPTEMBER

- Keep maturing vegetables picked to keep the plants producing.

- As long as containerized herbs or vegetables are producing, continue to fertilize them at half-strength at every watering.

- When temperatures fall below 65 degrees F., pinch out tomato blossoms to keep nutrients flowing to the remaining ripening fruits.

- If mildew starts or continues to be a problem, clear the bed, rake out the plant remains, and dispose of them in the trash (do not compost).

- Help cold-tender late crops through a cold spell by sheltering them from the first night frosts with row covers or old sheets.

- Clear out the remains of crops that have been harvested, and turn the rows. If you anticipate another six to eight weeks without freezing weather, replant with seedlings of cool-season crops that mature in a short time—lettuce, arugula, mache.

- In Zone 3, try wintering sage, oregano, savory, and other cold-tender perennial herbs in a cold frame.

OCTOBER

- Continue the battle to prolong your harvest! Pick from plants that are still producing, and protect them from the first frosts if you can.

- Beets and carrots must be harvested before the ground freezes. The flavor of mature rutabagas and turnips are improved by a light frost; parsnips are sweeter after a couple of frosts and can winter in the ground.

- Warm Zones 6 and 7 can plant garlic cloves now for harvest next spring.

- Buy a few young basil, parsley, chives, and rosemary plants and grow them on a sunny sill indoors.

- Clear the rows of vegetables that have been harvested.

- Discard any remaining insect- or disease-infected garden debris in the garbage. Where infestations have been severe, turn the soil over; air destroys many of the organisms there.

- In empty rows, plant a cover crop to improve the fertility, texture, and water-holding capacity of the soil.

NOVEMBER

- If your soil is sandy or lacking in humusy material, take the time now to incorporate aged horse manure or chopped composted leaves. There are stables and farms in our region, so locating a source should not be difficult. Or dig in seaweed. Fall storms at sea usually leave drifts on the shore.

- About the only thing you can plant at this point are Egyptian onions.

- Clear the rows of everything but parsnips, which are improved by wintering in the garden. Turn the soil by hand or with a rototiller.

- Maintain the soil moisture of herbs grown in containers indoors.

- Save wood ashes to use as fertilizer for the kitchen garden.

- Basil indoors may be attacked by whitefly. Shower the undersides of the leaves every two days for ten days. If the problem persists, spray four times every seven days with pyrethrum or Neem.

DECEMBER

- Check over your garden log for ideas for the coming season. Look over the accessories for kitchen gardens offered in garden catalogs, then do friends and family a favor by telling them about the seeds, tools, and accessories you'd enjoy receiving. A soil thermometer would be good to have.

- Organize a seed-saver file, so you can organize leftover seeds. Many seeds are considered viable for several years, especially the larger seeds such as beans and squash.

- Groom parsley and other herbs growing indoors. Maintain soil moisture for all potted herbs growing indoors now.

- Maintain the moisture of herbs growing in your cold frame or hot bed for as long as they are growing.

- Continue whitefly alert for indoor-grown basil plants. Showering the plants, especially the undersides of the leaves, may lick the problem.

SHRUBS
for New England

Shrubs wed the other elements of the landscape to the buildings and the trees. Given a minimum of maintenance they provide flowers, foliage, fragrance, fruits, and interesting structures—pyramidal, columnar, arching, rounded, upright, or sprawling.

The leaf-losing flowering shrubs bring color to the garden early in the year. Forsythia turns to gold in March, and the beautiful quinces follow. The spicily fragrant viburnums bloom later. In mid-spring, mature mock oranges perfume our gardens, and the roses described in the Roses chapter come out full force. Summer has its stars, among them shore-loving hydrangeas, and butterfly bush—a prime attraction for those beautiful insects. Daphne fills summer afternoons with perfume. The foliage of some deciduous flowering plants also contributes to the beauty of the garden. When shrub borders are a mass of dark green in summer, the colorful foliage of variegated daphne lightens the overall effect. In cold weather, spirea and the silver-backed leaves of willowleaf cotoneaster, *Cotoneaster salicifolius* 'Autumn Fire', take on a purplish cast that blends beautifully with autumn's russet tones. The structure of the deciduous shrubs is an important winter asset, especially very twiggy plants like the barberries.

A few broadleaved evergreens flourish here, and we recommend them highly because they not only add color, they green the garden at other seasons. Evergreen rhododendrons and mountain laurels bloom in spring. Boxwood can be sheared for centuries, literally, so it's ideal for topiary accents, low hedges, and to edge formal beds. The needled evergreen shrubs we find most beautiful and valuable are included in the Conifers chapter.

WHEN, WHERE, AND HOW TO PLANT

When we are choosing shrubs, our first concern is whether the places we have in mind will suit them as they mature. To develop well, a shrub needs air and space. Small young shrubs may look cozy in a deep, airless corner, but they become cramped as they mature, and can fall prey to certain insects and diseases under the stressful conditions.

Light isn't usually a problem. Many are "understory" plants that developed in partial shade of taller trees, so they thrive in partial sun.

Early spring and fall before Indian summer are the best planting seasons; early spring is best for shrubs that don't transplant easily. Container-grown plants can be set out any time, spring, summer, or fall. Mail-order suppliers deliver some shrubs bare root and in time for spring planting—the roots need to be soaked six to twelve hours before planting. Young shrubs tend to be more vigorous than bigger, older plants that may have been in their containers for some time. Before buying a bargain plant, make sure the rootball has a healthy, earthy smell and is vigorous looking, not irretrievably locked in wound-around roots. When the color of a shrub's blossoms or its foliage is important to you, buy a plant whose flower or leaf color is evident.

A generous planting hole is the best send-off you can give a plant. Make the hole three times as wide and twice as deep as the rootball, and plant the shrub so the crown will be an inch above the ground level. Loosen the soil on the sides, and blend the soil taken from the hole with the organic amendments. Never replace existing soil with potting soil. Half-fill the bottom of the hole with the improved soil, and tamp it down to make a firm base for the shrub to rest on. Then proceed with the planting.

Before placing a bare-root shrub in its planting hole, make a firm mound in the center of the hole. Drape the plant roots over and around the mound and proceed with the instructions for planting a container-grown shrub. To free a containerized shrub, tip the container on its side and roll it around until the rootball loosens, or slit the pot open. If roots wrap a rootball, before planting make four deep vertical cuts in the sides and slice the matted roots off the bottom 1 to 2 inches. Set the shrub in the hole and half-fill with amended soil. Tamp it down firmly. Fill the hole with improved soil and once more tamp it down firmly. Shape the soil around the crown into a wide saucer. Water the soil slowly, gently, and thoroughly with a sprinkler, a soaker hose, a bubbler, or by hand.

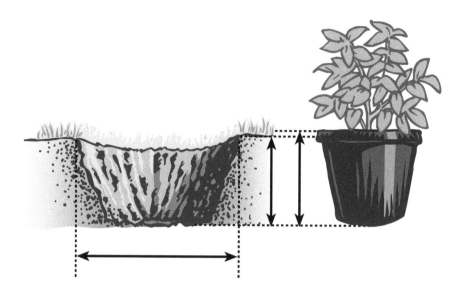

You need to put down 1½ inches of water measured in a regular-sized coffee can, or 10 to 15 gallons of water poured slowly from a bucket. Mulch newly planted shrubs 2 to 3 (for bigger shrubs) inches deep, starting 3 inches from the main stem. Replenish the mulch as needed to maintain it 2 to 3 inches deep.

CARE GUIDELINES

For a shrub's first season, unless there's a soaking rain, in spring and fall slowly and gently pour two to three bucketsful of water around the roots every two weeks; in summer, every week or ten days. Even after summer heat is gone and cold sets in, during fall droughts continue the watering program sufficiently to keep the soil from drying out. Once established, most shrubs will require less extra watering than perennials; they slow their growth in high heat so they adapt unless forced by shallow watering and inappropriate fertilizing to grow when the weather isn't supporting growth.

Fertilize shrubs twice a year. Avoid fertilizing flowering shrubs with chemical fertilizers shortly before blooming: that stimulates growth at a time when you want the plants to direct their energy into flowering.

More complete details on maintaining and nurturing your shrubs start on page 267.

More complete details on maintaining and nurturing your shrubs start on page 267.

MORE OPTIONS

Other beautiful shrubs that flourish here include

- Amur Privet, *Ligustrum amurense*
- Golden Privet, *Ligustrum × vicaryi*
- California Privet, *Ligustrum ovalifolium*
- Bayberry, *Myrica pensylvanica*
- Bush Cinquefoil, *Potentilla frutescens* 'Abbotswood'
- Harry Lauder's Walking Stick, *Corylus avellana* 'Contorta'
- Highbush Blueberry, *Vaccinium corymbosum*
- Inkberry Holly, *Ilex glabra*
- Merserve Holly, *Ilex × merserveae* 'Blue Boy' and 'Blue Girl'
- Korean Stewartia, *Stewartia koreana*
- Oregon Grape Holly, *Mahonia aquifolium*
- Red Twig Dogwood, *Cornus seriacea*
- Slender Deutzia, *Deutzia gracilis*
- Scotch Broom, *Cytisus scoparius*
- Warminster Broom, *Cytisus × praecox*
- Spicebush, *Lindera benzoin*
- Witchhazel, *Hamamelis × intermedia*

SOIL. The ideal container soil is a fertile semisoil-less mix, one part good topsoil, one part horticultural perlite, and two parts coarse peat moss. For every 7 inches of planter height, add ⅓ cup slow-release organic fertilizer, and 1 cup dehydrated cow manure. Adding a soil polymer can reduce watering by as much as 50 percent. Soak the polymer before adding it, and soak the growing medium before you plant. After planting, water until water runs out the bottom. Apply and maintain a 2- or 3-inch layer of mulch.

WATERING. From late spring to mid-autumn, plan to water weekly or bi-weekly. The larger the container, the less often you will have to water it. Containers with built-in water reservoirs, or with water rings that let the plant soak up the water from the bottom, help to keep the soil moist.

FERTILIZING. Once a month during the growing season, add a water-soluble fertilizer, seaweed, or manure tea to the water.

Next season, in late winter before growth begins, top-dress the soil. Tip the container on its side, and gently remove the top two inches of soil. Replace it with fresh fertile potting mix that includes Holly-Tone® slow-release fertilizer, and renew the mulch.

GROWING SHRUBS IN CONTAINERS

You can grow almost any shrub successfully in a container as long as it has good drainage and is big enough to hold the soil needed to protect the roots from our winter weather. Casters on the bottom of the larger containers make moving easier.

CONTAINER. For a small shrub, a container 14 to 16 inches in height and diameter is enough. Start a youngster of a larger shrub, like Japanese maple, in an 18- to 20-inch tub, and plan to move it to a 30-inch tub.

Insulation can keep containers from cracking in winter's cold. Wrap the interior of containers that will remain outdoors with a double row of large bubble wrap or Styrofoam™ before filling them with soil. You can provide added winter protection by packing bags of leaves around the containers in fall.

SHRUBS FOR THE SEASHORE

These plants tolerate salt spray and sandy situations at the shore and inland, too. Most require well-drained soil.

- Adam's-needle (*Yucca filamentosa*). Big, dramatic evergreen rosette of sword-like leaves that sends up 6-foot flower spikes.

- Bayberry (*Myrica pensylvanica*). For Zone 6 and north. Beautiful big shrub with gray-green, semievergreen leaves that are aromatic when crushed.

- Beach Plum (*Prunus maritima*). Round bush that bears clusters of white blooms followed by purplish fruit.

- Hydrangea (*Hydrangea* species and varieties). Deciduous shrubs with huge flower heads in mid- and late summer.

- Inkberry (*Ilex glabra* 'Compacta'). Black berries, usually evergreen, up to 3 feet high.

- Vicary Golden Privet (*Ligustrum × vicaryi*). Small-leaved evergreen for tall hedges.

169

BARBERRY
Berberis thunbergii 'Atropurpurea'

Hardiness—Zones 4 to 8

Color(s)—Vivid fall foliage

Bloom period—Spring (insignificant)

Mature Size (H × W)—2 to 3 ft. × 3 to 5 ft.

Water needs—Water regularly when establishing, and maintain soil moisture thereafter. If you plant it close to a wall where it will miss normal rainfall, watering is especially important.

Planting/Care—Plant a bare-root shrub before the buds start to break. Plant a container-grown in spring, summer, or fall. Slightly acidic, well-drained, loose or loamy humusy soil is best. Maintain a mulch. Fertilize in early spring and fall with a fertilizer for acid-loving plants. Prune to control the height or shape of a hedge immediately after flowering.

Pests/Diseases—None serious

Landscaping Tips & Ideas—Good for hedges, because their spiny leaves and thorns discourage pets and wildlife. Some good varieties include 'Crimson Pygmy', 'Rose Glow', and yellow-tinged 'Aurea'.

BOXWOOD
Buxus spp. and cultivars

Hardiness—Zones 5 to 8

Color(s)—Bright green foliage

Bloom period—Spring (insignificant)

Mature Size (H × W)—4 to 10 ft. × 4 to 10 ft.

Water needs—Water regularly during establishment, and maintain a moist soil thereafter. Boxwood doesn't tolerate wet feet.

Planting/Care—Plant a container-grown boxwood in spring, summer, or fall. Well-drained, humusy, moist soil is preferred. Maintain a mulch to keep the temperature even around the roots. Fertilize in early spring and fall. Protect over the winter with a burlap screen. Prune out elongated shoots in late spring. Reshape overgrown plants by cutting back to within 18 inches of the ground in spring.

Pests/Diseases—Prevent rot and insect attacks by providing good growing conditions.

Landscaping Tips & Ideas—Use as foundation plants, topiary, hedges, or to frame a rose or herb garden. May survive in colder areas with proper winter protection.

BURNING BUSH
Euonymus alata 'Compactus'

Hardiness—Zones 3 to 8

Color(s)—Bright crimson fall foliage

Bloom period—Spring (insignificant)

Mature Size (H × W)—8 to 10 ft. × 8 to 10 ft.

Water needs—Water regularly during establishment, and maintain a moist soil thereafter.

Planting/Care—Container-grown plants can be planted spring, summer, or fall. It succeeds even on dry, rocky slopes; any soil that isn't swampy will do. Maintain a mulch. Fertilize in fall and early spring. Most attractive when allowed to develop naturally with some thinning to keep the plant structure open. To maintain a 4- to 6-foot hedge, cut back branch tips of older wood in spring.

Pests/Diseases—While all euonymus are subject to scale, it's less of a problem with this species and its cultivars.

Landscaping Tips & Ideas—Good for informal hedges or as a featured lawn specimen. Superb planted with evergreens or forsythia.

BUTTERFLY BUSH
Buddleia davidii

Hardiness—Zones 5 to 9

Color(s)—Lilac, white, pink, lavender, dark purple, purple-red

Bloom period—Late summer

Mature Size (H × W)—5 to 8 ft. × 4 to 7 ft.

Water needs—Water regularly during establishment. Soak well every week to ten days if weather is dry.

Planting/Care—Container-grown plants transplant easily in early spring or early fall. Thrives in humusy, fertile, well-drained soil. Maintain a mulch. Fertilize in fall and early spring. In early spring, cut back to 12 to 18 inches. Revival growth will be slow, but it will flower on new wood.

Pests/Diseases—None serious

Landscaping Tips & Ideas—Large ones are best as specimen plants or at the back of a border. Dwarf varieties are easier to place, some small enough even to place next to the kitchen steps. May also be grown in a container and treated as an annual.

CARYOPTERIS
Caryopteris clandonensis

Hardiness—Zones 5 to 9

Color(s)—Shades of blue

Bloom period—Midsummer

Mature Size (H × W)—2 to 3 ft. × 3 to 4 ft.

Water needs—Water regularly during establishment. Soak well every week to ten days if weather is dry.

Planting/Care—Transplants easily in spring or early fall. Best in well-drained, loose, loamy, humusy soil. Maintain a mulch. Fertilize lightly in the fall and again in early spring. It blooms on new wood. In spring, just as the buds are breaking, prune back to within an inch of living wood all the growth that starts from the short woody branches at the base of the plant. Severe pruning in early spring vastly improves the flowering.

Pests/Diseases—None serious

Landscaping Tips & Ideas—Include in your butterfly plantings. A nice addition to mixed summer flower borders. Recommended varieties include 'Blue Mist' and 'Dark Knight'.

COTONEASTER
Cotoneaster apiculatus

Hardiness—Zones 4 to 8

Color(s)—White or pinkish flowers; bright red berries; colorful fall foliage

Bloom period—Spring, summer

Mature Size (H × W)—2 to 3 ft. × 5 to 8 ft.

Water needs—Water regularly during establishment. Established plants handle some drought.

Planting/Care—Set out container-grown plants in early spring or early fall. Succeeds in well-drained, humusy soil, acidic or alkaline. Maintain a mulch. Fertilize in early spring and again in the fall. Minimal pruning is needed, and best undertaken after the berries are over. Keep an informal hedge in bounds with light, selective pruning during the growing season. A formal hedge may be sheared as needed.

Pests/Diseases—Mites (in too-dry conditions) and fireblight are occasional problems.

Landscaping Tips & Ideas—Use for hedges and to clothe slopes, steps, and rocky places with attractive foliage, interesting branching, and bright berries.

DAPHNE
Daphne × burkwoodii 'Carol Mackie'

Hardiness—Zones 4 to 8

Color(s)—Pale pink flowers; foliage is variegated

Bloom period—Late spring

Mature Size (H × W)—3 ft. × 3 ft. or more

Water needs—Water regularly during establishment. Soak well every week to ten days if weather is dry.

Planting/Care—Plant in early spring. Choose a site with protection from hot noon sun and cold north winds. By the shore it may be able to take full sun. Best in well-drained, sandy loam with lots of leaf mold. Maintain a mulch. Fertilize lightly in fall and spring. When it finishes flowering, prune the branches back to outward-facing buds. Where snow cover is uncertain, cover for the winter with evergreen boughs.

Pests/Diseases—Rot and insect pests can afflict stressed plants.

Landscaping Tips & Ideas—Plant by garden paths or anywhere its fragrance can be appreciated.

DECIDUOUS AZALEA
Rhododendron spp. and hybrids

Hardiness—Zones 4 to 7

Color(s)—Pink, rose, rose-magenta, white; wider range of colors in the many hybrids

Bloom period—Early spring

Mature Size (H × W)—4 to 8 ft. × 4 to 8 ft.

Water needs—Water regularly during establishment. Soak well every week to ten days if weather is dry.

Planting/Care—Azaleas are shallow-rooted and transplant well even when quite large. Plant in early spring or early fall, in well-drained, humus-rich, acidic soil. Best in dappled light but tolerate full sun if the soil is moist. Maintain a mulch. Fertilize in early spring and fall with a fertilizer for acid-loving plants. After blooming, prune branches back to outward-facing buds.

Pests/Diseases—Mildew and other problems can occur; get advice from your nursery.

Landscaping Tips & Ideas—Good with broadleaved evergreen shrubs such as rhododendrons and mountain laurels. Especially nice with early-blooming forsythia.

FIRETHORN
Pyracantha coccinea

Hardiness—Zones 5 to 9

Color(s)—White flowers; orange or red berries follow

Bloom period—Late spring

Mature Size (H × W)—6 to 10 ft. × 8 to 10 ft.

Water needs—Water regularly during establishment. Soak well every week to ten days if weather is dry.

Planting/Care—Transplants with difficulty, so plant a container-grown shrub in early spring. A full-sun site with well-drained soil is best. Maintain a mulch. Fertilize lightly in the fall and early spring. Becomes very spreading if not pruned; cut just after flowering. Flower buds form on old wood, so spare some of the flowers for fall berries.

Pests/Diseases—Watch for fireblight, and also for scab on the fruits; seek advice at your local nursery.

Landscaping Tips & Ideas—Can be used as a freestanding specimen or as a thorny protective hedge. Striking when espaliered against a wall or grown on a trellis.

FLOWERING QUINCE
Chaenomeles speciosa

Hardiness—Zones 4 to 8

Color(s)—White, peach, pink, coral, rose, orange, red, ruby red

Bloom period—Early spring

Mature Size (H × W)—6 to 10 ft. × 6 to 10 ft.

Water needs—Water regularly during establishment. Soak well every week to ten days if weather is dry.

Planting/Care—Plant a balled-and-burlapped quince in early spring or fall, a container-grown one in spring, summer, or fall. Best in full sun, adapts to many soil types. Maintain a mulch. Fertilize lightly in the fall and spring with a fertilizer for acid-loving plants. When the blossoms fade, cut back older canes and suckers to the ground.

Pests/Diseases—Leaf spots can occur in wet weather; aphids attack young growth.

Landscaping Tips & Ideas—Makes an attractive informal hedge. Because quince only adds to the appeal of garden when in bloom, it's not ideal for smaller landscapes.

FORSYTHIA
Forsythia × intermedia

Hardiness—Zones 4 or 5 to 8

Color(s)—Yellow

Bloom period—Spring

Mature Size (H × W)—8 to 10 ft. × 10 to 12 ft.

Water needs—Water regularly during establishment. Soak well every week to ten days if weather is dry.

Planting/Care—Container-grown plants transplant readily in spring, summer, and fall. It thrives in full sun, in almost any soil that is well-drained, loamy, and has enough humus to maintain moisture. Maintain a mulch. Fertilize lightly in fall and early spring. To keep in bounds, wait till blooming is over, then cut back mature branches to outward-facing buds, and take the oldest canes out all the way down to the ground.

Pests/Diseases—None serious

Landscaping Tips & Ideas—Use as a screen, informal hedge, or tall groundcover. Attractive as specimen in the lawn, or grouped with evergreens and other flowering shrubs.

FOTHERGILLA
Fothergilla gardenii

Hardiness—Zones 5 to 8

Color(s)—White flowers; colorful fall foliage

Bloom period—Spring

Mature Size (H × W)—2 to 4 ft. × 2 to 4 ft.

Water needs—Water regularly during establishment. Soak well every week to ten days if weather is dry.

Planting/Care—Plant balled-and-burlapped ones in early spring or fall, container-grown ones in spring, summer, or fall. In hot areas, it needs protection from noon sun. It requires acidic soil. Apply and maintain a mulch. Fertilize lightly in the fall and again in the spring with a fertilizer for acid-loving plants. Before growth begins in the spring, cut back old branches to the ground.

Pests/Diseases—None serious

Landscaping Tips & Ideas—Lights up small gardens! A huge asset in shrub borders with azaleas, rhododendrons, and evergreens. Place near the house or along paths where its sweet honey scent can be appreciated.

GLOSSY ABELIA
Abelia × grandiflora

Hardiness—Zones 5 to 9

Color(s)—Pink flowers; purplish fall foliage

Bloom period—Summer

Mature Size (H × W)—3 to 6 ft. × 5 ft.

Water needs—Water regularly during establishment. Soak well every week to ten days if weather is dry.

Planting/Care—Plant in fall before Indian summer, or in early spring while dormant. The ideal soil is well-drained, humusy, sandy, and acidic. Full sun is best, shade is tolerated. Maintain a mulch. Apply a fertilizer for acid-loving plants in fall and spring. In late winter, prune back dead branch tips to outward-facing growth. Prune to restrict its size after flowering is over.

Pests/Diseases—None serious

Landscaping Tips & Ideas—Use as a twiggy asset in flowering borders, or as a bank cover. 'Edward Goucher' makes an informal hedge or handsome specimen. 'Prostrata' is a good compact-growing variety with smaller leaves.

HYDRANGEA
Hydrangea spp. and cultivars

Hardiness—Zones 4 to 9

Color(s)—White, shades of pink, shades of blue

Bloom period—Mid- to late summer

Mature Size (H × W)—3 to 5 ft. × 3 to 5 ft.

Water needs—Water regularly during establishment. Soak well every week to ten days if weather is dry.

Planting/Care—Plant in early spring, in well-drained or sandy soil with enough humus to maintain moisture. Some require acidic soil; some require shade—get the information you need at your local nursery, matching your site to your selection. Fertilize lightly in the fall and again in the spring. Maintain a mulch. Pruning also varies according to type, as some hydrangeas flower on newly pruned branches, some on old ones—get advice about your selection.

Pests/Diseases—None serious

Landscaping Tips & Ideas—Yes, you can alter the flower color (pink or blue) on some hydrangeas by altering the soil pH; get full information on when and how to do this at time of purchase. As for placement, hydrangeas should be featured specimens.

JAPANESE ANDROMEDA
Pieris japonica

Hardiness—Zones 6 to 8

Color(s)—White flowers (some varieties have pink buds)

Bloom period—Spring

Mature Size (H × W)—5 to 8 ft. × 6 ft.

Water needs—Water regularly during establishment. Soak well every week to ten days if weather is dry.

Planting/Care—A young plant transplants easily in early spring. The ideal site is out of the wind, in well-drained, humusy, moist, acidic soil. Maintain a mulch. Remove spent blooms when the plant is young to encourage growth and flower production. Fertilize lightly in fall and early spring with a fertilizer for acid-loving plants. Prune back damaged wood in early spring before new growth begins.

Pests/Diseases—In full-sun sites, it is more susceptible to damage from azalea lace bugs.

Landscaping Tips & Ideas—Because of its rather formal appearance, it makes an excellent foundation plant. Nice in groups with rhododendrons and azaleas.

JAPANESE KERRIA
Kerria japonica

☼ ☀ 🌱 🐝 💧

Hardiness—Zones 4 to 9

Color(s)—Yellow

Bloom period—Spring

Mature Size (H × W)—6 to 8 or 10 ft. × 6 to 8 ft.

Water needs—Water regularly during establishment. Soak well every week to ten days if weather is dry. Established plants become heat- and drought-tolerant.

Planting/Care—Plant in spring or fall. It will flourish in well-drained soil that is moderately moist and fertile. Maintain a mulch. Fertilize lightly in fall and early spring. To keep it shapely, wait till the followers have faded, then trim the old flowering stems back to strong young shoots or ground level.

Pests/Diseases—None serious

Landscaping Tips & Ideas—Use as a wall plant in a cottage garden, or mass in naturalistic plantings or on slopes. Nice where paths intersect, as a marker. The flowers are long-lasting in the garden and in a vase.

LILAC
Syringa vulgaris and hybrids

☼ ☀ ⟡ ⟡ 🌱 🐝 💧

Hardiness—Zones 3 to 8

Color(s)—Shades of blue and purple, white, pink, wine-red

Bloom period—Spring

Mature Size (H × W)—5 to 20 ft. × 8 to 20 ft.

Water needs—Water regularly during establishment. Soak well every week to ten days if weather is dry. Established plants tolerate some drought.

Planting/Care—Transplants easily in early spring and fall. They succeed in open, airy sites in full sun or light shade. Soil should be well-drained, moist, and neutral. Maintain a mulch. Fertilize lightly in fall and early spring. Deadhead to encourage flowering. Regularly prune out the oldest branches and all but two or three suckers.

Pests/Diseases—Mildew is often an issue; choose a resistant variety.

Landscaping Tips & Ideas—Taller ones can be pruned to grow as single-stemmed or multistemmed plants. Classic as lawn specimens, used for tall hedges, and nice lining walks.

MOCK ORANGE
Philadelphus × virginalis

☼ ☀ ⟡ 🌱 🐝 💧

Hardiness—Zones 4 to 8

Color(s)—White

Bloom period—Late spring, early summer

Mature Size (H × W)—10 to 12 ft. × 12 to 16 ft.

Water needs—Water regularly during establishment. Soak well every week to ten days if weather is dry. Established plants tolerate some drought.

Planting/Care—Plant a blooming container-grown plant in spring, summer, or fall. Does best in a moist, well-drained site. Maintain a mulch. Fertilize lightly in fall and early spring. After blooming, prune out older branches lightly. In winter or early spring, remove woody stems that are over five years old.

Pests/Diseases—None serious

Landscaping Tips & Ideas—This is a big shrub that needs a large garden to show off its beauty, such as a specimen position in the middle of a lawn. It's also attractive in a mixed shrub border with weigela, forsythia, spirea, and deutzia.

MOUNTAIN LAUREL
Kalmia latifolia

Hardiness—Zones 4 to 8

Color(s)—White, pink, red, bicolors

Bloom period—Spring

Mature Size (H × W)—7 to 12 ft. × 5 to 6 ft.

Water needs—Water regularly during establishment. Soak well every week to ten days if weather is dry.

Planting/Care—Plant a container-grown one in fall before Indian summer or early spring while the shrub is still dormant. It does best in light, open woodlands. Prospers in well-drained, acidic, humus-rich soil. Maintain a mulch. Provide a light feeding with a fertilizer for acid-loving plants in fall and early spring. Recovers slowly from pruning, which is unnecessary anyway in healthy plants.

Pests/Diseases—In poor, dry soil and full sun, develops leaf spot and dies.

Landscaping Tips & Ideas—Use at the back of shaded shrub borders. Ideal for naturalizing at a woodland edge, perhaps with rhododendrons and azaleas as companions.

PRIVET
Ligustrum vulgare

Hardiness—Zones 4 to 7

Color(s)—White

Bloom period—Spring

Mature Size (H × W)—5 to 15 ft. × 5 to 15 ft.

Water needs—Water regularly during establishment. Soak well every week to ten days if weather is dry.

Planting/Care—Transplant container-grown ones in fall or spring. Takes any soil and adapts to full sun or partial shade. Fertilize annually in spring. Prune dead or damaged stems promptly. Shear back only some of the new growth each pruning to assure some new leaves remain at all times.

Pests/Diseases—Blights, cankers, and mildew can occur; seek resistant cultivars.

Landscaping Tips & Ideas—A reliably tough, long-lived, adaptable, functional plant. Plant as a hedge along walks and property lines, and in the lawn to divide the yard into "rooms." If you want a smaller plant or less pruning, try 'Lodense', a dwarf deciduous form.

RHODODENDRON
Rhododendron spp. and hybrids

Hardiness—Zones 4 to 8

Color(s)—White, pink, rose, lavender, purple-red, yellow, some marked with contrasting colors

Bloom period—Spring

Mature Size (H × W)—3 to 8 ft. × 3 to 8 ft.

Water needs—Water regularly during establishment. Soak well every week to ten days if weather is dry.

Planting/Care—Plant in early fall or early spring. Does best in bright dappled light of tall trees with protection from high winds. Ideal soil is well-drained, humusy, and acidic. Apply a fertilizer for acid-loving plants in fall and early spring. Deadhead. Prune after blooming, removing individual branches that have grown ragged or as required to achieve the desired shape.

Pests/Diseases—Minimize disease and insect damage with good siting and care.

Landscaping Tips & Ideas—Plant in a transitional area to a woodland, backing a border of acid-loving shrubs, for screening, or as rural hedges.

ROSE-OF-SHARON
Hibiscus syriacus

Hardiness—Zones 4 to 10

Color(s)—White, pink, lavender, blue, lilac, deep red

Bloom period—Midsummer to fall

Mature Size (H × W)—8 to 12 ft. × 6 to 10 ft.

Water needs—Water regularly during establishment, and during prolonged periods of drought.

Planting/Care—Choose a young—under 6 feet—container-grown shrub and plant it in fall before Indian summer or in early spring. Provide a full-sun site that is well-drained and humusy. Maintain a mulch. Fertilize lightly in fall and early spring. In early spring before the buds break, prune the branches back heavily to the first or second pair of outward-facing buds.

Pests/Diseases—Leaf spots and various insect pests, including aphids and scale, can appear. Consult your local nursery.

Landscaping Tips & Ideas—Looks great anchoring the corner of a mixed border, fronting a building, or backing a group of shrubs. Can also be used for screening or to create a tall hedge.

SMOKEBUSH
Cotinus coggygria

Hardiness—Zones 5 to 8

Color(s)—Yellow flowers; pinkish-gray plumes

Bloom period—Early summer

Mature Size (H × W)—15 ft. × 10 to 12 ft.

Water needs—Water regularly during establishment. After, smokebush copes with drought.

Planting/Care—Plant container-grown shrubs anytime over the growing season. Accepts soils from dry and rocky to moist and clay-filled; it even handles alkaline and compacted soils. Maintain a mulch. Spring fertilizing is optional. To maintain it as a smallish shrub, cut back stems to the ground in late winter. Protect stems from nibbling rodents by wrapping in hardware cloth for the winter.

Pests/Diseases—Thwart overwintering scale insects with an annual late-winter cut-back.

Landscaping Tips & Ideas—Makes a handsome shrub when pruned, as a specimen, as foundation plants, or as part of a mixed shrub border. The purple foliage is dramatic in contrast with silver companions such as artemisia and lamb's ears.

SPIREA
Spiraea japonica

Hardiness—Zones 4 to 8

Color(s)—Rose-pink; wine-red fall foliage

Bloom period—Midsummer

Mature Size (H × W)—2 to 4 ft. × 3 to 5 ft.

Water needs—Water regularly during establishment. Soak well every week to ten days if weather is dry.

Planting/Care—Plant a balled-and-burlapped spirea in spring or fall; plant a containerized one in spring, summer, or fall. It handles all but very wet soil, and is best in full sun and an airy site. Maintain a mulch. Fertilize lightly in fall and early spring. Snip off stem tips before spring growth begins to maintain the shape and increase flowering.

Pests/Diseases—Though a tough plant, it can be subject to blight, mildew, and various insects.

Landscaping Tips & Ideas—Used to cover sloping beds and banks. The twiggy mass adds texture and color to perennial beds. The 'Goldflame' selection has glorious fall foliage.

SWEET PEPPERBUSH
Clethra alnifolia

Hardiness—Zones 3 to 8

Color(s)—White, pink

Bloom period—Mid- to late summer

Mature Size (H × W)—3 to 8 ft. × 4 to 6 ft.

Water needs—Needs moisture at the roots. Maintain a moist soil (if the site is rather moist, extra watering may not be needed).

Planting/Care—Plant in spring, summer, or early fall in rich, moist, humusy, somewhat acidic soil. It tolerates wet feet, dryish soil, and salty seashore conditions. Maintain a mulch. Fertilize lightly in the fall and in early spring with a fertilizer for acid-loving plants. In winter, cut bare older branches back to ground level, and remove the weakest suckers.

Pests/Diseases—None serious

Landscaping Tips & Ideas—It's a good candidate for wild or wet spots. Other uses include foundation plant, in a shrub border, or along paths or other much-frequented places where its perfume can be enjoyed.

VIBURNUM
Viburnum spp. and hybrids

Hardiness—Zones 4 to 9

Color(s)—White, pink, scarlet flowers, followed by red or black fruits

Bloom period—Spring

Mature Size (H × W)—6 to 15 ft. × 9 to 12 ft.

Water needs—Water regularly during establishment. Soak well every week to ten days if weather is dry.

Planting/Care—Plant in fall before Indian summer, or in early spring. Most prefer well-drained, humusy soils that are slightly acid. Maintain a mulch. Fertilize lightly in fall and early spring; use low-analysis organic fertilizers that don't force or stimulate excessive growth. Shortly after blooming, shape by pruning protruding branches back to outward-facing buds, and cut old branches to the ground.

Pests/Diseases—None serious

Landscaping Tips & Ideas—Plant by a porch, patio, near house windows, or along a well-traveled path so the fragrance can be enjoyed. There are many beautiful selections—match yours to the site.

WEIGELA
Weigela florida

Hardiness—Zone 4 to 8

Color(s)—White, pink, rose

Bloom period—Late spring, early summer

Mature Size (H × W)—6 to 10 ft. × 8 to 12 ft.

Water needs—Water regularly during establishment. Soak well every week to ten days if weather is dry.

Planting/Care—Plant in spring or fall in any type of well-drained soil. Maintain a mulch. Fertilize in spring. Because it blooms on previous year's wood, prune immediately after flowering. Cut branches that have just bloomed, as close to the base of the shrub as possible. To renew, either cut entirely to the ground in early spring or cut out the oldest, woodiest stems every few years.

Pests/Diseases—None serious

Landscaping Tips & Ideas—Older varieties are content to serve unobtrusively in shrub borders or as hedges. The newer, more flamboyant compact varieties are more versatile, fitting happily into mixed borders or serving as foundation plants.

SHRUBS

Regular maintenance of this type, and its timing, is easy to understand and provide. The only little glitch in this rosy picture is—most shrubs need pruning to stay shapely and productive.

When choosing a shrub for a New England garden, make sure it really is winter hardy in your zone. A shrub that is borderline hardy might survive many winters and mature into a handsome specimen, then break your heart by succumbing in an especially bad year. Our winters are uncertain—some years deep snow insulates the roots and keeps the plants safe; other years there's little snow cover, and the soil is bare to a biting cold that can last many weeks. Another possibility is that flowering shrubs planted north of their hardiness zone may grow well enough but not bloom satisfactorily. An example of this type is common forsythia, hardy in Zone 5, which lived in our northern Vermont garden but seldom bloomed. (Happily, some modern cultivars flower reliably in the north.)

DESIGN

Because of a shrub's size and mass, it makes a major impact on garden design. The shrub's structure—the branching and central stems—is the first thing you notice. Some shrubs we tend to think of as being arched (bridal wreath), others as rounded (barberries), others as upright (Japanese kerria 'Pleniflora'), others as drooping (Japanese andromeda), yet others as conical (dwarf Alberta spruce).

You will find your garden most interesting if you include shrubs that introduce considerable variety in structure and size, in flower, foliage, berry texture, and color. A thoughtful mix of evergreen and deciduous types will keep your grounds appealing in all four seasons.

Since few properties can accommodate every shrub you fall in love with, when adding a shrub to your foundation plantings or designing a shrub border, look for species that have more than one asset. In addition to lovely flowers, some shrubs enchant with their fragrance—the lilacs, mock orange, and Burkwood viburnum are outstanding examples. Some broadleaf evergreen shrubs bear beautiful flowers—among them are the rhododendrons and mountain laurel. Some shrubs delight the gardener and the birds with berries late in the season—the hollies and cotoneaster.

PLANTING ADVICE

The best planting seasons are in early spring when the ground becomes workable, and especially, fall. For deciduous shrubs, that's from the time the leaves start to turn in October through November. Evergreens are best planted or moved late August, September, and early October, depending on your zone. How a shrub is packaged has everything to do with when it can be planted. Shrubs are sold bare root, container grown, and balled and burlapped—B&B.

Bare-root shrubs. In early spring before growth begins, mail-order suppliers ship some shrubs bare root. Ascertain the size of a mail-order purchase before deciding it's a bargain since you'll have to pay shipping. Follow the nursery's instructions for planting exactly.

Container-grown shrubs. You can plant container-grown shrubs from early spring through summer and fall into November, when fall lingers. Buying locally allows you to select shrubs whose flower, foliage color, and structure are exactly what you expect.

Balled-and-burlapped shrubs. You can plant B&B shrubs from early spring into November. Evergreens are best moved August, September, and early October. In summer, avoid buying B&B shrubs dug in spring that have been sitting for months in the open air with their bare rootball drying and baking. B&B shrubs dug in spring and "heeled in," that is protected by mounds of mulch or soil, stay in good condition. We recommend paying extra to have large B&B shrubs planted and guaranteed by the supplier.

LIGHT AND SPACING

Many shrubs got their start in light shade under tall trees in a forest or at its edge. So most can do with less than a full day of sunlight. Azaleas, rhododendrons, and mountain laurel do very well in the tall shade at the edge of a woodland area.

Spacing is critical. Shrubs planted at distances that allow plenty of space for the lateral development of branches grow into beautiful mature specimens. To calculate the best spacing for two or more young shrubs, add together the widths given on the plant tags, and divide by the number of plants. To occupy the bed while young shrubs fill out, plant shade-tolerant hostas or ferns, and annuals such as impatiens, pentas, and caladiums.

Soil. The information on Soil Preparation and Improvement and pH given in the Introduction to the book applies to shrubs. Suitable pH varies widely. For azaleas, it's between pH 4.5 and 6.0; for dwarf burning bush (*Euonymus alatus* 'Compactus'),

---

PRUNING GUIDE FOR DECIDUOUS SHRUBS

- **Dead or damaged wood.** Prune any time between late winter and early autumn.

- **Flowering shrubs that bloom on new wood.** Prune in late winter or early spring, well before growth begins.

- **Flowering plants that bloom on old wood.** Prune right after they bloom to avoid removing next year's flower buds that develop on this year's new growth.

- **To encourage dense branching.** Prune during active growth; cut back by half succulent stems beginning to grow lateral shoots.

- **To control height.** Prune after new growth has fully developed. Extend the cuts into the old wood.

- **To slow or dwarf growth.** Prune after the season's new growth is complete.

pH 6.0 to 7.5 is suitable. Most lilacs thrive when the soil pH is near 8.0, a figure attainable in acidic soils by applying a bi-annual dusting of lime; instead of liming lilacs, in spring we sprinkle wood ashes around them—to raise the pH.

You can grow a small shrub successfully in soil whose pH is not perfect because its roots are modest. A big shrub needs lots of growing room and will have an edge if it is growing in soil with composition and pH compatible to its needs.

Digging the hole. Make the planting hole three times as wide and twice as deep as the rootball. Loosen the sides of the hole, and blend the soil taken from the hole with the organic amendments described in Soil Preparation and Improvement in the Introduction to the book. Half-fill the bottom of the hole with improved soil, and tamp it down to make a firm base for the roots.

Set the shrub so the crown will be an inch above ground level. Half-fill the hole once more with improved soil. Tamp it down firmly. Finish filling the hole with improved soil, and tamp it down firmly. Shape the soil around the crown into a wide saucer so water won't run off as quickly.

After planting, water the soil slowly, gently, and thoroughly with a sprinkler, a soaker hose, a bubbler, or by hand. You need to put down 1½ inches of water (see Watering). Or, slowly pour on 10 to 15 gallons of water from a bucket.

Mulch newly planted shrubs 2 to 3 inches deep, starting 3 inches from the main stem. Replenish the mulch as needed to keep it 2 to 3 inches deep.

Growing shrubs in containers. You can grow a shrub in a container outdoors indefinitely—a hardy shrub, that is—providing the container is large enough to insulate the roots from winter cold.

Transplanting shrubs. Spring and especially fall through November are the best seasons to move deciduous shrubs. Evergreen shrubs can be transplanted spring and fall through October. Move flowering shrubs well before, or after, they have bloomed.

MAINTENANCE AND PRUNING

The major maintenance involved in growing shrubs is pruning. Correct pruning and pinching or deadheading enhances a shrub's "habit" or natural form, and it encourages productivity. Pruning a shrub takes thought because when and how differs with each species and variety. We urge you to get a really well-illustrated guide to pruning shrubs and trees.

You can reduce the amount of pruning your shrubs will need by selecting dwarf and slow-growing varieties. This is most important when choosing shrubs for hedges. But even dwarfs grow, albeit slowly, so they may need some pruning to maintain their size.

We prune shrubs with a variety of goals in mind:

- **To rejuvenate.** Prune drastically in late winter while still dormant to rejuvenate leggy shrubs. Take away no more than a third or a quarter of the branches in one season. Make the cuts about a foot from the ground. Repeat the process the next two years until the pruning project is complete.

- **To encourage flowering.** Prune shrubs that flower on the current season's wood—butterfly bush and vitex, for example—well before growth begins to encourage the production of many new flowering shoots. Prune shrubs that bloom on last year's wood—azaleas, for example—when they finish blooming, because they soon start initiating flower buds for the next season.

- **To stimulate fullness.** Prune shrubs when they are growing actively to encourage more, bushier growth. Fresh, young shoots that are cut back by half immediately begin to grow lateral shoots.

- **To encourage branching.** To encourage more foliage in broadleaf evergreens that branch—azaleas and abelias, for example—prune succulent new shoots while they are growing actively back by half. Rhododendrons are different; cut just above a whorl.

- **To limit growth.** Prune leafy plants after the season's growth to reduce the leaf surfaces, which limits the sugar synthesized and sent to the roots, because that limits next year's growth.

- **To top a plant.** Top a shrub or a hedge after the season's growth has been completed to maintain the height.

FERTILIZING AND MULCHING

Fertilizing. A new shrub in improved soil rich in long-lasting organic fertilizers doesn't need fertilizing until the following year. The first annual application of fertilizer should be made before growth begins in spring. The last application should be as growth slows toward the end of the growing season. The number of applications in between depends entirely on the type of fertilizer you are using.

The rule of thumb is to make a final application of fertilizer as growth slows at the end of the growing season—in Zones 3 and 4, usually about August 15; in Zone 5, early September; and in Zones 6 and 7, early September to early October.

Mulching. Mulch shrubs 3 inches deep (no more!) after planting, starting 3 inches from the central stem(s). Top it off as needed to maintain the 3-inch height in spring after fertilizing, and again before summer heat arrives, and once more before winter cold sets in.

Watering. Once established, most shrubs will require less extra watering than perennials; when the weather isn't supporting growth, they adapt by slowing down unless forced by shallow watering and inappropriate fertilizing to grow. Always water slowly and gently, and try to pour on 1½ inches. Set a one-pound coffee can or other container under the sprinkler or the hose, and record how long it takes to put 1½ inches in the can—then you'll know for future waterings.

Newly planted and transplanted shrubs need sustained moisture. For the first eight weeks, apply two or three 5-gallon buckets of water around the roots once a week unless you have sustained soaking rains. In summer, every week or ten days, unless you have a soaking rain, slowly and gently lay down 1½ inches of water. In fall, even after cold sets in, shrub roots continue to develop, so water often enough to prevent the soil from drying out. In fact, one of the most important winter preparations is a deep and thorough watering before the ground freezes.

PEST CONTROL

Weeds. In naked earth, weeds sprout from April to October. Mulch helps keep them out, and the few that do get started are easy to hand-pull.

Critters. Bears harvest the berries of the handsome highbush blueberry (*Vaccinium corymbosum*), which we plant for its autumn color. Deer graze on rhododendrons, arborvitae, hydrangeas, shrub althea, and many other favorite shrubs. Rabbits can girdle stems, especially above the snow line.

Insects and diseases. Choose shrubs that are disease-resistant, and be willing to accept a normal amount of insect damage.

Good garden practices help keep problems away—air, space, light, good soil, and water as needed. Avoid planting shrubs in airless corners. Whitefly and spider mites love hot, airless spots and will spoil the leaves even if they don't do permanent damage. Neem-based products control pests; spray the plants two or three times at intervals of ten days or so.

PRUNING GUIDE FOR EVERGREEN SHRUBS

- Winter and snow damage is best pruned before growth begins.

- Dead or damaged wood on evergreen conifers can be removed at any time.

- Flowering broadleaf evergreens that bloom on new wood, like abelia, should be pruned in late winter or early spring before growth begins.

- Flowering broadleaf evergreens that bloom on old wood—azaleas and rhododendrons, for example—should be pruned immediately after they bloom and before they initiate new growth to avoid cutting off buds being initiated for the following season.

- To slow or dwarf a broadleaf evergreen, after its main spurt of growth, remove up to a third. You can cut the main stem (leader) back to the first side shoots, but don't take off more than has grown the last year or two.

- To reduce the size and to encourage dense branching in evergreens whose growth is initiated by candles (new, candle-like growth), pines, for example, cut the candles back by half when growth is complete. Prune the tips of yews, junipers, and hemlocks lightly any time during the growing season.

- To establish a shape, prune evergreen shrubs and hedges when they are three to five years old.

- Save a little pruning of your evergreens for the holidays.

JANUARY

- Free evergreen branches burdened by snow or ice. Use a broom to brush away accumulations of snow and ice that might harm hedges.

- Take the garden catalogs arriving now to a comfortable chair by a window, and consider what a few new shrubs or a hedge could do for your view.

- Give your out-of-bloom gift azalea a sunny spot on a sill since it, along with mums and poinsettias, is among plants that test high as air purifiers.

- Renew the anti-desiccant spray on broadleaf evergreen shrubs growing in exposed locations. If the winter is very bad, wrap them in Reemay® for protection.

- Remove branches damaged by heavy snowfall and winter storms.

- Water any shrubs wintering inside as needed. Also monitor them for signs of spider mite, whitefly, and other problems.

- Repair or renew deer deterrents and sprays.

- Check and adjust burlap covers and chickenwire cages protecting shrubs.

FEBRUARY

- Moving very large shrubs is a two-year project. Known as root pruning, the process slows growth during the first year by depriving the plant of nutrient uptake.

- Keep an eye on shrubs that flower in early spring. When buds begin to swell, harvest branches to force into bloom indoors.

- Place your catalog mail orders for shrubs now.

- Clear snow, dead branches, and winter debris from shrubbery.

- Prune evergreen branches damaged by winter storms any time.

- Fertilize gardenias and other tender shrubs brought indoors last fall at every second watering.

- As the ground thaws, voles get lively and they can damage young shrub roots. If vole runs appear, bait the main runway with a rodenticide.

- Before buds break on plants that you suspect of insect infestation, spray them with horticultural oil. The oil smothers insects and their eggs.

MARCH

- Fertilize all shrubs before growth begins. Halve the amount of fertilizer for mature hedges; do not overstimulate when you no longer have a lot of room for growth.

- After the last real snowstorm, remove winter covers and winter mulches from protected shrubs.

- To regenerate a multistemmed deciduous shrub that is overgrown, before it begins to grow in the spring, take out a third or a quarter of the branches. Make the cut about a foot from the ground.

- Prune back flowering shrubs that bloom on this year's growth now.

- Save wood ashes to sprinkle over the ground around lilacs to sweeten the soil and add potassium.

- Check the evergreens, and euonymus, for scale, and spray now with ultra-fine horticultural oils if it is present.

- In deer country, apply a new and different spray to vulnerable shrubs such as rhododendron, arborvitae, and other broadleaf evergreens, and replace old deterrents with new ones.

APRIL

- For a shrub's first season, unless there's a soaking rain, slowly and gently pour two or three 5-gallon buckets of water around the roots once a week throughout spring.

- You can transplant container-grown and balled-and-burlapped shrubs now and in the months ahead. Right now the stock at your garden center is likely to be in top condition.

- Repot florist's azaleas, gardenias, citrus, and other tender shrubs that are outgrowing their containers. Don't move them outdoors, however, until the thermometer stays above 60 degrees F. at night, then place them in bright, indirect light for the summer; they'll be happier for it.

- When flowers fade on the spring-flowering shrubs that bloom on last year's wood, prune back older non-productive wood and the branches that are compromising the natural form of the shrub.

- Prune azaleas when they finish blooming. Try for a layered "cloud" look; don't just shear off the branch tips.

MAY

- Spring is in full bloom! It's a wonderful time to visit public and private gardens.

- May is a fine month for planting new shrubs and transplanting shrubs that have finished blooming.

- To keep summer's downpours from eroding the soil around your shrubs, and to protect their roots from heat and drought, replenish the mulch. Make it 3 inches deep, starting 3 inches from the main stem.

- If your watering or spring rains have eroded the soil on sloping shrub borders, shovel it back up the slope, and re-establish saucers around the plants to catch and hold the rain.

- Twice a month, add a water-soluble fertilizer, or diluted seaweed or manure tea, to the water for shrubs growing outdoors in containers.

- If you are using organic fertilizers, the late-winter application is enough until fall. If you are using granular chemical fertilizers, fertilize every six weeks.

- Keep your shrubs free of weeds.

JUNE

- When the color of a shrub's blossoms matter, buy it from a local garden center at a time when you can see the plant in bloom.

- If shrubbery borders look bare, fill gaps with potted flowering maples (Abutilon spp.) and tropical hibiscus (in September you can pot them up and winter them indoors as houseplants).

- Keep the mulch around hedges and shrubbery 3 inches deep to save yourself weeding later.

- Cut the succulent new shoots on deciduous hedges in half.

- Soak newly planted shrubs every week to ten days.

- Check rhododendrons and azaleas for lace bug damage. The leaf surfaces will be dull, speckled, and pale, and the undersides will show dark specks of the insect excrement. Spray the foliage above and below at intervals with horticultural oil or insecticidal soap.

- Keep your shrubs clear of weeds, for if they mature and go to seed, there will be an army to rout later.

JULY

- Before going on vacation, group shrubs growing in containers in light shade; make sure each one has a generous saucer, and water them thoroughly.

- You can continue to plant container-grown shrubs this month. (Don't buy balled-and-burlapped shrubs that have been sitting unmulched and baking at a garden center since they were dug in early spring.)

- After heavy summer storms, check, and if needed, top off the mulch around shrubs and prune out broken branches.

- Groom and prune around the hedges and spring-flowering shrubs.

- Late July is drought season. If you go a week to ten days without rain, water the shrubs slowly and deeply.

- If shrubs fertilized with time-release chemical fertilizer are failing to bloom or looking peaked, supplement with foliar feedings.

- Check lilac for the grayish film that is a sign of powdery mildew. Controls are sulfur, ultra-fine horticultural oil, copper fungicide, and others.

AUGUST

- You will probably need to water all the shrub beds two or three times before September rains. The ideal is to apply 1½ inches of water at each session. Overhead watering is fine as long as you water deeply.

- In Zones 3 and 4, if you are using organic fertilizers, make a final application to inground shrubs as growth slows—usually about mid-month. If you are using chemical fertilizers, you should be fertilizing every six weeks.

- Clear the beds of all weeds; don't let them grow up and go to seed!

- Give hedges their final trimming for the year.

- If you are interested in adding a hedge to your yard, lay it out and order the plants now, so you can start planting when summer heat and drought ends.

- Continue to water shrubs growing in containers as needed.

- Change deer deterrents and spray around in the garden.

SEPTEMBER

- Many consider the period from Labor Day into late October as the best planting and transplanting season for shrubs in New England. It's the perfect time to plant spring-flowering shrubs.

- When the thermometer hits 60 degrees F., prepare to move tropical hibiscus, flowering maple, and other tender shrubs indoors. Hose them down, and then spray them with an insecticidal soap before the move.

- In Zones 5, 6, and 7, if you are using organic blend fertilizers, make a final application now. If you are using only granular chemical fertilizers, fertilize garden and container shrubs for the last time just as the growing season ends (depending on your zone, that will be some time between early September and early October).

- Even after cold sets in, the soil stays warm, and roots continue to develop, so water both established and new shrubs sufficiently to keep the soil from drying out.

- Continue to search for and destroy weeds.

OCTOBER

- The most important preparation for winter is a deep and thorough watering of all shrubs—new, established, inground, and in containers—before the soil freezes. If the sky doesn't provide rain, you will have to.

- When the leaves first start to change color is a good time to dig and transplant, or plant, deciduous shrubs.

- In Zones 6 and 7, the last application of fertilizer can be made in early October.

- In Zones 6 and 7, move container shrubs that are borderline-hardy and still out in the open to a frost-free shed or garage.

- After the second hard frost, cover low-growing shrubs, like dwarf evergreen azaleas, with a light winter mulch of pine boughs.

- For now until next spring, the only pruning you should do is to remove diseased or dead wood.

- If vole runs appear around shrubs, bait the main runway with a rodenticide. They are most active October through March.

NOVEMBER

- It's a good idea to provide winter protection to a newly planted shrub to protect the wood from drying in bitter winds and to avoid damage to the crown when alternate thawing and freezing cycles cause the soil to heave it.

- Protect rhododendrons and other broad-leafed evergreen shrubs growing in exposed locations by applying an anti-desiccant spray and/or wrapping them in burlap.

- To see the beauty of a New England garden at this season, train your eye to discern the wonderful structures nature bares when foliage is gone.

- In Zones 6 and 7, if the weather holds, you can still plant deciduous shrubs that are either container-grown or balled and burlapped. The air is cold, but the earth still has warmth.

- Shrubs need moisture until the plants are completely dormant. Prepare your inground shrubs for winter by giving them a deep and thorough watering just before the ground freezes.

DECEMBER

- Gifts that gardeners deeply appreciate—and never have too many of—are superior pruning tools. Inexpensive ones don't cut well and don't last. Good ones cost more, but with care they last a lifetime.

- After storms, check and adjust the protective covering on shrubs.

- Use only snowmelt products that don't harm plants, turf, and concrete.

- Shrubs being overwintered indoors should be watered as needed. Do not fertilize them until you see new growth late next month.

- Watch shrubs growing indoors for signs of whitefly and spider mites.

- The scent-carrying oils in evil-smelling deer deterrents don't volatize in cold areas. If you see a lot of deer, wrap rhododendrons and other endangered shrubs in chickenwire cages for the winter.

- If vole runs appear around your shrubs, bait the main runway with a rodenticide.

- As soon as possible after a heavy snowfall, use a broom to free evergreen shrubs that are weighed down.

VINES
for New England

Vines create lush vertical accents, invaluable when you want a real visual impact taking up little space in the ground. The leafy greens soften, beautify, transform, and hide problems. You can create an (almost) instant shade garden by training a leafy vine—trumpet vine, for example—to cover a pergola or a trellis. A climbing rose romances a balcony. Ivy greens ugly stumps. Vines climbing wires between the railing and the roof of a porch make a privacy screen. A vine can frame an attractive view and draw your eye to it. You can clothe a barren slope with a waterfall of vines by planting several at the top of a slope and training the runners to grow down. Fragrant vines belong where you can enjoy the scent. Sweet autumn clematis is especially fragrant—it grows like a tidal wave all summer then covers itself with a foam of small, sweetly fragrant white flowers in fall.

Vines grow rapidly—up, down, or sideways, according to how you train the leading stems, and the supports you provide. When choosing a vine consider how you are going to prune it when it gets to the top. How a vine climbs dictates what it needs as support. Vines that climb by twining stems require something narrow such as a wooden post, a pipe, wires, or strings. Vines that climb by twining tendrils or leaf petioles—clematis, for example—require a structure of wires, or wire mesh. Vines that climb by aerial rootlets that secrete an adhesive glue, like English ivy, need only a rugged surface, such as a brick or stucco wall, or a rough, unpainted fence.

Vines that eventually will be very heavy—climbing hydrangea, and wisteria—need the support of heavy timbers, or a dead tree, to hold them up.

Vines hold moisture: make sure the lumber that will support a vine is pressure-treated. Don't set a vine to growing up a wooden wall, because its moisture can cause rot. Allow 3 inches or more air space between foliage and a house wall—vines need air circulation all the way around. Avoid planting vines that climb by tendrils near trees, large shrubs, windows, or shutters.

PLANTING AND CARE GUIDELINES

Cultivated vines can be as invasive as any local weed vine—so plant a vine only where it won't escape into the wild. You plant a container-grown vine the same way you plant a shrub.

The first year, slowly and gently pour two to three bucketsful of water around the roots every week or ten days unless there's a soaking rain. Maintain the mulch throughout the summer. If the vine is sheltered from rain, hose it down now and then in summer—but don't hose it when it is coming into, or already in, bloom. In early spring before growth begins, broadcast an organic fertilizer around the plant and scratch it in. Replenish the mulch if necessary. Repeat in fall.

See pages 292 and 293 for more complete details.

SUPPORT FOR VINES

Vines are versatile in New England landscapes, and can be relied upon to contribute vertical interest for up to three seasons, depending on your selection.

Here are some ideas for ways to use vines:

On a fence: Whether it's to disguise an ugly fence or view, or just for decoration, many vines do very well on fences. Plant at the base and a little away, and train the vine up onto the fence.

On a house, shed, or other building: Be careful! A bad match may mean the vine straggles or damages a building, while a good match makes an enchanting sight. Choose the vine for this job with care and with an eye to how willing you are to intervene as needed to train or prune the growth.

On a tree: This is best done on a dead tree that you'd rather not remove, but still appears stable. Live trees can get choked by vigorous vines, or the vine may struggle to get the sunlight and air it needs to thrive. In general, lighter-weight vines are best for this job.

On a trellis or lattice: Whether homemade or store-bought, a flat support can make a beautiful support for the right vine. Make sure the two are a good match, that the vine is not too vigorous or heavy for the support. Also be sure to anchor or secure the support very well—the earlier the better.

On an arch, arbor, or pergola: Flowering and fragrant vines are especially wonderful on these sorts of stylish supports. Again, make sure the vine is not too heavy for the support, and make sure the support is strong enough for the job. Access is also an issue—at times, you may have to climb a ladder to prune or to harvest flowers or fruit.

On the ground: Some vines with no handy support can make a decent groundcover. English ivy is often in this role, but Virginia creeper and wintercreeper can also do. This could be a good solution for a steep bank or embankment.

In a pot: Smaller and lighter vines can be very pretty in a large pot, provided they are in an appropriate location and that support is close by or even inserted into the pot itself. Remember that potted plants dry out quickly; be diligent about watering a potted vine or it can wilt dramatically. Growing a vine this way, of course, is a way to have one that might not be cold hardy where you garden.

MAKING MORE VINES: MULTIPLY BY DIVIDING

Many vines, including wisteria and trumpet vine, are easily multiplied by ROOTING CUTTINGS of parent plants. Here's how:

1. Prepare a rooting box about the size of a seed flat and 5 to 6 inches deep. It must have drainage. Fill the box with 4 inches of a moist mix of ½ peat and ½ perlite or coarse sand.

With a pencil, make twelve equidistant planting holes.

2. Cover the bottom of a saucer with rooting hormone powder.

3. In early morning, cut a dozen semi-hardened branch ends 4 to 8 inches long at a point about 1 inch below a leaf cluster. Remove the leaves from the bottom 3 inches. Mist the foliage.

4. Working in shade, remove a strip of bark ½- to 1-inch-long on the side of each branch, cutting close to the cut end. Lightly coat the cut ends and the wounds in the rooting powder.

5. Insert the cut ends 2 to 3 inches in the rooting box, deep enough to fully cover the wounds. Press the soil up around the cuttings.

6. Water well, and enclose the box in clear plastic. You can use hoops made of wire coat hangers to support the plastic. Punch a few holes in the plastic for ventilation.

7. Place the box in a shaded, sheltered location. Check the soil moisture every five days; the cuttings mustn't dry out.

8. In about six weeks, test the cuttings to see if they are rooted. Very gently tug on a couple of the cuttings; when you meet real resistance, they are rooted.

9. Transplant the rooted cuttings to pots filled with ½ potting soil and ½ peat.

10. Gradually expose the pots to increasingly strong light while keeping the soil moist. In September, transplant them to the garden, and protect them with a light mulch of hay or open evergreen boughs.

Annual vines and some perennial vines will grow from seed. Some need stratification (chilling) to germinate. Seeds of trumpet vine sown in the fall will germinate some months later. Some seeds are programmed to withhold germination in the fall when they can be killed by winter frosts. They will germinate only after being exposed for a specific time period in the garden—typically four to eight weeks—to winter cold and moisture. Seed packets designate these seeds as needing "stratification" to germinate and tell you for how long. You can sow the seeds now in the garden, and they will germinate in the spring.

For more control of the stratification process, you can start them in containers. Here's how that works:

1. Sow the seeds in pots or trays. Label and date the containers. Cover them with plastic film (plastic bags from the drycleaners, for example) to keep the moisture from evaporating.

2. Keep the containers for the period designated on the seed packet in an unheated garage, shed, porch, or cold frame where they will be exposed to cold temperatures of less than 40 degrees Fahrenheit but safe from snow, rain, and wind.

3. When the temperature climbs to between 45 and 60 degrees Fahrenheit, the seeds will begin to germinate—each species in its own time frame. Once the seedlings pop, remove the plastic, and care for them as you would any indoor-started plants.

4. Plan to have enough large containers for each seedling so you can grow them on until outdoor planting weather arrives in May or June.

ALL ABOUT CLEMATIS

Clematis species and hybrids have a lot to give. The vines are deciduous and climb by attaching leaf petioles (stalks) to their supports. Once established, clematis species expand at a rate of 5 to 10 feet in a single season and will cover other vegetation, walls, trellises, posts, fences, and arbors. The big beautiful flowers of the clematis hybrids are especially lovely planted with climbing roses.

SITE. Clematis vines need to have their heads in the sun, but the roots need to be in cool, moist earth. If the roots aren't in shade, mulch heavily. A site with protection from strong winds is best; avoid hot, dry, airless sites.

SOILS. A pH between 6.5 and 7.5 is best, but clematis tolerates somewhat acid soils.

SUPPORT. Provide a structure of twine or wire for support; use twine or wire to lead the vines to a fence, a tree, or other support.

PRUNING. Pruning affects the way clematis blooms, and the timing is important. When you buy a clematis, ask for pruning instructions.

Prune clematis that blooms in spring on old wood—for example, anemone clematis (*C. montana*) hybrids rosy-red 'Rubens' and white 'Alba'—immediately after flowering to control rampant growth.

In late winter or early spring, prune back large-flowered hybrids like 'Duchess of Edinburgh', a double white; 'Henryi', a large single white; 'Jackmanii Superba', a dark purple; and 'Nellie Moser', a mauve pink. These bloom on old and new wood. Take dead stems back to the ground. Prune weak stems back to a healthy stem and the remaining stems back to a pair of strong buds.

To keep its growth in check, in early spring remove congested shoots of sweet autumn clematis (*C. terniflora* {formerly *C. maximowicziana*}), a rampant vine that bears a froth of tiny, fragrant, whitish flowers on new wood.

BLACK-EYED SUSAN VINE
Thunbergia alata

Hardiness—Zones 9 to 10; grown as an annual

Color(s)—Orange, yellow, white

Bloom period—Summer

Mature Height—to 8 ft.

Water needs—Water regularly when establishing; keep soil moist throughout the growing season, especially during dry spells.

Planting/Care—Direct-sow in spring after all danger of frost is past (or start seeds indoors in peat pots a good eight weeks before last frost). Plant in full sun in moist, well-drained soil. Install a support at planting time, and once or twice a week train or twine the tendrils where you want them to go.

Pests/Diseases—None serious

Landscaping Tips & Ideas—When happy, this vine grows exuberantly, so make sure it has good support (such as string, wire, or a trellis) or you will have a dense mass. May also be grown in a hanging basket. 'Alba' is the white version; 'Suzie' has orange-yellow flowers.

BOSTON IVY
Parthenocissus tricuspidata

Hardiness—Zones 4 to 8

Color(s)—Scarlet fall foliage

Bloom period—Early summer (insignificant)

Mature Height—to 60 ft. or more

Water needs—Water well when establishing, and regularly thereafter, especially during long dry spells.

Planting/Care—Transplant container-grown plants anytime during the growing season. It prefers well-drained, woodsy, moist, slightly acidic soil. Mulch. Once established, it does not need fertilizing. Prune away broken or discolored stems. Control either by pruning lightly and frequently, or by occasionally cutting back hard.

Pests/Diseases—Potential problems include scorch, mildew, leaf spot disease, and scale insects.

Landscaping Tips & Ideas—Though it can handle full sun, it is sensitive to bright light and extreme heat, so an eastern- or northern-exposed wall is best. Train on trellises or lattice panels as a screen. It dresses up chain- link fencing, and is handsome climbing up a tree. Not suitable on wooden buildings (inter- feres with regular painting, leaves rootlet marks).

CLEMATIS
Clematis spp., cultivars, and hybrids

Hardiness—Most are Zones 3 to 9

Color(s)—White and shades of blue, mauve, pink, red, lavender, purple, yellow, plus bicolors

Bloom period—Spring, summer, or fall

Mature Height—8 to 20 ft.

Water needs—Water well when establishing, and regularly thereafter, especially during long dry spells.

Planting/Care—Set out container-grown plants in mid-spring in a protected, airy site where they will be in sun but the roots will be somewhat shaded (they need to be cool—help this by applying a mulch). Check the vines often and prune to train them in the desired direction. Fertilize in fall and again in spring. Different clematis have different bloom times, and thus different pruning times—inquire at your nursery.

Pests/Diseases—Leaf spot and stem rot can occur. Various insects may attack; healthy plants are most resistant.

Landscaping Tips & Ideas—The big-flowered hybrids are lovely paired with open-branched shrubs or roses.

CLIMBING HYDRANGEA
Hydrangea anomala var. *petiolaris*

Hardiness—Zones 5 to 7

Color(s)—White bracts

Bloom period—Spring, early summer

Mature Height—60 to 80 ft.

Water needs—Water well when establishing, and regularly thereafter, especially during long dry spells.

Planting/Care—Set out container-grown plants in early spring, disturbing the rootball as little as possible. It will be slow to re-establish and show new growth. It tolerates salt air and can be used by the sea, but will need protection from direct salt spray. Provide deeply dug, rich, moist, loamy soil. Lead it to its support with soft twine. Maintain a mulch. Fertilize in fall and spring. Prune after flowering.

Pests/Diseases—None serious

Landscaping Tips & Ideas—Ideal for enhancing a high brick or stone wall, as well as trees, arbors, and other free-standing structures so long as they are strong enough to support its eventual bulk.

CORAL, OR SCARLET, HONEYSUCKLE
Lonicera sempervirens

Hardiness—Zones 4 to 9

Color(s)—Red, orange, yellow

Bloom period—Late spring to fall frost

Mature Height—to 15 ft. or more

Water needs—Water when first planted and during periods of severe drought.

Planting/Care—Plant bare-root plants in the spring; container-grown ones, anytime. Likes moist, good gardensoil but is adaptable. Because it has sparse roots, can be tricky to transplant. Choose 1- to 2- foot-tall plants. Space 2 feet apart, 1 foot from the support; a support should be at least 8 feet tall. Prune stems just after flowering or in winter after foliage drops.

Pests/Diseases—Aphids may be attracted to tender new growth; spray them off every day or two with a blast from the hose. Help prevent powdery mildew by thinning out branches for better air circulation.

Landscaping Tips & Ideas—Train a fence or trellis as a garden backdrop or to mask eyesores.

CROSSVINE
Bignonia capreolata

Hardiness—Zones 6 to 9

Color(s)—Red-orange and yellow

Bloom period—Late spring, early summer

Mature Height—30 to 50 ft.

Water needs—Water to establish and thereafter during long dry spells; mature plants are fairly drought-tolerant.

Planting/Care—Plant in spring after all danger of frost is past. It flowers best in full sun, but tolerates shade. Does best in moist, well-drained soil but is otherwise adaptable, tolerating heat, humidity, and wind. Maintain a mulch. It flowers on new growth, so you may cut it back to several feet in spring to renew it. At minimum, prune out deadwood and weak branches. It is not frost-tolerant, so must be grown as in annual in colder zones.

Pests/Diseases—None serious

Landscaping Tips & Ideas—Easily trained on a wall (wood or masonry), porch, fence, tree, or side of a house or other structure.

ENGLISH IVY
Hedera helix

Hardiness—Zones 5 to 9

Color(s)—Evergreen foliage

Bloom period—Spring (insignificant)

Mature Height—25 to 50 ft., or more

Water needs—The first season, water the plants deeply every week in hot and dry weather. Water during droughts.

Planting/Care—Plant flats of rooted cuttings in early spring or early fall in part shade or sun. Thrives in soil that is rich, fairly humusy, and well-drained. Set the plantlets 6 inches apart. Do not fertilize established plants unless the foliage yellows. Shear it back every few years for renewal/denser foliage.

Pests/Diseases—Prevent rot at the base of the vines by removing foliage that is low to the ground.

Landscaping Tips & Ideas—Easily trained on a fence or trellis. Or allow it to climb a wall or tree. Over time, can damage mortared-brick walls. Keep it under control and attractive with judicious pruning.

GOLDFLAME HONEYSUCKLE
Lonicera × heckrotti

Hardiness—Zones 4 to 8

Color(s)—Carmine buds open yellow, change to pink

Bloom period—Late spring to fall

Mature Height—10 to 20 ft.

Water needs—Water regularly when establishing; thereafter, maintain a moist soil.

Planting/Care—Plant in fall before Indian summer or in early spring. Set in moist, loamy soil in the neutral range. Performs best in full sun, but keep the roots shaded and cool. Maintain a mulch. Fertilize lightly in the fall and spring. In late winter, cut out weak, crowded, and dead growth, and trim shoots back to a pair of buds near the main stem.

Pests/Diseases—None serious

Landscaping Tips & Ideas—Perfect in a cottage garden, and shows well climbing archways, fences, arbors, mailboxes, and lampposts. Combined with a climbing rose and a clematis, it makes a beautiful flowering pillar display. Not as vigorous, easier to manage than some other honeysuckles.

HARDY KIWI
Actinidia kolomitka

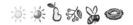

Hardiness—Zones 4 to 8

Color(s)—White

Bloom period—Late spring

Mature Height—to 30 ft.

Water needs—Water regularly when establishing. Once established, they are fairly self-reliant.

Planting/Care—Plant container-grown kiwi anytime during the growing season, in average, well-drained soil. Maintain a mulch to retain moisture and discourage weeds. Annual fertilizing is not needed. Prune in late winter to establish a few main stems and to control the number of subsidiary stems. Cats love the taste of kiwi foliage, so spray young vines with pet repellent and/or shield the young stems with chicken wire until they become woody.

Pests/Diseases—Fungal disease may occur where sunlight is insufficient or in other adverse environmental conditions.

Landscaping Tips & Ideas—Turns an ordinary wall into a showpiece. Needs a sturdy trellis set a few inches out from the wall surface, or a vine grid fastened to hooks embedded in wood or masonry.

HYACINTH BEAN
Lablab purpureus

Hardiness—Grown as an annual in New England

Color(s)—Lavender

Bloom period—Midsummer to fall

Mature Height—to 10 ft.

Water needs—Water regularly when establishing and thereafter when rainfall is particularly scarce.

Planting/Care—Sow seeds outdoors in late spring. It tolerates virtually any soil, but is most vigorous in well-drained garden soil near a post, trellis, or other intended support—provide a place to climb, or it will find one. Space 1 foot apart. Mulch to keep down weeds and retain soil moisture. Fertilizing is not needed. Needs no special pruning. Pick off the seedpods when they start to dry up.

Pests/Diseases—None serious

Landscaping Tips & Ideas—This vigorous vine is decorative and fun. Use to mask a chain-link fence, to create decorative enclosures around vegetable gardens, and to screen out noise and views. Plant them in children's gardens.

MANDEVILLA
Mandevilla spp. and cultivars

Hardiness—Grown as an annual in New England

Color(s)—Bright pink

Bloom period—Summer

Mature Height—to 20 ft.

Water needs—It is important to keep the soil evenly moist throughout the growing season.

Planting/Care—Available as young plants from garden centers in the spring. Pick a site in full sun. Continue to raise in a pot, or plant in rich, humusy, moist soil and fertilize regularly. Keep lush by pinching back the growing tips from time to time. Provide a lightweight trellis or lattice for it to climb on, and tuck or fasten the twining stems to train them.

Pests/Diseases—Scale, whiteflies, mealybugs and spider mites are all possible, mainly on struggling plants.

Landscaping Tips & Ideas—Makes a focal point on a patio or deck. To overwinter indoors, reduce watering as fall approaches and bring indoors to a bright room and treat it like a houseplant until spring returns.

MOONFLOWER
Ipomoea alba

Hardiness—Grown as an annual in New England

Color(s)—White

Bloom period—Midsummer to fall

Mature Height—to 15 ft.

Water needs—Water to get started. Once established, water only during periods of extended drought.

Planting/Care—Because seedlings are tricky to transplant, sow seed directly in the garden after the last frost (cut or scrape the hard seed coating to aid germination). Choose well-drained, average soil in a sunny spot. Soil that is too rich will favor foliage at the expense of flowers. Prune only if it exceeds its bounds. In fall, when frost kills it, pull down the dead stems.

Pests/Diseases—None serious

Landscaping Tips & Ideas—It twines with abandon on fences, arbors, and trellises. It is useful for covering landscape eyesores such as decaying stumps, drainpipes, and utility boxes. If placed near a doorway or an arbor so people can enjoy the scent, all the better.

MORNING GLORY
Ipomoea tricolor

Hardiness—Grown as an annual in New England

Color(s)—Blue, red, white, purple, bicolors

Bloom period—Summer

Mature Height—10 to 12 ft.

Water needs—Water to get started, and thereafter when weather turns dry.

Planting/Care—Sow seed in spring after last frost (because the seeds germinate slowly, soak them in warm water or nick or scrape them beforehand). Average, well-drained soil is fine, and sun is a must. Plant them a few inches from their support and stop by often to direct their ascent. Redirect or cut back wandering stems.

Pests/Diseases—None serious

Landscaping Tips & Ideas—A popular choice for easy coverage of a trellis or fence. Can be trained on string or thin wire. Aptly named 'Heavenly Blue' has nice, large flowers; those of 'Scarlett O'Hara' are bright red. They don't mix easily with other plants—they will ramble through and eventually overwhelm most flower bed favorites.

SWEET AUTUMN CLEMATIS
Clematis paniculata

Hardiness—Zones 5 to 9

Color(s)—White

Bloom period—Midsummer to mid-fall

Mature Height—15 to 20 ft.

Water needs—Water regularly to establish; soak well in prolonged dry spells.

Planting/Care—Set out container-grown plants in mid-spring in a protected, airy site where they will be in sun but the roots will be somewhat shaded (they need to be cool—help this by applying a mulch). Check the vines often and prune to train them in the desired direction. Fertilize in fall and again in spring.

Pests/Diseases—None serious

Landscaping Tips & Ideas—For a good privacy screen on a fence or porch, or for thorough coverage of an arbor, this beautiful vine is ideal. Position where its fragrant blooms can be savored and its decorative seedpods that follow can be enjoyed.

SWEET PEA
Lathyrus spp.

Hardiness—Grown as an annual in New England

Color(s)—White, shades of purple and pink, bicolors

Bloom period—Early summer—hotter weather brings blooming to a halt

Mature Height—6 to 8 ft.

Water needs—Maintain a moist soil throughout the growing season.

Planting/Care—Sow seeds outdoors in spring, or indoors a few weeks early (presoak the seeds or nick the hard seed coats to hasten germination). As the stems elongate, provide support and training. Tear them out when they are spent.

Pests/Diseases—Prolonged damp weather or soggy soil can lead to fungal diseases and bud drop.

Landscaping Tips & Ideas—Sweet peas attach easily to supports with grasping tendrils, which appear quickly, so install a support or guiding string at planting time. Beautiful on any sort of trellis, lattice, or fence. Position where the lovely fragrance can be enjoyed. Pinch back tops to encourage strong side-growth.

TRUMPET VINE
Campsis radicans

Hardiness—Zones 4 to 9

Color(s)—Orange, yellow, red

Bloom period—Spring to early fall

Mature Height—10 to 25 ft.

Water needs—Water regularly when establishing. Do not allow the roots to dry out in summer.

Planting/Care—Set out container-grown plants in early to mid-spring, or in early fall. Grows anywhere in almost any soil or light, but flowers best when positioned against a warm wall in full sun. Maintain a mulch, and replenish it every spring. Prune in early spring, taking out the secondary stems back to a few buds to encourage new flowering spurs.

Pests/Diseases—None serious

Landscaping Tips & Ideas—Really doesn't need companion plants. Give it solid support. It grows into a floriferous, heavy green roof for a pergola or terrace. Can also be used to soften corners, hide drainpipes, and screen ugly structures.

VIRGINIA CREEPER
Parthenocissus quinquefolia

Hardiness—Zones 3 to 9

Color(s)—Crimson foliage with blue berries in fall

Bloom period—Early summer (insignificant)

Mature Height—30 to 70 ft.

Water needs—Water regularly when establishing and thereafter when rainfall is particularly scarce.

Planting/Care—Plant in fall before Indian summer or in early spring while still dormant. It tolerates pollution, city life, almost any soil. Set the crown an inch above soil level, and tie it to the structure that will support it with some soft twine. Broadcast a little organic fertilizer over the planting area. Maintain a mulch.

Pests/Diseases—Mildew, leaf spots, and various insects can occur.

Landscaping Tips & Ideas—Have it cover unsightly objects or clothe a dull wall, especially in a spot where its fall coloration can be enjoyed. It can damage masonry and, if you decide to remove it, the traces are hard to wipe out.

WISTERIA
Wisteria floribunda

Hardiness—Zones 4 to 8

Color(s)—Pink, purple, lilac, white

Bloom period—Spring

Mature Height—30 to 50 ft.

Water needs—Water regularly when establishing and thereafter when rainfall is particularly scarce.

Planting/Care—Set out a container-grown plant in early mid-spring while the vine is still dormant. Provide soil that is deeply dug and well-drained. With soft twine, tie the stem(s) to a strong support. Fertilize annually in early spring. Prune back ruthlessly to the desired branching structure and to inspire bloom. When it reaches the desired height, cut back main stems so laterals will develop, and tie/train these to the support.

Pests/Diseases—Various diseases and insects can attack, especially stressed plants.

Landscaping Tips & Ideas—A strong support, such as a pillar or arbor, is key because a mature plant is heavy. Beware: it can invade and damage attics and gutters. It can destroy trees.

VINES

Vines soften bare corners, dress up balconies, clothe naked walls, and hide eyesores without taking up a lot of space on the ground. For the amount of foliage it produces, a vine requires relatively little watering. Most vines will grow up, down, or sideways, according to how you train the leading stems and the supports you provide.

Caution: Even cultivated vines can be as invasive as weed vines—so plant even the vines we recommend only where they won't escape and invade native plants.

Perennial vines. Generally deep-rooted, the perennial vines grow vigorously and thrive for years rooted in a modest planting hole or a large planter or tub. Cold hardiness in your area has to be there in a perennial vine. The top of the vine will be up in the wind, so you want to make sure it will withstand the coldest winters your region can throw at it. If a vine's cold-hardiness is doubtful, place it where it will have the protection of a north-facing wall at its back. Most are heavy when mature and need a strong support.

An evergreen vine is a good choice when you want year-round greening and screening. A deciduous vine is a better choice when you want summer screening coupled with access to sun in winter. While a perennial vine's major contribution is its foliage, some maximize your investment. Wisteria and sweet autumn clematis produce masses of blooms and add a sweet fragrance to the garden. Climbing hydrangea produces flowers, and the foliage takes on a nice color in fall. (One of the most beautiful of all vines, the climbing hydrangea takes its time growing, rare for most vines.)

Annual vines. The annual vines grow at the speed of light—instant effect. That gives you an opportunity to see whether a vine is the right answer to a given situation. Annual vines are useful for summer screening, and they're also good choices to clothe walls and fences that will need repainting periodically. Most annual vines need only light support. Many are easily grown from seed planted in spring. Where the growing season is short, the annual vines are usually started indoors early or purchased as seedlings. Some have fragrance, such as sweet peas, for example; the lovely hyacinth bean is somewhat scented, and its handsome purple pods are edible when boiled to a mush.

Tropical and semi-tropical vines. In late spring, tropical vines like passion flower, mandevilla, and bougainvillea are sold in big pots already blooming. They're great accent plants for patios and porches. Perennial in warm climates, they can live through winter in a greenhouse or a bright window as houseplants, or in a frost-free attached garage or root cellar.

TRAINING, PLANTING, AND MAINTENANCE

Training. Vines need supports. How a vine climbs—the plant parts it uses to hold itself to advancing positions—dictates the type of support it needs. When you are choosing a vine, that's an important consideration. Cross vine climbs by twining itself around its support. Climbing hydrangea uses aerial rootlets to cling to its next position. Clematis holds on with twisting leaf-stalks (petioles).

Perennial vines also require pruning in spring, summer, autumn, and winter. You prune a new vine lightly the first year or two to direct its growth and develop a graceful framework. Then you prune it annually to control growth and encourage flowering. So another important consideration when you are choosing a vine is how you will prune it when it gets up on whatever you want it to climb.

Caution: Don't plant a vine where it can get into shutters, gutters, windows, the attic, or other areas of your house. Vines get into things. It's their nature. They grow over things. That's their nature. Don't plant a vine near trees or large shrubs; if you fail to keep a vine pruned, it will smother everything within reach.

Planting and maintenance. Vines, like shrubs, are sold bare root and also as container-grown plants and are planted and maintained much like shrubs.

Because a vine makes considerable growth in a single season, the best time to plant one is early spring before growth gets underway. A perennial vine can be planted in fall after it has been dormant and cut back.

Transplanting vines. You can transplant a perennial vine planted a year or two ago fairly easily. Before you dig it up, cut the stems back to within 2 or 3 feet from the crown, and tie them together. If the vine is a flowering plant, move it shortly after it blooms to avoid cutting off next year's blooms.

PRUNING VINES

We can't give instructions for pruning vines that will apply to all. Wisteria requires special handling, as do some others. But to keep all vines healthy and good looking, remove dead, extraneous, or weak wood. Prune large, fast-growing vines severely every year.

When to prune depends on the plant itself. The rule of thumb is, before growth begins, prune flowering vines that bloom on wood that grows in the current year. Prune flowering vines that bloom in spring on last year's wood right after the flowers fade. Prune vines that do not flower in summer right after the major thrust of seasonal growth. Avoid pruning in the fall: wounds heal slowly then and pruning stimulates growth, which may come too late to harden off before the first frosts. It isn't necessary to paint, tar, or otherwise cover a pruning cut.

Perennial vines need a regular schedule of pruning to lead the branches in the direction you want them to grow and to contain their growth. Those vines that flower on last year's growth—spring bloomers usually—should be pruned as soon as they finish blooming in late spring or early summer. Flowering vines that bloom on new wood are pruned before they begin to grow, and that means pruning in late winter or early spring; they usually bloom late in the season.

MORE ABOUT PRUNING VINES

All vines need pruning to develop a strong beautiful framework and to enhance production. But the rules vary with the vine. Wisteria needs pruning two or three times a year; clematis varieties have individual pruning requirements. Here are some general guidelines:

- Prune a newly-planted vine lightly the first year or two to direct its growth so that it develops a graceful framework.

- Prune all vines to remove dead, extraneous, or weak wood now and then throughout the growing season.

- Prune large, fast-growing rampant vines like trumpet creeper and sweet autumn clematis severely in spring and again as needed. When depends on the plant.

- In late winter and spring, prune flowering vines that bloom on new wood. These typically bloom late in the season. Any time just after the coldest part of the season and before growth begins is good. Cut back shoots that bloomed last year to a strong bud(s) near the base of the shoot, leaving the framework of the vine intact.

- In late spring and early summer, right after the flowers fade, prune flowering vines that bloom on wood produced last year. These bloom in spring. Cut branchlets that have flowered back to strong replacement shoots or buds; they will carry the next year's flowers. That gives the plant time to mature the wood that will flower the following year.

- In summer, prune vines grown for their foliage—like ivy— right after the major thrust of seasonal growth. It's best to avoid pruning vines in fall. The wounds heal more slowly, and pruning may stimulate growth, which could come too late to harden off before the first frost.

VINES & THEIR SUPPORTS

The plant part each vine uses to attach itself to its support tells you what type of support it will need. The support it will need tells you whether a vine is suited to the job you have planned for it. The table of plants in the introduction to this chapter indicates which uses which. There are variations, but here's the general idea:

Twining stems. For vines that climb by twining stems, cross vine and wisteria, for example, suitable supports are narrow—a slim but strong post, a pipe, or wires.

Tendrils (twisting petioles). Vines that climb by twisting tendrils—clematis, for example—require a structure of wires or wire mesh to climb on.

Clinging aerial rootlets. Vines that climb by aerial rootlets that secrete an adhesive glue, like English ivy, need only a rugged surface, such as a brick or stucco wall or a rough, unpainted fence for support.

However they climb, vines that eventually will be very heavy—like climbing hydrangea, bittersweet, trumpet vine, and wisteria—need very strong supports to hold them up.

Vines hold a lot of moisture. It is essential that the lumber you buy to create their support be pressure-treated.

JANUARY

- Winter winds are going to keep blowing for weeks, so check and adjust the ties and support of mature vines. Tie down branches whipping in the wind. Free lower branches buried in snow.

- Take your garden catalogs to a window with a view of the garden, and consider whether plantings of vines can solve problems or make some tired old things new. Imagine a vine blooming on a garage corner, the garden shed, hiding a tree stump, or covering an unsightly garden structure. Resolve to try a fast-growing annual climber such as hyacinth bean, moonflower, or morning glory.

- Late this month or in February, sow seeds in a cold frame or hot bed for vines that need to be stratified (chilled) to germinate. You can multiply trumpet vine this way.

- Prune away broken vine branches.

- Water cold-tender vines wintering in containers in a shed or garage often enough to keep the soil slightly damp.

FEBRUARY

- Start seeds of annual vines late this month or next, about eight to ten weeks before the outdoor air warms to 60 degrees F. Annuals such as morning glory and many of the perennial vines grow readily from seed.

- If you plan to move a mature vine, root-prune it when the ground becomes workable, to prepare it for the change. A vine that has been in the ground a year or two can be moved any time before growth begins.

- Place your order for mail-order catalog plants this month.

- When the weather permits, prune weak stems of big-flowered clematis, including the Jackmanii group, back to a healthy stem. Take dead stems back to the ground. Prune the remaining stems back to a pair of strong buds.

- When the ground thaws, check the soil moisture of vines growing under overhanging structures. If the soil is not frozen, and if it is dry, water the plants.

MARCH

- Continue watering seedlings started indoors. Water your vines wintering in containers in a shed or garage often enough to keep the soil slightly damp.

- Vines hold moisture, so make sure the lumber you acquire to make a support for a vine is pressure-treated; untreated wood rots in the presence of constant moisture.

- Before growth begins, prune back vines that will bear flowers on shoots that will develop this year. Remove wandering and crowded shoots of sweet autumn clematis and trumpet vine; they bloom on new wood late in the growing season.

- Make sure the soil of vines growing under overhangs and pergolas has sufficient moisture.

- Fertilize your vines. If you are using organic fertilizers, apply four to six weeks before growth begins. If you are using chemical fertilizers, apply them just before growth begins.

- Apply a new and different spray to vines that deer come to browse on.

APRIL

- As the flowering vines come into bloom, record those dates in your garden log as prompts for next year's pruning dates.

- The ground is usually ready for planting in early April in warm Zone 7, toward the end of April in Zone 6, and in May in cooler gardens. Now through May are excellent vine-planting times.

- When you have prepared the soil for this year's growth, replenish the mulch.

- Sweet peas are cool-weather plants. When the weather permits, string supports for them and start seeds indoors in individual peat pots.

- Check and repair supports for vines. Provide training wires or strings for annual vines.

- Maintain the soil moisture of seedlings started indoors and of vines wintering in containers in a shed or garage.

- Pinch out the tips of leggy seedlings, and transplant the bigger ones to larger pots if the weather is still too cold for transplanting out to the garden.

MAY

- Check out your garden centers' offerings of tropical and semi-tropical vines—like mandevilla and bougainvillea. They're great accent plants for patio or porch.

- When the weather warms, move seedlings started indoors to a protected, shaded spot outdoors to harden off for a week or so, and then transplant them to the garden.

- When vines start to grow vigorously, carry twine with you out to the garden, and tie new shoots to training strings or wires headed in the direction you want them to follow.

- Early this month, move overwintered tropical and semi-tropical vines back to their spot outdoors. Remove the top 2 inches of soil in the pot, and replace it with compost and a slow-release fertilizer in an eight-month formulation.

- Check the new shoots on all vines; cut back to the main framework all shoots not headed in the direction you intend.

- Prune—deadhead and pinch back—vines that have finished blooming.

JUNE

- Good-sized container-grown vines may be on sale this month, so make a point of visiting the garden centers.

- Top up the mulch around your vines. Make sure the roots of the clematis vines have enough mulch to stay cool. The heads can be in sun, but the roots need to be cool.

- As blooms fade, lightly prune stems and shoots of vines that have finished blooming.

- Sweet peas tend to yellow when summer comes—pull the roots up and compost them. The vines add nitrogen to the soil, as do all legumes. A leafy annual vine, Dutchman's pipe, for example, would be a good follow-on plant, or you can plant seedlings of large marigolds. If you grow sweet peas in the kitchen garden, a good follow-on crop is a big leafy vegetable such as kale.

- Check the moisture level in vines growing in containers; even if it rains, their foliage keeps the rain from the soil beneath.

JULY

- Prune and retie new shoots of vigorous vines to keep the plants growing in the directions that will improve the framework.

- Wisteria needs pruning two or three times a year to keep its exuberant growth in bounds and to make it produce a sumptuous show of flowers. Trumpet creeper can use an extra trim when it gets unruly. The time to do it is soon after the blooms begin to fade. Prune both to establish the framework and to encourage flowering. Cut the long lateral (side) branches back to two or three buds. You will need to prune again in the fall.

- Many vines, including wisteria and trumpet creeper, can be multiplied by rooting cuttings taken now.

- Vines sheltered from rain benefit from being hosed down now and them in summer. But don't hose a vine when it is coming into, or already in, bloom as that may bruise flowers that are open and make them soggy.

AUGUST

- Summer heat and drought reveal the vulnerabilities of plants, sites, and your annual soil maintenance efforts. Young vines whose leaves are showing crisped edges here and there may need more consistent watering.

- After summer thunderstorms, check the vines and make sure they are securely fastened to their supports.

- By now, aggressive vines like sweet autumn clematis, trumpet creeper, and wisteria will have made a lot of new growth. Prune to thin excess growth and to keep the main stems developing a desirable framework.

- This month is usually dry, so expect to compensate for the missing rain by watering your vines every week to ten days. Put down 1½ inches of water at each session.

- If vines fertilized with a time-release chemical fertilizer are failing to grow as expected, supplement with a foliar feeding of water-soluble organic or fast-acting liquid fertilizers.

- Now and then, hose down and water the vines that are sheltered from rain.

SEPTEMBER

- Now and as the first leaves begin to fall is an excellent planting season for vines and their companion plants. Warm Zone 7 gardeners can plant into October.

- When temperatures head below 60 degrees F., move cold-tender and tropical vines to a greenhouse or try them as houseplants. Or move them to a frost-free shed, attached garage, or root cellar.

- Give wisteria its second trim now or in October. Cut the laterals back again, leaving only two or three buds to each shoot.

- If your vines are sheltered from rain, even when rainfall is plentiful, make sure the soil doesn't dry out.

- If you are using organic-blend fertilizer, fertilize your vines for the last time this month. If you are using chemical fertilizers, do it by the end of this month or early next month.

- Weed around vines, scratching up the soil so that fall rains can give the plants a deep watering.

OCTOBER

- Continue to divide, move, and transplant vines.

- Limit any pruning to removing dead or diseased material.

- Check the soil around vines sheltered from rain, and make sure it's moderately damp. The roots are still growing even if the air is good, and water is essential.

- If you are using organic fertilizers and didn't feed your vines last month, do it now. If you are using only chemical fertilizers, the last fertilization should be before the final weeks of Indian summer. If you are using time-release fertilizers, a spring application of an eight-month formulation should carry the plants through the end of the growing season—no fertilizer need be added at this time.

- Apply or change whatever deer deterrents you are using.

NOVEMBER

- Before the first anticipated hard freeze, water all your vines slowly, deeply, and thoroughly.

- In deer country, wrap susceptible evergreen vines with Reemay®, or circle them with bird netting or chickenwire cages. Change whatever deer deterrents you are using.

- Harvest strands of clematis several feet long while they are still pliant, prune away small shoots, and twine the stems into a circle to make a wreath. Tie the circle with raffia and let the wreath dry, and then you can use it as is or use raffia to tie on dried herbs, flowers, or seedheads from your ornamental grasses.

- If you have unplanted containers of vines, water them thoroughly, and sink the pots up over the container rims in empty spaces in the kitchen garden or elsewhere. With a winter mulch of evergreen boughs, they should still be good to go in late winter when the ground dries for planting.

DECEMBER

- Planting is over for this year. Take the time to assess what did and did not grow well for you last year, and consider whether to move or replace vines.

- Prune wisteria laterals back again if you haven't done it a second or third time. Leave only two or three buds to each shoot.

- Peruse garden catalogs to see if there are any new pruning tools that would make your job easier next year. Family and friends would probably appreciate knowing your holiday gift wishes.

- Keep the soil for tropical and semi-tropical vines wintering indoors moderately damp.

- The scent-carrying volatile oils in deer deterrents don't volatize in cold air. If you are concerned, wrap still-green vines in Reemay® for the winter.

- Nothing left to fertilize this month. Be sure any leftover fertilizers are tightly sealed and stored away from children and pets.

TREES
for New England

A tree is such a large presence in a landscape, its every aspect—habit, color, and texture—can contribute to your pleasure in fall and winter as well as in spring and summer. In this chapter we have included large and small deciduous trees, trees we plant for their flowers, for fall foliage color, and for beauty of bark and form. Needled evergreen trees and shrubs can be found in the Conifers chapter.

In choosing a tree, beauty is the first thing we look for, and we think of foliage. A maple's flaming fall color can be breathtaking. But when the leaves go, it's the bark, bole, and branch structure that lend beauty to your garden view. Imagine white birches against a stand of evergreens.

A tree's silhouette, whether columnar, pyramidal, oval, vase-shaped, round, clumping, or weeping, also makes a deep impression. By repeating the same silhouette, color, and texture—the symmetry of paired blue spruces flanking an entrance, or an allée of columnar flowering apple trees—you create an air of gracious formality.

By combining a variety of forms, such as a symmetrical incense cedar and a stylized Serbian spruce with a wide-branching maple and a clump of birches, you create a natural, informal effect, adding a hint of mystery and a little excitement.

When it's shade we need, we look to wide-branched trees whose silhouettes are oval, pyramidal, vase-shaped, or round. Maples and oaks are excellent shade trees, and some evergreens make good shade trees too—hemlocks, for example. Limbed-up, small flowering trees can provide all the shade a small urban garden needs—take dogwoods and some flowering fruit trees, for example.

For style and for the fun of something different, we look to columnar trees. Many species now are offered in this form—red maple, European hornbeam, beech, and apple. 'Princeton Sentry'® is a beautiful columnar ginkgo. Small columnar forms even grow well in big tubs, adding style to patios, roof gardens, and decks.

For romance, grace, and movement, weeping trees are tops. They're especially effective planted where their drooping branches will be reflected in water. The graceful weeping willow loves wet places. A weeping birch or a weeping beech, or the gorgeous weeping crabapple 'Red Jade', can be very beautiful. And weeping varieties of the flowering and the kousa dogwoods are lovely.

To create a seasonal parade that is a true delight, we plant small flowering trees. The flowering fruit trees—almond, plum, cherry, pear, crabapple, apple—open the season. Some flowering trees bear colorful fruits—the fruits of the dogwoods and flowering crabapples are among many that attract birds.

For more choices than those we offer in this chapter, look into some of the tall shrubs in the Shrubs chapter—lilac, rose-of-Sharon, hydrangea, viburnum, and shrubs that can be trained as trees, or standards. Dwarf fruiting trees make pretty specimens too: dwarf apple, pear, peach, and plum. A few big trees rival the show staged by the small flowering trees. In early spring the maples are outlined in tiny garnet-red buds. In summer a mature Japanese pagoda tree bears showy panicles of creamy-white, fragrant, pea-like flowers followed by beautiful showers of winged, yellow-green seedpods. It takes years to bloom, but it's worth the wait.

Size can be an asset, or a debit. A tree that will grow out of scale with a dwelling is a debit. The heights we give in this chapter are for trees in cultivation—in the wild and in arboreta they can often be twice as big.

WHEN, WHERE, AND HOW TO PLANT

Young trees knit into their new environments quickly: a tree 7 to 8 feet tall can overtake the growth of a 15-foot tree set out at the same time. Early spring and early fall are the best planting seasons for trees. Fall-planted trees need two months of good weather ahead to begin to adjust. Choose early spring for trees difficult to transplant. Most large trees need full sun; many small flowering trees are understory plants that developed in the partial shade of a forest, and do well with part sun.

Make the planting hole for a tree three times as wide as the rootball and twice as deep. Mix into the soil from the hole the amendments described in Soil Preparation in the introduction. Half-fill the

bottom of the hole with improved soil, and tamp it down to make a firm base for the tree to rest on.

Trees are sold balled and burlapped, or growing in containers. To free a containerized tree, tip the container on its side and roll it around until the rootball loosens, or slit the pot open. If roots wrap the rootball, before planting make four deep vertical cuts in the sides and slice the matted roots off the bottom 2 inches. A balled-and-burlapped tree goes into the hole in its wrapping, then you cut the rope or wires and remove as much of the burlap as you can. Set the tree in the hole so the crown will be 1 to 2 inches above ground level (the weight on unsettled soil will cause it to sink some after planting). Half-fill the hole again with improved soil and tamp it down. Fill the hole to the top with improved soil and tamp it down firmly. Shape the soil around the trunk into a wide saucer. Water the soil slowly and gently with a sprinkler, a soaker hose, a bubbler, or by hand. Put down 1½ inches of water measured in a regular-sized coffee can, or pour 10 to 15 gallons of water slowly from a bucket.

ABOUT GROWING TREES IN CONTAINERS

Small hardy trees succeed in containers big enough to allow for growth and insulation. For insulation, wrap the interior with a double row of large bubble wrap or Styrofoam™ before you add soil. Bags of dry leaves placed around the containers for winter add extra protection.

Soil. The ideal container soil is a fertile semi soil-less mix. Mix one part good topsoil, 1 part horticultural perlite (or ½ perlite and ½ PermaTill®), and 2 parts coarse peat moss. For every 7 inches of planter height, add ⅓ cup slow-release fertilizer, and 1 cup dehydrated cow manure. Adding a soil polymer, such as Soil Moist, can reduce watering by as much as 50 percent.

Containers. A young tree can withstand most winters if grown in a container 14 to 16 inches in height and circumference. A larger tree needs a 14- or a 16-inch tub, and eventually one 30 inches high and 24 inches in circumference. Line the bottom of these large containers with 4 to 5 inches of PermaTill® for drainage. It's lighter than gravel.

Water and mulch. Before planting, soak the tub until water runs out of the bottom. After planting, top-dress the soil with 2 or 3 inches of mulch.

Some good choices to consider:

- American Hornbeam, *Carpinus caroliniana*
- American Smoketree, *Cotinus obovatus*
- Amur Maple, *Acer ginnala* 'Flame'
- Flowering Autumn Cherry, *Prunus subhirtella* 'Autumnalis Rosea'
- Flowering Weeping Cherry, *Prunus subhirtella* 'Pendula'
- Caroline Silverbell, *Halesia caroliniana*
- Chinese Dogwood, *Cornus kousa* var. *chinensis*
- Eastern Redbud, *Cercis canadensis*
- Hawthorn, *Crataegus viridis* 'Winter King'
- Foster Hybrid Holly, *Ilex attenuata* 'Fosteri #2' and others
- Flowering Cherry, *Prunus serrulata* 'Kwanzan', 'Shirotae'
- Flowering Cherry, *Prunus yedoensis* 'Akebono'
- Fragrant Snowbell, *Styrax obassia*
- Goldenrain Tree, *Koelreuteria paniculata*
- Japanese Flowering Crabapple, *Malus floribunda*
- Japanese Maple, *Acer palmatum* cultivars
- Japanese Snowbell, *Styrax japonicus*
- Japanese Tree Lilac, *Syringa reticulata*
- Pink Princess Crabapple, *Malus* 'Parrsi'
- Sargent Cherry, *Prunus sargentii*
- Sourwood, *Oxydendrum arboreum*
- Southern Black Haw, *Viburnum rufidulum*
- Trident Maple, *Acer buergeranum*
- Washington Hawthorn, *Crataegus phaenopyrum*

Apply 3 inches of mulch starting 3 inches from the trunk and extending to the edge of the saucer. Stake a young tree so the trunk will grow up straight, and wrap the lower trunk to protect the bark from sunscald and deer rubbing. Remove the stake and wrapping as the trunk fills out. Or, paint the trunk with whitewash, which is calcium carbonate with resins in it.

CARE GUIDELINES

The first year, unless there's a soaking rain, slowly and gently pour two to three bucketsful of water around the roots every two weeks in spring and fall; in summer, every week or ten days. Maintain the mulch.

The slow-release organic additives mixed into the soil at planting time are sufficient fertilizer for that year. For flowering trees, use a slow-release organic fertilizer. For trees whose flowers are not the show, use a complete, slow-release, long-lasting lawn fertilizer. In the following years, in late winter or early spring apply one of these fertilizers from the drip line outward to a distance that equals the height of the tree, plus half again its height. And compost the leaves you rake up in the fall. The nutrients they contain should go to enriching your soil, not clogging a landfill!

OTHER CHOICES

While the trees in this chapter are recommended for New England gardens, here are a few others we like:

SMALL FLOWERING TREES

- Carolina Silverbell, *Halesia tetraptera*
- Chaste Tree, *Vitex agnus-castus*
- Mountain Silverbell, *Halesia monticola*

LARGE DECIDUOUS TREES

- Kentucky Coffee Tree, *Gymnocladus dioicus*
- Yellowwood, American Yellowwood, *Cladrastis kentuckea*

AMERICAN BEECH
Fagus grandifolia

Hardiness—Zones 3 to 8

Color(s)—Fall foliage is russet-gold-brown; flowers insignificant

Bloom period—Spring

Mature Size (H × W)—50 to 70 ft. × 60 ft.

Water needs—Water a new tree regularly to establish and thereafter whenever there's a long drought.

Planting/Care—Transplant a young container-grown or balled-and-burlapped tree with great care in early spring. Don't break the rootball. Best in somewhat acidic, well-drained, loose soil that is humusy enough to hold moisture. Staking may help the tree grow straighter, but remove the support once the tree is established. Maintain a mulch. Fertilize each spring.

Pests/Diseases—None serious

Landscaping Tips & Ideas—Needs space all around. The brow of a low hill, or toward the top of a slope, are likely sites. This tree has high surface roots that are hard to cover, but they're attractive when interplanted with small flowering bulbs.

BIRCH
Betula spp. and cultivars

Hardiness—Zones 2 to 6

Color(s)—Green catkins; white bark

Bloom period—Spring

Mature Size (H × W)—30 to 40 ft. × 12 to 15 ft.

Water needs—Birches require ample water when establishing and regular watering thereafter.

Planting/Care—Plant in early spring or fall. Thrives in full sun but accepts bright shade. Provide soil that's fertile, humusy, and well-drained. Staking might help the tree grow straighter, but remove when the tree is established. Maintain a mulch, replenishing each spring. Fertilize in early spring. In summer or fall, prune out limbs that threaten to cross others or grow in the wrong direction.

Pests/Diseases—Certain birches are susceptible to various maladies and insect pests; inquire at your local nursery about resistant selections.

Landscaping Tips & Ideas—Beautiful birches like 'Whitespire' are at their best as specimens with a background of evergreens.

CALLERY PEAR
Pyrus calleryana

Hardiness—Zones 4 to 8

Color(s)—White flowers; wine-red fall foliage

Bloom period—Early spring

Mature Size (H × W)—30 to 50 ft. × 15 to 20 ft.

Water needs—Water regularly to establish, and thereafter during periods of drought.

Planting/Care—Plant in late winter or early spring before the plant leafs out. Set the tree so the crown will be an inch or two above soil level. It might grow straighter if staked, but remove the stake once the tree is established. Maintain a mulch. Fertilize in early spring. In late winter or early spring, prune to keep the tree open and airy.

Pests/Diseases—None serious

Landscaping Tips & Ideas—Tolerant of urban conditions and a superb street tree. 'Bradford' unfortunately tends to split as it matures, but it is being replaced with stronger varieties such as 'Whitehouse'—inquire at your local nursery.

DOGWOOD
Cornus spp., cultivars, and hybrids

Hardiness—Zones 5 to 8

Color(s)—White, pink, pink-red flowers; red-plum fall foliage

Bloom period—Spring

Mature Size (H × W)—20 to 30 ft. × 25 to 30 ft.

Water needs—Water regularly when establishing, and thereafter during drought periods.

Planting/Care—Plant in early spring while the young tree is still dormant. Handle the rootball with care. Ideal in a well-drained site with acidic soil that is humusy. Set the crown an inch or two above soil level. Mulch, and replenish each spring. Fertilize once a year in early spring.

Pests/Diseases—Dogwood anthracnose and powdery mildew can be serious issues. Healthy trees are more resistant. Get resistant varieties and/or advice from your local nursery.

Landscaping Tips & Ideas—Beautiful at the edge of a woodland, centering a lawn, or by a stone wall—almost anywhere.

EASTERN REDBUD
Cercis canadensis

Hardiness—Zones 4 to 8

Color(s)—Red-purple, lavender-pink, magenta, white

Bloom period—Early spring

Mature Size (H × W)—20 to 30 ft. × 25 to 35 ft.

Water needs—Water regularly when establishing. Does not like wet feet.

Planting/Care—Plant a balled-and-burlapped redbud in early spring—it can be difficult to transplant. Choose a protected spot to avoid winter dieback. Succeeds in well-drained sites in either acidic or alkaline soil, but not in a permanently wet location. Mulch, and replenish each spring. Fertilize annually in early spring.

Pests/Diseases—Canker, and certain insect pests, may pose problems. Get advice from your local nursery.

Landscaping Tips & Ideas—Small enough to use at the back of a shrub or flower border. Also a good specimen tree for a smaller yard. Especially charming naturalized at the edge of a woodland. Some lovely cultivated varieties are available, including white 'Alba'.

EUROPEAN HORNBEAM
Carpinus betulus

Hardiness—Zones 4 to 7

Color(s)—Insignificant white florets

Bloom period—Spring

Mature Size (H × W)—30 to 40 ft. × 30 to 30 ft.

Water needs—Water regularly during establishment, and slowly and deeply during periods of drought.

Planting/Care—Plant a young, dormant container-grown or balled-and-burlapped tree in early spring. This tree is not easy to transplant, so handle the rootball with care, digging an ample hole and setting it so that the crown is an inch or two above soil level. Mulch, and replenish every spring. Fertilize annually in early spring.

Pests/Diseases—None serious

Landscaping Tips & Ideas—An excellent choice for naturalizing near streams, as it tolerates pollution, wet soil, and periodic flooding. It makes an attractive street tree. Two varieties that lend character to a landscape are 'Columnaris', a narrow form of European hornbeam, and 'Pendula', a weeping tree.

FLOWERING CHERRY
Prunus spp. and hybrids

Hardiness—Zones 5 to 8

Color(s)—Pink

Bloom period—Spring

Mature Size (H × W)—20 to 50 ft. × 20 to 50 ft.

Water needs—Water regularly during establishment, and thereafter if there is a prolonged dry spell.

Planting/Care—Transplant a balled-and-burlapped tree in early spring, in well-drained, sandy loam, pH 6.0 to 7.5. Maintain a mulch. Fertilize in early spring. After the tree has bloomed, remove any sprigs that will become branches headed for the center of the tree or that will ultimately cross other branches. Roots are close to the surface, so weed by hand.

Pests/Diseases—None serious

Landscaping Tips & Ideas—This is a specimen tree, best featured where it can be seen from a distance. Cultivars of the Sargent cherry make excellent street trees and beautiful specimens in lawns, large or small.

FLOWERING CRABAPPLE
Malus spp., cultivars, and hybrids

Hardiness—Zones 4 to 7

Color(s)—Pink or carmine buds, opening to white; colorful fruits follow

Bloom period—Mid-spring

Mature Size (H × W)—10 to 25 ft. × 10 to 25 ft.

Water needs—Water regularly during establishment and more often in hot, dry weather.

Planting/Care—A young container-grown or balled-and-burlapped plant transplants readily in the early spring or fall, in well-drained, heavy, loamy soil on the acidic side. Maintain a mulch. Apply fertilizer in early spring. Prune after the tree has bloomed, removing branches heading to the center of the tree or crossing others.

Pests/Diseases—Don't plant within 500 feet of red cedar, which can lead to fungal diseases.

Landscaping Tips & Ideas—Should be set out as a featured specimen. There are many fine hybrids; one of the best is 'Donald Wyman'.

FRANKLIN TREE
Franklinia alatamaha

Hardiness—Zones 5 to 8

Color(s)—Showy white flowers; fall foliage is bronze, orange, red

Bloom period—Late summer into fall

Mature Size (H × W)—15 to 20 ft. × 6 to 15 ft.

Water needs—Water regularly during establishment, and thereafter during prolonged dry spells.

Planting/Care—Not always easy to transplant. Set out a container-grown or balled-and-burlapped tree from a reliable nursery, in early spring while it's still dormant. Even in Zone 5, it needs a site protected from cold north winds. It thrives in well-drained soil that is acidic, fertile, loose, and humusy enough to hold soil moisture. Feed early every spring with a fertilizer for acid-loving plants. Maintain a mulch.

Pests/Diseases—Wilt can be a problem; buy quality stock.

Landscaping Tips & Ideas—An exceptionally lovely plant that belongs out in the open where its flowers and fall color can be appreciated.

209

FRINGE TREE
Chionanthus virginicus

Hardiness—Zones 4 to 9

Color(s)—White flowers; pure yellow fall foliage

Bloom period—Mid-spring

Mature Size (H × W)—15 to 25 ft. × 15 to 25 ft.

Water needs—Water regularly and deeply, during establishment and beyond.

Planting/Care—Set out a young container-grown or balled-and-burlapped tree in early spring while it is still dormant. Handle the rootball with care. The ideal site is in full sun (for best flowering) and near water, in slightly acidic soil. Apply a fertilizer for acid-loving plants annually in spring. Maintain a mulch. Flowers on the previous season's growth; prune immediately after flowering.

Pests/Diseases—None serious

Landscaping Tips & Ideas—Beautiful as a specimen where you will see it at a slight distance—in the center of a lawn or by a pond. Underplant with periwinkle, ajuga, and small spring-flowering bulbs.

GINKGO
Ginkgo biloba

Hardiness—Zones 4 to 9

Color(s)—Golden fall foliage

Bloom period—Spring (flowers insignificant)

Mature Size (H × W)—30 to 50 ft. × 30 to 50 ft.

Water needs—Water regularly during establishment, and thereafter during dry spells.

Planting/Care—Ask for and make sure you get a male ginkgo (the females produce messy, smelly fruits). Transplants readily in the spring while the plant is still dormant, and in fall before Indian summer. It thrives in sandy, deeply dug, well-drained, moist soil with a pH between 5.5 and 7.5. Maintain a mulch. Apply a fertilizer annually in early spring. Cut away any young branches that will grow into the center of the tree or rub against other branches.

Pests/Diseases—None serious

Landscaping Tips & Ideas—Too tall to look well in a small garden once it begins to mature—give it a large space.

GOLDENRAIN TREE
Koelreuteria paniculata

Hardiness—Zones 5 to 9

Color(s)—Blooms in yellow; orange-yellow fall foliage

Bloom period—Late spring to summer

Mature Size (H × W)—30 ft. × 30 ft.

Water needs—Water regularly during establishment, and thereafter during dry spells.

Planting/Care—Transplants easily in spring. Young trees look gaunt at first, but fill out quickly. They appreciate full sun and decent soil, but are tolerant of poor soil, drought, pollution, and wind. Six months after planting, feed lightly; feed again for the next few years. Prune damaged branches promptly. Self-sows—pull out unwanted seedlings.

Pests/Diseases—Stressed trees develop dieback or wilt disease.

Landscaping Tips & Ideas—Fast growers initially, these trees stay relatively small and are suitable for lawns under utility wires or nearer the house to provide some shade. They also work well in smallish yards (they do not overpower one-story homes).

HONEYLOCUST
Gleditsia triacanthos

Hardiness—Zones 4 to 9

Color(s)—Yellow flowers; golden fall foliage

Bloom period—Spring

Mature Size (H × W)—70 ft. × 50 ft.

Water needs—Maintain soil moisture, especially during establishment.

Planting/Care—Plant at almost any season. Best in full sun, in rich, moist soil with a high pH, but tolerates other situations, and once established, handles drought and salt (a consideration where roads are salted in the winter). Fertilize in early spring before growth begins; repeat in November.

Pests/Diseases—Stressed trees are vulnerable to various insects and fungal problems; webworms can defoliate a tree.

Landscaping Tips & Ideas—An excellent lawn and street tree. The variety 'Shade Master' is recommended for fast growth, a short trunk, an open crown, and best of all, it is thornless and produces few seedpods, so you can plant it where there is foot traffic or children will play.

JAPANESE MAPLE
Acer palmatum

Hardiness—Zones 5 to 9

Color(s)—Fiery red fall foliage

Bloom period—Spring (insignificant)

Mature Size (H × W)—6 to 20 ft. × 6 to 20 ft.

Water needs—Water new transplants well their first spring and fall; in droughts, water slowly and deeply every two weeks.

Planting/Care—Take special care in transplanting as you set out container-grown or balled-and-burlapped specimens in early spring. Does best in a well-drained site and humusy, rich, moist, slightly acidic soil, but it is fairly adaptable. Maintain a mulch. Fertilize in early spring. Rarely requires pruning to develop a beautiful form.

Pests/Diseases—None serious

Landscaping Tips & Ideas—An elegant tree. Nice underplanted with vinca and ajuga. If the shade cast is dense, you can thin a few branches. There are many fine and varied cultivars; the best upright deep-red variety is probably 'Bloodgood'.

JAPANESE PAGODA TREE
Sophora japonica

Hardiness—Zones 4 to 7

Color(s)—Creamy white flowers; lime-green winged pods follow

Bloom period—Midsummer

Mature Size (H × W)—40 to 50 ft. × 30 to 40 ft.

Water needs—Water regularly during establishment. Once mature, it is drought-tolerant.

Planting/Care—Plant in spring while still dormant. It is somewhat tender to cold while still young. Flowers best in full sun. A well-drained site with space all around is ideal. Adapts to a wide range of soils and pollution. Maintain a mulch, and fertilize every spring and late fall. In the fall after the leaves go, prune to a strong central leader.

Pests/Diseases—Canker and various blights can attack; seek advice from your local nursery.

Landscaping Tips & Ideas—Lovely when underplanted with periwinkle or ajuga. Other good choices include hosta, liriope, small spring-flowering bulbs, and wood hyacinths. 'Regent' is a superior cultivar.

JAPANESE STEWARTIA

Stewartia pseudocamellia

Hardiness—Zones 4 to 8

Color(s)—White flowers; colorful fall foliage

Bloom period—Mid- to late summer

Mature Size (H × W)—30 to 40 ft. × 20 to 30 ft.

Water needs—Water a young transplant regularly; water established trees during droughts.

Planting/Care—Plant a small, young, container-grown or balled-and-burlapped tree in early spring while it's still dormant. It thrives in soil that is fertile, moist, organically rich, and acidic. Maintain a mulch. Fertilize annually in early spring, using a fertilizer for acid-loving plants. It needs some protection in colder areas, Zone 4 and 5.

Pests/Diseases—None serious

Landscaping Tips & Ideas—Beautiful as a lawn specimen, grouped in a shrub border with low-growing azaleas, and at the edge of an open woodland. For small gardens, the very similar Korean stewartia, *S. koreana*, may be a better fit.

JAPANESE ZELKOVA

Zelkova serrata

Hardiness—Zones 5 to 8

Color(s)—Reddish-purple fall color

Bloom period—Spring (insignificant)

Mature Size (H × W)—60 to 70 ft. × 50 to 55 ft.

Water needs—Water regularly when young; established plants are drought-tolerant.

Planting/Care—Zelkovas transplant well. They are agreeable to any well-drained soil except sand. Do not plant where a diseased elm was growing. Site in full sun. Stake for their first year. After six months, fertilize lightly. Prune young trees to establish a single stem and branching framework and to remove rubbing branches.

Pests/Diseases—Highly resistant to Dutch elm disease, but have occasional problems with Japanese beetles.

Landscaping Tips & Ideas—Use wherever shade is desired—over porches and walks. Their vaselike profile of fanning upright branches above a short trunk makes them good street trees.

LINDEN

Tilia cordata

Hardiness—Zones 3 to 7

Color(s)—Pale yellow

Bloom period—Early to midsummer

Mature Size (H × W)—0 to 00 ft. × 0 to 00 ft.

Water needs—Water if rainfall is unreliable over the one or two years it takes for them to get established, and then during periods.

Planting/Care—Lindens transplant easily. They prefer good well-drained soil rich in organic matter. Maintain a mulch. Fertilize lightly after six months; after three years, fertilizing won't be necessary. They accept pruning well and can be hedged. Prune off suckers that appear below the graft.

Pests/Diseases—Aphids and Japanese beetles can be problems; seek advice from your local nursery. Older, established trees can withstand defoliation.

Landscaping Tips & Ideas—Good as specimens in a lawn, or along the street (space 40 feet apart if planting several). Underplant with an evergreen groundcover rather than turfgrass.

MAPLE
Acer spp. and cultivars

Hardiness—Zones 3 to 9

Color(s)—Greenish-yellow to red buds; vivid fall foliage

Bloom period—Spring

Mature Size (H × W)—60 to 75 ft. × 40 ft.

Water needs—Maintain a moist soil throughout the growing season, especially during dry spells, for maples have shallow root systems.

Planting/Care—Choose a container-grown or balled-and-burlapped tree and plant it in the fall before Indian summer or in early spring while dormant. Most any well-drained, rich, moist soil will do. Maintain a mulch. Fertilize annually in early spring before growth begins.

Pests/Diseases—In some maples, anthracnose (especially in rainy spells) and verticillium wilt are problems; others may be attacked by various insects. Ask your local nursery to help you choose a locally resilient one.

Landscaping Tips & Ideas—Most large maples are better in large landscapes. The vigorous roots will buckle cement sidewalks and patios.

OAK
Quercus spp.

Hardiness—Zones 4 to 8

Color(s)—Colorful fall foliage, depending on the species

Bloom period—Spring (insignificant)

Mature Size (H × W)—40 to 95 ft. × 40 to 60 ft.

Water needs—Water regularly to establish; water deeply during droughts until the plant is growing well.

Planting/Care—Plant while still dormant in early spring. Buy a young container-grown or balled-and-burlapped tree and handle carefully—most oak species have taproots that can be damaged. Prefers full sun, moist, fertile, somewhat acidic, well-drained sandy loam. Maintain a mulch. Fertilize annually in early spring. In late winter, prune to develop a strong central leader.

Pests/Diseases—Various maladies, galls, and insects are possible; get advice from your local nursery on the healthiest locally adapted ones.

Landscaping Tips & Ideas—Red oaks are the best choice for quick growth and smaller landscapes. For larger settings, the white oak is recommended.

RED HORSE CHESTNUT
Aesculus × *carnea* 'Briotii'

Hardiness—Zones 4 to 7

Color(s)—Rose-red, salmon-red

Bloom period—Mid- to late spring

Mature Size (H × W)—45 to 60 ft. × 35 to 45 ft.

Water needs—Water when establishing. Even after it is established and growing well, water deeply during droughts.

Planting/Care—Transplant in early spring. The most successful plants are grown in moist, well-drained soil whose pH is around 6.5, but they are tolerant of other soils. Maintain a mulch. Fertilize early every spring. Prune out any young branches that will grow into the center of the tree or rub against other branches.

Pests/Diseases—Not as susceptible to blotch and mildew as the common horse chestnut

Landscaping Tips & Ideas—This is an excellent choice for a large yard, and it is used extensively for shade in street plantings, in parks, golf courses, and on campuses. It is quite cold hardy.

RUSSIAN OLIVE
Eleagnus angustifolia

Hardiness—Zones 2 to 7

Color(s)—Cream-yellow

Bloom period—Spring

Mature Size (H × W)—20 ft. × 15 to 20 ft.

Water needs—Water when establishing; established plants are fairly drought-tolerant.

Planting/Care—Set out a container-grown or balled-and-burlapped tree in the spring while the plant is still dormant. It likes sun, and can handle a windy location (in fact, will end up looking quite picturesque there). It thrives in light, sandy loam but succeeds in almost any soil, including salty coastal soils. Fertilize annually in early spring. Maintain a mulch.

Pests/Diseases—Verticillium wilt can wreak havoc; your local nursery will know if it is a concern in your area.

Landscaping Tips & Ideas—Naturalized, or planted as a tall hedge and neglected, Russian olive stays 12 to 15 feet high. Provided with care and space to expand, it can reach 40 feet.

SAUCER MAGNOLIA
Magnolia × soulangiana

Hardiness—Zones 4 to 9

Color(s)—White with pink

Bloom period—Mid-spring

Mature Size (H × W)—30 ft. × 30 ft.

Water needs—Water to establish, and then during dry spells.

Planting/Care—Magnolias' fleshy roots are tender and sparse. Damage delays recovery from transplant shock. Plant in early spring. They do best in full sun out in the open (sheltered sites heat up too soon, encouraging flower buds to open early and risk frost-damage). Provide soil that is slightly acidic, organically rich, and well-drained. Fertilize lightly after six months. Prune for size and shape immediately after flowering.

Pests/Diseases—Stressed trees may experience various leaf-spot diseases. Deer generally ignore magnolias.

Landscaping Tips & Ideas—Site front and center in a spacious yard, and underplant with hardy bulbs such as snowdrops, squill, or grape hyacinth (cultivating the soil for annuals damages their shallow roots).

SERVICEBERRY
Amelanchier arborea

Hardiness—Zones 4 to 9

Color(s)—White flowers; vivid fall foliage

Bloom period—Early spring

Mature Size (H × W)—15 to 25 ft. × variable spread

Water needs—Water regularly when young. For established plants, maintain a moist soil.

Planting/Care—Plant a container-grown or balled-and-burlapped plant in early spring while still dormant or in fall before Indian summer. It is at its best in full sun and thrives in moist, well-drained, acidic soil. Maintain a mulch. Fertilize in late fall and again in early spring.

Pests/Diseases—Rust and leaf spot can occur; the newer varieties are resistant

Landscaping Tips & Ideas—These trees are most effective in groups at the edge of a woodland or as a backdrop for an island of shrubs where the fall color will be seen. They're excellent near streams and ponds. 'Autumn Brilliance' and 'Robin Hill Pink' are recommended cultivars.

SOUR GUM
Nyssa sylvatica

Hardiness—Zones 4 to 9

Color(s)—Greenish-white flowers; vivid fall foliage

Bloom period—Spring

Mature Size (H × W)—30 to 50 ft. × 20 to 30 ft.

Water needs—Water regularly when establishing, and maintain a moist soil thereafter, especially in dry spells.

Planting/Care—The sour gum has a taproot, making it difficult to transplant successfully. Choose a thriving, young container-grown plant and set it out with the utmost of care. It requires moist, well-drained, acidic soil and some protection from wind. Maintain a mulch. Apply a fertilizer for acid-loving plants in early spring. In late fall, cut away branches that grow into the center or rub against others.

Pests/Diseases—None serious

Landscaping Tips & Ideas—Looks best featured at the edge of a lawn or near a stream or pond where its autumn foliage can be admired. Also successful at the seashore.

SOURWOOD
Oxydendrum arboreum

Hardiness—Zones 5 to 9

Color(s)—White flowers; yellow, orange, red, and purple fall foliage

Bloom period—Early summer

Mature Size (H × W)—25 to 30 ft. × 20 ft.

Water needs—Water regularly when establishing and thereafter during periods of drought.

Planting/Care—Does not transplant easily. In early spring, buy a young, still-dormant, container-grown plant from a reliable nursery, and handle the transplanting with great care. It requires a well-drained site, and acidic soil. Maintain a mulch. Fertilize early every spring with a fertilizer for acid-loving plants.

Pests/Diseases—Leaf spots and twig blight; neither is serious.

Landscaping Tips & Ideas—This lovely, slow-growing native tree deserves to be made a prominent feature of your landscape in a spot where it can be enjoyed all year long. It naturalizes fairly easily; it does not tolerate urban pollution.

STAR MAGNOLIA
Magnolia stellata

Hardiness—Zones 4 to 8

Color(s)—Creamy white

Bloom period—Spring

Mature Size (H × W)—15 to 20 ft. × 10 to 15 ft.

Water needs—Water regularly to establish, and thereafter during periods of drought.

Planting/Care—Transplant a young container-grown or balled-and-burlapped magnolia with care, before new growth begins in early spring. Full sun is best. Pick a site that is protected from north winds but not particularly warm (too-early blossoms can be ruined by late frosts). Ideal soil is acidic, fertile, humusy, and well-drained, but not dry. Maintain a mulch. Fertilize early every spring with a fertilizer for acid-loving plants. Prune right after the tree has bloomed, if at all.

Pests/Diseases—None serious

Landscaping Tips & Ideas—Needs space to develop all around. Excellent as tall foundation plants for grounds around large buildings.

SWEET GUM
Liquidambar styraciflua

Hardiness—Zones 5 to 8

Color(s)—Fall foliage is true yellow, red, and purple.

Bloom period—Spring (insignificant)

Mature Size (H × W)—50 to 60 ft. × 35 to 45 ft.

Water needs—Water well when establishing. Grows quickly in moist soil, slower in dry.

Planting/Care—Plant in early spring while still dormant. Handle the rootball with care, as it takes a while to recover even in the best of circumstances. Provide ample space for the developing root system. Well-drained, moist, acidic soil is best. Maintain a mulch. Fertilize in early spring and in the fall. If any pruning is required, do it in late winter before the buds swell.

Pests/Diseases—Various scale insects and leaf spots can occur; get advice from your local nursery.

Landscaping Tips & Ideas—A superb lawn tree (but its prickly fruit must be removed before mowing near it).

TULIP TREE
Liriodendron tulipfera

Hardiness—Zones 4 to 9

Color(s)—Chartreuse flowers; yellow fall foliage

Bloom period—Late spring

Mature Size (H × W)—70 to 90 ft. × 35 to 50 ft.

Water needs—Water regularly when establishing. In periods of drought, water even well-established trees deeply every week.

Planting/Care—Requires care in transplanting. Plant in early spring when the young tree is still dormant. Does well in most soils, but thrives in sandy, deeply dug, well-drained, moist ground that is slightly acidic. Maintain a mulch. Do any pruning in winter.

Pests/Diseases—Aphids and associated sooty mold is a common problem. Yellowing leaves are often caused by inadequate watering.

Landscaping Tips & Ideas—A majestic tree, suited to larger landscapes with enough space all around to be seen. Can tolerate city conditions and is handsome in a park, but can be too big for street planting.

WINTER KING HAWTHORN
Crateagus viridis 'Winter King'

Hardiness—Zones 4 to 7

Color(s)—White flowers; gold, scarlet purple foliage in fall; showy orange-red berries in winter

Bloom period—Spring

Mature Size (H × W)—20 to 30 ft. × 20 to 30 ft.

Water needs—Water regularly to establish; maintain soil moisture thereafter.

Planting/Care—Plant in early spring when the plant is still dormant. At their very best when planted in full sun. Thrive in well-drained soil with enough humus to sustain moisture. Maintain a mulch. Fertilize annually in early spring. The best seasons for pruning are winter and early spring.

Pests/Diseases—More resistant to rust than other hawthorns.

Landscaping Tips & Ideas—Especially picturesque in naturalized areas with ornamental grasses, or in a meadow where birds can enjoy the fruits. Choose a site where children won't be tempted to climb it, because of the sharp thorns.

TREES

Healthy trees need little maintenance. Most will be fertilized as you fertilize the surrounding lawns and gardens. Newly planted trees need watering as often as you water perennials, but once mature, they need watering only in periods of deep drought—two or three weeks without rain—and pruning now and then to remove misplaced or damaged limbs. Maybe a treatment for tent caterpillars or webworms. But that's about it.

Established trees. Established trees that aren't doing well usually suffer from crowding, loss of light, compacted soil, and lack of nutrients and water. Pruning the trees to open the crown up to air and light, clearing surrounding vegetation, fertilizing, and watering in times of drought will bring them back. The prompts in the month-by-month pages ahead will help you to get them growing well again.

CHOOSING NEW TREES

When you are adding a new tree to your property, look for a species whose habit, color, and texture will add variety to existing plantings and the view. Look for trees that have several assets. An example is the American holly (*Ilex opaca*). It is hardy in Zone 5, has a handsome silhouette, evergreen foliage with an interesting texture, produces bright red berries, and has few enemies.

Habit and size. A tree is the largest plant in the garden, so its silhouette—habit—makes an important difference to your yard and to your neighborhood. Each species has a recognizable volume and sculptural structure—spreading, pyramidal, oval, vase-shaped, round, columnar, clumping, or weeping. When adding—or deleting—trees, aim for a variety of silhouettes.

Avoid trees that will grow so big they dwarf your house or garden and rob neighbors of light.

EVERGREEN OR DECIDUOUS?

Choose evergreens to keep the yard green and block unwanted views all year round. Conifers that have flat scale-like leaves—American arborvitae, for example—are very dense. The needled evergreens—hemlock and pine—have an airier presence.

Choose deciduous trees that bring change to your garden view with spring's baby leaves, summer's rich green canopy, fall's grand finale—which ranges from buff in the oaks, to gold in the willows, to the flames of the sugar and swamp maples. In winter, a deciduous tree's bare branches and twigs frame the sky, and the bark presents arresting textures—think of the silky gray kid of the American beech, for example, and the chalky white of river birch.

Both evergreen and deciduous trees shade the house and protect it from the sweep of winter wind, thereby saving on the costs of cooling and heating.

Flowering trees. A flowering tree in bloom is a sky-high bouquet. Your property, if big enough, can host a flowery parade from early spring when the ornamental cherries bloom until mid-fall when the last fragrant blossom falls from the little Franklin tree (*Franklinia alatamaha*). Selecting flowering trees that bear colorful fruits will double your pleasure. The flowering crabapples and dogwoods are two of many whose flowers are followed by plentiful fruits. Some are fragrant—for example, the five-foot Sargent crab (*Malus sargentii*), which is truly charming in big perennial beds and shrub borders.

PLANTING

Make healthy choices. However perfect a tree is for its site, if it is susceptible to pests and diseases, it's a poor choice.

Location. Site large trees where they will reach full sun as they mature. Many small flowering trees are understory plants that developed in the partial shade of a forest, and they will thrive in partial light. If you are trying a tree that is borderline hardy in your yard, give it a spot sheltered from the north wind. The lovely little Loebner magnolia (*Magnolia* × *loebneri*) can make it in some Zone 4 gardens but only with protection.

Don't plant a tree, large or small, in an airless corner, or close to a wall or overhang.

Place trees at distances from each other that allow plenty of space for the lateral development of branches. Columnar trees can be set more closely than pyramidal trees. Large shade trees are best set 75 feet apart. The absolute minimum for a street tree is 8 feet in every direction, and 12 feet is better. Staggered plantings achieve greater density in less space.

Don't plant tall trees near electric or phone lines, and avoid proximity to pipes and septic systems.

TREES WITH EXCEPTIONALLY COLORFUL FALL FOLIAGE

- American Smoke Tree, Chittamwood (*Cotinus obovatus*)
- American Sweet Gum (*Liquidambar styraciflua*)
- Amur Maple (*Acer ginnala*)
- Black Gum, Sour Gum (*Nyssa sylvatica*)
- Bradford Pear (*Pyrus calleryana* 'Chanticleer', 'Aristocrat')
- Chinese Dogwood (*Cornus florida* hybrids; *C. kousa, C.* × *rutgersensis* Stellar Series)
- Golden Larch (*Pseudolarix kaempferi*)
- Japanese Zelkova (*Zelkova serrata*)
- Katsura Tree (*Cercidiphyllum japonicum*)
- Maidenhair Tree (*Ginkgo biloba*)
- Mountain Ash, Korean Mountain Ash (*Sorbus alnifolia*)
- Northern Red Oak (*Quercus rubra*)
- Red Maple, Swamp Maple (*Acer rubrum* 'October Glory', 'Red Sunset')
- Sassafras (*Sassafras albidum*)
- Scarlet Oak (*Quercus coccinea* 'Superba')
- Sugar Maple (*Acer saccharum* 'Bonfire', 'Green Mountain')
- Sweet Gum (*Liquidambar styraciflua*)
- Tatarian Maple (*Acer tataricum*)
- Tulip Tree (*Liriodendron tulipifera*)
- Washington Hawthorn (Crataegus phaenopyrum)
- Witchhazel (Hamamelis × intermedia 'Diane')

Before placing a large tree near a garden, consider the effect on the plants of the shade it will cast at various times of the day and the year. Don't plant so close to a sidewalk or patio that the roots will heave the paving.

When to plant. You can plant trees as soon as the ground becomes workable, April for most of us, but the truly ideal planting season begins when the leaves start to change color and ends in November. Choose early spring for planting trees difficult to transplant, Florida dogwoods and magnolias, for example. Plant trees that bloom in spring in the fall. Plant trees that bloom in summer and early fall in the spring.

Bare-root trees. In early spring before growth begins, mail-order suppliers ship young trees bare root. Before placing your order, check on the size and the age of a bargain sapling so you know what to expect. The tree will be shipped when it is time to plant in your area. Follow the shipper's instructions for planting exactly.

Container-grown and B&B trees. Container and balled-and-burlapped trees are more costly than bare-root trees. B&B packaging is usually reserved for very large trees. But big trees are also being grown now in 10-, 15-, and even 50-gallon containers. Container and B&B trees may be planted from early spring through summer and into fall. B&B trees dug in spring and protected in the months since by mounds of mulch or soil can stay in good condition.

Costs. Buying young trees saves on costs, and they knit into their new environments quickly. Trees 7 to 8 feet tall soon overtake the growth of 15-foot trees set out at the same time. If you are buying a large, expensive specimen, we recommend buying from a full-service nursery or garden center and paying extra to have it planted and for a warranty in case of loss.

Soil and pH. Within a year or two, a new tree will send roots out well beyond the amended soil of its planting hole. That means your easiest successes will be with species growing in native soil that has a pH matching their pH needs. However, amending the pH of the planting hole helps, especially with hard-to-transplant specimens like the American hornbeam and sour gum.

Digging the hole. If you plant your trees correctly, they will have a much better chance of success. Here's how:

1. Make the planting hole for a tree three times as wide and twice as deep as the rootball.

2. Loosen the sides of the hole, and blend the soil taken from the hole with the organic amendments described in Soil Preparation and Improvement in the Introduction to the book.

3. Half-fill the bottom of the hole with improved soil, and tamp it down very firmly to make a solid base. Instructions for planting bare-root trees usually call for the creation of a cone in the center of the hole over which the roots are to be spread.

4. Set a container or B&B tree in the hole so the trunk is straight and 2 inches above the level of the surrounding earth. The weight on unsettled soil will cause the tree to sink after planting.

5. Half-fill the hole once more with improved soil. Tamp it down firmly. Finish filling the hole and tamp the soil down. Shape the soil around the crown into a wide saucer.

6. Water the area slowly, gently, and thoroughly with a sprinkler, a soaker hose, a bubbler, or by hand. (See Watering on the facing page.)

7. Mulch newly planted trees 3 inches deep, starting 3 inches from the trunk out to the edge of the saucer. Replenish the mulch as needed to keep it 3 inches deep.

Ground covers such as pachysandra, ivy, myrtle, hostas, drought-tolerant rudbeckias, and small flowering bulbs may be planted outside the water basin (saucer) around a tree when it is first set out. The ground covers will move in around the trunk and become a living mulch that keeps weeds out and spares you hand trimming the lawn grasses.

Staking and protecting the trunk. It isn't essential to stake a young tree unless the stem or trunk shows a tendency to lean or to grow at an odd angle. Remove the stake when the tree is growing straight and true.

In Zones 3 through 6, a burlap windbreak helps a young tree through its first winter. You can either wrap the tree loosely in burlap or place a burlap screen between the tree and the sweep of the wind. Where wildlife is active, wrapping a tree trunk with a protective tape or a plastic casing may keep the critters from chewing through the bark; remove the wrap in spring when growth starts. If your concern is the injury winter sun can inflict on a young trunk, paint it with whitewash, which is calcium carbonate with resins in it, or envelop it in a tree wrap.

FERTILIZING

Established trees surrounded by a lawn or growing in a shrub border receive all the nutrients they need when you fertilize the ground around. Groves of trees benefit from an annual fertilization with an organic lawn food high in nitrogen, for example, Espoma organic lawn food 18-8-6. Woodland trees get their nutrients from the decomposition of their fallen leaves.

New trees growing in improved soil rich in organic fertilizers will benefit from fertilization twice a year for the next eight or ten years. The first annual application of fertilizer should be made before growth begins in spring. For flowering and fruit trees, use Holly-Tone® or Plant-Tone®. In the following years, in late winter or early spring, apply fertilizer from the drip line (the outer ring of leaves on the tree) outward to a distance that equals the height of the tree, plus half again its height. The last application should be as growth slows toward the end of the growing season—in Zones 3 and 4, that's usually about August 15; in Zone 5, early September; in Zones 6 and 7, early September to early October. The number of applications in between depends entirely on the type of fertilizer you are using.

Compost the leaves you rake up in the fall. The nutrients they contain should go to enriching your soil, not clogging a landfill!

MULCHING AND WEEDING

A 3-inch-deep mulch spread around newly planted trees keeps weeds out and buffers trees from the weather. For the first two or three seasons, top the mulch off in spring after fertilizing, and once more before winter cold sets in. The last application helps maintain moisture in the ground, which retains its warmth for some time after the air turns freezing cold.

Start the mulch 3 inches from the trunk, and spread it to the outer edge of the tree's saucer. If you pile mulch right up against the trunk, that prevents it from drying out after rain and may harm the bark. Deep mulch right against the trunk also makes a cozy home for field mice that may girdle the tree—eat through the outer layer of the trunk—which can kill a young tree. Keep the mulch free of weeds.

If lawn grasses or ground covers move in around to the trunk, they will act as a living mulch, and you can stop mulching.

WATERING

Newly planted and transplanted trees must have sustained moisture for the first couple of years. After planting and during spring, summer, and fall in weeks where there is no rain, pour two or three 5-gallon buckets of water around the roots. Or use a sprinkler to lay down 1½ inches of water slowly and gently. Set a one-pound coffee can or other container under the sprinkler or the hose, and record how long it took to put 1½ inches in the can—then you'll know.

In summer when the weather isn't supporting growth, young trees adapt by slowing down unless forced to grow by shallow watering and inappropriate fertilizing. In fall, even after cold sets in, roots continue to develop, so water often enough to prevent the soil from drying out even after it gets cold.

After the first year or two, most trees require watering only in times of severe drought.

PRUNING DECIDUOUS TREES

You prune a tree to encourage its natural structure, to keep the center open, to get rid of suckers, and to remove damaged wood. Never remove more than 25 percent of a tree's growth at one time. It's called "dehorning" and causes "water sprout" growth. Water sprouts shoot straight up at a 90-degree angle from the branch, and must be removed to maintain the tree's natural shape and keep the center airy and healthy.

The best time to prune a shade tree is when it is dormant, after the coldest part of the winter. If sap starts to flow, it will stop when the tree leafs out. Light pruning and thinning in summer will not promote unwanted growth in trees, and you can see what you're doing. However, heavy pruning and dehorning in summer can stimulate new unwelcome growth.

Prune a spring-flowering tree that blooms on last year's wood after the flowers fade. Prune a summer-flowering tree that blooms on current growth shortly before growth begins.

Most new trees require periodic light pruning. The first few years are the most important times to prune and shape a new tree. When needed, remove branches growing into the center of the tree, or crossing other branches. Never remove more than 25 percent.

Before cutting a branch, find the collar or ring at its base, where it springs from the trunk. Taking care not to damage the ring, make the cut just to the outside of it. From the collar an attractive, healthy covering for the wounded area can develop. Current wisdom says "no" to painting or tarring these cuts.

That said, our main consultant, nurseryman André Viette prefers to paint with orange shellac any wounds caused by removing big branches: it disinfects and seals the cuts.

Nurturing a beautiful tree for years and then losing it leaves a gap in the heart as big as the gap in the garden. For an extra fee, nurseries will plant your purchase and guarantee replacement if it fails, but usually only the first year. The best protection against loss or disappointment is to choose disease-resistant trees and to plant, water, and feed them wisely.

THE BASICS OF PRUNING CUTS

When you remove a large limb, follow the three-cut pruning method to avoid stripping bark from the trunk:

1. About a foot out from the trunk, cut from the bottom of the branch upward about a third of the way through the limb.

2. A couple of inches out, or beyond the first cut, cut from the top of the branch down. The branch will break away cleanly.

3. Find the collar or ring at the base of the limb where it springs from the trunk. Taking care not to damage the ring, remove the stub. From the collar an attractive, healthy covering for the wounded area can develop.

WHEN AND HOW TO PRUNE DECIDUOUS TREES

New trees may need some shaping, and they will shape up best if you follow the supplier's instructions for pruning after planting and for pruning the next two or three years.

- **Winter damage.** Prune any time.

- **Damaged branches.** Prune them before the leaves fall—they're easier to spot.

- **Flowering trees that bloom on new wood.** Prune in late winter or early spring before growth begins.

- **Flowering trees that bloom on old wood.** Prune immediately after they bloom to avoid cutting off branches where buds are being initiated for the following season.

- **To control height.** Prune after the season's new growth has fully developed.

- **To slow or dwarf growth.** Prune in summer when the plant has stopped growing.

- **Trees that need regular shaping.** Prune while the tree is still dormant, just after the coldest part of the season.

- **Don't get carried away, but don't be timid.** Focus on supporting the tree's natural outline, its growth "habit." Never prune away more than 20 percent at one time.

PESTS AND DISEASES

Choose trees that are disease-resistant, and be willing to accept a normal quota of insect damage.

You can spray young and small trees, but if full-sized trees have problems, we recommend you get professional help from a tree company or a full-service garden center or nursery.

PRUNING EXAMPLES

Open center for peaches

Central leader for apples

JANUARY

- January winds bring a big sky and the possibility of a new vision for your landscape. So take your mail-order catalogs to a window overlooking the garden, pull up a comfortable chair, and consider what adding or subtracting a tree or two can do for the scenery.

- Prune away winter and snow damage any time before growth begins. Cut down old and injured trees. Cut the wood of deciduous trees into logs the size of your fireplace, and stack them to dry.

- Renew the anti-desiccant spray on broadleaf evergreens in exposed locations.

- Maintain the soil moisture of your indoor trees. Mist and air the room daily or often.

- Repotting large indoor trees is difficult, and necessary only every three or four years. Other years, in late winter as new growth appears, remove the top 2 inches of soil, and replace it with 2 or 3 inches of compost or fertile potting soil.

FEBRUARY

- The best time for pruning trees is as winter comes to an end. So, on days when the sun is warm enough to linger outdoors, spend some time studying your trees and making a plan for those that need it.

- Keep an eye on flowering trees as the weather warms. The swelling of leaf buds tells you pruning time is coming up. Damaged branches should be pruned first, before growth begins, and well before they bloom. Then prune summer-flowering trees, which will be slower to bed.

- Place catalog orders for new trees this month.

- Bare-root trees can be planted about a month before the last freeze. Mail-order suppliers will ship them dormant at your planting time.

- Continue to prune back damaged and dead tree branches, especially after major snowstorms.

- Check whether cycles of thawing and freezing have heaved roots. Press heaved roots back into place and replenish the mulch to insulate the soil.

MARCH

- Consider planting a tree in your yard or a street tree to enhance your neighborhood. If you want to plant a street tree, get municipal permission and their recommendations for trees that tolerate urban conditions.

- You can plant dormant trees when the earth loses its winter wet.

- When winter storms are over, remove trunk covers from protected trees.

- If a tree that was staked is growing straight and not being heaved, you can remove the stakes.

- Before buds break, prune newly planted trees lightly the first few years to control the development of the limb structure. Remove branches heading into the center of the tree or crossing others, water-sprout growth, and suckers.

- Prune summer-flowering trees before growth begins this month or in early April. Never take more than 20 to 25 percent of a tree's growth.

- If, in its third or fourth season or later, a tree isn't growing well, fertilize.

APRIL

- Mow around the trunks of trees young or old. If the mower consistently gets too close, keep it away by surrounding the trunk with a ring of mulch 3 inches deep.

- Spring, right now, is an excellent time to plant trees that bloom in summer and early fall and trees difficult to transplant.

- You can move newly planted container-grown trees their first two years without trauma.

- Before trees leaf out, remove the water-sprout growth from tree limbs, and suckers from around the base of the tree and on tree trunks and branches.

- Maintain the soil moisture in all your container trees.

- Inground trees growing in lawns and flower and shrub borders will get all the fertilizer they need when you fertilize the surrounding lawns and borders.

- Continue protecting your trees from the deer.

- Late this month, tent caterpillars emerge. Spray trees with Bt or other controls as suggested by your local nursery.

MAY

- This is a fine month to plant new trees.

- For newly planted and transplanted inground trees, pour two or three 5-gallon buckets of water around the roots once a week throughout spring unless you have rain.

- Renew the mulch under newly planted trees. Get rid of weeds sprouting in the mulch around established trees.

- When you see the first signs of gypsy moths, spray trees showing signs of infestations with a biological control such as Bt or other control suggested by your local nursery.

- Look for and destroy the cone-shaped nests of bagworms.

- Since frequent watering leaches nutrients from the soil, once a month give all the trees growing in containers a light application of water-soluble organic fertilizer—seaweed or manure tea, for example.

- Deer sightings may subside now that the woods are full of browsing materials. Even so, continue to discourage them from visits to your yard looking for treats.

JUNE

- As the spring burst of growth ends, prune trees you want to keep small or dwarf. Reducing the leaf surface reduces the sugar synthesized and translocated to the roots, and that limits next year's growth in the tree.

- Pour two or three 5-gallon buckets of water around new trees every week or ten days, unless you have a soaking rain.

- Container-grown and balled-and-burlapped trees transplant well even after they have leafed out.

- Make sure the mulch around new trees is a full 3 inches deep to avoid weeding.

- Maintain the soil moisture of the indoor trees moved outdoors for the season—citrus, ficus, palms. Water once or twice every week or so, or when the soil seems dry. Since frequent watering leaches nutrients from the soil, give the plants a light feeding at every second watering.

- June is the spray time for bagworms. If you spot bagworm tents, remove and destroy them now.

JULY

- Study the shade enveloping your gardens. Where you are losing too much light to tree branches, mark upper limbs that can be removed to thin the canopy so more light comes through.

- You can plant container-grown trees even now. Just be sure to keep them well-watered.

- Remove the water sprouts and suckers from around the base, the trunks, and the branches of flowering fruit trees. The flowering cherries usually need repeated attention.

- Use a string trimmer to keep down undergrowth in woodlands and groves. Leave the debris in place, and it will decompose and nourish the trees growing there.

- If there has been two weeks without rain, water established trees. Slowly and gently lay down 1½ inches of water.

- Indoor trees growing outdoors for the summer need regular attention in hot weather. Keep their soil moist, and at every second watering, add a half-strength dose of fertilizer to the water.

AUGUST

- Use lazy summer days to consider where you would like to see a tree or trees that are winter assets. In winter, a tree's major assets are its silhouette against the sky and its bark.

- For trees, from late this month until December is the best planting season. Container-grown ones should do well.

- Small trees can be transplanted as soon as their leaves color up and fall.

- Woodland trees will likely make it through any drought typical of New England. That said, you should water new trees every week to ten days, unless there is a soaking rain. Water established ones if there has been more than two weeks without rain.

- Bagworms and tent caterpillars are usually very active right now. Physically remove and destroy their nests, and spray as needed.

- In Zones 3 and 4, fertilize trees (except those planted this year) after August 15 as growth slows.

SEPTEMBER

- Check out the changing color of the trees in your neighborhood and at public gardens, where the names of those you admire are sure to be available. Then look in your own garden for a spot that would be much more exciting if it had a glow of red, coral, or yellow in the fall.

- Plant sales and pleasant September weather combine to make this a fine time to plant trees.

- If you've been wanting a too-expensive tree—a good-sized Japanese maple, for example—take advantage of the seasonally discounted prices sometimes offered now. If you are buying a balled-and-burlapped tree, choose one that has just been dug.

- You may need to wrap new trees as a protection from deer rubbings, critter nibbling, and sunscald this fall and winter.

- The time for the second application of fertilizer for newly planted trees is as growth slows toward the end of the growing season.

OCTOBER

- In Zone 6 and northward, it's time to move outdoor trees growing in containers from exposed locations to more protected spots for the winter.

- Save all of your fallen leaves, and heap them in and out-of-the-way place for composting or insulation around plants. Or grind them to use as mulch and bag them for spring use.

- When the leaves start to change color is the best time for transplanting or planting trees. The air is cold, but the earth still has warmth.

- You may prune out dead or diseased tree limbs now, but delay any major pruning until winter.

- Trees benefit from fertilization twice a year for the first eight or nine years of their lives. However, a tree just planted this year is not likely to need fertilizing until next spring. In Zones 6 and 7, the time for the last application of fertilizer is between early September and early October.

NOVEMBER

- As long as the ground isn't frozen, you can plant trees in November.

- In Zones 3 to 5, move hardy trees growing in containers to a sheltered corner out of the wind for the winter, or store them in a shed or garage.

- The earth remains warm even after the leaves fall and the air cools, so roots continue to develop. That's why watering is recommended when fall is dry. Be sure to water newly planted trees thoroughly before the ground freezes.

- Do not fertilize trees now, indoors or out.

- Deer will eat almost any tree when they are hungry, and young trees are especially vulnerable. So if deer nibble your plantings regularly, cage your new trees with chickenwire to keep them safe.

- Change whatever deer deterrents you are using to something new to them and obnoxious. Deer disregard deterrents they become accustomed to.

DECEMBER

- Maintain the soil moisture of your indoor trees—citrus, ficus, and palms—and mist them and air the room often.

- If there's no rain, water all new outdoor plantings thoroughly.

- Trees growing indoors come under attack from mealybugs and spider mites. Frequent showers and spraying with horticultural soaps discourages these pests.

- Make a New Year's resolution to stick to non-polluting fertilizers and biodegradable controls. Decades of nursery experience have shown that trees that are inherently healthy—planted in a suitable climate, in properly prepared soil, and given all the water they need for their first years—are strengthened by normal stresses.

CONIFERS
for New England

Delayed leaf drop is one of the advantages you gain by planting evergreens: practically no leaves to gather and grind in the fall. It's reassuring to know that yellowing needles most often are a normal part of a needled evergreen's cycle and not symptomatic of a problem.

The term "evergreen" is misleading. Every plant must renew its foliage. White pines shed aging needles every year. Most other evergreens shed some aging needles every year, but they don't, like the deciduous trees, lose all their older needles at once—so they appear to be "ever green."

Evergreens are key foundation plants. In this chapter we've grouped together the needled and scale-leaved evergreens, large and small. The shrub sizes of familiar species—pines, yews, cedars, junipers, spruces, and hemlocks—are discussed on the same pages as the tree sizes.

We find the small, shrubby conifers extremely useful for anchoring color and as backgrounds in flower beds and shrubbery borders. The shrubby evergreens also make the best dense hedges and windbreaks, and provide sturdy edgers for paths and driveways. For tall privacy screening and windbreaks we use big, naturally columnar evergreens, such as American arborvitae. To furnish neglected corners, and for mid-height or low screening, we like the bold branching of the sprawling dwarf junipers, and upright little yews like 'Pygmaea', which stay under 2 feet. Elegant columnar junipers, such as 'Skyrocket', are ideal where a stylish accent is wanted, and they make great verticals for small spaces.

A big, needled evergreen that has considerable presence in New England landscaping is the fast-growing native white pine. The Canadian hemlock, a pyramidal conifer with short needles, is another handsome shade tree for our region (though it has severe problems in Rhode Island), and a hemlock hedge can be pruned for decades before the central stems become too thick to be attractive. White pine, hemlock, and blue spruce make a lovely background for the white-barked birch that flourishes here, and for azaleas and ornamental grasses.

A hurry-up tree for really tall screening is the Leyland cypress, which grows at least 3 feet a year. It can be pruned for many years without losing its beauty. Mature, it becomes a big stately tree with graceful, feathery, bluish green, scale-like foliage and red-brown bark. Weeping evergreens, like the blue Atlas cedar, *Cedrus libani* ssp. *atlantica* 'Glauca Pendula', add grace notes to the landscape.

CONIFERS CARE GUIDELINES

Evergreens need well-drained soil—for some this is very critical—and most prefer an acid, or somewhat acid, pH. They are moderate drinkers. The information on planting and care for shrubs in the Shrubs chapter, and for trees in the Trees chapter, applies to evergreen shrubs and trees.

LANDSCAPING WITH NEEDLED EVERGREENS AND CONIFERS

- The shrub-sized needled evergreens and conifers are dwarf or slow-growing species and varieties of evergreen trees that grow everywhere in New England. Some are perfect for keeping green all year round in perennial beds and shrubbery borders. Others make fine dense hedges, wind breaks, and edgers for paths and driveways.

- Among small evergreens we use to anchor beds of perennials are the dark, chunky little Mugho pine and dwarf blue spruces. Narrow conical dwarf Alberta spruce is a sensational accent in a large flowering border. (Alberta spruce is attacked by spider mites, so make a note to keep it sprayed periodically with horticultural soaps.) Others for perennial beds and shrub borders are pyramidal—for example the dwarf Colorado blue spruce 'Fat Albert', shrubby Hinoki false cypress, and the dwarf golden Sawara false cypress. A cluster of small, clipped, ball-shaped juniper topiaries in a perennial border adds greenery and a smile.

- Evergreen shrubs that are excellent for hedges and edging include dwarf spruce cultivars, the dwarf junipers, the Japanese yew 'Meyeri' and cultivars, and the Meserve hybrid hollies 'Blue Boy' and 'Blue Girl', which are hardy in Zone 4. In Zones 6 and 7 even the handsome dwarf variegated hollies can be grown.

- To furnish neglected corners, and for low and mid-height screening, consider some of the sprawling Chinese junipers, the Pfitzer cultivars, dwarf false cypresses, and upright little yews like 'Pygmaea'. Some of the slow-growing Japanese pines are hardy in Zone 5.

Most often we prune an evergreen only to shape the plant or to make it bushier. To encourage dense branching to the ground, begin pruning when the evergreen is three to five years old. Summer after its main spurt of growth is the time to prune an evergreen to slow, dwarf, or maintain its shape. The rule is to prune strong growth lightly, and weak growth hard. Never trim more than a third from an evergreen.

You should not remove more of the top growth (the leader) than the growth of the last year or two. You can cut the main stem back to the first side shoots. This doesn't apply to trimmed hedges.

Additional information appears on page 343.

MORE ABOUT DWARF CONIFERS

Sometimes less is more. For New England gardeners with less space or those who are tired of shearing out-of-scale needled evergreens to a more manageable size, there are dwarf evergreens to consider.

These plants will bring landscape interest from several standpoints. They offer the eye-catching appeal of unusual shapes, colors, and textures. They provide literally hundreds of forms. They can be attractive all year long. They have admirably low upkeep requirements. More and more nurseries have recognized the value of these plants, so now you can choose from field-dug nursery specimens, potted garden-center offerings, and wide mail-order selections.

Most dwarf conifers originate from full-sized trees—mainly fir, cypress, pine, and spruce progenitors. This dwarfness is not the result of cultural manipulation (as with bonsai) or of grafting (as with dwarf fruit trees). Rather, dwarf conifers result from apparently spontaneous flukes of nature that produce variations of or even radical departures from the normal habit and appearance of a parent plant. Such mutants, or "sports," can have tiny needles, unusual coloration, and, most important, greatly slowed growth habits.

Dwarfism in conifers can arise from the seed, buds, or branches of a normal tree. Only occasionally can such mutant material be reproduced sexually since seed, when it is produced at all, is often sterile. This is why nurseries, when they come across such a plant and see potential in it, use cuttings (vegetative reproduction) to make more. This takes time and effort, which is why these nifty plants are sometimes in short supply or expensive!

Of course, "dwarf" is a relative term, and some evergreens marketed this way may not seem so to you. Or they may not remain so; they may grow slowly at first, but in time, become too tall for their chosen spot. For instance, the dwarf concolor fir, *Abies concolor* 'Compacta' grows slowly but may eventually reach 9 feet tall. It's still significantly smaller than its 150-foot mature ancestor, but it may not be right for your rock garden.

TIPS FOR SUCCESS:

- Pick a spot first and a plant second. This way, you won't be pruning back, shearing, or even removing your selection in a few years.
- Don't surround conifers with fast-growing, exuberant plants that may not only distract from their natural beauty but overwhelm them physically, growing into their space or running right over them. Instead, grow them with other small or low-growing plants or groundcovers that are in scale with their size and personalities.
- Grow them in groupings. Small gatherings of dwarf conifers are charming. Find matches of size or coloration, or make contrasts.

ARBORVITAE
Thuja occidentalis

Hardiness—Zones 2 to 7

Color(s)—Dark green

Mature Size (H × W)—12 to 15 ft. × 3 to 5 ft.

Water needs—The first season, water deeply every two weeks. Water deeply during periods of drought.

Planting/Care—Container-grown or balled-and-burlapped arborvitae transplants easily in early spring and fall. It flourishes in soil that is slightly acidic, fertile, well-drained, and moist. When planting, set the rootball so the crown will be an inch or two above ground level. Lay down and maintain a mulch. Fertilize lightly in fall and again in spring. Generally does not need pruning.

Pests/Diseases—Deer crop arborvitae to the core at grazing height; the radical solution is 8-foot wire fencing.

Landscaping Tips & Ideas—Excellent as a formal specimen in the lawn, as a backdrop for deciduous trees and flowering shrubs, and in windbreaks and hedges.

BLUE ATLAS CEDAR
Cedrus libani ssp. *atlantica* 'Glauca'

Hardiness—Zones 5 to 9

Color(s)—This cultivar has icy-blue foliage.

Mature Size (H × W)—40 to 60 ft. × 25 to 30 ft.

Water needs—Water regularly to establish.

Planting/Care—Set out young containerized plants in spring, handling the rootball with great care. Choose a site protected from prevailing winds. Does best in acidic soil and tolerates clay or sand, so long as it is well-drained. Set the tree so the rootball is an inch or two above ground level; shape the soil around the crown into a wide saucer. Water slowly, deeply, thoroughly. Maintain a mulch. Using a slow-release fertilizer for acid-loving plants, fertilize lightly in the fall and again in the spring.

Pests/Diseases—None serious

Landscaping Tips & Ideas—Use as a handsome specimen tree in a large landscape.

CANADIAN HEMLOCK
Tsuga canadensis

Hardiness—Zones 3 to 7

Color(s)—Deep green

Mature Size (H × W)—40 to 70 ft. × 25 to 36 ft.

Water needs—Water regularly the first season, unless there are good soaking rains.

Planting/Care—Plant in fall before Indian summer, or in early spring. It thrives in cool, moist, acidic soil. Set so the crown will be an inch or two above ground level. Maintain a mulch. Fertilize lightly in spring with a slow-release, acidic, organic fertilizer. Prune away deadwood anytime, and prune lightly or shear after the main growth spurt (never when the plant is dormant).

Pests/Diseases—The woolly adelgid is a serious threat; avoid planting this tree if it is a problem in your area.

Landscaping Tips & Ideas—An excellent tall foundation plant. Limbed up, it becomes a graceful evergreen shade tree. Trimmed, it makes a superb tall hedge.

229

COLORADO BLUE SPRUCE

Picea pungens 'Glauca'

Hardiness—Zones 3 to 8

Color(s)—Soft blue-gray

Mature Size (H × W)—30 to 50 ft. × 10 to 20 ft.

Water needs—Water regularly when the tree is getting established.

Planting/Care—Plant in early fall or spring, in well-drained, acidic, moderately moist ground. Set the tree an inch or two above the ground level, shape the soil around the crown into a wide saucer, and water well. Mulch, and replenish annually. Fertilize in early spring before growth begins.

Pests/Diseases—Vulnerable to a fungus in warmer parts of New England.

Landscaping Tips & Ideas—Best featured as a specimen out in the open in a large landscape. To encourage density or to change the shape of the plant, periodically trim the tips back by half. It can also be grouped with smaller evergreens, becoming the anchor for an evergreen screen.

DOUGLAS FIR

Pseudotsuga menziesii

Hardiness—Zones 4 to 6

Color(s)—Green to blue-green

Mature Size (H × W)—40 to 50 ft. × 12 to 20 ft.

Water needs—Water regularly when establishing, especially if rains are sparse.

Planting/Care—Transplants well in early spring. The ideal site is open and sunny with moist air and space all around it. Set the crown 1 or 2 inches above ground level, shape the soil around the crown into a wide saucer, and water well. Mulch, maintain the mulch through the summer, and replenish as needed. Fertilize lightly in the fall and again in early spring.

Pests/Diseases—Various cankers, mites, and beetles can be problems where the tree is not thriving.

Landscaping Tips & Ideas—This is a large, dramatic ornamental tree for large landscapes such as parks, golf courses, and estates. Note that it does not succeed in dry, windy locations.

DWARF HINOKI CYPRESS

Chamaecyparis obtusa 'Nana Gracilis'

Hardiness—Zones 4 to 8

Color(s)—Deep green

Mature Size (H × W)—6 ft. × 3 to 4 ft.

Water needs—Needs moisture around the roots, so water regularly when establishing and thereafter as required.

Planting/Care—Plant in fall before Indian summer or in early spring, while it is still dormant. Requires full sun and protection from the wind. It prefers humusy, well-drained soils that are neutral to slightly acidic. Fertilize in late fall and again in early spring. Pruning is hardly ever needed.

Pests/Diseases—None serious

Landscaping Tips & Ideas—This is a first-rate, shrub-sized evergreen, great for use in hedges, as a background to a shrub border of azalea, or as a foundation plant. The golden foliage of the cultivar 'Crippsii' is striking against darker evergreens.

EASTERN WHITE PINE
Pinus strobus

Hardiness—Zones 2 to 8

Color(s)—Medium to light green

Mature Size (H × W)—50 to 80 ft. × 40 ft.

Water needs—Water regularly the first year, and during dry spells once established.

Planting/Care—Early spring is best. Provide well-drained, acidic soil. Set the crown an inch or two above ground level, create a wide saucer of soil around it, and water well. Mulch. Using a slow-release fertilizer for acid-loving plants, feed lightly in the fall and again in early spring.

Pests/Diseases—In some areas, white pine blister rust and the white pine weevil are serious problems; check with your local nursery.

Landscaping Tips & Ideas—Makes an excellent specimen plant, a first-rate divider, screen, windbreak, or dense tall hedge. To encourage density, or to change the shape, cut back the candles by half in June when they are fully grown.

JUNIPER
Juniperus spp. and hybrids

Hardiness—Zones 2 to 9

Color(s)—Shades of green and blue-green, depending on the selection

Mature Size (H × W)—Varies, according to the species and cultivar

Water needs—Water regularly when establishing; established plants are fairly drought-tolerant

Planting/Care—Set out container-grown plants in spring or fall. Most prefer soil acidic, light, even sandy, and moderately moist. Apply a slow-release organic fertilizer lightly in the fall and early spring. Maintain a mulch. Minimize shearing and pruning by choosing one whose growth habit suits your purpose. If you must prune or shape, the best time is just after a spurt of new growth.

Pests/Diseases—Some are subject to blights and cedar-apple rust and various insects; inquire when making your selection at your local nursery.

Landscaping Tips & Ideas—There's a juniper to fill every garden need: tough groundcover, stately specimen, columnar accent, and graceful focal point.

LEYLAND CYPRESS
x *Cupressocyparis leylandii*

Hardiness—Zones 5 to 10

Color(s)—Bluish-green

Mature Size (H × W)—60 to 70 ft. × 25 to 30 ft.

Water needs—Water regularly when establishing. Maintain soil moisture during droughts.

Planting/Care—Plant in fall or early spring. Allow plenty of room, as it is too vigorous for narrow spaces. Adapts to a variety of soils, but grows most rapidly in moist, humusy, fertile soil. Set the crown an inch or two above the ground, create a basin for watering, and soak well. Periodically prune or shear during July.

Pests/Diseases—None serious

Landscaping Tips & Ideas—Fast-growing: good for screening, makes a fine tall hedge. In shade, branching is more open and informal; in full sun, the foliage grows densely and close to the trunk. Sometimes planted with a desirable but slow-growing evergreen and removed when the second plant reaches its desired height.

UMBRELLA PINE
Sciadopitys verticillata

Hardiness—Zones 4 to 8

Color(s)—Medium to dark green

Mature Size (H × W)—20 to 30 ft. × 15 to 20 ft.

Water needs—Water regularly when establishing, especially if there are no soaking rains.

Planting/Care—Plant a young container-grown or balled-and-burlapped plant in early spring, and handle the roots with great care. The ideal site is a steep, rocky, well-drained place that has rich, moist, somewhat acidic soil. Needs protection from hot late-afternoon sun and sweeping winds. Set the crown an inch or two above ground level, water well, and mulch. Use a fertilizer for acid-loving plants in fall and early spring. Should not be sheared, should not need pruning.

Pests/Diseases—None serious

Landscaping Tips & Ideas—Best used as an accent in a group of trees and shrubs, or as a specimen out in the open.

WHITE FIR
Abies concolor

Hardiness—Zones 3 to 7

Color(s)—Rich blue-green

Mature Size (H × W)—30 to 50 ft. × 15 to 30 ft.

Water needs—Water regularly when establishing and thereafter during times of drought.

Planting/Care—Plant in early spring. Ideal soil is a rich, moist, sandy loam. Prepare the soil well! Set the crown an inch or two above the ground, create a basin, and soak well. Maintain a mulch throughout the summer, and replenish it every spring. Feed lightly in the fall and spring with a slow-release, acidic fertilizer.

Pests/Diseases—None serious

Landscaping Tips & Ideas—The evergreen needles make a handsome backdrop for ornamental plants, and in fall and winter they lend life to a sleeping garden. It is generally used as a specimen in lawns or parks.

YEW
Taxus × media

Hardiness—Zones 4 to 8

Color(s)—Dark green

Mature Size (H × W)—Varies, depending on the cultivar. Many are as wide as, or wider than, they are tall.

Water needs—Water regularly, but remember that yews do not tolerate wet feet at all.

Planting/Care—Plant in fall or early spring. The ideal site has excellent drainage and fertile, humusy soil. Set the crown an inch or two above ground level, create a saucer, and water well. Maintain a mulch. Fertilize in fall and spring. Prune away deadwood anytime, but do not cut beyond the area where green needles are growing. Yews accept shearing of the branch ends throughout the growing season.

Pests/Diseases—Though very tough, yews may be attacked by certain blights and insects if stressed.

Landscaping Tips & Ideas—Yews are enduring foundation plants.

CONIFERS

Choose evergreens to keep the yard green and block unwanted views all year round. Conifers that have flat scale-like leaves— American arborvitae, for example—are very dense. The needled evergreens—hemlock and pine—have an airier presence.

Just as with many of the larger deciduous trees, conifers will shade the house and protect it from the sweep of winter wind, thereby saving on the costs of cooling and heating.

CHOOSING NEW CONIFERS

When you are adding a new tree to your property, look for a species whose habit, color, and texture will add variety to existing plantings and the view. Look for trees that have several assets.

A tree is the largest plant in the garden, so its silhouette—habit—makes an important difference to your yard and to your neighborhood. Each species has a recognizable volume and sculptural structure—spreading, pyramidal, oval, vase- shaped, round, columnar, clumping, weeping. When adding—or deleting—trees, aim for a variety of silhouettes.

Avoid coniferous trees that will grow so big they dwarf your house or garden and rob neighbors of light.

CARE OF CONIFERS

For general information on planting and maintenance, please consult the "Trees" chapter.

Light pruning of the branch ends of many evergreens, including hemlocks, junipers, and yews, is acceptable throughout the growing season, but not when they are dormant. Yews and junipers can take heavy pruning and fill out again very quickly. Firs, pines, spruces, and other evergreens whose growth is initiated by candles should be pruned in spring when the candles appear at the branch tips. Cutting back the new candles by one-half to two-thirds will make the tips branch. Heavy pruning in fall isn't a good idea, because the wounds heal more slowly in seasons of reduced activity and the pruning may stimulate a new flush of growth, which could be damaged by winter weather.

HOW TO PRUNE EVERGREEN TREES

Pruning woody plants stimulates growth, so avoid heavy pruning in summer when the plant is preparing to go dormant.

Dead or damaged wood on evergreen conifers can be removed at any time.

Winter and snow damage is best pruned before active growth.

To encourage dense branching in evergreens with candle-like new growth, cut the candles back by half. Prune the tips of hemlock branches lightly any time during the growing season. Prune yews and junipers lightly or heavily any time during growth.

To establish a shape, prune evergreens (sparingly) when they are three to five years old.

To slow or dwarf a broadleaf evergreen tree—hollies, for example—when growth ends, cut back no more than 20 percent of the new growth. You can reduce the main stem back to the first side shoots, but don't remove more than has grown the last year or two.

When you are pruning evergreens, remember to save some new growth on hemlocks, hollies, spruce, and cedars to prune in December for holiday trimmings.

GOOD CHOICES FOR EVERGREEN HEDGES

- Canadian Hemlock (*Tsuga canadensis*)

- Cripp's Golden Hinoki Falsecypress (*Chamacyparis obtusa* 'Crippsii')

- Dwarf Alberta Spruce (*Picea glauca* 'Conica')

- Dwarf Chinese Juniper (*Juniperus chinensis* 'Mas', 'Spartan')

- Dwarf Colorado Blue Spruce (*Picea pungens* 'Glauca', 'Glauca Montgomery', 'Fat Albert')

- Sawara False Cypress (*Chamaecyparis pisifera* 'Boulevard', 'Filifera Aurea')

- Yew, Dwarf Japanese Yew (*Taxus cuspidata* 'Nana', 'Densa'); Hick's Japanese Yew (*Taxus × media* cultivars)

JANUARY

- Use a broom to brush off accumulations of snow and ice on the lower branches of the evergreens.

- Renew the anti-desiccant spray—a coating that keeps leaves from losing moisture—on evergreen trees.

- Check and adjust the burlap that is protecting trees.

- Prune away winter and snow damage any time before growth begins. Cut down old and injured trees. Evergreen wood is soft and bad for your chimney, so compost it or chip it and use it to top paths.

- A live Christmas tree can begin to deteriorate after ten days indoors in a heated house. As soon as possible, move the tree outdoors. As soon as you can, dig a hole, plant the tree, and then mulch the area.

- Deer go for the tips of reachable branches of arborvitae, cedars, yews, and other evergreens. Spraying may deter them, but wrapping with burlap or chickenwire is a surer safeguard.

FEBRUARY

- Remove snow that is weighing down evergreen limbs and prune back damaged and dead branches.

- Check the stakes and ties of recerntly planted trees. If the ties are damaging the bark, loosen them. If the tree is growing straight and true, you can remove the stakes.

- Check whether cycles of thawing and freezing have heaved roots. Press heaved roots back into place and replenish the mulch to insulate the soil.

- If you have planted a live Christmas tree, maintain the soil moisture.

- Deer are hungry. Spray evergreen foliage that is munching-height with deer repellents. Check and adjust burlap covers and chickenwire cages.

- Root-pruning evergreen trees to check growth can be undertaken now before growth begins. Use a spade to sever the roots in a circle around the trunk. Go out to where the roots are about the size of your little finger. Water well and fertilize after root-pruning.

MARCH

- You can plant dormant trees when the earth loses its winter wet. Handle a balled-and-burlapped one with care! Avoid disturbing the burlap, twine, or wire basket as you put the rootball into the planting hole. Once it is in, cut the twine around the trunk, and cut off or push the ends of the burlap into the hole. If the cover is plastic, cut away as much as possible, and poke holes in what remains.

- When winter storms are over, remove covers from protected trees.

- For trees growing in containers, before the seasonal growth begins, top-dress the soil. Remove the top 2 inches and replace it with enriched soil.

- The ends of hemlock branches can be lightly pruned throughout the growing season. Prune yews and junipers any time during the growth cycle.

- Maintain soil moisture around a live Christmas tree, or any container-grown conifer. Water weekly unless you have a good soaking rain.

APRIL

- Need more colorful trees? Check out the yellow and yellow-green evergreens. Cripp's gold Hinoki cypress is fast-growing and the new foliage is rich golden yellow. Enter the names of trees that catch your fancy in your garden log, and plan to buy them at a local nursery late in the season.

- Mow with care round the trunks of trees. If the mower consistently gets too close, keep it away by surrounding the trunk with a ring of mulch 3 inches deep.

- For new and transplanted inground trees, including a Christmas tree, pour two or three 5-gallon buckets of water once a week throughout spring unless there's a good rain.

- Maintain the soil moisture in all your container-grown trees.

- Inground trees growing in lawns and flower and shrub borders will get all the fertilizer they need when you fertilize the surrounding lawns and borders.

- Continue protecting your trees from deer.

MAY

- This is a fine month to plant new trees.

- To furnish your yard with song—and to keep insects down—look for places to plant a few trees that meet the needs of birds. They nest in the branches of evergreens like Canadian hemlock and white pine.

- Prune to encourage dense branching to the ground in pines, firs, spruces, and other evergreens whose growth is initiated by candles (new candle-like growths at the ends of branches). Cut the candles back by half when they appear at the branch tips.

- Prune yews and junipers any time during their growing season. The ends of hemlock branches can be lightly pruned throughout the growing season.

- Woody adelgid attack Canadian hemlock and can do severe damage. Spraying twice a year with horticultural oil is the preferred control. These lightweight botanical oils also control aphids, cankerworms, leafhoppers, leaf rollers, mealybugs, mites, psyllids, scale, tent caterpillars, and webworms.

JUNE

- After the first flush of new growth in evergreen hedges, trim the top and sides to keep the height down and greenery full. Keep the top narrower than the bottom so light can reach the flower branches.

- Make sure the mulch around new trees is a full 3 inches deep to avoid weeding.

- Water trees growing in containers once or twice every week or so, or when the soil seems dry. Since frequent watering leaches nutrients from the soil, once a month during the growing season, give the plants a light application of a water-soluble organic fertilizer—seaweed or manure tea.

- Pour two or three 5-gallon buckets of water around new trees every week to ten days, unless you have a soaking rain.

- Coniferous evergreens can be rooted from semi-hardwood cuttings taken in June and July. New green growth that is just turning brown and hardening is what is meant by "semi-hardwood."

JULY

- At the shore, evergreens are the best plants for windbreaks. Needled evergreens that work well include Japanese black pine, hemlock, and the junipers. If they get exposed to heavy spray during a storm, wash off as much salt as possible with the hose.

- Prune deadwood on evergreen conifers at any time.

- Study the shade enveloping your gardens. Where you are losing too much light to tree branches, mark the upper limbs that can be removed to thin the canopy so more light comes through. Consider whether removing a few lower branches will help; late winter is a good time to do that.

- Established trees need watering in times of severe drought—which is more than two weeks without rain. Water new trees every week to ten days.

- Use a string trimmer to keep down undergrowth in woodlands and groves. Leave the debris in place, and it will decompose and nourish the trees growing there.

AUGUST

- For conifers, from late this month until December is the best planting season. Use the lazy days of summer to consider where you would like to see a tree or trees that are winter assets. The symmetrical winter silhouettes of the incense cedar, and the stylish Serbian spruce, are arresting. The spruces are especially beautiful outlined by snow.

- Evergreen trees do well moved August through October.

- Plant container-grown or balled-and-burlapped conifers. If your choices come balled-and-burlapped, be careful. Don't buy ones that have been sitting unmulched and baking at a garden center since they were dug early in spring.

- August can be hot and dry. Continue to water your trees every week or ten days, unless you have a soaking rain.

- Give hedges their final trimming for the year.

- If you are putting in an evergreen hedge, buy young plants. They are inexpensive and adaptable.

SEPTEMBER

- In Zone 6 and northward, get ready to move outdoor trees growing in containers from exposed locations to more protected spots for the winter.

- If rainfall is not sufficient, continue watering your conifers. The air may be cooler, but the earth is still warm and roots are still growing.

- Late plant sales and perfect planting weather combine to make this a fine time to install a hedge. Make the width of the bed equal to the height of the plants at maturity. Columnar plants need less space. Prepare a trench 12 to 18 inches deep, and improve the soil. After planting is complete, finish the bed with 3 inches of mulch.

- You may need to wrap new trees as a protection from deer rubbing, critter nibbling, and sunscald this fall and winter. Plan to remove wrappings come spring.

OCTOBER

- Evergreen shrubs may do better planted this month rather than next.

- You may prune out dead or diseased tree limbs, but delay any major pruning until winter.

- Maintain the soil moisture of indoor trees, mist them often, and air the room daily if you can.

- Water newly planted trees every week to ten days if the season runs dry.

- Consider enclosing newly planted conifers with chickenwire cages to keep them safe from deer. Or, at least, change whatever deer deterrents you are using to something new and obnoxious. Deer disregard deterrents they become accustomed to.

- The most important preparation for winter is deep and thorough watering of all shrubs and trees—new, established, inground, in containers—before the soil freezes. If the sky doesn't provide the rain, you will have to.

NOVEMBER

- If you plan to buy a live Christmas tree for the holidays, choose a permanent home for it now, one suited to the tree's mature width and height, and dig the planting hole while the weather is pleasant and the ground easy to work. Cover the areas with 12 to 18 inches of leaves held down with evergreen boughs to keep them from blowing away.

- Don't be concerned for their health when evergreens show some yellow in the interior of their branches—pines, arborvitae, juniper, and yews among them. These lose some of their older leaves at more or less regular intervals, but look green year-round because they don't drop them all at once. So chances are that some yellowing is a normal part of a cycle and not a problem.

- Apply an anti-desiccant spray to the foliage of newly planted evergreens growing in exposed locations, or wrap them in Reemay® or burlap.

DECEMBER

- The most popular Christmas trees are the Douglas fir and the fragrant balsam fir, which stay fresh longest. Balsam fir looks like a spruce, the traditional evergreen with short, stiff needles.

- If you would like to have a live Christmas tree, consider a Colorado blue spruce. Before buying, give the plant a health check: is the rootball moist? Do needles drop off when you shake it?

- Before bringing a tree indoors, to keep the needles fresher longer, spray with an anti-transpirant like biodegradable Wilt-Pruf. One application before you decorate the tree should last. When you bring it indoors, stand it away from heat sources and keep the room temperature under 65 degrees F.

- Spray an anti-desiccant on young evergreens in exposed locations. Protect them from bitter winds by erecting a burlap screen.

- Lightly harvest mature evergreens with cones and berries for use in holiday decorations—pines, firs, hollies, spruces, and junipers.

APPENDIX

PESTS, DISEASES, & CONTROLS

New England gardens, like gardens everywhere, can host problems. In this section, we give you an overview of some of the problems you might encounter and how to control them. This section includes the sound environmental approach to handling pests, which is known as Integrated Pest Management. That is followed by sections describing common problems and controls that are considered okay now.

INTEGRATED PEST MANAGEMENT

Known as IPM, integrated pest management is an environmentally friendly approach to dealing with the pests that bug your plants.

The goal of IPM is to try to handle problems by taking into account the environment in which the problem occurs. To disrupt the environment as little as possible, we try to encourage and some-times even release certain predatory "beneficial" insects that are natural enemies of the destructive insects. We also employ some physical barriers, such as row covers, to keep plants safe.

BENEFICIAL INSECTS. The first line of defense in IPM is to encourage beneficial insects and to use biological controls, rather than poisons—pesticides—to control the others.

There are two groups of beneficials, the predators and the parasites. The most familiar predators are praying mantids, lady beetles, green lacewings, and spiders. They hunt and feed on the others. The parasites are primarily various tiny wasps that hatch inside other insects and . . . you can imagine!

Several mail-order houses offer batches of the beneficial insects with instructions on releasing them. Successfully established in your garden, the beneficials help control the bad guys. To keep beneficials with you season after season, you must not use broad-spectrum insecticides.

HORTICULTURAL OIL SPRAYS. If you need more control than the beneficials provide, look into horticultural oils. Sprayed on infected plants, these dense oils smother insects and their eggs. Some are based on petroleum and others on vegetables such as cottonseed and soybeans. They're environmentally okay. Applied in early spring before plant buds break, they control the undesirables and have a limited effect on the beneficials. Sprayed on in summer, they control whiteflies, mealybugs, scale, spider mites, and aphids.

BOTANICAL PESTICIDES AND INSECTICIDAL SOAPS. Safer as far as the beneficials are concerned, some of these are derived from plants. From Pyrethrum, a daisy-like flower, manufacturers extract an insecticidal chemical. The tropical Neem tree provides a very effective insecticide that is also a fungicide; it even can help with Japanese beetles. (The main control for Japanese beetles is to treat the soil with milky disease spores in late summer. The spores harm the larvae. To be effective, the treatment must be repeated the following year.) Insecticidal soaps are milder than the sprays—they are effective when they come into contact with the insects.

COMMON INSECT PESTS AND CONTROLS

Many factors play a role in how light or heavy your insect problems will be.

1. The presence of natural parasites and predators cuts down on pests and diseases, as explained under Integrated Pest Management (IPM).
2. Dry or wet seasons encourage certain problems.
3. Very cold winters can reduce insect populations.

By choosing pest- and disease-resistant plants that thrive in our climate and by being faithful to the healthy garden practices we recommend, you can avoid many of the most common problems—spider mites, whitefly, Japanese beetles, blackspot, mildew, rust, and nematodes.

What you can't avoid, try to control. Identify the problem and apply controls early in the developmental cycle, not late. The development stage of each species is affected greatly by warm early seasons and cool late seasons. Just as the growth of the plant on which an insect or disease preys is delayed or stimulated by the weather, so is the insect affected.

Keep an eye on plants that hosted problems in previous years. The colder the zone and the season, the later the infestation will come. Blackspot, mildew, mites, whitefly, and Japanese beetles will appear earlier in gardens in Zone 6 and 7 than in yards in Zones 3 and 4. Warm climates may face more broods of insects per year.

Here are various controls for certain stages in the development of pests and diseases:

- With aphids, leafhoppers, earwigs, thrips, crickets, grasshoppers, scale, and similar insects, the metamorphosis to adulthood is simple. All stages of larvae and adults are similar to each other and all feed on the host plant. The egg hatches, and there is a series of nymphs, which shed their skin (molting), getting larger each time until the final adult stage. A little cricket molts and molts and becomes a large adult cricket. You use the same control from beginning to end of the cycle.
- For other creatures, metamorphosis requires an egg stage, a larval stage, a pupal stage (resting stage), and then there is a miraculous transformation into a very different adult.
- With some insects such as beetles, the grub stage feeds on the roots of plants, and the adult beetle feeds on the leaves, stems, and flowers of the host plant.
- In the case of moths and butterflies, nectar feeds only the adult butterfly. For the larval stage—the caterpillar—most butterfly species must locate a specific host plant because the caterpillar would die rather than eat anything else. After mating, a female butterfly flutters slowly near plants, touching down and tasting them through organs on her front legs. When she finds a plant acceptable for her kind, she

will deposit one or more eggs, and then wander off looking for other host plants.

Here is a list of pests and their controls:

APHIDS

Small, pear-shaped insects, they have piercing, sucking mouthparts and, in some cases, can transmit diseases. Aphids stunt and deform leaves and stems and produce a sugary, sticky substance called honeydew. A black fungus quickly spreads on the honeydew and slows down photosynthesis. This fungus is called sooty mold. *Controls:* Aphids usually can be sprayed off with a strong jet of water from a hose. Repeat if they return. If they persist, try a soap-based insecticide or products with malathion or Pyrethrin. Some biological controls are green lacewings, lady beetles, and aphid lions. Some natural controls are applying rubbing alcohol with cotton swabs, horticultural soap, and ultrafine horticultural oil.

BEETLES

Beetles and weevils belong to a group called Coleoptera. Weevils, or curculios, are beetles that have jaws at the end of long snouts. Some have a larval stage that feeds on plants. An example is the black vine weevil, which is most destructive to garden plants. Many other species of beetles, including the June beetle and the rose chafer, affect garden plants. The Japanese beetle, a metallic green and coppery maroon insect, is one of the most destructive pests east of the Mississippi. They chew the leaves and stems of some 200 species of perennials, ruin roses, basil, and other favorites, completely devouring those they like. If there are wild grape vines on your property, root them out; they are an attractive host plant for the Japanese beetle. The grub stage is devastating to lawns and gardens. Apply milky spore disease control or a grub control product to the lawn and gardens now and again next year, and there should be fewer Japanese beetles in the future. But that won't stop them from flying in. *Controls:* Japanese beetle traps are effective, providing they are placed far away from the plantings you are trying to protect rather than among them. If the infestation is minor, beetles can be picked off by hand. Insecticides containing Neem, rotenone, or Sevin insecticide control many of the negative beetles.

BUGS

True bugs belong to the Hemiptera family and do their damage by piercing and sucking. Examples are squash bugs, stink bugs, and the tarnished plant bug. *Controls:* Products containing Sevin insecticide are best, along with Pyrethrin or malathion. These are most effective when the bugs are in an early stage of development.

CATERPILLARS

Caterpillars are the immature stage of moths and butterflies. Their mouthparts chew holes in the leaves, stems, and flowers of most everything. Caterpillars may be smooth or fuzzy and range in size from very small to the huge tomato hornworm. They include leaf rollers and tent makers. Among them are other destructive pests such as the gypsy moth and tent caterpillar. *Controls:* One of the best ways to get rid of a minor infestation is to pick the critters off by hand. The other way is to spray with a biological control such as Bacillus thuringiensis. Other controls are Sevin or malathion insecticide, Pyrethrin, or rotenone.

LEAFMINERS

Leafminers can be the larval stage of small flies, moths, and beetles. Over seven hundred kinds of leafminers affect plants in North America. Leafminers burrow between the upper and lower epidermis of the leaf, making irregular serpentine tunnels. *Controls:* Spray with a product containing malathion or Pyrethrin. Sprays must be applied before the larvae hatch out and enter the leaf. Once inside, the only effective control is a leaf systemic insecticide. An alternative is to cut off the affected foliage; columbine and some plants affected by leafminers generally grow back healthy.

MEALYBUGS

Mealybugs are one-eighth of an inch long and have a mealy, waxy covering. They lay eggs on the undersides of leaves and affect stems, roots, and foliage. Like aphids, they exude honeydew. The presence of sooty mold is an indicator that mealybugs, aphids, or soft scale is present. Mealybugs affect a wide range of hosts, including ferns, ficus, and African violets. *Controls:* Lady beetles are a predator control and are available from biological companies. Spraying with horticultural soaps and ultra-fine horticultural oils also controls mealybugs.

SCALES

Soft and hard scales have piercing, sucking mouthparts. The crawler stage is mobile. After that the insect becomes stationary. Hard scales resemble tiny oyster shells and occur in great numbers. Soft scales are larger, more cup-shaped, and are especially destructive to houseplants. *Controls:* Ultra-fine horticulture oils and horticultural soaps are effective controls.

WHITEFLIES

These tiny whiteflies erupt into clouds of insects when the plant is touched, and then settle back. Their piercing, sucking mouthparts stunt and yellow the host plant. Sooty mold may follow. *Controls:* The most effective control is to spray four times with an insecticide, five to seven days apart. Ultra-fine horticultural oil or insecticidal soaps may be used. Pyrethrin and malathion are also effective. The undersides are where whiteflies cling, so be sure to spray there most thoroughly. Insecticidal soap can handle small infestations. For persistent infestations, use insecticides based on seeds of the Neem tree.

BOTANICAL AND NATURAL CONTROLS FOR COMMON INSECT PESTS AND DISEASES

COPPER

Use fungicidal formulations. *Use to control:* Blackspot, peach leaf curl, powdery mildew, rusts, and bacterial diseases such as fire blight, bacterial leaf spots, and wilt.

CRAB SHELLS

Crab shells (Chitin) is the crushed shells of crabs, crab meal, and is currently sold only by wholesalers. A source of nitrogen must be provided, such as dried blood or cottonseed meal. *Use to control:* Harmful nematodes. Apply crab meal at the rate of 5 pounds per 100 square feet.

DIATOMACEOUS EARTH

This is a powdery substance mined from fossilized silica shells that are the remains of an algae. Physical contact destroys soft-bodied insects. Rain and high humidity may render it less effective. *Use to control:* Ants, aphids, caterpillars, cockroaches, leafhoppers, slugs, snails, and thrips.

HORTICULTURAL OILS

These are botanical oils sprayed on the egg and immature stages of insects to smother them. *Use to control:* Woolly adelgids (which do so much damage to Canadian hemlocks), aphids, cankerworms, leafhoppers, leaf rollers, mealybugs, mites, psyllids, scale, tent caterpillars, and webworms. Note: Spraying with horticultural oils can temporarily remove the blue in blue hostas and Colorado blue spruce. Never spray during droughts, and always water deeply before applying.

HORTICULTURAL SOAPS

This control dates back to the late 1800s. *Use to control:* Soft-bodied insects such as aphids, fruit flies, fungus gnats, lace bugs, leafhoppers, mealybugs, psyllids, scale, scale crawlers, spittle bug, thrips, and whiteflies. Note: Water deeply before using. Do not use on plants under stress, especially drought. Do not use on plants you have just set out, or on delicate plants such as ferns and lantana.

NEEM

These products are derivatives of various parts of the Neem tree (*Azadirachta indica*). Neem is a broad-spectrum repellent, growth regulator, feeding inhibitor, and contact insect poison. It is partially systemic. The most effective formulation is made from the extract of the Neem seed. It also controls certain diseases. *Use to control:* Aphids, leafminers, gypsy moths, loopers, mealybugs, thrips, mites, crickets, mosquitoes, lace flies, and flea beetles.

PYRETHRIN

This is an extract of the flowers of *Chrysanthemum cinerariifolium. Use to control:* Many piercing, sucking, and chewing insects such as ants, aphids, beetles, cockroaches, coddling moths, grasshoppers, leafhoppers, Japanese beetles, leafminers, loopers, Mexican bean and potato beetles, spider mites, stink bugs, ticks, thrips, weevils, and whiteflies.

ROTENONE

Rotenone is a very old botanical pesticide, first used in the mid-1800s. It is prepared from the roots of the tropical plant Lonchocarpus. *Use to control:* Aphids, beetles, caterpillars, Colorado potato beetle, and thrips.

RYANIA

This is a powdered extract from the roots and stems of the South American shrub, *Ryania speciosa. Use to control:* Caterpillars, corn earworms, European corn borer, leaf beetles, and thrips.

SABADILLA

Sabadilla is made from the grinding of the seeds of the Sabadilla plant. *Use to control:* True bugs, caterpillars, Mexican bean beetle, and thrips.

SULFUR

This is a mined mineral. *Use to control:* Blackspot, leaf spot, mites, powdery mildew, rusts, and other plant diseases.

ULTRA-FINE HORTICULTURAL OILS

These are dense refined oils, some based on petroleum and others on vegetables such as cottonseed and soybeans. When sprayed on plants, they smother insects in the egg and immature stages, and they control certain diseases. *Use to control:* Blackspot, mildew, and certain insects including adelgids, aphids, leafhoppers, mealybugs, mites, scale. Note: A Cornell University control for mildew is to spray with a solution consisting of 1 tablespoon of ultrafine oil and 1 tablespoon of baking soda dissolved in 1 gallon of water.

CHEMICAL CONTROLS FOR COMMON INSECT PESTS AND DISEASES

CARBARYL (SEVIN)
Use to control: Beetles, caterpillars, Japanese beetles, mealybug, and thrips.

MANCOZEB, MANZATE
Use to control: Fungal diseases (especially rust on asters and hollyhocks), anthracnose, and botrytis blight.

SEVIN
(See Carbaryl).

MALATHION
Use to control: Aphids, beetles, leafhopper, leafminer, mealybug, spider mites, thrips, and whitefly.

PARZATE
(See Mancozeb, Manzate).

PERMETHRIN
Use to control: A wide range of insects, including whitefly.

COMMON NON-INSECT PESTS AND CONTROLS

NEMATODES
Nematodes are microscopic worm-like creatures. Some feed on roots, others feed on foliage. Endoparasitic nematodes enter the root, causing galls. An example is root-knot nematode. Others are cyst nematodes, such as the golden nematode of potatoes. There are also ectoparasitic forms that feed on the outside of the roots. Symptoms are a yellowing and stunting of the plant, lack of vigor, and wilting during hot weather. *Controls:* Growing orange French marigolds for three months and tilling them into the soil before planting has been effective. Also effective is the application of ground crab shells, which are sold only by wholesalers at this writing. However, you can make your own. Save up and grind lobster and crab shells and scatter them around and dig them into the soil around affected plants.

SPIDER MITES
Spider mites are so tiny you need a magnifying glass to see them. They can attack all parts of a plant but are most prevalent under the leaf. These piercing, sucking pests cause a yellowing of the plant, and finally result in a rusty and sometimes silvery look to the leaf. For a positive identification, shake the perennial over a white pad, and if little dots move on the paper, you have spider mites. Roses, indoor plants in hot dry conditions, and evergreens in dry airless corners are especially susceptible. *Controls:* Hosing the plant down regularly discourages spider mite activity. Insecticidal soaps, ultrafine horticultural oils, and miticides can be used.

SLUGS AND SNAILS
These plant pests feed on lush foliage, leaving holes in the leaf. Irregular, shiny, slimy trails are a telltale sign. Complete defoliation can occur on some lush-leaved annuals and perennials, hostas, for example. *Controls:* Diatomaceous earth, iron phosphate (Sluggo), slug and snail bait, beer in shallow aluminum plates or tuna fish cans, or commercially available traps.

COMMON DISEASES AND CONTROLS

BACTERIAL DISEASE
Bacteria is not a fungus, and although the symptoms may be similar, in order to control the causative agent, you must use a bacteriacide such as copper fungicide. *Controls:* Copper fungicide, Kocide 101, Agri-Strep.

BOTRYTIS GREY MOLD (BOTRYTIS BLIGHT)

Symptoms are a grayish-to-brown powdery covering on buds, leaves, and stems. This disease affects many perennials, including peonies. *Controls:* Sulfur, Daconil 2728.

FOLIAR DISEASES

Symptoms on perennials are leaf spots and blight that can be bacterial or fungal in origin. *Controls:* Sulfur, copper fungicides, Daconil, Mancozeb, Immunox.

LEAF SPOTS

Most gardeners encounter this as blackspot. Leaf spots can be caused by a bacterial or fungal agent. Examples are blackspot of roses and leaf spot on tall bearded iris. *Controls:* Copper fungicide, Daconil, horticultural oil, Immunox, sulfur.

POWDERY MILDEW

This fungus covers buds, stems, and leaves with a white-gray powdery substance. High humidity increases the severity of powdery mildew. If you water often with underground sprinkling systems, you may find this disease difficult to control. Powdery mildew is commonly found on asters, monarda, and phlox. *Controls:* If it appears in your garden, when buying new plants, go for those advertised as mildew resistant. Roses, lilacs, and many other garden favorites are also susceptible. Wide spacing for good air circulation and air movement helps. Apply sulfur, ultrafine horticultural oil, copper fungicide, Immunox, Bayleton.

ROOT AND STEM ROT

Symptoms are the wilting and rapid death of the plant. The crown or rhizome of the plant may be wet or slimy. The cause may be bacterial or fungal. *Controls:* For fungal causes, use Terrachlor or Mancozeb. For bacterial causes, use copper fungicides, Kocide 101, Agri-Strep.

RUST DISEASE

This form of fungus may be a single- or double-host disease. The first indication is yellow or pale spots on the upper surface of the leaf, with powdery orange spores visible on the bottom of the leaf. Asters, chrysanthemums, lily-of-the-valley, and hollyhocks are common hosts. *Controls:* Any fungicidal control labeled for rust. Also, sulfur, copper fungicide, Daconil, Immunox, Mancozeb.

VIRAL DISEASES

These diseases are not fungal or bacterial in origin but in fact are particles of protein and genetic material so small that an electron microscope is needed to see the virus. Piercing, sucking insects commonly spread viral diseases. Viral diseases may be difficult to diagnose. Symptoms are a mottling or mosaic discoloration of the leaf or ring spots. *Control:* No known control except removing the infected plant.

COMMON ANIMAL PESTS AND CONTROLS

BEARS

Where bears are a problem, they may come to bird and hummingbird feeders. They harvest berries and sometimes take your pets. If there are bear sightings near you, take in bird feeders and other attractions.

BIRDS

Our feathered friends are beautiful, lovable, inspiring, and useful in that they eat insects, some good and some bad. They also eat berries and fruit, your kind as well as theirs; seeds you give them and seeds you don't; and sunflowers.

A bird mesh cover is almost the only way to protect fruit that birds want to eat.

- Cover ponds with bird netting to keep the fish safe from herons and other expert fishermen.

DEER

The most destructive of all the wild creatures that visit our gardens is the deer. New repellents come on the market every season, but at this writing we know of none that has proven to be a permanent deterrent.

When deer really want what you've got, they come on in and get it in spite of flashing lights, jets of water, ultra sound devices, evil smelling egg and protein sprays, predator odors, hot pepper wax, bitter Bitrex, garlic, and systemic repellants. Deer-Off® can be used on fruits and vegetables as well as flowers, trees, and shrubs; when tested by Rutgers University, it lasted for up to three months. Some nurseries successfully protect clients' plants with their own deterrent sprays and may sell you their version. Some gardeners have luck discouraging deer by hanging old pantyhose containing human or canine hair around the property. However, most deterrents of this type fail to keep deer away once they get used to it. Here are approaches that have some effect:

- Don't invite deer by planting Class A fatal attractions: Apple or pear trees. If you have fruit trees, be sure to harvest the fruits daily before the deer get to them. Arborvitae, rhododendrons, and broadleaved evergreens are winter favorites, along with shrub althea and hydrangeas. Hostas and other big, lush-leaved plants, phlox, 'Autumn Joy' and other *Sedum spectabile* varieties, tomatoes, peas, beans, and other leafy vegetables are summer favorites. Roses, raspberries, and other members of the *Rosa* family—deer relish them all.
- Protect small endangered plantings, beds of hostas and daylilies for example, by screening them with enclosures of deer fencing or chickenwire supported by wooden or metal stakes. Deer generally avoid small, enclosed spaces that could be traps. Protect large plantings with bird netting.
- Enclose your property or gardens. A single strand of electric wire 30 inches high with a stake every 20 feet and baited with peanut butter can be effective. Close the peanut butter into a square of tinfoil, and crimp it on to the wire every 20 feet. The deer nibble the peanut butter and, without being really hurt, learn to avoid the fence.
- Enclose your property with a deer fence 8 to 10 feet high supported by a post every 40 feet.

This high, tensile steel fencing can be unobtrusive.
- Train a dog to run deer off your property, without leaving it himself.
- Discourage visits by positioning a variety of alarming and distasteful smells where deer customarily enter your grounds, and change the smells often. For example, hang at the height of a deer's nose tubes of crushed garlic, or predator urine, or Irish Spring or lavender soap, or human hair dampened with odorous lotions. Place a different scent at each entry point. And, this is crucial, change each deterrent every four to six weeks while the weather is warm enough to volatilize scents.
- For winter, wrap rhododendrons, arborvitae, and other species that deer love in burlap or chickenwire.
- Try new plants from those on the list of deer-resistant plants at André and Mark Viette's site, www.inthegardenradio.com.

MOLES AND VOLES

You think "moles" when you see tunnels heaving the lawn and blame them when perennials disappear and bulbs move around. But they are innocent. Moles eat bugs, grubs, and worms only. The culprits are voles, *Microtus* species. Often called pine and meadow mice, these small rodents are reddish-brown to gray, 2 to 4 inches long, and have short tails, blunt faces, and tiny eyes and ears. They live in extensive tunnel systems usually less than a foot deep with entrances an inch or two across.

Protecting the plant is easier than getting rid of voles. They dislike tunneling through coarse material. Keep them away by planting with VoleBloc™ or PermaTill®, which are bits of non-toxic, light, long-lasting aggregates like pea gravel with jagged edges. The stuff promotes rooting. Here's how to apply it:

ESTABLISHED PLANTINGS—Dig a 4-inch-wide, 12-inch-deep moat around the drip line of perennials under attack, and fill it with VoleBloc™, and mulch with VoleBloc™.

NEW PLANTINGS—Prepare a planting hole 2 inches deeper than the rootball(s), and layer in 2 inches of VoleBloc™. Set the rootball in place, and backfill with VoleBloc™. Mulch with more VoleBloc™.

If vole damage appears in winter, bait the main area around the plants with a rodenticide, pull the mulch apart, spray the crown lightly with a repellent, and put the mulch back in place.

Tunnels heaved in the lawn between March and October are apt to be moles hunting for grubs. Apply a grub control such as Merit or Marathon® to kill off the grubs, and the moles will find another supermarket.

RABBITS, WOODCHUCKS, RACCOONS, AND OTHER RODENTS

Try chemical fungicide formulations such as Thiram (Arasan) and hot pepper wax. Or fence gardens with 6 foot high chickenwire that starts 24 inches underground. If you have woodchucks to deal with, leave the chickenwire loose and floppy, not stiff enough to climb. Keeping raccoons out of the vegetable garden requires enclosing your garden overhead as well.

MORE ABOUT FERTILIZERS AND PLANT NUTRITION

Our all-purpose recipe for fertilizing, followed by an explanation of why and when we use which product:

FLOWER AND SHRUB GARDEN

For each 100 square feet of new garden space add the following:

	SUN GARDEN	SHADE GARDEN
Plant-Tone®	5-10 lbs.	5-10 lbs.
Holly-Tone®	5-10 lbs.	14-7 lbs.
Rock Phosphate	5-10 lbs.	5-10 lbs.
Super Phosphate	5-10 lbs.	13-5 lbs.
Greensand	5-10 lbs.	5-10 lbs.
Gypsum (for clay soils)	5-10 lbs.	5-10 lbs.
Osmocote® (8 month)	2-02 lbs.	5-02 lbs.

Till all these amendments plus organic matter into the soil, rake smooth, and your bed is ready to be planted.

KNOW WHAT'S IN YOUR FERTILIZER

In our experience, plant health depends on more than just the three essential nutrients, nitrogen, phosphorous, and potash, provided in an all-purpose chemical fertilizer. The Viette family has been growing plants for over eighty years using natural, organic, blended fertilizers made up of at least ten to fourteen ingredients. These are earth-friendly products that include the three essential nutrients, and, in addition, have beneficial effects on the environment and the soil.

Adding natural organics to the soil has a positive effect on soil microorganisms, the micro-fauna and micro-flora of the soil, and beneficial earthworms. The soil structure and aeration is improved. Natural organics don't dissolve quickly and do not easily run off into rivers and lakes.

Their breakdown is dependent on three factors—soil moisture, temperature, and microbial activity. The nutrient microbial release is a slow, gradual process that makes nutrients available exactly when the plants need them and over an extended period of time. The result is overall plant health, and plants with luxuriant and robust foliage and superb flowers.

In the past, we mixed our own blends of organic fertilizers in the nursery garage. Today the marketplace offers packaged fertilizers that are blends of natural organics. Bulb-Tone®, Holly-Tone®, Plant-Tone®, and Rose-Tone® are the most complete on the market at this writing. Here's what they contain:

HOLLY-TONE® 4-6-4

Ingredients: dehydrated manure, animal tankage, crab meal, cocoa meal, cotton seed meal, dried blood, sunflower meal, kelp, greensand, rock phosphate, sulfate of potash, ammonium sulfate, single superphosphate (1 pound = 2⅔ cups)

Application Amounts: New Bed—10 lbs. per 100 sq. ft., 100 lbs. per 1000 sq. ft.; Established Bed—5 lbs. per 100 sq. ft., 50 lbs. per 1000 sq. ft.

PLANT-TONE® 5-3-3

Ingredients: dehydrated manure, animal tankage, crab meal, cocoa meal, bonemeal, dried blood, sunflower meal, kelp, greensand, rock phosphate, sulfate of potash

Application Amounts: New Bed—10 lbs. per 100 sq. ft., 100 lbs. per 1000 sq. ft.; Established Bed—5 lbs. per 100 sq. ft., 50 lbs. per 1000 sq. ft.

BULB-TONE® 4-10-6

Ingredients: bonemeal, crab meal, dehydrated manure, animal tankage, cocoa meal, dried blood, sunflower meal, greensand, rock phosphate, ammonium sulfate, single super phosphate

Application Amounts: New Bed—10 lbs. per 100 sq. ft.; Established Bed—5 lbs. per 100 sq. ft.

ROSE-TONE® 6-6-4

Ingredients: dehydrated manure, animal tankage, crab meal, cocoa meal, dried blood, cottonseed meal, sunflower meal, kelp, greensand, bode phosphate, sulfate of potash, ammonium sulfate, single super phosphate

Application Amounts: New Plant—4 cups per plant; Established Plant—2 cups per plant

GREENSAND

Greensand is a mined mineral-rich marine deposit, also known as glauconite. These ancient sea deposits are an all-natural source of potash. It is an iron potassium silicate in which the potassium is the important element in the potash. Thirty-two or more microingredients are contained in greensand. There is 0.01 percent soluble potash in what is a total of 6 percent total potash K20. Greensand is non-burning and helps to loosen heavy clay soil. It also binds sandy soil for a better structure. It increases the water-holding capacity of soils and it considered an excellent soil conditioner. Greensand promotes plant vigor, disease resistance, and good color in fruit. Greensand contains nitrogen, phosphorus, potassium, calcium, magnesium, sulfur, chlorine, cobalt, copper, iron, manganese, molybdenum, sodium, and zinc. Greensand also contains silica, iron oxides, magnesia, and lime. Dr. J.C.F. Tedrew, Rutgers University Soil Specialist, mentions that glauconite may have a considerable capacity for gradual release of certain plant food elements, particularly the so-called trace elements (micronutrients). Once greensand is impregnated with micronutrients it will later release them at a very slow rate.

GYPSUM

Gypsum is a hydrated calcium sulfate. The actual amounts of calcium and sulfur can vary, but 22% calcium and 17% sulfur occurs in some formulations. Gypsum replaces sodium in alkaline soils with calcium and improves the drainage and aeration.

Gypsum is an effective ammonia-conserving agent when applied to manured soils or other rapidly decomposing organic matter. The escaping ammonia is changed to ammonium sulfate, which is stable. Gypsum is applied at the rate of 10 lbs. per 100 sq. ft. in heavy clay soil and 5 lbs. per 100 sq. ft. in moderately clay soil. Gypsum improves the structure of the heavier soils rather than the sandy soils.

OSMOCOTE®, SCOTTS AND SCOTTS-SIERRA ALL-PURPOSE FERTILIZERS

All-purpose chemical fertilizers contain balanced proportions of the three essential plant nutrients— nitrogen (N), phosphorus (P), and potassium (K). The numbers on the packaging, 5-10-5 and 10-10-10 for example, refer to the proportions of each element present. When you apply a granular all-purpose chemical fertilizer to the soil, the nutrients last a short time—five or six weeks. To keep the plants nourished using only chemical fertilizers, you must repeat the applications. Because they dissolve easily in water, these elements can contribute to the pollution of nearby streams and rivers, and eventually harm bigger bodies of water like the Chesapeake Bay. Somewhat similar are the soluble chemical fertilizers you mix with water and apply in a hose-end sprayer or a watering can. We use these fertilizers when a plant shows symptoms of nutrient deficiency, as a quick pick-up, or as a starter fertilizer. But for a general liquid fertilization there are organic counterparts of the chemical fertilizers: for example, fish emulsion and liquid seaweed, manure teas made by steeping dehydrated manure, and the compost teas that are becoming popular today.

Scientists have packaged the chemical fertilizers so they act like tiny little time pills, releasing their nutrients over a specified period. Examples are Osmocote® controlled release fertilizers, which come in 3-4 month, 8-9 month, and 12-14 month formulations. A similar product is Scotts controlled-release Agriform™ fertilizer tablets, which can last up to two years.

MORE ABOUT PRUNING TREES AND SHRUBS

Pruning is part of regular garden maintenance, not just a solution to things gone wrong. The thing to keep in mind when you prune is that it stimulates growth, and that dictates what you should prune, and when.

WHAT TO PRUNE

To keep trees and shrubs looking their best and growing well, regularly remove weak, crowded stems; branches that will eventually cross each other; suckers, which are shoots growing at the base of a tree or shrub; and water sprouts, which are vigorous upright shoots that develop along a branch, usually where it has been pruned. Pruning is sometimes needed to open up the canopy of a tree or a shrub to let in air and sun. Pruning also causes denser growth, and can be used to encourage height and to control size. For the most appealing results, when you prune, follow the lines of the plant's natural growth habit.

WHEN TO PRUNE

Our plant pages suggest a best time for pruning each plant. The rule is that trees and shrubs that bloom on this year's growth—hydrangeas for example, rose-of-Sharon, chaste tree, butterfly bush—are pruned early in the year, before growth begins. The growth that pruning encourages provides more places for flowers. Plants that bloom on wood from the previous year—ornamental fruit trees and most spring-flowering trees and shrubs such as azaleas—are pruned as soon as possible after they bloom. Shade and evergreen trees typically are pruned every three or four years.

Flowering and evergreen shrubs may need maintenance pruning every season. Young vigorous plants will need more pruning than mature plants. Winter and early spring pruning stimulates plants to produce more unwanted suckers than late spring or summer pruning. So if it's a plant's nature to sucker heavily, as with lilacs and crabapples, summer is a better time to prune. On the other hand, pruning in late summer or early fall can cause growth that won't have time to harden off before winter.

PRUNING LARGE TREES

When a large limb is involved, pruning is best undertaken in spring just before growth begins, or after maximum leaf expansion in June. Pruned then, the tree will likely roll calluses over the external wound, and, internally, it will protect itself by walling off the damaged tissue. Painting a wound has fallen out of favor but the Cornell Cooperative Extension Illustrated Guide to Pruning says "certain materials such as orange shellac may provide a temporary barrier to certain pathogens until a tree's natural barrier zones form." The alcohol in shellac is a disinfectant.

Evergreen trees are usually allowed to develop naturally, but deciduous trees may need pruning to grow up to be all they can be. After planting a balled-and-burlapped, or a container-grown, deciduous tree, remove any weak and injured branches, and those that will eventually rub across each other. For bare-root trees, some experts recommend thinning out a quarter of the branches so the canopy will be in better balance with the reduced root system. The year after planting, pruning to shape a deciduous tree begins, and that continues over the next three to five years. The first step is to identify the strongest terminal leader, unless the tree is naturally multistemmed: the leader will become the trunk. Then prune all but the main limbs—the "scaffold branches"—that will define the structure of the tree. Choose as scaffolding those branches whose crotch is at a wide angle to the trunk. The height of the lowest scaffold branches depends on the activities planned under the tree. You can leave them in place for the first few years to protect the bark from sunscald and to provide more leaves to nourish the root system. The scaffold branches at each level should be a fairly equal distance from each other: spaced evenly all around the trunk, they make for better balance. For each next level of scaffold branches, choose limbs developing between or offset from, not directly over, the branches of the level below. In the following years, watch the growth of the tree and trim back any side branches growing taller than the leader.

PRUNING AND REJUVENATING SHRUBS

At planting time prune out weak and injured branches, and any crossing each other. To keep the shrub airy, then and later, you may need to remove a few branches from the base and to head back others. "Heading back" means cutting an unwanted branchlet back to where there is an outward facing branchlet or bud on the main stem. Shearing shrubs, unless they are growing as a hedge, is discouraged because it stimulates dense growth at the tips of the branches and distorts the natural shape of the plant.

You can use pruning to rejuvenate older shrubs grown leggy or out of scale with their place in the garden. There are three ways to rejuvenate deciduous shrubs, all initiated before growth begins in early spring. The most drastic way is to cut the whole plant back to within 6 to 10 inches of the ground: by July it will be a mass of upright canes. Remove half or more of these, and head the others back to outward facing buds at half or less of the height you want the shrub to be. A slightly less drastic way is to cut half, or more, of the older branches, including any that cross, and all suckers, back to the ground: at midsummer, remove all new canes and head back branching that develops on the canes you kept. The least drastic method is to remove a third to a quarter of the older branches over three, or even four, years, each year removing unwanted suckers and heading back crowded branching. You can rejuvenate broadleaved evergreen shrubs that have grown out of scale—rhododendrons, mountain laurels, and boxwoods for example—by cutting them back to within 2 to 4 feet of the ground in late winter or early spring before growth begins. Leave branch ends at various heights so regrowth will appear natural. Regrowth will take two to four years.

GARDENING WITH WILDLIFE, WELCOME AND OTHERWISE

BIRDS

Birds adopt gardens that provide food, water, and shelter. To attract birds, plant trees and shrubs that have berries and small fruits. Let stand the seedheads of ornamental grasses and various flowers for fall and early winter. Provide a water basin/birdbath near a shrub, preferably a dense evergreen, where birds can check for predators before flying in. Plant, or keep, tall trees for perching and nesting: pines and hemlocks provide nesting materials as well. Finally, if you have space, allow milkweed and other wild plants useful to birds to develop in a bramble away from house traffic.

To deter birds: Our feathered friends are beautiful, lovable, inspiring, and useful in that they eat insects, some good and some bad. They also eat your berries and your garden and grass seeds. A mesh cover is almost the only way to protect berries. Remember when planting for birds that they drop seeds everywhere. Bears are eager for birdseed: if there are bears in your area, stocking a bird feeder may not be a good idea.

HUMMINGBIRDS

Hummingbirds rely on sight, not scent, to locate their food. They are attracted by tubular, brightly colored flowers, and prefer single-petaled varieties to doubles. Like butterflies, hummingbirds require a continuous supply of nectar.

BEARS, BEES, AND WASPS

Bears, bees, and wasps love nectar, too: think twice before putting out sugared water.

BUTTERFLIES

Ideal for a butterfly garden is the sun-warmed side of a south-facing fence, a wall, or a windbreak.

Because this lovely thing is cold-blooded, it can fly only when warmed by the sun and in air that is 55 to 60 degrees Fahrenheit. On sunless days and at night, butterflies roost in deeply fissured bark, or a butterfly hotel: a wooden box with perches and an entrance big enough for a butterfly with folded wings to slide through, a slot about ¼-inch wide by about 3½ inches high. For basking, butterflies also need tall verticals that hold warmth—statuary, stones, standing logs. And a puddling place—a patch of damp sand or drying mud where male butterflies can gather and take up moisture and dissolved salts, which we believe are helpful for mating. The food for adult butterflies is the nectar in flowers. They are drawn to brightly colored flowers—purple, yellow, orange, and red. The caterpillars of most species need a specific host plant: Peterson Field Guide to Eastern Butterflies can tell you which. Learn to recognize the caterpillars of butterflies, and even many moths, so that you won't be tempted to eliminate them from the garden when you see them eating your plants.

DEER

To attract Bambi and company, plant fruit trees. They relish apples and pears. They also adore hostas, rhododendrons, and other large, succulent leaves, and roses, raspberries, impatiens—anything that doesn't have itsy bitsy leaves or flowers. Provide a salt lick and water in a secluded spot, and for winter put out bales of hay.

To deter these oversized white-tailed rats: Every commercial deterrent we have tried so far has succeeded only until the deer decided it wasn't a sign of danger. Wrapping evergreens with burlap in late fall and winter works: for summer, use chicken wire—at a distance you won't see it. Or plant in small, fully enclosed spaces.

To protect a large property, try fencing high enough for a tennis court, or double fences 4 to 5 feet apart. If you can't fence, you may be able to discourage them this way: at places where they enter your garden, hang tubes of crushed garlic, or predator urine, chunks of Irish Spring soap, or human hair damp with strongly scented lotions such as Avon's Skin So Soft. Hang them at the height of the deer's nose, a different scent at each entry point. Replace these scents with new different ones every four to six weeks of the gardening season.

RABBITS, WOODCHUCKS, AND OTHER RODENTS

To attract these sweet critters, develop a wilderness bramble with fallen logs far enough from the beaten path to let them feel safe. Provide a source of water. Time and nature will do the rest.

Chicken wire fencing that starts 24 inches underground keeps out most rodents: for woodchucks, make it 4 to 6 feet tall as well and leave it loose and floppy, not stiff enough to climb. Keeping raccoons out requires enclosing your garden overhead as well.

STARTING SEEDS INDOORS

New England's growing season is unpredictable. We can have a heat wave in March, late frosts in May, just enough chill in early September to ruin the tomatoes, followed by a glorious lingering Indian summer. So we extend the growing season by starting seeds early indoors—in winter for spring planting, in summer for early fall planting. Seedlings of plants labeled "hardy" can be transplanted to the garden after the last frost. Others must wait until night temperatures reach 50 to 55 degrees Fahrenheit. But you can start seedlings outdoors early under a plastic cone called a "hot cap," an elegant, bell-shaped "cloche," strips of filmy tenting like Reemay®, or in a cold frame or a hot bed—projects beyond the scope of this book.

The seed packet tells you whether you can start the plants indoors, and how much ahead of the outdoor planting season to plant. For fast growers four to six weeks is usual; for slow-growers, ten to twelve weeks is typical. We recommend starting seeds in moistened, *sterile* commercial seed starter mix. We use the flats that have individual planting pockets and plastic covers.

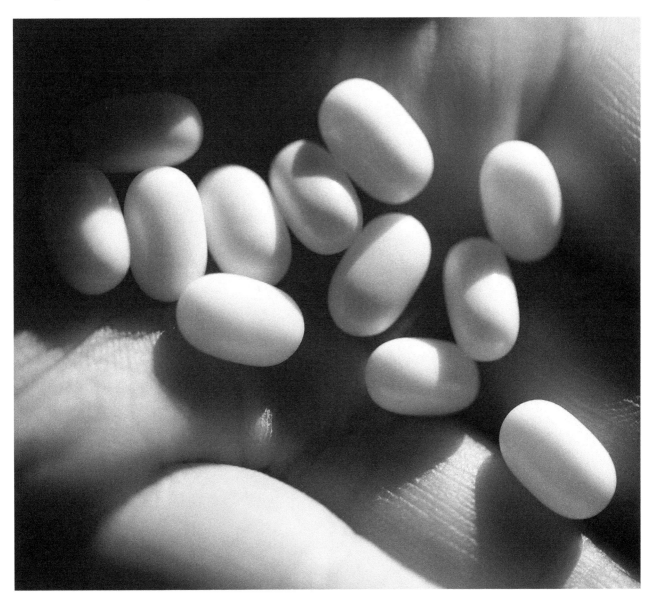

A humusy *fertile* planting mix is best for plants that will be indoors six weeks or more. Seed packets recommend planting depths. Use a pencil or a pointed stick to make planting holes: for medium-size seeds, ¼-inch-deep; for large seeds, 1-inch-deep is better. To sow very fine seeds, mix them half and half with builder's sand and broadcast them evenly over the planting mix from a saltshaker. The seed packet will tell you whether the seeds germinate best in the dark covered with soil, or uncovered so they get light.

Label the seeds—don't forget!—and cover the flat with its plastic top for the germination period.

To speed germination, set it on a heat mat, or an old heating pad on "Low" and covered with plastic. Perennials tend to be slow to germinate, and require more attention than annuals. "Seed" leaves, called cotelydons, appear first. They contain starches and proteins the embryo draws on until the "true" leaves open and begin producing food. The cotyledons are present within the seed, along with an embryonic stem, a root, and all else necessary to create a new plant.

When all the seeds in the flat are sprouted, remove the cover and move the flat to good light. Seedlings that will go out to the garden in four or five weeks do well with the light on a sunny sill. They will eventually bend toward the sun: to keep them growing straight, rotate the container.

Seedlings that will be indoors six weeks or more do best under grow lights, one cool and one warm white fluorescent bulb burned fourteen to sixteen hours a day. A fluorescent light garden is a worthwhile investment if you plan to start seeds indoors every year. Many gardeners keep their grow lights in the basement.

To keep the seedlings growing strongly during this period, maintain soil moisture. Water from the bottom, or mist the seedlings; pouring water over hair-thin stems flattens them. Add only as much water as the seedlings take up within an hour. Tip out any excess water. Air the room often if you can. The cotyledons are followed by the true leaves, which are more complex. Their unfolding indicates the plant has begun to grow. At that point, however tiny, the seedling can be transplanted successfully. As the seedlings become crowded, transplant each to an individual 4-inch pot filled with sterile potting mix. Fertilize seedlings that will be indoors six weeks or more every two weeks: we use a soluble houseplant fertilizer (20-20-20) at half strength.

Seedlings sulk in cold soil. Before moving them to the open garden, wait for daytime temperatures to reach 55 degrees Fahrenheit. Four or five days before transplanting to the garden, set the pots outdoors in a spot sheltered from direct sun and wind. The soil will dry more quickly outdoors, so check the pots often and water as needed.

GLOSSARY

ACIDIC SOIL: soil whose pH is less than 7.0. A pH of 6.0 to 7.0 is mildly acidic . The pH in which the widest range of flowers thrive is slightly acidic , in the pH 5.5 to 6.5 range. Except for areas where limestone is prevalent, most garden soil in America is in this range. This pH is also suited to most plants described as acid-loving.

ALKALINE SOIL: soil whose pH is greater than 7.0. It lacks acidity, often because it has limestone in it. Mid-Atlantic soils tend to be alkaline.

ALL-PURPOSE FERTILIZER: available in three forms: powdered, liquid, or granular. It contains balanced proportions of the three important nutrients—nitrogen (N), phosphorus (P), and potassium (K). It is suitable for most plants.

ANNUAL: a plant that lives its entire life in one season. It germinates, produces flowers, sets seed, and dies the same year.

BALLED AND BURLAPPED: a tree or shrub grown in the field and dug, whose soil- and rootball is wrapped with protective burlap and tied with twine.

BARE ROOT: describes plants without any soil around their roots, often packaged by mail-order suppliers. The rule of thumb is to soak the roots ten to twelve hours before planting.

BEDDING PLANT: usually annuals that are planted in large groups in a bed for maximum show.

Beneficial insect: insects and their larvae that prey on pest organisms and their eggs. Some that are well known include the ladybug and praying mantis.

BOTANICAL NAME: plant names given in Latin accurately identifying the genus, species, subspecies, variety, and form. Here's an example: *Picea abies* forma pendula is the 1) genus, 2) species, and 3) form (pendula, meaning "pendulous" or "weeping") that is the botanical name for weeping Norway spruce. *Picea abies* 'Nidiformis' is the 1) genus, 2) species, and 3) variety. When the varietal name is between single quotation marks, it's what is

called a "cultivar"—a cultivated variety, or a variety that has been cultivated and given a name of its own.

BRACT: a modified leaf structure resembling a petal that appears close behind the flower or head of flowers. In some flowers, that of flowering dogwoods for example, the bract may be more colorful than the flowers themselves.

BUD UNION: a thickened area above the crown on the main stem of a woody plant. This is the point at which a desirable plant has been grafted, or budded, onto the rootstock of a plant that is strong but less ornamental.

CANOPY: the overhead branching area of a tree, including its foliage.

COLD HARDINESS: the ability of a plant to survive the winter cold in a particular area or zone.

COMMON NAME: there is no such thing as an accurate "common name" for a plant. Names commonly used for plants are rarely common the world over, or even in a single country or state. Because they can vary from region to region, they are not as much help in locating plants as the scientific botanical names. Many are British "antiques" which continue to be used for their charm—for example, love-in-a-mist, fleabane, and lady's mantle. Botanical names find their way into common gardener language. Examples are: impatiens, begonia, petunia, salvia, zinnia, aster, astilbe, phlox, iris. In time, you will find yourself remembering many of the botanical names of the plants that interest you most.

COMPOST: organic matter, such as leaves, weeds, grass clippings, and seaweed, that has undergone progressive decomposition until it is reduced to a soft, fluffy texture. Soil that has been amended with compost holds air and water better and also has improved drainage.

CORM: an energy-storing structure, similar to a bulb, but actually a specialized stem, found at the base of a plant, such as crocosmia and crocus.

CROWN: the base of a plant where the roots meet the stems.

CULTIVAR: the word stands for "cultivated variety." Cultivars are varieties named by gardeners and gardening professionals. They are developed, or selected, variations of species and hybrids.

DEADHEAD: the process of removing faded flower heads from plants in order to improve their appearance, stop unwanted seed production, and most often to encourage more flowering.

DECIDUOUS: refers to trees and shrubs that lose their leaves in fall, a sign that the plant is going into dormancy for the period of weather ahead.

DIVISION: the splitting apart of perennial plants in order to create several smaller plants. Division is a way to control the size of a plant, multiply your holdings, and also to renovate crowded plants that are losing their vitality.

DORMANCY: the period, usually the winter, when plants temporarily cease active growth and rest. However, heat and drought can throw plants into summer dormancy. Certain plants, for example Oriental poppies, spring-blooming wildflowers, and certain bulbs, can have their natural dormancy period in summer.

ESTABLISHED: the point at which a new planting begins to show new growth and is well rooted in the soil, indicating the plants have recovered from transplant shock.

EVERGREEN: plants that do not lose all their foliage annually with the onset of winter.

EXFOLIATING: to peel away in thin layers, as with bark.

FERTILITY/FERTILE: refers to the soil's content of the nutrients needed for sturdy plant growth. Nutrient availability is affected by pH levels.

FLORET: a tiny flower, usually one of many forming a cluster, comprising a single flower head.

FOLIAR: refers to the practice of making applications to just the plant's foliage of dissolved fertilizer and some insecticides. Leaf tissue absorbs liquid quickly.

GERMINATE/GERMINATION: refers to the sprouting of a seed, the plant's first stage of development.

GRAFT/UNION: the point on the stem of a strong, woody plant where a stem (scion) from another plant (usually one that is more ornamental) has been inserted into understock so that they will join together into one plant.

HARDSCAPE: the permanent, structural, non-plant part of a landscape, such as walls, sheds, pools, patios, arbors, and walkways.

HERBACEOUS: plants with soft stems, as opposed to the woody stem tissue of trees and shrubs.

HUMUS: almost completely decomposed organic materials such as leaves, plant matter, and manures.

HYBRID: a plant that is the product of deliberate or natural cross-pollination between two or more plants of the same species or genus.

LEADER: the main stem of a tree.

LOAM: a mix of sand and clay. When humus is added, loam is the best soil for gardening.

LOW-WATER DEMAND: describes plants that tolerate dry soil for varying periods of time. They are often succulent and may have taproots.

MICROCLIMATE: pockets on a property that are warmer or cooler than the listed climatic zone. Hilly spots, valleys, nearness to reflective surfaces or windbreaks, proximity to large bodies of water can all contribute to altering the surrounding temperature.

MULCH: a layer of material (natural or man-made) used to cover soil to protect it from water or wind erosion, and to help maintain the soil temperature and moisture. Mulches also discourage weeds.

NATURALIZED: a plant that adapts and spreads in a landscape habitat. Some plants we think of as "native" are imports that have "naturalized", for example, *Phlox drummondii,* the annual phlox, self-sows and has naturalized in sand in the Outer Banks of North Carolina.

NECTAR: the sweet fluid produced by glands on flowers that attract pollinators such as bees, butterflies, and hummingbirds.

ORGANIC FERTILIZER: a fertilizer that is derived from anything that was living, such as bonemeal, fish emulsion, manure, plants.

ORGANIC MATERIAL/ORGANIC MATTER: any substance that is derived from plants.

PEAT MOSS: acidic organic matter from peat sedges (United States) or sphagnum mosses (Canada) often mixed into soil to raise its organic content and sometimes as a mild acidifier.

PERENNIAL: a flowering plant that lives for more than one season; the foliage often dies back with frost, but their roots survive the winter and generate new growth in the spring.

PERENNIALIZE: sometimes confused with "naturalize." The two words are not synonymous. Tulips many perennialize, that is come back for four years or more, but they don't become wild plants. "Naturalize" applies to a garden plant that becomes a wildflower of a region that is not its native habitat. It could be a native plant or an exotic plant.

PH: pH stands for potential of hydrogen. A measurement of the relative acidity (low pH) or alkalinity (high pH) of soil or water. Based on a scale of 1 to 14, pH 7.0 being neutral.

PINCH: to remove tender stems and/or leaves by pressing them between thumb and forefinger. The purpose is usually to deadhead, or to encourage branching and compactness. Hand shearing achieves the same purpose on plants whose blooms are too small to pinch out one at a time, pinks for example.

PLANTING SEASON: refers to the best time to set out certain plants. The most vigorous growth occurs in spring. Early spring is the preferred planting time in cold zones, particularly for woody plants and for species that react poorly to transplanting. Early fall, after summer's heat has gone by and before cold comes, is an excellent time for planting in the Mid-Atlantic, provided the climate allows the roots two months or so to tie into the soil before cold shuts the plants down. Traditional planting seasons are spring and fall: availability of plants in containers/pots has added a new and valuable season to plant—the summer.

POLLEN: the yellow, powdery grains in the center of a flower which are the plant's male sex cells. Pollen is transferred by wind and insects, and to a lesser extent by animals, to the female plants, whence fertilization occurs.

RACEME: describes a flower stalk where the blossoms are an arrangement of single-stalked florets along a tall stem; similar to a spike.

RHIZOME: an energy-storing structure, actually a specialized stem, similar to a bulb, sometimes planted horizontally near the soil surface (iris), or beneath the soil surface (trillium). The roots emerge from the bottom, and leaves and flowers grow from the upper portion of the rhizome.

ROOTBOUND/POTBOUND: the condition of a plant that has been confined in a container too long. Without space for expansion, the roots wrap around the rootball or mat at the bottom of the container.

ROOT DIVISION/ROOTED DIVISIONS: sections of the crown of a plant, usually of a perennial, that has been divided. This is most often the source of containerized perennial plants. A root division will perform exactly like the parent plant.

ROOTED CUTTINGS: cuttings taken from foliage growth perennials, usually, or from woody plants, that have been handled so as to grow roots. Rooted cuttings will perform exactly like the parent plant.

SELF-SOW: some plants mature seeds, sow them freely, and the offspring appear as volunteers the following season.

SEMIEVERGREEN: tending to be evergreen in a mild climate but deciduous in a colder climate.

SHEARING: the pruning technique where plant stems and branches are cut uniformly with long-bladed pruning shears or hedge trimmers. Shearing is also a fast and easy way to deadhead plants with many tiny blooms, pinks for example.

SLOW-RELEASE FERTILIZER: fertilizer that does not dissolve in water and therefore releases its nutrients gradually. It is often granular and can be either organic or synthetic.

SOIL AMENDMENT: anything added to change the composition of the soil. Most often the element called for is humus—compost.

SUCCULENT GROWTH: the production of (often unwanted) soft, fleshy leaves or stems. Can be a result of over-fertilization.

SUCKERS: shoots that form new stems which can be useful, or not, depending on the plant. Removing lilac suckers keeps the parent plant strong and attractive.

SUMMER DORMANCY: in excessive heat some plants, including roses, slow or stop productivity. Fertilizing or pruning a partially dormant plant will stimulate it into growth.

TUBER: similar to a bulb, a tuber is a specialized stem, branch, or root structure used for food storage. It generates roots on the lower surface while the upper portion puts up stems, leaves, and flowers. Dahlia and caladium are examples.

VARIEGATED: foliage that is streaked, edged, or blotched with various colors—often green leaves with yellow, cream, or white markings.

VARIETY: the only accurate names for plants are the scientific botanical names, and these are given in Latin—genus, species, subspecies, variety, and form. In botany, "variety" is reserved for a variant of a species that occurs in the wild or natural habitat. It should not be used instead of, or confused with "cultivated variety," which has been shortened to "cultivar."

WINGS: the tissue that forms edges along the twigs of some woody plants such as winged euonymus; or the flat, dried extension on some seeds, such as maple, that catch the wind and enable the seeds to fly away to land and grow in another place.

BIBLIOGRAPHY

Aden, Paul. *The Hosta Book: Second Edition*. Timber Press, 1992.

American Horticultural Society A-Z Encyclopedia of Garden Plants, The. Christopher Bricknell and Judith D. Zuk, eds. DK Publishing, 1997.

André Viette Gardening Guide. Viette Staff.

Annuals: 1001 Gardening Questions Answered. Editors of Garden Way Publishing. Storey Books, 1989.

Armitage, Allan M. *Herbaceous Perennial Plants: Second Edition*. Stipes Publishing Co., 1997.

Armitage, Allan M., Asha Kays, Chris Johnson. *Armitage's Manuel of Annuals, Biennials, and Half-Hardy Perennials*. Timber Press, 2001.

A-Z of Annuals, Biennials & Bulbs (Successful Gardening). Reader's Digest, 1997.

Bales, Suzanne Fruitig. *The Burpee American Gardening Series: Annuals, Reissue Edition*. Hungry Minds, Inc., 1993.

Ball, Liz. *Pennsylvania Gardener's Guide*. Cool Springs Press, 2002.

Barash, Cathy Wilkinson. *Edible Flowers: From Garden to Palette*. Fulcrum Publishing, 1993.

Bar-Zvi, David, Kathy Sammis, Chani Yammer, Albert Squillance. *American Garden Guides: Tropical Gardening, Fairchild Tropical Garden*. Pantheon Books, 1996.

Bath, Trevor and Joy Jones. *The Gardener's Guide to Growing Hardy Geraniums*. Timber Press, 1994.

Bloom, Adrian. *Conifers for your Garden*. John Markham & Associates, 1987.

Boland, Tim, Laura Coit, Marty Hair. *Michigan Gardener's Guide: Revised Edition*. Cool Springs Press, 2002.

Bost, Toby. *North Carolina Gardener's Guide: Revised Edition*. Cool Springs Press, 2002.

Bradley, Fern and Barbara Ellis. *Rodale's All-New Encyclopedia of Organic Gardening*. Rodale Press, 1992.

Bridwell, Ferrell M. *Landscape Plants, Their Identification, Culture and Use: Second Edition*. Delmar Learning, 2002.

Brown, Deni. *The Herb Society of America Encyclopedia of Herbs and Their Uses*. DK Publishing, 2001.

Brown, George E. *The Pruning of Trees, Shrubs and Conifers*. Timber Press, 1995.

Bush-Brown, Louise, James Bush-Brown, Howard Erwin, Brooklyn Botanic Garden. *America's Garden Book: Revised Edition*. MacMillan, 1996.

Clarkson, Rosetta E. *Herbs, Their Culture and Uses*. MacMillan Publishing Co., 1949.

Clausen, Ruth Rogers and Nicolas Ekstrom. *Perennials for American Gardens*. Random House, 1989.

Colborn, Nigel. *Annuals and Bedding Plants*. Trafalgar Square Publishing, YEAR MIA.

Cooke, Ian. *The Plant Finders Guide to Tender Perennials*. David & Charles Publishers, 2001.

Coombes, Allen J. *Dictionary of Plant Names*. Timber Press, 1985.

Courtright, Gordon. *Tropicals*. Timber Press, 1995.

Darke, Rick. *Ornamental Grasses for Your Garden*. Little Brown and Co., 1994.

Davis, Brian. *The Gardener's Illustrated Encyclopedia of Trees and Shrubs*. Rodale Press, 1987.

Den Ouden, P. and B.K. Boom. *Manual of Cultivated Conifers*. Martinus Nijhoff, 1982.

Dictionary of Horticulture, National Gardening Association: Reprint Edition. Penguin USA, 1996.

Dirr, Michael A. *Manual of Woody Landscape Plants: Fifth Edition*. Stipes Publishing Co., 1998.

DiSabato-Aust, Tracy. *The Well-Tended Perennial Garden*. Timber Press, 1998.

Edinger, Philip, Janet H. Sanchez, Sunset Books. *Annuals and Perennials*. Sunset Publishing Company, 2002.

Everett, Thomas H. *The New York Botanical Garden Illustrated Encyclopedia of Horticulture*. Garland Publishing, 1980.

Field Guide to North American Trees: Revised Edition. (Grolier).

Foster, Gordon. *Ferns to Know and Grow: Third Edition*. Timber Press, 1993.

Good Housekeeping Illustrated Encyclopedia of Gardening, The. William Morrow Hearst and Company, 1972.

Grey-Wilson, Christopher. *Poppies*. Timber Press, 2001.

Grey-Wilson, Christopher and Victoria Matthews. *Gardening with Climbers*. Timber Press, 1997.

Griffiths, Mark. *Index of Common Garden Plants: The New Royal Horticultural Society Dictionary.* MacMillan Press, 1994.

Grissel, Eric. *Thyme on My Hands: Reprint Edition.* Timber Press, 1995.

Halfacre, R. Gordon and Anne R. Shawcroft. *Landscape Plants of the Southeast: Fifth Edition.* Sparks Press, 1989.

Halpin, Anne. *Morning Glories and Moonflowers.* Simon & Schuster, 1996.

Harper, Pamela J. *Designing with Perennials.* Lark Books, 2001.

Hearst Garden Guides: Annuals. Ted Marston, ed. Hearst Books, 1993.

Hériteau, Jacqueline. *Glorious Gardens.* Stewart Tabori & Chang, 1998.

Hériteau, Jacqueline. *Virginia Gardener's Guide.* Cool Springs Press, 1997.

Hériteau, Jacqueline, H.M. Cathey, Staff of the National Arboretum. *The National Arboretum Book of Outstanding Garden Plants.* Simon & Schuster, 1990.

Hériteau, Jacqueline and André Viette. *The American Horticultural Society Flower Finder.* Simon & Schuster, 1992.

Hortus Third. Staff of L. H. Bailey Hortorium, Cornell University. John Wiley & Sons, 1976.

Hoshizaki, Barbara. *Fern Growers Manual.* Random House, 1975.

Hudak, Joseph. *Gardening with Perennials Month by Month: Second Edition.* Timber Press, 1993.

Irwin, Howard S. *America's Garden Book.* Brooklyn Botanic Garden. John Wiley & Sons, 1996.

Iverson, Richard R. *The Exotic Garden, Designing with Tropical Plants in Almost Any Climate.* Taunton Press, 1999.

King, Michael and Piet Oudolf. *Gardening with Grasses.* Timber Press, 1998.

Leach, David G. *Rhododendrons of the World.* Scribner, 1961.

Loewer, Peter. *Growing and Decorating with Grasses.* Walker & Co., 1977.

Lowe, Judy. *Tennessee Gardener's Guide: Third Edition.* Cool Springs Press, 2002.

Massey, A.B. *Virginia Ferns and Fern Allies.*

Mazeo, Peter F. *Ferns and Fern Allies of Shenandoah National Park.*

McEwen, Currier. *Japanese Iris.* University Press of New England, 1990.

McEwen, Currier. *Siberian Iris.* Timber Press, 1996.

McVicar, Jekka. *Jekka's Culinary Herbs.* William Morrow Hearst and Co., 1997.

Moskowitz, Mark, Thomas Reinhardt, Martina Reinhardt. *Ornamental Grass Gardening.* Mark Moskowitz, 1994.

Naamlijist Van Vaste Planten. Van der Laar, Fortgens, Hoffman, and Jong

Opler, Paul A. and Roger Tory Peterson. *A Field Guide to Eastern Butterflies (Peterson Field Guides).* Houghton Mifflin Co., 1998.

Ottesen, Carol. *Ornamental Grasses: Second Edition.* McGraw-Hill, 1995.

Poor, Janet M. and Nancy Brewster. *Plants That Merit Attention: Volume 1, Trees.* Timber Press, 1984.

Rice, Graham. *Discovering Annuals.* Timber Press, 1999.

Rice, Graham and Elizabeth Strangman. *The Gardener's Guide to Growing Hellebores.* Timber Press, 1993.

Rodale, J.I. and Staff. *Encyclopedia of Organic Gardening.* Rodale Press, 2000.

Rogers, Allan. *Peonies.* Timber Press, 1995.

Rohde, Eleanor Sinclair. *A Garden of Herbs.*

Shaver, Jesse M. *Ferns of the Eastern Central States.* Dover Publications, 1970.

Snodsmith, Ralph. *The Tri-State Gardener's Guide.* Cool Springs Press, 2001.

Southern Living Garden Guide: Annuals and Perennials. Lois Trigg Chaplin, ed. Oxmoor House, 1996.

Thomas, Graham Stuart. *Perennial Garden Plants, or, the Modern Florilegium: Third Edition.* Saga Press, 1990.

Trehane, Piers. *Index Hortensis: Volume 1, Perennials.* Timber Press, 1990.

Tripp, Kim and J.C. Raulston. *The Year in Trees.* Timber Press, 2001.

Van Gelderen, D.M. and J.R.P. van Hoey Smith. *Conifers: The Illustrated Encyclopedia.* Timber Press, 1996.

Viette, André and Stephen Still. *The Time Life Complete Gardener: Perennials.* Time Life.

Wyman, Donald. *Easy Care Ground Covers.*

Wyman, Donald. *Shrubs and Vines for American Gardens: Revised Edition.* Hungry Minds, 1996.

Wyman, Donald. *Wyman's Gardening Encyclopedia: Second Edition.* Simon and Schuster, 1987.

Yeo, Peter F. *Hardy Geraniums, Second Edition.* Timber Press, 2002.

INDEX

MEET THE AUTHORS

JACQUELINE HERITEAU and her daughter HOLLY HUNTER STONEHILL have gardened and cooked together since Holly was young. They have co-authored the *New England Gardener's Guide and Month-By-Month™ Gardening in New England,* as well as two cookbooks and the popular *"Herbs & Spices"* grow-and-cook-it recipe calendars. Cooking is their second passion.

Jacqui, whose background is journalism, is known for her many books featuring environmentally sound plants and gardening methods. She was the General Editor for the *Good Housekeeping Illustrated Encyclopedia of Gardening.* Her first book, *The How to Grow and Cook It Book* was a book club selection and her *National*

Arboretum Book of Outstanding Garden Plants, brought her the American Nurserymen and Landscape Association Communicator of the Year Award. In 1999 she was made a Fellow of the Garden Writers Association (GWA) in recognition of her leadership of the Plant A Row for the Hungry campaign.

The mother and daughter team live about a mile apart as the crow flies in the Litchfield Hills of Northwestern Connecticut. Their joint kitchen garden, designed by Holly, has been featured in national magazines. In 2007, Jacqui and Holly's love for good, fresh food led them to open the Country Bistro in Salisbury, Ct, now a popular gathering place where "everybody knows your name."

LIZ BALL is a horticultural writer, photographer, researcher, and teacher. Over the past 20 years her articles and photographs have appeared in numerous catalogs, magazines and books. She has co-authored nine books on plant and landscape care for Rodale and other publishers. She is the sole author of many others, including these Cool Springs Press titles: *My Pennsylvania Garden, a Journal* (2000); *Month-by-Month*™ *Gardening in Pennsylvania* (revised 2007) and *Pennsylvania Gardener's Guide* (2002). Liz writes about a wide range of gardening topics, and specializes in issues that concern non-gardening homeowners who have lawns and plants to care for, but limited time and interest in working in their yards. Her weekly "Yardening" column has appeared in her local newspaper for 18 years. A former high school teacher, she has taught courses on gardening or writing at Philadelphia area adult schools, college and arboretum programs, and Longwood Gardens. She is a member of Garden Writers Association.

JAMES FIZZELL has more than 50 years of hands-on horticultural experience, making him the source other experts turn to with their toughest turf, vegetable, landscape and plant problems.

Fizzell is well known to Midwest gardeners through numerous appearances on radio and TV and from articles for neighborhood weekly newspapers. He has been the popular host of his own radio and TV gardening programs. Mr. Fizzell has been featured often in leading trade journals, and as a celebrated speaker at industry seminars and horticultural associations throughout the Midwest. Jim has written twelve books for Midwest gardeners for Cool Springs Press. Jim and his wife Jane currently reside and garden on Garden Street in Northern Illinois.

JOE LAMP'L, (aka joegardener®) is the host of two National television shows: GardenSMART on PBS and DIY Network's Fresh from the Garden. His latest project includes producing and hosting a brand new series on PBS, Growing a Greener World. He's also a syndicated columnist and author, including his latest book, The Green Gardener's Guide: Simple Significant Actions to Protect & Preserve Our Planet. Joe's passion and work related to gardening, sustainable living, and environmental stewardship through multiple media platforms has positioned him as one of the most recognized personalities in the "green" sector today. Find out more information about Joe and his work online at www.joegardener.com.

CPSIA information can be obtained
at www.ICGtesting.com
Printed in the USA
LVHW01s0335310318
571780LV00005BA/5/P

9 781591 865445